Why Conserve Nature?

How we view nature transforms the world around us. People rehearse stories about nature which make sense to them. If we ask the question 'why conserve nature?', and the answers are based on myths, then are these good myths to have? Scientific knowledge about the environment is fundamental to ideas about how nature works. It is essential to the conservation endeavour. However, any conservation motivation is nested within a society's meanings of nature and the way society values it. Given the therapeutic and psychological significance of nature for us and our culture, this book considers the meanings derived from the poetic and emotional attachment to a sense of place, which is arguably just as important as scientific evidence. The functional significance of species is important, but so too is the therapeutic value of nature, together with the historic and spiritual meanings entwined in a human feeling for landscape and wildlife.

STEPHEN TRUDGILL is an Honorary Vice-President of the Field Studies Council and Emeritus Fellow in Geography at Robinson College, Cambridge University, where he is Chair of the Gardens Committee and a member of the Visual Arts Committee. He formerly lectured on the social engagement with nature, biogeography, soils, nature conservation and environmental management in the Department of Geography at Cambridge University. He has experience of community conservation near Cambridge and nature reserve management at Slapton Ley National Nature Reserve, Devon. He has written, edited and co-edited seven books to date. He was also a contributor to the recently published Cambridge University Press book, *Curious about Nature* (Burt and Thompson, 2019).

ECOLOGY, BIODIVERSITY AND CONSERVATION

The world's biological diversity faces unprecedented threats. The urgent challenge facing the concerned biologist is to understand ecological processes well enough to maintain their functioning in the face of the pressures resulting from human population growth. Those concerned with the conservation of biodiversity and with restoration also need to be acquainted with the political, social, historical, economic and legal frameworks within which ecological and conservation practice must be developed. The new Ecology, Biodiversity and Conservation series will present balanced, comprehensive, up-to-date and critical reviews of selected topics within the sciences of ecology and conservation biology, both botanical and zoological, and both 'pure' and 'applied'. It is aimed at advanced final-year undergraduates, graduate students, researchers and university teachers, as well as ecologists and conservationists in industry, government and the voluntary sectors. The series encompasses a wide range of approaches and scales (spatial, temporal and taxonomic), including quantitative, theoretical, population, community, ecosystem, landscape, historical, experimental, behavioural and evolutionary studies. The emphasis is on science related to the real world of plants and animals rather than on purely theoretical abstractions and mathematical models. Books in this series will, wherever possible, consider issues from a broad perspective. Some books will challenge existing paradigms and present new ecological concepts, empirical or theoretical models, and testable hypotheses. Other books will explore new approaches and present syntheses on topics of ecological importance.

Ecology and Control of Introduced Plants
Judith H. Myers and Dawn Bazely

Invertebrate Conservation and Agricultural Ecosystems
T. R. New

Risks and Decisions for Conservation and Environmental Management
Mark Burgman

Ecology of Populations
Esa Ranta, Per Lundberg, and Veijo Kaitala

Nonequilibrium Ecology
Klaus Rohde

The Ecology of Phytoplankton
C. S. Reynolds

Systematic Conservation Planning
Chris Margules and Sahotra Sarkar

Large-Scale Landscape Experiments: Lessons from Tumut
David B. Lindenmayer

Assessing the Conservation Value of Freshwaters: An International Perspective
Philip J. Boon and Catherine M. Pringle

Insect Species Conservation
T. R. New

Bird Conservation and Agriculture
Jeremy D. Wilson, Andrew D. Evans, and Philip V. Grice

Cave Biology: Life in Darkness
Aldemaro Romero

Biodiversity in Environmental Assessment: Enhancing Ecosystem Services for Human Well-Being
Roel Slootweg, Asha Rajvanshi, Vinod B. Mathur, and Arend Kolhoff

Mapping Species Distributions: Spatial Inference and Prediction
Janet Franklin

Decline and Recovery of the Island Fox: A Case Study for Population Recovery
Timothy J. Coonan, Catherin A. Schwemm, and David K. Garcelon

Ecosystem Functioning
Kurt Jax

Spatio-temporal Heterogeneity: Concepts and Analyses
Pierre R. L. Dutilleul

Parasites in Ecological Communities: From Interactions to Ecosystems
Melanie J. Hatcher and Alison M. Dunn

Zoo Conservation Biology
John E. Fa, Stephan M. Funk, and Donnamarie O'Connell

Marine Protected Areas: A Multidisciplinary Approach
Joachim Claudet

Biodiversity in Dead Wood
Jogeir N. Stokland, Juha Siitonen, and Bengt Gunnar Jonsson

Landslide Ecology
Lawrence R. Walker and Aaron B. Shiels

Nature's Wealth: The Economics of Ecosystem Services and Poverty
Pieter J. H. van Beukering, Elissaios Papyrakis, Jetske Bouma, and Roy Brouwer

Birds and Climate Change: Impacts and Conservation Responses
James W. Pearce-Higgins and Rhys E. Green

Marine Ecosystems: Human Impacts on Biodiversity, Functioning and Services
Tasman P. Crowe and Christopher L. J. Frid

Wood Ant Ecology and Conservation
Jenni A. Stockan and Elva J. H. Robinson

Detecting and Responding to Alien Plant Incursions
John R. Wilson, F. Dane Panetta and Cory Lindgren

Conserving Africa's Mega-Diversity in the Anthropocene: The Hluhluwe-iMfolozi Park Story
Joris P. G. M. Cromsigt, Sally Archibald and Norman Owen-Smith

National Park Science: A Century of Research in South Africa
Jane Carruthers

Plant Conservation Science and Practice: The Role of Botanic Gardens
Stephen Blackmore and Sara Oldfield

Habitat Suitability and Distribution Models: With Applications in R
Antoine Guisan, Wilfried Thuiller and Niklaus E. Zimmermann

Ecology and Conservation of Forest Birds
Grzegorz Mikusiński, Jean-Michel Roberge and Robert J. Fuller

Species Conservation: Lessons from Islands
Jamieson A. Copsey, Simon A. Black, Jim J. Groombridge and Carl G. Jones

Soil Fauna Assemblages: Global to Local Scales
Uffe N. Nielsen

Curious about Nature
Tim Burt and Des Thompson

Comparative Plant Succession among Terrestrial Biomes of the World
Karel Prach and Lawrence R. Walker

Ecological-Economic Modelling for Biodiversity Conservation
Martin Drechsler

Freshwater Biodiversity: Status, Threats and Conservation
David Dudgeon

Joint Species Distribution Modelling: With Applications in R
Otso Ovaskainen and Nerea Abrego

Natural Resource Management Reimagined: Using the Systems Ecology Paradigm
Robert G. Woodmansee, John C. Moore, Dennis S. Ojima and Laurie Richards

The Species–Area Relationship: Theory and Application
Thomas J. Matthews, Kostas A. Triantis and Robert J. Whittaker

Ecosystem Collapse and Recovery
Adrian C. Newton

Animal Population Ecology: An Analytical Approach
T. Royama

Why Conserve Nature?

Perspectives on Meanings and Motivations

STEPHEN TRUDGILL

Robinson College, University of Cambridge

CAMBRIDGE
UNIVERSITY PRESS

University Printing House, Cambridge CB2 8BS, United Kingdom

One Liberty Plaza, 20th Floor, New York, NY 10006, USA

477 Williamstown Road, Port Melbourne, VIC 3207, Australia

314–321, 3rd Floor, Plot 3, Splendor Forum, Jasola District Centre, New Delhi – 110025, India

103 Penang Road, #05–06/07, Visioncrest Commercial, Singapore 238467

Cambridge University Press is part of the University of Cambridge.

It furthers the University's mission by disseminating knowledge in the pursuit of education, learning, and research at the highest international levels of excellence.

www.cambridge.org
Information on this title: www.cambridge.org/9781108832526
DOI: 10.1017/9781108961059

First published 2022

Printed in the United Kingdom by TJ Books Limited, Padstow Cornwall

A catalogue record for this publication is available from the British Library.

Library of Congress Cataloging-in-Publication Data
Names: Trudgill, Stephen T. (Stephen Thomas), 1947– author.
Title: Why conserve nature? : perspectives on meanings and motivations / Stephen Trudgill, University of Cambridge.
Description: Cambridge, United Kingdom ; New York, NY : Cambridge University Press, 2022. | Series: Ecology, biodiversity and conservation | Includes bibliographical references and index.
Identifiers: LCCN 2021019841 (print) | LCCN 2021019842 (ebook) | ISBN 9781108832526 (hardback) | ISBN 9781108958578 (paperback) | ISBN 9781108961059 (epub)
Subjects: LCSH: Nature conservation. | BISAC: NATURE / Ecology
Classification: LCC QH75 .T78 2022 (print) | LCC QH75 (ebook) | DDC 333.72—dc23
LC record available at https://lccn.loc.gov/2021019841
LC ebook record available at https://lccn.loc.gov/2021019842

ISBN 978-1-108-83252-6 Hardback
ISBN 978-1-108-95857-8 Paperback

In memory of Mum, Dad, my godfather 'Uncle' Henry, Ted Ellis and Janet Smith who taught me so much about natural history, art and literature.

Contents

Colour plates can be found between pages 106 and 107.

Foreword

As this magnificent living planet we are privileged to call home whirls through time and space, humanity's relationship with it has become ever more complex. Although we have been inhabitants of Planet Earth for a mere 300,000 years of its 4.5 billion-year history, in that minuscule time we have literally transformed the face of the earth. People are ingenious, creative and driven beings. Our large brains combined with dexterous hands and an overwhelming desire to improve our lot has seen us grow in number and transform the earth's resources into goods and services. Other life on earth has had to either fit into our agenda or be eradicated. In the blink of an eye it has taken to transform us from cave dweller to city banker, we have carried out a systematic re-shaping of the surface of the earth. Science now tells us we are at a tipping point where the natural world's ability to adapt to humanity's demands may be fatally compromised. As ecosystems collapse, so too will humanity. This oft-told story is being heard with increasing urgency. Not a single one of us wants this to happen – we are survivors not self-destroyers – but our sheer numbers and demands have been too much. It is clear that if we are to have a future, we have a collective job to do to turn this around. The big question is – how?

Like so many of us, I worry and ponder on this question of survival. When I read *Why Conserve Nature?* my angst-ridden soul stopped fretting for a while and jumped up and down punching the air. The words rang out true and bright from the first page. I found myself agreeing with every sentence and every quote. This book is about engagement, about positive collaboration, about drawing deep on our collective love of story and meaning and turning that into action. It is about recognising the validity of the many different perspectives we have on the world and bringing them into union to create solutions to the earth's ills. As the art historian E. H. Gombrich observed, "There is no reality without interpretation; just as there is no innocent eye, there is no innocent ear."

At heart we are creative problem-solvers. There is nothing humanity likes more than a challenge, and we always have, and hopefully we always will, get to grips with what needs to be done. But the clever truth that this book explores is that the motivation to make good is not just found in explaining the problem through facts and science, it is embedded in touching our souls. Ever since we sat around fires as hunter-gatherers and told each other what was important, we have used metaphor and simile, we have woven tales that are as fantastical as they are true. We constantly play with words, image, movement, sound and meaning and we present them in ways which delight us, scare us, shock us or humour us – all of them make us think. And humanity loves to think. We love to dream. We love to present reality in non-real terms. As the author surmises from his wide-ranging research, to get people involved you have to tell stories that reach into their hearts and ignite the spark that will light the fire of action. People don't always react to ideas alone but to stories that incorporate those ideas, and those stories come in very many forms.

To ignore the cultural aspect of our nature is to deny a huge part of what makes us human. Yet, so often, we present the problems faced by the earth as being solvable by technology and equations alone. While telling, showing and demonstrating what needs to be done are important, it is finding our own meaning which is always more effective at producing action. The key proposition of this book is, "that without meanings, we have no motivation". What we need now more than ever are clever motivated people who act from both their souls and their heads. Not a single one of us is merely a processor of fact. We are not a collection of Mr Spocks from Star Trek; we rarely act on purely rational grounds. Everyone is a mixture of many different roles – child, sibling, parent, lover, consumer, believer, activist, friend and neighbour. We are spiritual beings as much as we are scientific and very often it is our relationships, culture, traditions and beliefs that dictate our actions, not pure logic. It is why conservation needs "collective crisis leadership" that draws on a range of experiences and world views that is both inclusive and enabling to a wide range of people.

No one has the single answer to the environmental crises we face. Our continued presence on earth requires that not only conservationists and scientists tell their truths but also artists, poets, musicians, writers, financiers, indigenous teachers, grassroots organisations, business leaders, religious leaders and politicians. It is imperative that young and old from every sector of society find who they are in the stories we tell. The route to success is to gather these ways of seeing the earth, and then act.

It will need a near-miracle to save many parts of the world from destruction, but then the interplay of science and culture has always created magic. It is an honour to be asked to write the foreword to this most important book.

Mary Colwell

Producer and writer; author of *Curlew Moon*. Chair of the Steering Group and a trustee of New Networks for Nature, an alliance of scientists, conservationists and artists. 2019 WWT Marsh Award for Wetland Conservation, 2018 David Bellamy Education Trust NGO Award, 2017 BTO Dilys Breese Award for Outstanding Science Communication. Books: *Beak, Tooth and Claw: Living with predators in Britain* (William Collins, 2021). *Curlew Moon* (William Collins, 2018). *John Muir: The Scotsman who saved America's wild places* (Lion Hudson, 2014).

Preface

This book derives from my part in The Social Engagement with Nature course which I used to lecture on in the Department of Geography, University of Cambridge. I can't thank enough the other lecturers on the course and the students who took the course. Your inputs helped to shape my ideas.

In an earlier book I acknowledged the debt I felt to Robinson College Cambridge, a place where I became a Fellow in 1996. I was given a room for teaching and study which was neither home nor University Department but, while independent of either, gave me elements of both. This helped me to produce my *Terrestrial Biosphere* book on science, attitudes and values (Trudgill, 2001b). I had hitherto kept my more cultural and literary interests about nature and art at home as part of my personal life. However, now I managed to combine my arts interests with my scientific work from the Geography Department (where I started by teaching physical geography in the guise of soils, water quality and environmental management as well as some geomorphology) and brushing shoulders with other College Fellows in the arts and sciences alike helped enormously. When writing the *Terrestrial Biosphere*, as I recorded in the acknowledgements for that book, I was greatly encouraged by a review of my earlier *Barriers to a Better Environment* book (Trudgill, 1990) by Ian Simmons, then Professor of Geography at Durham. He had kindly written a piece (Simmons, 1993b) indicating that I had moved from physical to social science in a particularly seamless way handling "a wide variety of material with a facility many of us would envy". A Cambridge College enabled me to build on this further and it was, I feel, not something I could have done without an appropriate 'neutral' space of a College room in which to operate – and the stimulus of the breadth of interests which surrounded me.

Some years on, I now have to acknowledge a debt to Cambridge Geography Department and especially Bill Adams who enabled me to emerge in the Department as an environmental geographer – even allowing me to be some kind of human geographer – and join the course which Bill had invented called The Social Engagement with Nature. Here he, together with Tim Bayliss-Smith, Gerry Kearns, Phil Howell, Piers Vitebsky and me, formed a varied association exploring the themes of the social construction of nature.

I rapidly emerged with a term's worth of lectures on the representation of nature in art, poetry and other literature and explored how this related to the social construction of nature in ecological science – and then how both of these influence what we do to nature in gardens, nature reserves and the wider environment. Earlier in the development of the course Gerry Kearns talked about North American constructs of nature and Bill Adams lectured on ecology and literature and later Piers Vitebsky contributed from his knowledge of Arctic peoples and their relation with nature. For many years Phil Howell lectured on the social construction of animals, including his famous talk on dog cemeteries, and Tim Bayliss-Smith lectured on Paradise and other such constructions in the Pacific. Tim, Phil and Jim Duncan were always admirable colleagues on the Mallorca Field Trip where I learnt so much from them and it was during one of those visits I coined the term psychobiogeography (Trudgill, 2001a). I also greatly appreciated the visits to Wicken Fen with Tim Bayliss-Smith and Steve Boreham, teaching second-year students about conservation. Our field trips were greatly enhanced by the competence and efficiency of the late Adrian Hayes, much missed. I must also mention Laura Cameron who helped me with her many insights in the world of Sir Arthur Tansley and of course Keith Richards who, while we were standing on Scolt Head island in Norfolk, brought to my attention a lectureship available in my area of interest in Cambridge. All these colleagues have of course influenced me greatly and I am grateful for that experience.

I am no less grateful to the students who coped with the first line of my first lecture each year when I looked out of the window and said: "That tree doesn't know it is Tuesday." Inevitably two students would leave but those who stayed rapidly caught on to the point about the tangible existence of something which we call 'tree' and the constructed world of concepts like 'Tuesday' – and I am grateful that they stayed and joined in the fun of exploration in lectures and supervisions.

In terms of personal friendships and support, apart from those in the Geography Department mentioned above, I can but turn to College and village. Mary Stewart has been an especially invaluable friend to me during the past twenty-five years. Prior to being in College I certainly would not have guessed that I would have become interested in oncology, family law and theology – but thanks to Gary Doherty, Brian Sloan, Simon Perry and Morna Hooker for that. Gary has also been great in the way that, as Chair of the College Visual Arts Committee, he curated an exhibition of my artworks and also an exhibition of my father's paintings. I have also greatly appreciated working as Chair of the Gardens Committee with Guy Fuller as Head Gardener and with Helen Cornish and Sarah Westwood as successive Heads of Development in my role as President of the Robinson College Alumni Association (Pegasus). Lord Lewis and then David Yates as the Founding and Second College Wardens have both provided fundamental support for me and my interests. At this stage I am now conscious that I should mention about another seventy people in College which space precludes except to say thank you to my former students who continue to stay in touch in such a supportive way, especially Nikolai Koval-Radley and Josh Lomax. Nikolai's love of art and nature has been especially motivational.

In the village I can but mention my colleagues on the Parish Council on which I served for twenty-three years, especially the late Willy Brown and Jane Chater (who shares my interest in natural history), and also Mike Boagey, our village newsletter editor, together with those who work on the Wellcome Trust Liaison Committee, especially the Hinxton Sanger Centre Wetlands Nature Reserve Management Committee. I certainly wish to celebrate those wonderful people of the Village Hall Committee. They have given me some of the best moments in committee work, especially by all volunteering at once to make the onion gravy for a sausage and mash meal at the village history evening. In my immediate neighbourhood, I have usually had a yearly meal in my house with those who live more or less next door. Many have come and gone except Jill-next-door and it has been such a privilege to be surrounded by such good people who are so happy and willing to do things for other people. There are also then all the other lovely people in the village, all of whom seem to know me and are tolerant when I inevitably forget some of their names.

I cannot express my debt enough to the Field Studies Council (www.field-studies-council.org/about-us/) and especially my PhD supervisor Dingle Smith from Bristol Geography Department (and then ANU Canberra) who introduced me to the Executive Committee of the Council. My memorable experiences have often been at Malham, especially when Adrian Pickles was there, and very much at Slapton

Ley Field Centre. The people I have met in and around there have given me many treasured memories, like the late Keith Chell, Jim and Di McPetrie, Tim Burt (together with Liz Burt and my godson Tom Burt), Nigel Coles, Hilary Gibson, Ali 'Crash' Cadle, Liz Cole, Tim Mitcham, Keith Orrell, Tim Orrell, Karen Scadeng, Mark Ward, Maggie Jarman and Sue Townsend now Dancy. Many of these people have been friends for life, especially Nigel who got me into cycling in France and Spain, often happily with Alistair Kirkbride, and particularly Hilary Gibson who has encouraged and inspired me and my art in so many ways. I started attending Hilary's art courses and ended up running some with her, which has been one of life's enriching experiences. For many years I was a member of the Executive Committee of the Field Studies Council. Special thanks to Neil Emery who, aged nine, attended one of my family natural history courses at Slapton and then found me out years later to say how much it had meant to him. And I still try to raise money for the FSC Kids fund: www.field-studies-council.org/about/fsc-kids-fund.aspx. Slapton Ley Field Centre has been a special place for me, particularly in helping to run the National Nature Reserve and working with Nigel Coles and Tim Burt, not to mention the pivotal input of Jimmy McPetrie ('Jimmy the Farmer') who challenged my talk on nitrate years ago and has made me think about what I was doing ever since – the times in Jim and Di's kitchen are treasured memories. Without knowing Tim Burt as both president of the FSC and a friend, I may well not have met Des Thompson and put this book forward for this series. I have had the benefit of Des's enthusiasm and of the wisdom of Series Editor Michael Usher, especially with his invaluable comments on the first draft, and the insightful feedback on the book proposal from the Editorial Board – together with the inputs of Dominic Lewis and the efficient help and guidance from Aleksandra Serocka from Cambridge University Press.

For help in my endeavours to write, I am grateful to David Stonestreet for his guidance during an earlier version of this book and to Nuala Johnson for positive comments on that earlier version. I am also grateful, as ever, to my sociolinguist brother Peter Trudgill and Jean Hannah for their support and especially to Simon Perry who, in return for me reading the draft of his book on Christendom and atheism, read though the draft of this book for me. There is much in this book which reflects his challenging inputs to what I had written. For help on specific sources and other aspects of this book I am particularly grateful to Terry Hartig from Uppsala Psychology Department for sharing his work on restoration with me, Miles Burnyeat for his insights into Bernard Williams, Tom Lynch for discussions of ecocriticism and Mary Colwell for encouragement about the spiritual aspects of nature and, not least, for her work on the emblematic importance of the curlew. Lucy Rhymer of Cambridge University Press is thanked for her invaluable advice and encouragement during the early stages of the writing of the book. Sharing an Emeritus Fellows Room with Morna Hooker and Mary Stewart has been an interesting experience and has meant that there is usually someone around to comment helpfully on what I am doing.

I thank Rogelio Luque-Lora of the Department of Geography, University of Cambridge (and Ben Peacock for introducing us). Not only am I very grateful for his proofreading skills, he has helped me with his challenging and thoughtful questions, insightful discussions, suggested readings and constructive comments on this book – and this together with his much appreciated companionship on nature walks as we looked around us together. With encouragement from Chris Sandbrook, we had thought that he would contribute a section to this book on the results of his work on why people conserve nature but pandemic travel restrictions curtailed his fieldwork on this. However, this means we can hope to look forward to reading about his work at some future date in another publication.

The endeavour of the current book is to examine a range of ideas and to neither stress nor deny the importance of science or of culture and to highlight the significance of values and the affective emotions. I can't claim to be uniquely placed to cover the entire science–culture/arts spectrum but enough people have told me that my ideas and my approach of examining narratives has changed their way of thinking to encourage me that this book is worthwhile. This is especially in relation to the reaction to my Psychobiogeography Guest Editorial in *The Journal of Biogeography* (2001), published with the encouragement of editor Philip Stott. I had positive feedback from many, including John Parker, former Director of Cambridge Botanic Gardens, ecological scientists at ecological institutes (including ITE Monkswood), attendees at geographical and ecological conference and emails from many countries. I would like to thank Tim Unwin for helping me to become an editor of *Ethics, Place and Environment* for a while. I would even like to thank the bean-counting morons who invented the RAE/REF (Research Assessment Exercise/Research Excellence Framework) stuff which made me think that taking advantage of the University early retirement scheme looked like a very good idea, thus giving me more time to write this book.

I would never have got anywhere I have without my parents' love of nature, art, poetry and literature, and I especially value the bird and nature books I inherited from my godfather Henry Smith, particularly his books by the Norfolk naturalist Arthur Patterson (who often wrote under the pen name John Knowlittle). Patterson and Henry corresponded with each other and the family kept some envelopes illustrated by Patterson with bird drawings as sent to Henry; the envelopes are now in the archives in the Norfolk Record Office in Norwich. My A-level learning from my Geography, Zoology and Botany teachers helped to enrich and consolidate my knowledge and my youth was imbued with nature trips and childhood memories of being on Blakeney Point and other well-known Norfolk places for nature. Many of my mother's ancestors came from North Norfolk and Dad, as manager of Jarrolds Colour Publishing, produced several books on local natural history, including *The Birds of Norfolk* by M. J. Seago, *The Flora of Norfolk* by C. P. Petch and E. L. Swann and many by Norfolk naturalist Ted Ellis. Ted had transcribed the books of Arthur Patterson when he was younger and I read, cut out and kept cuttings of Ted Ellis's nature column in the *Eastern Daily Press*. I thus grew up steeped in a love of nature, and Blakeney Point, Mum, Dad, Teddy Eales and Reggie Gaze all seem inextricably linked with childhood, as does adolescence and bird watching at Cley with people like Robin South, Michael Seago and Richard Richardson. Especially valuable were the Norfolk Naturalists outings led by Ted Ellis and where we were with a family friend and local librarian who did so much to foster my interests in natural history: Janet Smith.

At Bristol University I am pleased that while I studied Geography and Geology, I also wanted to study Botany but the timetable precluded the latter and so I had to study Sociology instead: this insight into society proved to be invaluable. The debt one owes to the lecturers, especially my tutor and then PhD supervisor Dingle Smith, is immeasurable. The same goes for the experience with the University of Bristol Speleological Society and the president E. K. Tratman – not forgetting Oliver Lloyd (brother of the garden writer Christopher Lloyd, with his tales of growing up in Great Dixter). Trat was a truly remarkable gentleman who inspired me greatly, especially his philosophical approach to life after surviving time in Changi prison. My time on Aldabra Atoll, Indian Ocean, for my PhD fieldwork was very formative – and I am grateful to David Stoddart and The Royal Society for the opportunity to spend a total of seven months in such a wild place immersed in nature and with the company of geologists and biologists Roger Gaymer, Tony Diamond, John Taylor, Colin Braithwaite, Jim Kennedy and Jack Frazier.

Finally, thank you to those who have been helping me through lockdown like Jill and Simon, Sarah, Sarah, Sara and the rest of the village – and especially Pete and Amy – and also other friends particularly Rogelio Luque-Lora, Simon Perry, Mary Stewart and Hilary Gibson.

Stephen Trudgill
Emeritus Fellow, Robinson College, University of Cambridge

Part I
The Experience of Nature

1 · *The Experience of Nature*

1.1 Perspectives on the Meaning and Significance of Nature

Why Conserve Nature?

Why do we[1] want to keep anything? Surely it is because it means something to us? Isn't it because we value qualities like usefulness and the ways in which we can cherish memories and meaningful associations? We may keep things which make life easier, help us in day-to-day living and might assist us in some future difficult time. We may also value those things with enriching associations – something we found on a memorable day; something which appealed to us for its form and beauty, its intricacy, diversity or simplicity; something inherited from an ancestor or given to us by a friend or parent. Or it can be something we did not know about but which we found out about in the media or which a teacher, parent or mentor told us was rare, valuable, a privilege to have. Thus, the meaning can be discovered by yourself or a meaning can be given to you by someone else which then becomes significant to you. Whatever the many reasons for keeping something, it is the value and the meanings which make us cherish it: the meanings vary widely, but meanings there have to be. Hence the subtitle of the book: *Perspectives on Meanings and Motivations*. Meanings are the key.

[1] When I use the word 'we' or 'our' in a text, critics and reviewers often rightly ask 'who is this we you are referring to – which society or group of people? Do you purport to speak for all of them and are you speaking with their endorsement?' This is highly relevant in particular contexts but there is a clear distinction between statements of opinion which can be contested such as 'we need to spend money on our own problems rather than those of others', where all the questions posed above are germane, and those which actually do speak for the whole of humanity without the need for further contextualisation, such as 'we need oxygen to breathe' and 'the evidence suggests that we evolved about two million years ago in Africa'. Thus, when I use the term 'we' the intention is to make reference to humanity – the human animal – in the context of the human relationship with nature. Any differentiation between particular sections, groups, societies or cultures of humanity will be indicated. In other places in the book, reference to the reader as in: 'we have already seen in an earlier chapter…' should be clear by context.

The very act of asking the question: 'Why conserve nature?' indicates that there can't be one universally agreed positive meaning of nature which motivates people to cherish it. Surely if nature meant something good to everyone – something significant, something valued – then people would all act to conserve nature and this book would not be needed. However, the view that conservation is needed is one that is not universally shared, despite all the exhortations which abound in scientific writings and the media. One person's idea of utility might be another person's idea of irrelevance; even if others seek to tell them that something is useful and with meaningful associations. One person's meaningful associations might be another's indifference if nature has no meaningful association for them. So, the interesting question might equally be: 'Why don't people conserve nature?' The answer must lie, if we follow the thread of the argument so far, in that a lack of personal meaning and significance means there is no sense of value and no motivation to cherish. Is this the case, and if it is, why should this be so? Is it that people don't see nature as useful? Is it that they have no associations with it? Is it just irrelevant, or at least not an important consideration for people? Are the meanings of nature too many and too complex? Do conservationists fail to get their point of view across? Or is it that people actually agree that nature should be conserved but they don't have – or feel they have – the means to do it?

One aspect of this discussion is that conservation could be made more engaging by heeding the approach of those who say that an answer lies in meaningful stories about practical situations and involving people in positive outcomes. There is a quotation attributed to Samuel Johnson (1709–1784, most well known for his dictionary of the English language): "Nothing has more retarded the advancement of learning than the disposition of vulgar minds to ridicule and vilify what they cannot comprehend." This starkly condescending condemnation, I would stand on its head. Rather than a failure of people to grasp the situation, maybe any failure to comprehend lies in a failure to involve people in a meaningful and relevant way. While telling, showing and demonstrating are important, it is finding your own meaning through being involved which is always more effective.

Organisations such as Action for Conservation (AFC) stand out in this sense (www.actionforconservation.org/about-us). AFC believes that all young people should feel moved and empowered to protect the natural world. It feels that if children and young people lose contact and involvement with nature, they are less likely to fight to protect it as they grow older. AFC's egalitarian belief is that a passion for conservation can flow through anyone's life. It has five core values that define its approach to creating the next generation of conservationists: Diversity, Wonder, Hope, Action and Change. It aims to effect this by creating a sense of wonder and fostering ongoing engagement through stories of hope and through direct involvement with nature. The importance of childhood experiences is emphasised by many studies, for example Daitch et al. (1996) and Vining (2003). Chawla (1999) found childhood experiences to be far more effective in formulating a positive attitude to effective environmental action later in life than the other subsequent experiences investigated. Significantly, such childhood experiences are now seen as lacking, with the media meme derived from surveys that 'prisoners now spend more time outdoors than children' and Louv (2005) lamenting the idea of the *Last Child in the Woods* in the title of his book and promoting the idea of positive childhood nature experiences in *Saving Our Children from Nature-Deficit Disorder* in the subtitle.

Involving people in nature means that there can be a more effective position of being able to argue that if we progressively lose nature, we then lose something of ourselves – mentally, emotionally, spiritually – and indeed, if we make conditions untenable for ourselves, maybe even physically. We can thus see that with nature there can indeed be aspects of utility and of having something inherited and given to us. We can also realise that meaning and significance can vary widely with the observer, the context and the situation – and indeed be highly contested – as well as realising that some people are just indifferent. Hence, the discussion in this book is justifiably about the way in which knowledge, attitudes, values and beliefs interact in cultural contexts to influence the connections between meanings, motivations and actions in nature conservation. This has to be both positive and negative about conservation – the reasons why people don't care are as important as the reasons why people should.

So, this is not a book on how and what precisely to conserve – there are many other books in this Cambridge University Press *Ecology, Biodiversity and Conservation* series which discuss these topics. In this volume the discussion is on the ways in which the meanings of nature matter for motivating us to conserve nature at all. The key proposition is that without meanings, we have no motivation. Botanist and ancient woodland expert Oliver Rackham (1991) promoted this idea when he wrote on 'Landscape and the conservation of meaning', discussing how we can cherish meanings which have evolved over time and are still evolving.

Thus, we focus in this book on the connections between the varied and diverse meanings of nature, the origins of motivations to cherish it and the taking of actions to conserve it. We also have to think what we include when we use the term 'nature'. This includes life forms and the environments in which they live and involves the consideration of the status of the actual life forms themselves and the dynamic processes and interactions between the life forms and between them and their environment. We find that the meanings are a complex fusion of scientific knowledge, pervasive myths, psychological perceptions and cultural contexts.

The scientific knowledge we have about plants, animals and environment is fundamental to giving us a set of ideas and associated values about how nature works and is thus essential to the conservation endeavour. However, this knowledge is produced by a society which holds a set of cultural values and, equally, any proposed action is nested within the context of that society and its values. Writing in *On the Future*, Astronomer Royal Martin Rees (2018: 227) concludes that, "Now is the time for an optimistic vision of life's destiny .... We need to think globally ... rationally ... long term – empowered by twenty-first-century technology but guided by values that science alone can't provide." So, while the knowledge is necessary, it is not sufficient. We have to understand that it is the cultural concepts of meaning and significance in relation to our emotions which actually lead to our actions involving nature.

There is a popular quote from Gus Speth, US Advisor on Climate Change, which is often cited as:

> I used to think that top environmental problems were biodiversity loss, ecosystem collapse and climate change. I thought that thirty years of good science could address these problems. I was wrong. The top environmental problems are selfishness, greed and apathy, and to deal with these we need a cultural and spiritual transformation. And we scientists don't know how to do that. (variously sourced, e.g. https://ncipl.org/environmental-crisis-not-environmental-spiritual)

This quote has been taken up by some as meaning that science doesn't have the answers but that a more spiritual approach does. To believe that, however, would be as limiting as the converse belief that as soon as science has a solution, then the problem is solved. Neither is true. Without science and technology we have difficulties proposing a viable solution but without due regard to cultural contexts – including psychological, economic, social and political factors – we have difficulties in implementing a solution. It should also be realised that scientific knowledge itself is produced in cultural contexts and is not value free in the way questions are framed, investigations formulated and answers derived. Many scientists are indeed aware of these contexts – and also many would find Speth's assertion somewhat pejorative in that they are indeed culturally and spiritually aware. The book edited by Brian Moss and Otto Kinne (2012): *Liberation Ecology: The reconciliation of natural and human cultures* springs to mind here as one example of the science–culture awareness.

Another notable milestone on this road to a wider view is to be found in a special issue of the 2018 journal *Methods in Ecology and Evolution* on qualitative methods for ecologists and conservation scientists, led by Sutherland et al. (2018). They use the self-evident though often ignored wisdom that "conservation of biodiversity involves dealing with problems caused by humans, by applying solutions that comprise actions by humans" (p. 7). They add: "Understanding human attitudes, knowledge and behaviour are thus central to conservation research and practice." There are papers from a range of disciplines (ecology, human geography, political science, land economy, management) and the authors feel that the ways forward involve "incorporating human values, perceptions, judgements and knowledge into conservation decision making". Of particular significance in the volume is the paper by Moon et al. (2019) on expanding the role of social science in conservation through an engagement with philosophy, methodology and methods.

Additionally, lack of conservation action is not just about "selfishness, greed and apathy", as above, it can also be about poverty and survival. Jane Goodall, the primatologist well known for her work on chimpanzees, expresses the situation well in an interview for *Deutsche Welle* (Baker, 2019). While the interview is entitled: '"The biggest problem is greed" says conservationist Jane Goodall', this, I submit, is not her key message. When asked "Why do you think it is that some aren't moved to take action to protect the environment?" she indeed replied, "The biggest problem is greed." However, more tellingly, while making reference to corporate greed, she went on to make her insightful observation on poverty and survival.

The interview focussed on the link she had made between connecting social justice with conservation efforts. She said how she learnt of poverty, the lack of good health and education and the destruction of the environment. The quote from her is: "Because when you're very poor, you cut down the last trees to try and desperately grow some more food or make charcoal." She recalled how in 1990 she flew over what had been a great equatorial forest to see that Gombe National Park was now "just a tiny island forest surrounded by completely bare hills and people were struggling to survive. That's when I realized if we don't help the people to find other ways of living than destroying the environment, then we can't even try to help the chimps." She then went on to engage people in simultaneously aiding the conservation effort and making a living – not only without cutting down further forest but also protecting the remaining forest and its wildlife. This theme is, for example, very much central to the discussions by Stocking, Perkin and Brown (2014) in 'Co-existing with nature in a developing world', a chapter in the key book edited by Morse and Stocking, *People and Nature: Development for the future*. People are seen as part of the solution rather than part of the problem. But there has to be some impetus – some leadership and structure – to make this possible, and to ensure that for the people involved conservation is not part of their problem but becomes a solution.

In this context, recently Ngwenya et al. (2020) have usefully made 'A call for collective crisis leadership': "To scale up conservation efforts . . . we need an inclusive, enabling approach involving everyone – from health and finance ministers to Indigenous Nations, grassroots organizations, NGOs, businesses and heads of state" (p. 432). They continue that, as conservationists, "Standing alone, we are being set up to fail . . . . Collectively, we must deal with the root causes of environmental crises. Only then will we see transformational change unfolding, perhaps with more ease than we ever imagined."

An additional point on motivation which can be usefully noted here is that Jane Goodall also said that she does not believe in aggressive activism, as explained in an interview on the power of reaching people's hearts (Hirsh, 2015). What she feels is that the way to get people motivated is through the emotions as revealed in stories. This is not the same as 'being emotional' but that something moves us – it has meaning. "With storytelling, you have to get to people's hearts. It's not about engaging them intellectually" (Shea, 2015). She feels that the trick to helping people understand that we can all make a difference is pretty simple: telling stories (Figure 1.1).

She said: "If you [get] aggressive . . . you don't get anywhere." She feels that if you watch two people talk from opposing sides, one just tries to refute the other, with neither listening, "and they get more and more aggressive, and nothing's accomplished at all. Except possibly to make it worse." She makes her key point: "Being angry and pointing fingers, you

Figure 1.1 Chimpanzees in their natural forest habitat. Jane Goodall on key aspects of conservation, caring enough to act and being practical: "It's not about engaging them [people] intellectually. . . . You just have to reach people's hearts. And the best way I know is to tell stories" and "If we don't help the people to find other ways of living than destroying the environment, then we can't even try to help the chimps" (guenterguni / E+ / Getty Images)

won't get anywhere. You just have to reach people's hearts. And the best way I know is to tell stories."

In a different discipline, in 'Earth stories: Context and narrative in the communication of popular geoscience', by Stewart and Nield (2013), the first author, having worked in television for some time, promotes exactly the same conclusion. He feels that people are not necessarily motivated by ideas alone, but they do tend to listen to stories which involve these ideas and they can find the narratives very engaging and motivational (Box 1.1).

The relationship between scientific evidence, the stories told and the motivations for human response and reaction are complex and interesting. But, simply put, a story is a way of making sense of something – a way of finding meaning – an explanation. "What is that?" or "Why is that creature doing that?" we might say. "Oh, it is so-and-so" comes the answer. "Ah, yes", we say. And, thus, something is understood through the answer which often conveys a meaningful sense of purpose and reason that is very attractive.

Box 1.1 *The importance of narratives*

Our ideas can often be effectively expressed as storylines – or narratives – which bring meanings to events and observations. As seen in the book description of *The Routledge Encyclopedia of Narrative Theory*: "[S]tories have come to be viewed as a basic human strategy for coming to terms with time, process, and change" (Herman, Jahn and Ryan, 2010). The American literary critic, Kenneth Burke (1941: 253) put it as: "stories are . . . equipment for living" and as such they are bound up with our identity (as discussed in Brockmeir and Carbaugh (2001), *Narratives and Identity*).

The analysis of narratives is common in cultural and literature studies but such analyses are less common in ecological science – but they are there nonetheless, especially in the field of conservation motivation. This is evidenced, for example, in the writings of Cronon (1992), 'A place for stories: Nature, history and narrative' and Rose et al. (2016) in 'Honest advocacy for nature: Presenting a persuasive narrative for conservation', published in the *Biodiversity and Conservation* journal.

In *The Power of Narrative in Environmental Networks*, Lejano, Ingram and Ingram (2013: 56) feel that environmental narratives reach from how we think things are to how we think things should be: "[N]arrative is the means by which we bridge the gap between describing the events . . . and prescribing." Narratives of the environment are also discussed by Palmer (2011) in terms of their fundamental involvement in the history of places; Satterfield, Slovic and Gregory (2000) in the context of policy judgement and Shanahan, Pelstring and McComas (2010) in terms of their significance to environmental attitudes and behaviour.

Human cultures do indeed have many stories about nature. We use these stories very effectively to make sense of nature, often giving meaning, value and purpose to the way we see things. Some of the stories don't necessarily stand up to closed scrutiny, so there is a possible dilemma of having something which is motivational but wrong. However, what is interesting is that the more that people can relate nature to their own human feelings, the more effective – the more motivational – the stories become.

But there is no necessity of meaning in nature itself. Nature is just doing what it is doing; things exist because they can. It is us who bring a sense of value: there are no meanings in nature other than those we bring to it. Things in nature don't have to be the way they are except in the sense that what is and what happens depend upon what has gone before and the way things interact. The world has been through many different states with many different life forms in geological time, all of them viable in the sense that they all existed and indeed life forms have come and gone as the states varied and evolution took place. Nature is indifferent to us and there is no necessity that we are here. However, the necessity of nature is that for us, the earth is our home. We depend upon nature and we should cherish it. This is not only a functional, utilitarian argument but also a spiritual one. We need nature for our culture and our intellectual and spiritual life to flourish as much as we do for oxygen, food and water. As Laurens van der Post (1986: 139 and 141) nicely expressed it: "[C]onservation is a deep need in the soul of man ... man needed it almost more than the animals did ... nature will always take care of itself even without man. But man without nature is unthinkable and, known or unknown, his spirit needs it: needs it for its survival, sanity and increase, as his body does." Loss of nature is thus a loss of culture and a loss of self.

Hence, we can argue that not only does our science have to be enacted through practical conservation in a cultural context, the proposition is that it is the cultural context which provides a set of persuasive arguments as to why we should conserve nature. We should also examine the counter-arguments which exist about why nature need not be conserved; otherwise we shall not understand why it doesn't happen. Such counter-arguments may involve indifference or hostile attitudes to nature, or selective views that some animals have more conservation value than others. One has only to think of the cultural attitudes towards pandas and mosquitoes, for example, to grasp the range of views. There are also many, more subtle, aspects as to why not everything needs to be conserved; for example, the selective control of predators to conserve a rare species and tackling pests which decrease our food stocks. In all cases, we have to think carefully about our justifications.

In the context of nature conservation endeavours, given the therapeutic and psychological significance of nature to our species and to human culture, we also consider the roles of poetic, emotional attachment to a sense of place which can be as important as scientific evidence. A sense of justification for action involves a wide range of approaches.

Not only are the functional significance of species important, as for example discussed by Jax (2010) in *Ecosystem Functioning*, but also the therapeutic value of nature together with the historic and poetic associations involved in a human feeling for landscape, including seascape, and wildlife. In a key book, *Why Care for Nature?* Postma (2006: 107) has chapter 3 entitled 'Because we are human' and a section 'In defence of an aesthetic account of the intrinsic value of nature' – to get away from the dichotomy between the anthropocentric and ecocentric views of nature. That is to say that it is neither an anthropocentric view of nature, where nature deserves moral consideration because nature affects humans, or an ecocentric view where nature deserves moral consideration because nature has intrinsic value. However, it is an endeavour to see the whole picture where both are viewed through the lens of aesthetics – an appreciation of nature for its beauty. This is very much the spirit of networks for nature: www.newnetworksfornature.org.uk. This is a broad alliance of poets, authors, scientists, film makers, visual artists, environmentalists, musicians and composers whose creative work draws on the natural environment. They feel that wildlife and landscapes are too often evaluated in economic or scientific terms when they should be seen as a resource at the very heart of human creativity with the natural world at the centre of the nation's cultural life.

In Andrea Wulf's (2015: 298) book on Alexander von Humboldt she has a chapter on 'Art, ecology and nature' where she describes the difficulty the biologist Ernst Haeckel (1834–1919; Figure 1.2) had in coming to terms with reconciling his scientific work with the cultural dimensions of nature. By contrast, Humboldt (1769–1859; Figure 1.3), who Haeckel looked up to, had written in his *Cosmos* about the bond which "united knowledge, science, poetry and artistic feeling". Earlier, Goethe (1749–1832) was well known for his literary botanical and anatomical work and his writings on colour. However, Wulf recorded how Haeckel "didn't know if he should use a paintbrush or a microscope" (2015: 299). Nevertheless, Haeckel's drawings are now widely regarded as great art, as in Hartman's (2010) book: *Ernst Haeckel: Art forms in nature*. Today, it is argued that earlier investigators had to deal with less knowledge so they could cover a wider range and that the proliferation of knowledge has inevitably led to specialism. However, in order to promote the conservation endeavour, it seems today that any scientists sticking to their narrower disciplines might usefully do more to embrace the wider outlook and awareness of Humboldt and others even as they focus on their specialism.

Figure 1.2 Ernst Haeckel "didn't know if he should use a paintbrush or a microscope" (Wulf, 2015: 298) (Hulton Deutsch / Contributor / Corbis Historical / Getty Images)

For a modern example of the unity of science, poetry and art, and how this motivates to conserve, one need look no further than Helen Macdonald's (2006) *Falcon*. Here scientific understanding and cultural history, including J. A. Baker's (1967) *The Peregrine*, merge in an appreciation of the speed, power, beauty and ferocity which make falcons so compelling.

The book thus embraces a range of scientific, artistic, creative, emotional and spiritual aspects of nature. This range then forms a basis for exploring an approach to nature which is both scientifically defensible and also humanistic and which can foster the widest possible diversity of reasons why we should wish to justify the conservation of nature and natural places.

Setting the Scene – Meaning and Significance

I used to start my lectures on the social engagement with nature by looking at a tree out of the window and saying that "that tree does not know it is Tuesday". I do remember at least one student walking out at this stage, understandingly at a somewhat ridiculous statement designed to be provocative. However, most of them readily grasped that there is a

Figure 1.3 Alexander von Humboldt "united knowledge, science, poetry and artistic feeling" (Wulf, 2015: 298) (ullstein bild Dtl. / Contributor / ullstein bild / Getty Images)

world of objects – for example, something to which we give the word 'tree' – and then a world which we have constructed: 'Tuesday' is our invention. We have many, many such inventions, including the words 'ecology' and 'ecosystem' (the latter by Sir Arthur Tansley, as discussed by Trudgill, 2007, 2020). People also often attach values to our constructions, like 'healthy ecosystem'. It is this invented world and the associated value systems which are of interest here because this is where the realms of meaning and significance lie. A tree is a tree is a tree – but we never see it that simply. What sort of tree? Do we value it? Is it in the way? Does it support birds, give shade, fruit, is it useful for timber? The constructed world around 'tree' is as large and diverse as it is revealing of our own thoughts and attitudes which act to transform the object 'tree' as we look at it.

The writer Paul Feyerabend (1999: 12; Figure 1.4) made an important proposition, which is discussed further later in the book but which is

Figure 1.4 Paul Feyerabend (1924–1994) (Photo: Wikimedia)

relevant here, that when we understand something, we transform it. This proposition relates to how we immediately account for something using narratives of meaning – and it is an interesting and important cultural process in society which changes both what is being observed and how we react to it.

People react to something which they find meaningful and significant – and this may well involve attributing a sense of purpose to an occurrence. The meanings may be significant in that how people see something can be highly motivational and lead to the justification of different courses of action. Depending on how we are situated, we might shrug our shoulders and walk away or we might complain and demand action. Any action following this reaction relates to the emotional response – whether neutral, negative or positive. It will follow that people will want to counteract something negative and cherish something when the meanings are positive. Deciding what to do and how to do it can follow but meaning and significance are fundamental to caring enough to be motivated to do something. If we are interested in motivation for conservation, it thus behoves us to explore this world of the meaning and significance of nature.

As a further example, a boulder falling off a cliff and hurtling down towards us is very real and can hurt us. The event is then transformed by meaning which is beyond the simple observation and it could be seen as significant according to the perceptions, assumptions and culture of the observer. Why did it fall off just as we are passing? Was it just bad luck? Was it dislodged by an animal? Loosened by the weather or a minor earth tremor? Or did it just fall off? Perhaps it was pushed? Is it aimed at us? What could have been done to prevent it? Is it someone's fault? Is it a sign? Is it a punishment? Is it God's will? Is it possessed by a spirit?

Finding meaning and significance in events thus transforms the events: the things which happen around us are changed by the way we think about them. In sociology, this can be referred to as a social construction – a meaning constructed by society which may be held by many people or contested and more individualistic. The boulder still fell, as any observer would agree, but when we construct meanings, the meanings are within us and not in the event itself and thus can vary with the individual.

If we follow this idea, it leads to the conclusion that reality is defined by our concept of reality: how we see something defines what we are seeing. What is real is imagined and what is imagined is real. It is akin to the writer Rorty's (1979) ideas in the 'mirror of nature' where he discusses how 'what is seen as true' amounts to 'what the observer wishes to say'. These ideas themselves can be examined more closely; however, as clearly one could argue the case that every observer will see a tree or a boulder falling but not all will agree on what it means – they are able to construct it differently. So, it is the 'truth' of meaning which varies rather than the 'truth' that some kind of object is present (these two notions are allied to the ideas of epistemology – knowing – and ontology – existence, though these terms are themselves much discussed and debated). However expressed, the ideas do elucidate the notion that there are no meanings in nature other than those which we bring to it ourselves. Thus, a tree will be a tree; a boulder will be a boulder; a fly will be a fly; a wet area of land will be a wet area of land – but how we construct them in terms of meaning can vary vastly – tree as useful or obstruction; falling boulder as omen or inconsequential; fly as nuisance or useful part of the ecosystem; wetland as biodiverse area or dismal swamp.

So, then, given that different people will see – or construct – the same things differently, we may ask: why is an observer thinking like they are? The philosopher Foucault asked a key question here (from Bernauer, 1987 and Bernauer, 1992: 270–271 on Foucault, as discussed in Darier, 1999: 224): 'How have I been situated to experience the real?' How have I been positioned by my upbringing? My culture? My circumstances and the contexts in which I exist? For us, the really interesting question becomes one of why and how have people come to see and perceive the meanings in nature that they do.

The answers clearly relate to people's knowledge, beliefs and culture. Equally interesting, is that if we ask: 'Why do we think the way we do?', this can be quickly followed by: 'Do we actually have to think the way we do?' And if we realise that we do have a choice – and have the power to change the way we think – how do we choose which ways might be better? What would the criteria for 'better' be? This gives both a sense of 'having been situated or positioned' to think in a certain way but also the liberation that 'I could think in a different way.'

One aspect of this is to be conscious of how we are supporting the ways in which we think. Beliefs can be cherished despite the evidence – and evidence can also be selected to reinforce a belief. This is known as 'confirmation bias' where we tend to see what we already agree with. If we are conscious of this process, it might help us to try to think and look differently.

In this context, the way we find justifications for proposed courses of action is particularly interesting. Evidence is often cited when we are finding meaning and significance and we are justifying actions. However, not only is the gathering of the evidence itself influenced by our approaches to deriving it, confirmation bias means that we might consciously or unconsciously selectively ignore or emphasise aspects of the evidence available. So, part of the self-awareness during the process of justifying our actions is to ask how far are knowledge and information selected, supressed or emphasised to fit a preferred meaning or belief? As we saw with the falling boulder, the interpretations are not entirely based on what we actually experienced. There is an important link between our beliefs, our justifications and our actions. As the philosopher Jacob Bronowski (1973, pp. 116) said: "the hand is the cutting edge of the mind" – what we do reveals what we have in mind.

Notwithstanding such attempts to be self-aware, thinking differently from the way we do is not easy. Towards the end of his book on the way in which societies see nature, Neil Evernden (1992) wrote:

> Perhaps there is only one conclusion a reflective naturalist can come to: that if we would protect nature from the perils of the 'environmental crisis', we must first acknowledge that those perils arose as a consequence of conceptual imprisonment. If we would save the world, we must set it free. This is a frightening prospect. To contemplate actually letting something be is very nearly beyond our ability. (Evernden, 1992: 129–130)

Tellingly, Shirley (2019) in 'Nature's place – what should live where?' the author writes:

> If we lift our eyes above the 'ecological horizon' we will see a world which, socially and culturally, is a borderless mix. Nature strives to be like this, but we constantly try to constrain it. Instead we need to harness nature's resilience, resourcefulness and chaos, and stop pretending that it is frozen and static. We need to create the conditions for natural processes to flourish and stop trying to impose our own 'designer solutions'.

These quotations raise many interesting points and the conceptual imprisonment, to me, refers to the transformations, inspirations and constraints which our ideas bring. This is rather more fundamental than the idea of 'setting nature free' and moving from 'management' of nature to 'letting nature take its course' – that is merely jumping from one conceptual imprisonment to another. What I gain from Evernden's writing is that the unthinking repetition of ideas can dominate our automatic responses and actions – and that this should not go unchallenged. It is the realisation that we don't actually have to live by the ideas we do live under which sets us free from the conceptual prison. If our ideas can turn out to be some form of cultural delusion, then we should realise that they are limiting our thoughts and actions, rather than just rehearsing them over and over again. We come to realise that we are looking through a cultural lens of perception, and that we should realise that the lens is there while we are thinking about the way we see things.

There is a German word, '*Kulturbrille*': *kultur* ('culture') and *brille* ('glasses' or 'spectacles') or 'culture-glasses', used by the German-born American anthropologist Franz Uri Boas (1858–1942) to mean acquired cultural associations ('lenses') that shape an individual's perceptions. It was seen as important for anthropologists when writing about cultures other than their own. In *Falcon* by Helen Macdonald (2006: 7–8), the author refers to the "the invisible mental lens" you acquire in your own culture and through which you view the world. In the book, our human *Kulturbrille* make falcons the "repository for human meanings" but Macdonald (2006: 8) writes: "Animals are so malleable a repository for human meanings that some modern critics see them as existing almost entirely within the realm of human representation." She then resists this: "But falcons are not merely imaginary receptacles for symbolic meaning. They live, breed, fly, hunt, breathe. As living animals real falcons constrain, undercut and sometimes resist the meanings people have attached to them."

This discussion of perceived worlds, lenses and meanings can be further illustrated by a quote from the script of a television programme written by Adam Curtis (2011) cited in a paper on 'The ecosystem' by Cameron and Earley (2015: 473): "This is a story about the rise of machines and our belief in the balance of nature. How the idea of the ecosystem was invented. How it inspired us. And how it wasn't even true."

How interesting. An ecosystem doesn't actually exist in the way a falling boulder does. It exists as a very important idea which we find extremely helpful in our way of thinking and it serves us well, we think. The term was invented by Sir Arthur Tansley (as discussed by Trudgill, 2007) and involves ideas of interrelationships and dependency. It remains, however, a concept not a tangible entity, as Tansley himself wrote – it is a way of seeing things – and we should see it as such. The writer John Steinbeck felt that science did not prove anything, but that it goes by something so long as it serves us well, though we can become very attached to our own hypotheses, as he discusses in *The Log from the Sea of Cortez* ([1951]1960: 234). The ecosystem concept seems to be serving us well, so we are going with it, but it may just also be a constraint on our way of thinking. This is not to challenge or to deny the importance of the ecosystem concept but the point is simply to make sure that we know that it is giving us a lens through which we are looking.

My ideas on this topic of looking through cultural lenses crystallised more on reading Stephen Bocking's (2015) article on 'Ecological concepts: Seeing, placing, imposing'. Yes, I thought, we impose so much on nature – that word in his title just about sums up what I wish to write about. Certainly, we might usefully be aware that the beliefs are impositions before we repeat them endlessly and use them to justify our actions.

In essence what I want to emphasise is that nature is just doing what it is doing. Maybe things happened just because they could – and that 'why' is the same as 'how'. However, we impose a multitude of ideas upon nature and, believing them to be true, we act upon the presumed implications of our beliefs. Think back to the falling boulder and you will see what I mean. It just fell, but our reactions tell us so much about the way we think and act.

I shall feel I have succeeded if this book helps the reader to think more carefully about our much-rehearsed ideas about the meanings of nature. Especially if this is to think about the way we impose them on the environment both consciously and unconsciously. And particularly to think about the way we may do this with or without any evidence – or despite the evidence which we choose to ignore and because of the evidence we are willing to see. In terms of imposing our ideas on events and objects, vindictive traffic lights are a good example.

Vindictive Traffic Lights: Explanations and Choice

Drivers in urban areas will immediately recognise what I mean about traffic lights changing to red just as you drive up to them. You *know* that they are just changing at set times but *why* do they *have* to change to red *just* as *I* am approaching? It seems personal and malicious, especially if you are in a hurry. In all reason, of course, the lights are just changing – they are just doing what they are doing, quite impassively. However, this common urban experience shows how we interpret the world about us in a way which readily involves attributing a story – or narrative – to a set of objects. Most important is that the story is formed in relation to our wishes and intentions. It is the same with nature – it is just impassively doing what it is doing, but we relate to it through our intentionality.

Sometimes, how the lights change doesn't matter at all. If we are not in a hurry we might just stop mechanically at a red light, thinking nothing of it. If they are green we might hardly notice – unless we are concerned that they will change before we get there. The key point is that our relationship with the traffic lights tells us a lot about ourselves and far less about the traffic lights. And so it is with the key proposition that our relationship with nature tells us far more about us than about nature itself.

In *Other Worlds: A portrait of nature in rebellion – space, superspace and the quantum universe* Davies (1980) writes on landscape, proposing that we do not experience an objective reality. Instead it is "the relationship between the observer and the observed which gives us the sensations of a surrounding reality". Our versions of this reality will be coloured by our model of the world "as constructed by previous experience, emotional pre-disposition and expectation" (after Davies, 1980, quoted from Sayer, 2005: 103 where the reference is erroneously attributed to Professor Paul Davis [*sic*]).

The proposition that our relationships with nature reveal more about us than about nature matters because these relationships control our approach to nature. A bird or animal eating some vegetation by a roadside we happen to be passing is very different to that same bird or animal eating our very own food crops which we have grown for ourselves in our garden or farm plot. The casual and incidental observation of eating is transformed into a malicious threat from a marauding creature. We pass the creature by in the former case and may seek to remove in the latter. That creature is, however, just like the red traffic light – it is just there doing what it is doing and we have constructed narratives involving positive or negative emotions – or indifference – according to our intentions. A scientist might say that the bird is just eating to stay alive but we can also empathise with the creature in its needs or think about eating it for our survival or invoke a host of other stories. A key point is how these ideas of meaning transform nature according to our perspectives. A further endeavour is to assess how the meanings act both to inspire and to constrain us.

Meaning and Seeing

Our perspectives do have a strong influence on perceptions, as many authors have emphasised. As Sheail (1995: 955) deduced from Simmons's (1993c) book on environmental history, "we are simply projecting onto the world what the author wanted to believe anyway" and Pimm (1991: 388) writes in *The Balance of Nature?* that "theories tell us where to look and when we readily find what we are looking for, we gain confidence in them" (see also 'Do theories tell us what to see?' by Trudgill, 2012a). Writing on 'Environmental thought and action' Denis Cosgrove (1990: 345) asserted that: "Metaphor and image are conceived not as surface representations of a deeper truth but as a creative intervention in making truth." In other words, what we already have in our mind as representations can become the object we are observing. This also concurs with a proposition from another writer arguing from a psychological perspective that "images do not raise consciousness, they force it to descend" (Bishop, 1992: 17). Thus, imagery can constrain what we are aware of.

The phenomena of seeing faces in non-human objects, such as rocks and clouds, is well known under the term pareidolia which can be defined as perceiving familiar patterns where none actually exists. As Mark Antony says to Eros in Shakespeare's *Antony and Cleopatra* (Act 4, Scene 14):

Sometimes we see a cloud that's dragonish;
A vapour sometime like a bear or lion,
A tower'd citadel, a pendent rock,
A forked mountain or blue promontory
With trees upon't, that nod unto the world
And mock our eyes with air.

This phenomenon, in its generalised sense, is perhaps far more widespread and fundamental than is generally acknowledged and involves not just seeing faces where there are none but also seeing what we think we perceive in everything from landscape views to beliefs about nature. We see a powerful idea and look no further. Indeed, Samuel Perry, a sociologist at the University of Oklahoma who writes on Christianity and the cognitive underpinnings of religious belief, is quoted (in Whipple, 2020) as saying: "Humans have an evolved tendency to perceive agency when there is none" and "That adaptation would help us to survive by allowing us to better detect danger. But it could also incline us toward attributing the random movements we observe in nature to spirits." So, we can attribute patterns to deities or other agencies and we can see a man in the moon if we are so minded. However, while we know that there is not actually a human face in the moon, we see the balance of nature and other concepts all around us but we all too rarely appreciate that this is a form of conceptual pareidolia and make the second step of looking to see what might actually be there. As J. A Baker (1967: 19) observed when writing about the peregrine falcon and the way it is portrayed, "the hardest thing of all is to see what is really there".

Perhaps we are like the travellers discussed by Andrews who, writing on *Landscape and Western Art*, cites the observation of Cézanne who wrote in 1902 that he felt that people had stopped looking at nature but were just recognising previously experienced pictures. Andrews (1999: 177) quotes Cézanne's words: "Today our sight is a little weary, burdened by the memory of a thousand images. We no longer see nature; we see pictures over and over again." Andrews reinforces this by noting (p. 131) that some early travellers in Europe recorded how they referred to the names of artists when they came to particular views "according to whether the subjects before our eyes reminded us of the manner and choice of one or other of the masters [artists] named". The mental image takes precedence over the landscape which is before the viewer.

I've often taught how landscape art can have wide interpretations. I had a painting (Figure 1.5) in my College room and I regularly asked students what they think what is being depicted.

Some saw it as positive as representing how life clings on despite adversity; others saw it as negative as showing something dying. It can thus be described as hopeful or gloomy. The response was usually about 50:50 each way. Either way it is seen as imbued with significance and purpose. Whatever the interpretations, there seemed to be some

Figure 1.5 Author's painting of a tree on a limestone pavement, Ingleborough, Yorkshire. Negative as the tree is partly dead or positive as the tree is surviving? (Photo: S. Trudgill). *A black and white version of this figure will appear in some formats. For the colour version, please refer to the plate section.*

emotional engagement and a search for meaning. As a physical entity, it is a half-dead, half-alive tree. We can say that the dead portion is on the exposed side where frost and wind have combined to kill the tree – and thus we can know the tree by that meaning. Our narratives of meaning can be emotional and/or scientific – but each is purposeful in some way.

The supervision students, not knowing initially that it is my painting, discussed the artist's intention, often with some relish and assumed insights which, for them, imbued the painting with a sense of purpose. When I revealed that I had painted it and I recognised very little of what they said as motivational for me, they were often crestfallen. However, when they pushed me, they felt comforted, I thought, when I said that I think the appeal for me is about the juxtaposition of the living and the dead parts. But that is a post hoc self-interpretation. In truth I just sat down and painted it without much conscious thought of why – it just appealed to me, perhaps compositionally and as a striking image as much as anything. This process told me that unless the artist was aware of and specifically stated their intentions, then not only is it easy to over-interpret the artist's intention but that all interpretations are possible – and untestable. The viewer is making up stories about the artist which are justifiable, and which then become true for the viewer. The fact that I created the image and then sat back and listened to a myriad of interpretations and assumed meanings which 'the artist must have intended' told me a lot. That many interpretations of images are possible – and untestable – and about how easy it is to over-interpret the intentionality of an artist. The lesson is the same when looking at nature and we read intentionality where there is none.

Meaning and Transformation

Just as with paintings, we can find meanings in landscapes themselves and nature derived from a blend of prior knowledge, associations and emotional responses. I also have no doubt that the understanding brought to bear by interpretations is not only transformative but also restrictive. This key point here is one introduced earlier in this book and is made by Feyerabend (1999: 12) in *The Conquest of Abundance: A tale of abstraction versus the richness of being*. Here he describes how we tend to reduce the myriad teeming complexity of nature through the process of trying to understand it. From his writings (p. 12) I find the following points particularly telling. First: "Variety disappears when subject to scholarly analysis. This is not the fault of scholars. Anyone who tries to make sense of a puzzling sequence of events, his or her own actions included, is forced to introduce ideas that are not in the events themselves, but put them in perspective." Second: "There is no escape: understanding a subject means transforming it, lifts it out of a natural habitat and inserts it into a model or a theory or a poetic account of it." The phrase 'understanding a subject means transforming it' is, I think fundamental. As we saw earlier, a bird eating a seed is a just bird eating a seed – but it can be a delight if we put the seed out to attract it or a pest if it is our food it is taking.

The 'model or a theory or a poetic account' he writes about are abstract notions we construct in our minds. Such mental constructs then become the means by which we give significance to the perceived world through the use of narratives of meaning. The proposition is that narratives are unavoidable in order that the world may have some interpretation and meaning: they provide necessary and comforting ways of making sense of the world. The idea of a 'bird eating a seed' is a simple enough construct but the emotive narratives of delight or theft give the transformative significance. In terms of what justifies environmental action, it is easy to see the different directions these transformations take us.

The transformations can be highly individual according to people's culture and experience. Feyerabend (1999: 12) writes: "Even the discovery of an immanent [pervading the universe, inherent] structure changes the scene, for the events-as-they-are and events-known-to-have-the-structure don't affect people in the same way. But one transformation may be better than another in the sense that it permits or even explains what for the other transformation remains an insoluble puzzle." However, each transformation can impoverish rather than enrich experience – directing our attention at the expense of other items which might be observable, focussing and constraining our thoughts. This also limits the range of possible actions.

We may emphasise here again how in detective stories, the crime writers not only lay the false trails of narrative traps during the unfolding of their work, but they also in the end make us fit all the detail into the concluding narrative, marginalising all other aspects as trivial. We thus omit or include so much when making sense of things according to our sense of significance. Feyerabend writes that "even the simple attempt to describe may throw a veil of illusion over the world" and he considers eighteenth-century travellers and naturalists described by Mary Louise Pratt (1992) in *Imperial Eyes* who "reduce and dismantle all they find while retaining the language of direct observation" (Feyerabend, 1999: 12).

Interactions between Facts, Evidence, Experience and Values

Consider the proposition that a 'fact' is meaningless unless it has a narrative of meaning. In terms of the role of evidence and experience, Kearns (1998: 379) writes how values and experience interact, terming experience "facts". Values prioritise or relegate facts and the feedback is that facts embarrass or endorse values (Figure 1.6).

A 'fact' can be endorsed as significant and taken as evidence to support the values or it can embarrass the value which we might change; in turn, our values may lead us to stress a 'fact' or to relegate it. Physical 'reality' can thus be played down or played up according to our values and also may change or reinforce our values according to the selectivity with which we play it up or down.

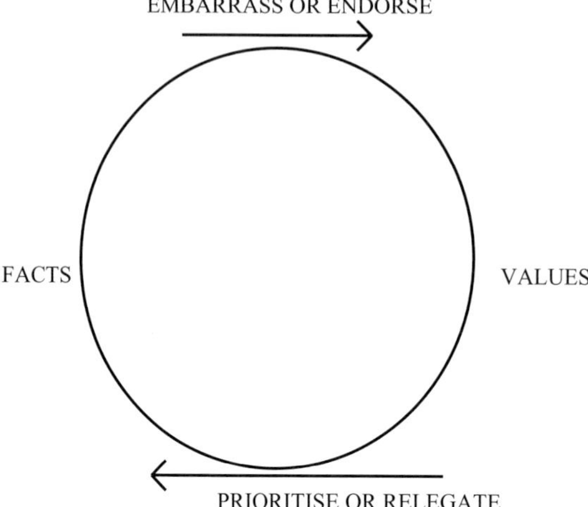

Figure 1.6 The virtuous circle of facts and values (modified from Kearns, 1998: 379 by permission from The Association of American Geographers, www.aag.org published by Taylor & Francis Ltd: www.tandfonline.com, and the author)

If 'facts' can have no meaning without a contextualising narrative, then what we call 'reality' can arguably be seen as having a fluid, reflexive relationship with our mental constructs and associated narratives by which we make sense of the world. In that sense, reality is defined by our concepts of reality.

What is interesting is the choice we have between whether to change our concepts to fit new evidence or whether to be selective about which evidence we find legitimate.

This choice is often not made consciously, and the situation is often rather messier than a simple duality of choice and so the purpose of this section is to raise awareness of these processes whereby constructs, narratives, meanings and judgements can become conflated.

It might be assumed that that Feyerabend's transformation and Kearns's prioritising/relegation is less marked the more we are dealing with tangible (e.g. 'hot') constructs because the facts might only allow a narrow range of narratives, allowing few other meanings and judgements. It is then arguable that meanings and judgements only really flourish in multitudes for constructs which are more diffuse, less easy to test. Thus, a woodland can be seen positively as a refuge or negatively as a place where threats lurk depending on the viewer's context. In this case we would have far more choice of values because the 'facts' can be constructed in many different ways and thus tend to embarrass our values less. However, while nature does cover the whole spectrum from the tangible to the more obviously judgemental, even the more tangible end of the spectrum can be just as readily transformed and constructed. 'Fire' does indeed have a latitude of conceptual interpretation – while it is always 'hot', it may be seen as beneficial or disastrous depending on what is burning, how controlled it is and in what context and thus we have to study both the range of descriptors and the range of meanings. Thus, with fire the basic descriptions (some form of 'hot') might be limited but the meanings and significance vary and this is so much so that even the descriptors become loaded: 'warming' or 'destructive inferno' because the meanings influence what we are perceiving.

For example, earthquakes are highly tangible as a construct but can be attributed with multiple meanings and judgements (Ludwin, 1999). They can be seen as an event or punishment or some kind of 'test' to be met. In Greek mythology, Poseidon was the cause and god of earthquakes. When he was in a bad mood, he struck the ground with a trident, causing earthquakes and other calamities. He also used earthquakes to punish and inflict fear upon people as revenge. In understanding the earthquake, it is transformed into an instrument of purpose.

In Norse mythology, earthquakes were explained as the violent struggling of the god Loki. When Loki, god of mischief and strife, murdered Baldr, god of beauty and light, he was punished by being bound in a cave with a poisonous serpent placed above his head dripping venom. Loki's wife Sigyn stood by him with a bowl to catch the poison, but whenever she had to empty the bowl the poison dripped on Loki's face, forcing him to jerk his head away and thrash against his bonds, which caused the earth to tremble.

In Japanese mythology, Namazu (鯰) is a giant catfish who causes earthquakes. Namazu lives in the mud beneath the earth and is guarded by the god Kashima who restrains the fish with a stone. When Kashima lets his guard fall, Namazu thrashes about, causing violent earthquakes.

It has often struck me at English Harvest Festival services, where we celebrate what we have grown and gathered, what a conceit there is underlying a lot of the otherwise appropriate gratitude: it seems curious to me that God's bounty is just for us. Everything is created especially for us and it is bestowed on us – and we are grateful, humble even. There is thus a curious anthropocentric view of creation pervading the narratives in the hymns and prayers. Curious when plants like grasses evolved, but it was we who cultivated the most productive varieties. The worship is as though wheat was suddenly created especially for us. Here we are at the centre of the universe and a benign God has created everything for our benefit.

The question of agency is also interesting and the fact that we don't have it all our own way. Yes 'we plough the fields and scatter the good seed on the land' but 'it is fed and watered by God's almighty hand'. It is the interaction which seems to be central here. There is something beyond our power – but what are we actually saying? This looks like a supplication, an entreaty because the Almighty hand might not bestow its grace upon us. We are grateful for the occasions when it does but, in reality, sometimes the weather is bad and the harvest is miserable – so it is not actually all for our benefit. Of course, we might conclude all sorts of things if the harvest has been bad – maybe it was our fault. Who knows? It depends what you wish to believe. So, which delusion would you like? Is the world created for us? It is all out of our control? It is all a struggle against the elements? It is all under our control – or at least to make the best of it? It is all ordained? It is all random?

Transformative narratives of purpose thus abound. However, while an earthquake is still an earthquake and a fire is still a fire, I think that the key point is that in nature the physical realities can be subordinate to the construction of meanings which readily dominate. Nature is passive and neutral but so often can have an imposed set of meanings. These meanings are often deeply held and the widely varied narratives can be contested, as Macnaghten and Urry (1998) describe in *Contested Natures*.

The Imperative of the Explanation

What we are really doing with nature, both in the way we see it and in what we do to it, is no more and no less than writing stories – finding narrative accounts which make sense to us. The crime writer P. D. James is attributed with the quotation that: "What the detective story is about is not murder but the restoration of order" (James, 1986). So, something ghastly has happened: a body lies in a room. It is the detective who is the hero. We twist and turn through the story, suspecting everyone until, at last, the killer is revealed. Most importantly we then discover the motive – the reason: money, love, jealousy or whatever. The logic is immensely comforting and we go back over the story and see how everything fits into the pattern. Order is restored and we are satisfied, no matter how awful the crime. Imagine, though, that there was no motive or reason. How immensely disturbing. The killer would then have to be 'insane'. No motive, no logic, no order. How unsatisfying – no wonder that detective stories do not characteristically end with this plot line. We may just cope with there being no killer (died of natural causes) but if there is a killer then there just has to be a motive.

The alternative to the reasoned narrative is, then, disturbing, unsatisfying and we quickly have to put in the narrative of un-reason – insanity. We may be satisfied with the provisional 'puzzling' but it never stops there – parallel and competing theories proliferate. It is the pursuit of order and reason, of the explanation, which we demand relentlessly. Without an explanation, we are lost.

It is the same with nature. We observe something. We ask why it occurred. We proffer explanations. We eliminate some possibilities till we complete the story by finding a cause or reason – and then we are happy to repeat this to others.

We are always telling stories – 'it is . . . this' or 'that', to explain. Passing a road accident, people crane their necks to see what happened – 'he must have swerved. . .', 'going too fast. . .' or some such follows, and we have order again. Everything is OK as long as there is a story. This is a pervasive and inescapable human trait: Marek Kohn (2004) encapsulates this in the title of his book on evolution: *A Reason for Everything: Natural selection and the English imagination*. We will argue over different types of reason and search for the most plausible given the evidence, but it almost doesn't matter what the reason is as long as we can find one – there has to be reason.

Even a sense of nothing has its own story – the narrative of emptiness. Victor Hugo's (1866) central character Gilliatt in *Toilers of the Sea* wakes at night on an island and peers into the indivisible darkness and there are thoughts of horror and terror hidden in the unreasoned nothingness. "Darkness has unity, hence arises horror; at the same time it is complex, and hence terror" writes Hugo ([1866]1911: 239–240), but then: "All is incomprehensible, but nothing is unintelligible." Even the darkness can be known and be read as a narrative. The words 'incomprehensible' and 'unintelligible' Hugo uses almost mean the same thing but the subtlety seems to be that you might not understand something but nevertheless you can say something about it: you can know or read something in it as some kind of construct without understanding what it is. Thus, he gives darkness, the epitome of unknowingness, narrative attributes of unity, horror, complexity and terror and so they become part of the story of darkness and unknowingness.

The imperative of the explanation is writ so large in the human relationship with nature. There has to be a story. A woodland can rarely be 'just' a collection of trees; even indifference has its logic. At the very least it has to be sights and sounds, light, shade, greens, birdsong. It may then be perhaps a retreat, as for Thomas Hardy in "Nature as soft release from men's unrest" (from 'In a Wood' of 1898; see Chapter 5). Equally, a wood may be an ecosystem, with form and function – layers, interdependence, food chains. Alternatively, it can be an impenetrable threatening place; 'wilderness' and even 'chaos'. Thus, there are always stories and descriptors which allow us to handle something and derive meaning. However, note that not only can there be a descriptive appreciation but also how many of the characterisations are purposeful, for example about the function of the wood in providing release, being a system or thwarting our intentionality.

Simply expressed we have a relationship between 'something which is there' and 'what it means to us'. This can be expressed as a relationship between what is 'ontological' – dealing with being or essence, and 'epistemological' – dealing with knowledge in terms of concepts, propositions and meanings. These words themselves can be used with various shades of meanings which can prompt lengthy debates, but here, for example, ontologically there might be a group of trees but epistemologically it might be seen as an ecosystem with the attached notions of inter-linkage, flows, pathways and so on. Notwithstanding any of this, and in short, narratives have to be there and in nature many of them are imbued with purpose.

'Appropriateness' and the Consequences of Meaning

Deciding what is an appropriate narrative is always going to be a sticking point. 'Appropriateness' includes our sense of significance and is always going to be particularly contested because judging appropriateness will be nested in our criteria and contexts. In science, appropriateness might putatively be judged in terms of verifiability and evidence. However, even then, what is interesting is the study of the conditions which allow multiple narratives to coexist and flourish. This is actually a normal phenomenon especially as many situations are multi-dimensional. Even if a case for a belief seems overwhelming to many, 'evidence' can always be selective. A temptingly easy route to understanding is that narratives can be interpreted in terms of the characteristics of who is espousing them (usually declared as "they would say that, wouldn't they") – deconstruction in terms of the source. However, one might caution that this attributive narrative is a very easy cliché to use and is often over-used when there is actually no necessity in applying it. So, the rejoinder to "they would say that, wouldn't they" could usefully be "not necessarily" or "that doesn't necessarily follow" as they didn't actually *have* to say that. In this context I do like the paper containing the words 'the view from nowhere' (Shapin, 1998) and Thomas Nagel's (1986) book *The View from Nowhere* – the notion of just that very concept is one worth entertaining.

While constructs can be strongly normative and held by many, others may be weak, ambiguous and varied with many contested coexisting narratives held by minorities, along with disputed claims of appropriateness. With any normative, accepted sense of appropriateness it takes mavericks, new events, situations or evidence to change any accepted such sense. Appropriateness is thus very context dependent and difficult to generalise about. However, one clear criterion I can see for judging the validity of narratives, and their associated value systems, is in terms of the consequences of holding them.

Examining the consequences of espousing particular meanings is important because meanings tell us where to look, what to see and thus how to act. Therefore, we should be careful to examine any sense of necessity which follows from them. This might be compared with reading a tour guide which constrains us by telling us where to go and what to see. Travellers all know that if we go to a foreign place and read a guidebook we tend to focus on the specific sights highlighted and feel a sense of satisfaction at actually seeing them; we might find other sights not mentioned – and really enjoy some kind of personal exclusivity at our discovery but the guidebook gives a sense of significance. May (1996) discussed this in the article 'In search of authenticity off and on the beaten track'. We recognise this process on holiday but it is scarcely recognised that it is happening all the time. We can, however, have such a self-awareness if we think of Foucault asking – "how have I been situated to experience the real?" (from Bernauer, 1992 on Foucault as discussed in Darier, 1999: 224). Narratives play a vital role in this situating.

What is liberating is realising that there is a necessity and imperative of having a narrative but there is no necessity in having the narratives we have. Realising the former is essential to understand how we relate to the world but realising the latter can and should be liberating as nothing has to be seen like it is. Equally we don't, then, actually have to see nature and treat the environment the way we do.

The questions focus on: how and why do we see and, most importantly: what effect does how we see affect what we do? What conceptual stores do we have in our minds to influence our vision – and how does this vision affect our environmental actions? It was the philosopher Immanuel Kant (1724–1804) who changed the view that the mind merely reflected the world about the observer. Kant maintained that the mind is active in playing a part in shaping the world of experience: objects confirm to our minds. We can turn to Wordsworth's observations where his lines contain the phrases: "How exquisitely the individual Mind . . . to the external world is fitted; and how exquisitely too . . . The external world is fitted to the Mind" (from 'Home in Grasmere', 1800, lines 1006–1111; see Wyatt, 1995: 124).

How far and how do we fit the external world to the mind? How far and how does our imagined world alter the physical world about us? This is as well as: how far and how does this relate to the way the imagined world in the mind might or might not be fitted to the external world?

In *Landscapes of the Mind: Worlds of sense and metaphor* Porteous (1990: 3) observes that: "While environmentalists strive to protect tangible landscapes, poets, artists and novelists preserve, restore, and express our landscapes of the mind." We might also well ask how those imagined landscapes of the mind influence the tangible landscapes. That is to say not only do landscapes exist in the mind, the landscapes we create reflect what is in our mind. And is what we call tangible actually a set of created signifiers which we selectively find significant? Do we thus focus on what we have created in an elusive illusion of reality produced by the interaction of selective action and vision?

In terms of fitting the landscape to the mind, mankind's attempts to control and influence nature are well documented (e.g. Thomas, 1956, 1970). A singular historical example of the imposition of an ideology on nature is provided by Blackbourn (2007) in *The Conquest of Nature: Water, landscape and the making of modern Germany*. Here, the book charts how from Frederick the Great of Prussia through to the Nazis, the idea of 'mastery over nature' led to river channelisation and dam building in Germany. Rivers were not allowed to wander in their natural state but had to be controlled. The theme is further extensively displayed in Lekan's (2004) *Imagining the Nation in Nature: Landscape preservation and German Identity, 1885–1945.*

Meanings, Stories and Narratives in Nature Conservation

One of the UK's first nature reserves was Wicken Fen in Cambridgeshire (www.nationaltrust.org.uk/wicken-fen-nature-reserve). As is discussed further in Chapter 6 in the section on nature reserves, the changing management of the Fen illustrates the theme of how the ideas people espouse become manifest in the landscape. In *Wicken Fen: The making of a wetland nature reserve* Friday (1997: 216) discusses how the management plans ranged from an earlier idea of "laissez faire . . . allowing the Fen to run wild . . . and . . . return to its original state". The meaning was thus one of wildness. However, doing nothing and 'keeping it wild' led to the gradual replacement of the distinctive wetland by commoner shrubby plants and trees and a loss of the local fenland flora and fauna the area was famous for. Thus, one promotion of one meaning, wildness, led to the loss of other meanings such as speciality, rarity and species-richness. This contestation of meanings led to a change of plan and the removal of woody vegetation to maintain the wetlands – which indeed had been maintained by reed and sedge cutting for thatch in earlier times. In many ways the existence of local assemblages of distinctive biota was very man-made. A concept of management for particular purposes came to the fore, with the negotiation of ideas involving several possible reference points from the historical and pre-historical past. Eventually the plans agreed were those which were both biologically and culturally significant. The justificatory narratives involved both enhancing biodiversity, especially of the species special to that wetland area, and maintaining the reed beds which had been important to the economy of the area in recent historical times. Both of these objectives are facilitated by scrub clearance and now selected areas are maintained by the use of Highland cattle and Konik ponies to keep areas open and diverse (https://nt.global.ssl.fastly.net/wicken-fen-nature-reserve/documents/wicken-fen-the-grazing-programme-explained.pdf). There are clear actions and clear objectives but they are rather obviously nested in meanings and concepts about desirability which were negotiated through discussion. In Friday's book there are many justificatory concepts and images which are involved either implicitly or explicitly – especially those which refer to ideas about what the place should look like and what should be there (Figure 1.7).

The place was not left alone but managed to suit what a collective set of minds agreed upon according to a set of criteria. Whatever we see in the nature reserve now reflects how the landscape was fitted to the mind. What is revealing is how Friday's book rehearses so many narratives in order to justify each set of actions. These narratives involve constructs of biodiversity, the roles of particular species and the significance of cultural heritage. The instrumental power of narratives which are invoked during

Figure 1.7 Cambridge University biogeography fieldwork class at Wicken Fen discussing habitat diversity – woodland left to grow in background, area maintained by cutting in the foreground (Photo: S. Trudgill)

the implementation of actions based on them is very evident. There was no letting nature exist – the whole project was imbued with a sense of purpose. The Fen guidebooks are now evocations of care with meanings of biodiversity, rarity and history.

Many natural history films are imbued with stories about creatures that are intended to raise concern about their future. Here we move on from simple observation (a falling boulder and possible interpretations) to more detailed stories about the relationships between animals, survival, predators and prey. The storylines involve strategies and often the purposefulness of the wildlife portrayed.

However, the search for purposes – the search for a story – can exert a kind of tyranny. We rather abhor the notion of 'well, it just happened'. But how far are we trapped in what one might call a 'tyranny of purpose'? The term 'narrative trap' is often understood in fiction – and especially drama – to indicate a false lead (for the use of the term in different contexts such as psychology and storylines in fiction see, e.g., Cayton, 2012; Dolan, 2019 and Lindenmuth, 2012). An example of a narrative trap in crime fiction involves a plot where we may be misled to suspect several innocent characters of a crime. However, in the finale the clever detective reviews the evidence and reveals the actual criminal, together with the way the narrative of the plot had trapped us into following false trails. Here indeed I wish to use the term in the sense of a narrative which appears attractive but may be misleading or constraining – indeed in the sense of Evernden's 'conceptual prison'. Thus, in the case of environmental narrative traps it may be that we keep on rehearsing the usual suspects without the revelation of the actual situation, possibly because it is difficult to see the actual situation as we find the narrative traps so attractive.

I became interested in stories about nature and where they lead us when I watched a natural history film and heard contradictory things. This made me wonder how far the statements made were illusions about nature which we only imagine to be true and it occurred to me that the ideas could both be narrative traps: meaningful, attractive, but misleading. In one part of the commentary I heard a speaker saying that nature is so fragile that if you take one species out then the whole ecosystem collapses. Later in the same film I heard a different commentator say that nature is so wonderfully robust because if you lose one species another steps in to take its place, keeping the whole system stable.

Much engaged me here: the evident incompatibility of these ideas as universally applicable generalisations together with the possibility that both these statements could be true depending on circumstances. For example, ecologists are used to citing Paine's 1966 and 1969 work on keystone species, where the removal of some species does matter far more than others, as examined further, below. However, what intrigued me was the fact that the two storylines could coexist in the same film and that both commentators genuinely believed what they were saying. Both also imply that species can have a purpose. This pervasive – and persuasive – sense of purpose is inherently woven throughout so much ecological language used, as discussed by Kohn (2004) in his book *A Reason for Everything: Natural selection and the English imagination*. It is also noticeable that the terms 'collapse' and 'stability' are not so much dispassionate observations as 'change' and 'not changed' might be; they have value-laden, judgemental overtones. One can see implicit instrumentality and morality in the words 'fragile', 'collapses', 'robust' and 'stability.

Additionally, as the film went on it showed that each speaker could present supporting evidence to confirm their assertions – in that sense both ideas could be made to be evidentially true or, to put it another way, both could be true if the speaker wanted them to be. There was no sense of questioning or testing, just the use of axiomatic statements.

Most tellingly, I realised that there were widely different implications of holding each of these views: the idea of fragility implies that we should have a mandate to step in to conserve each and every species; the idea of robustness implies that we have a reason for not doing anything as long as there is a range of some kind of species or other around. The real importance of these is that once stated, they constrain us in a delusion where evidence can be gathered to support them and, most importantly, the consequences of holding them are highly significant.

Two very different worlds revolve around the ideas. Fragility has a sense of wonder about nature's delicacy and allows a sense of responsibility for the loss: there can be a sense of guilt if it is we who have removed a species or damaged an ecosystem, a feeling of culpability and duty of care. Robustness allows a different sense of wonder about nature – 'isn't it amazing how it copes' – which also allows a lack of a sense of responsibility which in turn could foster a sense of indifference. But, I thought, which of these can lay any greater claim to truth? Both are clearly and sincerely held views which the proponents believed to be defensible. We can but question them as justifications for action.

In terms of evidence-based conservation – and specifically of seeking evidence to support an argument for which species 'matter' – we have the example of the oft-cited work of Paine (1966, 1969) where the removal of a top 'keystone' predator led to a complete change in a marine ecosystem. The removal of the sea star *Pisaster ochreous* converted a diverse rocky shore to a uniform mussel bed. Is this 'collapse' 'robust' or 'fragile'? It is certainly different. Life has carried on in some form, just as it has ever done through evolutionary changes in geological time, so it is robust. However, if it is human agency which has effected the change, we tend to view this negatively. Diversity has decreased so it is collapsed and fragile. The assessment is ours – but how do we justify our assessment?

When I read in Drury's (1998) book on *Chance and Change* that a species may become lost and there may be no discernible difference in an ecosystem, I was rather hooked into this debate. This did not assume that more was necessarily better and good. This was clinical, dispassionate: so, no species has a purpose. There is no preferable state. So, when a species is removed, there are narratives of 'collapse', 'replacement bringing stability' – but also 'no difference at all'. Is it just that we have a preference for diversity? It all seemed clear to me that viewing the world, finding evidence to support your views (confirmation bias) and justifying actions (or inaction) are all mediated through a set of assumptions and impositions which we often don't think about.

This makes me wonder what is going on. If different people can seriously propound different views of the way things are, how do we justify environmental actions if we can't agree on how nature works?

Are we to propose that it must be the case that different mechanisms leading to collapse, robustness or no difference occur in different situations, so the narratives are real but we need more careful scientific research to specify under what conditions each happens?

Or are we to recognise that the much-rehearsed attractive narratives are all just illusions?

If we don't work out the jurisdiction of these ideas, how can we predict what the consequences of our actions might be?

Certainly, we should not keep repeating them as uncontested axioms and acting on their assumed significance.

Finally, I also question whether caring about species loss is necessarily linked to their function in an ecosystem – and indeed even questioning how we go about identifying that function.

Even if is 'there is no difference' in function, does that mean that we should not care?

The possibility does begin to appear that we might be trying to justify actions with a set of assertions which might indeed be essentially unverifiable. However, what is interesting is that they must also be simultaneously not without foundation otherwise surely they would not exist at all. But if the powerful storylines and engaging motivators containing assertions like 'fragile', 'robust', 'collapse' are easy to repeat but remain untested, how do we know the extent to which they are defensible in the face of evidence or how far are they defensible because we wish them to be the case? Testing them more could readily dismiss them in the face of evidence – and certainly contrasting meanings could not readily coexist unless their jurisdictions were specified. Maybe, even if they are unverifiable but powerful motivators to conserve, then they are good myths to have? Additionally, if the detailed knowledge is already available there to test whether these ideas are viable or not, why do commentators keep repeating them in isolation from any evidence? Certainly, the aspect of attractive narrative trap seems to apply here, but does that matter?

Not for the first time, I am drawn to the idea that we should conserve species simply because we care – and just drop the functional arguments about how things do or don't work. Does a species have to have a function before we act to protect it? However, does that stance of 'just because we care', in itself, solve anything?

I once entered into a blog discussion about removing ancient woodland to provide housing. I was lambasted by those who had to rent and were waiting for houses and said that every time there was a proposal to build houses there was some Nimby protesting about some group of trees – and trees are everywhere and housing is scarce. I explained about the heritage of ancient woodlands inherited from probably medieval times at least and maybe much longer than that. At least when I replied that I sympathised but that I would not destroy St Paul's Cathedral to build your house, there was no reply from the original writer, though someone else wrote that, "well, trees can be replanted", rather missing the point about our heritage of woodlands which have evolved over long periods of time. Maybe an argument about a functioning ecosystem and species could have worked equally well – but there is still a reply that that could be the case anywhere. It seems perhaps that an argument about heritage and place might be persuasive.

The stance that we care, however, indicates that when we move to thinking about how to do something to protect nature, all we have is a mandate derived from an idea which indicates the need to protect as many species as possible in as many ways as possible. That seems virtuous but proclaiming that can itself present traps and restrictions. Take any one site and, for example, do we put a fence round it and keep people out, do we engage with promoting people's well-being and livelihoods in that area at the same time and how do we manage a habitat for the widest range of species as well as the rarest and most endangered species? Which meaning do we reach for then and why? So, let us not just say 'we should conserve because we care' and abandon the world of scientific ecology quite so lightly. It does obviously have a huge amount to offer, though it is also obviously necessary but not sufficient. The better conclusion is that we should examine our values and take more care with our justifications.

If we are dealing with a powerful set of meanings which can perhaps only survive because they are attractive, the interesting question then becomes one of how such attractive meanings come into being and then how they act to mediate in our relationship with nature. This is all important because the nature in our imagination does indeed exist only in our minds but it is so very real to us – and the storylines involved can have such immense power in directing our actions. However, there should be an awareness that the unquestioning use of justificatory narratives that have limitations we are unaware of has just as many pitfalls as deliberately selecting meanings to support what we want.

The 'Balance of Nature' and Responsibility

Let's continue our discussion with the proposition that one characteristic of narrative traps is that they can be self-sustaining; their propagation stemming from their compelling nature and consequent unthinking rehearsal rather than in any process of verification.

It seems that part of that uncritical propagation is that they often introduce attractive or otherwise compelling value judgements to nature. A classic example is the much-rehearsed and emotive concept of the 'balance of nature' – what John Kricher (2009) calls in the subtitle to his book *Ecology's Enduring Myth*. This is a highly motivating idea, and the very word 'balance' is one we greatly value (imbalance being regarded very negatively; people are said to commit suicide when the 'balance of the mind is disturbed'). However, who can precisely define the 'balance of nature'? If we examine this concept we often find that what is commonly rehearsed as 'the balance of nature being upset' is when things simply change. The unthinking story goes that when things change, things are not like they used to be (which was of course seen as right, even sacrosanct) and it has now been altered, which is wrong (as implied by the emotive term 'upset'). Can we here not also begin to see that some senses of 'hallowed state' and purpose, even, are exercising some kind of tyranny over our thoughts? Does this matter? Should we mind?

However, if the phrase means anything at all, what the balance of nature actually means to me is that there are processes by which components of a system will tend to interact and adjust to each other in some way. Any preference for a state or indeed any virtue ascribed to these interactions and adjustments speaks to us of our own judgement. Thus, the balance of nature, if such exists, is a (value-free, unemotive) process of adjustment to changed conditions rather than a state, and as such cannot be upset – merely altered. However, we find it compelling to add our values and to seek virtue and preferences. Clinically speaking, changes only bring effects and consequences – but then we insert a value judgement on to altered states and conflate this with notions of desirability – and so often, guilt, if we don't like the change and simultaneously think that we might be responsible. I am not saying that we should not have our preferences, ascribe virtue or express desirability (e.g. for species diversity or a food chain where the vegetation, herbivores and predators appear to be adjusted to each other sustainably) – I am trying to separate the components of a more clinical assessment of what is happening from the value judgements. This I see as important otherwise the value judgement tends to cloud the observation of process. Can we separate observation from value judgement? Can we not just specify how things have changed and then pause to think about what that might mean as a separate issue rather than automatically reach for the somewhat mythical 'balance of nature' being upset.

Climate change is the classic upsetter of the balance of nature. As is often rehearsed, it is changing everything, things are different from what we were used to, and worse still when it is our fault. However, nature is still out there adjusting, changing, moving on – species distributions are moving around, species are adjusting to different timings of events and so on, just as they have ever done. Yes, things will be different, interactions will change, some species will thrive in one place rather than another, some will decline, some will increase – certainly many changes – but we sit there observing these differences with our value judgements about things being not what we are used to which become conflated with our assumed causal guilt.

I remember a storyline in a film that climate change might mean that some things might happen at different times than they used to, as with emergence of caterpillars and the arrival of migrant birds which feed on them. Then, things might not be synchronised as they used to be, that is, it was said that the 'balance of nature' would be upset. No, it means that things would just be different and that the situation would evolve to a new state. You could say that a 'balance' would indeed be restored – but this would be in terms of everything adjusting to the new situation. The situation is not restored to what it was: things find a new mutual adjustment – that is what balance actually means in this context. A new balance would be found in the ways things interacted differently, but not in necessarily ever going back to how it was.

Yet still we love to rehearse how climate change is upsetting the balance of nature – when in fact climate change has been a feature of the planet ever since its origin and nature has not only just been reacting to and moderating it, it has indeed been as much shaped by it as by anything else and in many ways life can influence climate by a mutual interaction.

If we wish to take responsibility for climate change, this is a psychologically comforting idea as it means we can do something about it – and find someone or a group to blame and expect them to act. We find this infinitely preferable to powerlessness. Even when something we cannot control happens like an earthquake, and if we do not ascribe this to some kind of deity, we immediately set about blaming people who might have made better predictions and built better safeguards into an infrastructure to resist the effects. We then expect them to do better in the future. We have to be in control, if not physically then at least morally.

In terms of being able to do something, Richard Jefferies, a nature writer, wrote in *The Story of My Heart* in 1883 that nothing was subject to some over-arching entity. For this he was widely criticised for being a 'Shocking Atheist' (Harrison, 1938). Jefferies wrote: "This is a foundation of hope, because, if the present condition of things were ordered by a superior power, there would be no possibility of improving it for the better in the spite of that power. Acknowledging that no such direction exists, all things become at once plastic to our will" (Jefferies, [1883] 1938: 133).

This is the non-fatalistic, non-shrugging of shoulders and non-acceptance. He found this argument so encouraging, uplifting, inspiring and compelling when compared to fatalistic despair. It is perhaps ironic that his restricted view of such a superior power seemed to prevent him seeing that any superior power could also be responsible for the human will which he so cherished. However, the key point is that Jefferies found such comfort in being able to do something about things. My point is that similarly with climate change if it is not actually our fault then we can do nothing about it and that is so scary. However, if we don the mantle of guilt and culpability, immediately we can see the power of the route to salvation lies in our hands – and all the exhortations that are involved in the global warming meta-narrative follow.

Key Points about Meanings, Narratives and the Conflation of Observations, Preference and Value

- While scientific investigation can amass evidence and test out theories, meanings can be derived independently of this endeavour in relation to powerful stories. These narratives of meaning not only influence the way we see nature and therefore what we do to it, they can also influence the scientific endeavour itself. Attractive narratives can form a narrative trap which constrains our thinking and actions.
- Everything has a story. As William Cronon (1992: 1347) writes in 'A place for stories: Nature, history and narrative': "In the beginning was the story. Or rather: many stories, of many places, in many voices, pointing toward many ends."
- More explicitly, Harré, Brockmeier and Mühlhäusler (1999: 70) write on nature in *Greenspeak: A study of environmental discourse*: "Narratives, which appear in a variety of forms, constitute a linguistic, psychological, social and philosophical framework for our attempts to come to terms with the nature and conditions of our existence."

- Many narratives imbue nature with what almost seems like an intentionality – as Marek Kohn (2004: 9) writes in *A Reason for Everything: Natural selection and the English imagination*: "Life is intolerable without a sense of purpose."

This all tells us more about ourselves than it does about nature. Our minds are making the meanings, as illustrated by these three quotations:

1. "The mind is its own place, and in itself can make a heaven of hell, a hell of heaven." John Milton (1667), *Paradise Lost.*
2. "We don't see the world as it is, we see it as we are." Anaïs Nin (variously attributed; commonly *Seduction of the Minotaur*, 1961).
3. "Nature is there for its own sake and not for mine, though I make it what it is for me." Trudgill (2003a) from ch. 2 in *Contemporary Meanings in Physical Geography: From what to why?.*

These points are important in the triangular relationship between knowledge, cultural imagery and action (Figure 1.8).

We like to think that there is a relationship between our scientific knowledge and our considered environmental actions (albeit tempered by political/cultural preference). However, the third mediating factor is the mental image we have of what nature is like. This, in turn, is derived from the way we are culturally situated. This image, together with all the associated narratives, is actually the most telling aspect in our relationship with nature, but it is often the most unexamined.

A further point to make here is that while value-laden ideas like the 'balance of nature' can be seen as somewhat problematic, they are also extremely useful in providing motivations for doing something. Guilt-laden notions also bring the comfort that we don't feel powerless. Thus, if we debunk these ideas we lose motivation and a sense of virtue. So, perhaps we rather like such narrative traps? Perhaps they are really rather useful, flawed as they may be? Perhaps the 'balance of nature' is a good thing and we don't need to be disabused of it?

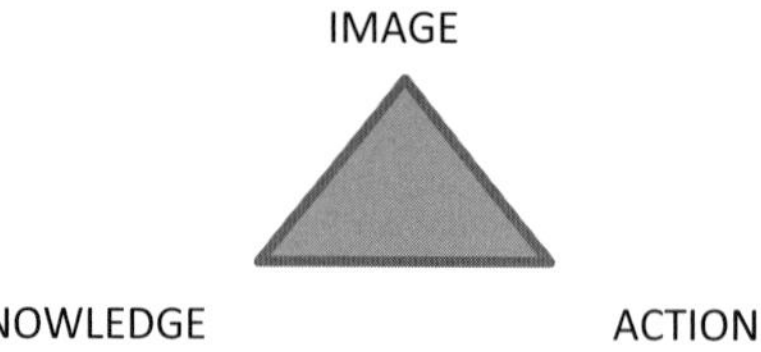

Figure 1.8 The triangular relationship between knowledge, cultural imagery and action

The caution comes in that the actual narrative trap is that the ideas involved can be so generalised that they don't actually tell us how nature works so we cannot necessarily predict any outcome of actions based upon them. Moreover, we should think about what may be done in their name. All narratives can be manipulated to suit different purposes. For example, cutting carbon emission by cleaner energy may look entirely laudable – but is placing a tidal power-producing barrage across a species-rich tidal estuary the best way to go about it? Maybe 'use less energy' would be a better slogan than 'produce energy with less carbon'.

Actions taken may not have the desired effect at all and may also have harmful unintentional side effects. That is why we should treat our enthusiasm for acting on value-laden narratives with some caution. We should also explore in rather more depth how readily we can become trapped by explanatory narratives which ascribe values, purpose and other human attributes to objects and events. In what can be seen as a 'tyranny of meaning', in the way we look at nature we tend to conflate observation, preference and value all too easily, seeing the latter two above all else.

Discussion Points

The discussion points which have arisen include:

- Where do ideas of imagined nature come from?
- How is it that people come to hold certain views and continually rehearse an associated set of meanings?
- Does this relate to some world view, a vested interest, some educational or personal experience or what?
- How are the ideas propagated – and, given that contrasting meanings can coexist, how far are they ever tested – if indeed they can be?
- Is their untestability part of their attraction?
- Indeed, are we dealing more with some kind of 'ecological faith'?
- What are the consequences and effects of our varieties of imagined natures?
- How are they used to justify environmental actions?

The key questions are, first, where do our narratives of explanation come from and how are they propagated? Second, how do our narratives – which involve imagery, metaphors, scientific constructs and other revelations of meanings – influence our approaches to nature, landscapes and ecosystems?

These are important considerations because when we interact with nature, the rehearsal of narratives about nature tells us the following:

1. where to look
2. what to see
3. how to behave and
4. what to do.

Justificatory narratives are a particularly interesting focus of study as they are routinely cited when deciding a course of action. Here information may be suppressed or emphasised to fit an ideological stance. There is a direct link between our beliefs, our justificatory narratives and our actions.

The American literary critic Kenneth Burke (1941) put it one way round as "stories are [or literature is] equipment for living". The philosopher Jacob Bronowski (1973: 116) put it the other way around that what we do reveals what we have in mind: "the hand is the cutting edge of the mind". For example, in nature conservation rarity seems to be valued so this is an oft-rehearsed justification for protection, with narratives such as 'unique to this area' and 'irreplaceable'. Equally there may be competing narratives of 'economic growth' and so on. What is not always predictable is which narrative will 'win' but what is certain is that we can't propose action without a justificatory narrative.

1.2 Psychogeography and Nature

Psychogeography and the Learnt Experience

I'm sitting by a pool. It is actually part of a river which gets wider at this point. To my right, where the river is flowing from, there is a bridge. The water flows through the arch and then slows down, spreading out as it reaches the pool. The water then moves rather slowly from right to left because there is little gradient in this flat land – the sea is not that far away and we are a long way from the headwaters. To my left, the water splits round a small island and then disappears behind some trees. There is lush vegetation growing next to the river. I can see that there is a grazing animal beyond the plants but I can't quite make out what it is. The plants are reflected in the water with some blue sky and clouds. The water looks quite deep. It hasn't rained lately so the river is not brown with mud but I can't see the bottom and it looks quite black down there.

There are aquatic plants in and floating on the water and water birds dabble around on the edges.

Now what kind of place have you been imagining? Indeed, where in the world am I? What might this place mean to you? What kind of narratives do you have in mind from reading the above paragraph? Certainly, you have already compared this place to places you know. We might be in parts of Africa where the thought about the occurrence of rains would be important. There are trees, but of what sort? The grazing animal might be a moose, gazelle or bison. We could be in Siberia and it would be the unfrozen summer when the rivers flow. Maybe South America, North America, Europe, Asia? There also could be any number of significances associated with the place but given the limited description above we, the readers, are all allowed multiple readings of the site. We very probably all only have one set of associations in common and this is to do with water. The common meanings might thus involve narratives to do with life giving and survival and also possible threats: maybe it floods, maybe it dries up. Whatever the manifestations, water has very basic psychological significance which all humanity can share. We might also find many other things – maybe tranquillity or unrest. We can't really tell unless we know some more.

Let me now tell you that the plants include reeds, rushes and iris, with water lilies on the water and pondweed in it. The grazing animal is a horse. Still not that specific in terms of place, maybe? But then let me say that the trees include willows and perhaps we are feeling something more specific like northern hemisphere or a place with European influence. Add in elms, chestnuts and also some oaks in the distance beyond the grass meadows and then say the mill is just beyond the bridge and we are indeed feeling more European or North American maybe, maybe even British or English but not necessarily so; maybe it is New Zealand – I remember seeing willows planted by a river in Christchurch. But each detail adds an associative significance – a new layer of meaning and significance. Note how the type of vegetation and animal can give a feeling of location and even possibly country.

I know myself that there is a deeper place here. I might have already been reminded of Constable's paintings by the willows, mill and water so I might be in Flatford Mill where Constable painted the *Hay Wain* picture. But when I look at the elm trees I am actually thinking of: "do the elm-clumps greatly stand" and "The chestnuts shade, in reverend dream." And as I look to the right I am thinking: "And laughs the immortal river still/ Under the mill, under the mill?"

And of:

To smell the thrilling-sweet and rotten
Unforgettable, unforgotten
River-smell, and hear the breeze
Sobbing in the little trees.
Oh, is the water sweet and cool,
Gentle and brown, above the pool?

What is now important is whether you have recognised these extracts from a poem or not. If not what about "The yet unacademic stream?" Or:

Say, is there Beauty yet to find?
And Certainty? and Quiet kind?
Deep meadows yet, for to forget
The lies, and truths, and pain? . . . oh! Yet
Stands the Church clock at ten to three?
And is there honey still for tea?

And if you still don't know those lines the final clue is: "Ah God! to see the branches stir/ Across the moon at Grantchester!" You either now know this so well and have found the place unambiguously – or maybe you have no idea what I am talking about or where Grantchester is. If the latter I then have to tell you that it is on the river Cam, just south of Cambridge in England and I am sitting by the pool next to the vicarage where the poet Rupert Brooke (1887–1915) lived for part of his early life. Here it was indeed that Rupert Brooke dived into and swam around the pool before which I now sit. This is the area about which he wrote the poem 'The Old Vicarage, Grantchester', from which these extracts come (Brooke, 1912, see, e.g., Marsh, 1942: 97). He wrote it in May 1912 just before the First World War (1914–1918) while he sat, homesick for England, in the Café des Westens in Berlin. I am also reminded of the later poem with the lines: "If I should die, think only this of me:/ That there's some corner of a foreign field/ That is for ever England" ('The Soldier', 1914). If you still have no idea what I am talking about, this can only be a reflection on your particular cultural upbringing. For me, I have read and loved Rupert Brooke's poems and one of the first things I did when I first came to Cambridge was to make a pilgrimage to this place which, by association, means so much to me.

So I can think of this:

In Grantchester, in Grantchester! —
Some, it may be, can get in touch
With Nature there, or Earth, or such.
And clever modern men have seen
A Faun a-peeping through the green,
And felt the Classics were not dead,
To glimpse a Naiad's reedy head,
Or hear the Goat-foot piping low: . . .
But these are things I do not know.
I only know that you may lie
Day long and watch the Cambridge sky,
And, flower-lulled in sleepy grass,
Hear the cool lapse of hours pass,
Until the centuries blend and blur
In Grantchester, in Grantchester. . . .

And the "Goat-foot piping low" makes me think of my favourite part of Kenneth Grahame's *Wind in the Willows*: 'The Piper at the Gates of Dawn' when the mole and rat drift downstream and are entranced by Pan, and I think of the biography of Kenneth Grahame by Matthew Dennison (2018): *Eternal Boy: The life of Kenneth Grahame* and how he came to write this. But nothing, nothing of this is in the scene. It is all in my mind, but is thus very real for me in this place.

So, I am sitting in a place which can be seen, by poetic association, as emblematic of what is quintessentially English. But if I didn't know the poem, I would simply be sitting by a pool, in England. Consider also there might be even fewer associations – just a bit of river we went past: we must always remember indifference as a reaction, with a complete lack of significance. Of course, it is what is in my mind which makes this place significant to me. Thus, we are reading the landscape – or a description of it – much as we read anything we come across: Wolfgang Iser describes how we read a text by taking a structure and filling in the gaps according to our histories and memories (see, e.g., Iser (1972), *The Reading Process* and De Bruyn (2012), *Wolfgang Iser: A companion*).

I have taken you through a generalised place with a generalised meaning to a more specific place, which is probably English and probably tranquil but might have other meanings – and both of these are purely visual and also related to the viewer's own experience. Then we are in a specific place due to a very specific association, which you will either sense or not sense, depending upon your prior knowledge. The place has meanings which grade from something any human being might sense through to specific cultural experiences which can only be learnt. These are the layers of psychogeography.

What we learnt from sitting by that pool applies everywhere. For every single moment of our lives we are in a place. Wherever we are, places can have meaning, significance and influence. Psychogeography can be defined as the effects of where you are on what you feel. This involves how your location can affect your thoughts and feelings and, equally, how your thoughts and feeling affect the perceptions of that place. Many psychogeographical writings have already focussed on the urban setting – for example on how architecture, street scenes and urban ambience inter-relate with people (Bonnett, 2003; Debord, 1956, 1977; Marcus, 1989; Pinder, 2001). Porteous (1990) felt that our visual sense dominates the experience of our surroundings, with hearing and sometimes tactile senses helping to give us a structured spatial awareness, while smell can give a sense of authenticity of place. Other authors have come to similar conclusions (Bell et al., 1996 and Macnaghten and Urry, 1998). Thus, it is the interiority of the retained image of our surroundings which becomes important in our relationship with our surroundings. Hence it is important to explore the ways in which we relate to the images of environment and nature in terms of a sense of place – and ask how we respond when the environments, nature and places change and become at variance with our retained images.

Imagine that we are back at the pool. Say I had written eucalyptus rather than elm, fir rather than chestnut, maple rather than oak. So, we could have been in Australia or Canada or somewhere where these grow – if we know it to be the case that this is where they grow. The Brooke poem becomes all wrong in these cases but consider this: if it had been originally the case that these trees were in the poem, then we would have learnt that significance and association – thus it just is a different set of ideas. There is no necessity in the association, only a specific learnt response.

But then, if the climate changes and the trees which are associated with the poem die out and any of these others start to grow in our lifetime, then is this all wrong because it is not what we have learnt? Say for the sake of argument that the climate becomes very hot and the willows die and eucalyptus grows. The poem crumbles and has less meaning: the new place starts to diminish in cultural association. This dissonance between what we expect and what we see may be so great that we might re-plant what was there before and try to maintain it despite changed conditions. However, young people growing up with the new trees will probably just accept them as the norm, seeing nothing wrong – and maybe find the old poem rather quaint and about what used to grow there – with no trace of personal nostalgia. They have no personal memory of former times.

This is where environmental change and the associated changes in vegetation become matters of challenges to our psychogeography of nature. How, then, are we to understand our psychogeography of nature and its relevance to nature conservation? How do we predict how we might react to change and, indeed, what is the right or defensible thing to do in the face of change? Is it just a stark choice between adapting and losing cultural associations or fighting to preserve cultural associations? That our personal associations are often learnt is evidenced by an outcry when "our open area" is forested over to grow timber which can be followed, a generation later, by an outcry about felling the trees and "losing our forests" and a call for re-planting. Our cultural associations, beyond our own experiences, obviously depend more on the heritage of literature, art and stories passed down between the generations. Here, narratives about "what it used to be like" and "natural" can often be cited. Either way, justifications for stances, attitudes and thus actions stem from a blend of personal experiences and cultural heritage.

How Have I Been Situated to Experience the Real?

The learnt relationships between the self, psychogeographic significance and nature in particular places are thus matters of dependency rather than necessity. They involve contingency and personalisation and relate to Foucault's thoughts of: "how has the path of my knowledge been determined?", "how have I been situated to experience the real" and "how have my questions been produced?" (from Bernauer, 1992 on Foucault as discussed in Darier, 1999: 224). This admits that "personal experience is a form of knowledge" (Harding, 1986: 240) and stresses the significance of 'one's own story' as revealed in auto-ethnographic studies (e.g. Reed-Danahay, 1997).

Personal stories can be difficult to generalise from, but we can venture that in our relationships with the environment, we can find meanings derived from a blend of prior knowledge, preconceptions, perceptions, reactions, feelings, emotional responses and, most importantly, associations which combine to give us meanings of our surroundings. This is exemplified in terms of environmental psychology by Bell et al. (1996: 45–59) on landscape perception. The relationship is very much a two-way process between perceived form and our concepts. The concepts themselves involve both generalised social and cultural responses to particular physical situations and our own individual thoughts and feelings which are derived from our own particular experiences. Both combine to condition our response in terms of what, why and how we find something significant. There are thus two linked aspects, one involving structural significance and the other concerning associative significance.

Structural aspects are concerned with the physical view before us and its spatial and dimensional configuration. This can be a response to something simple, for example, height. Where a cliff towers up, if we stand at its foot and look up it makes us feel small or, if we stand on top of it, we feel a sense of a 'commanding' view. Such basic psychological reactions are those often shared widely by humanity.

Associative significance is more personal, with a blend of shared cultural concepts and individual experiences. Involved are memories, experiences, personal and shared narratives, learned responses and mental images which make for what we find significant and meaningful in where we are. So, while we might stand at the foot of a cliff and feel dwarfed by it, we also might relish the situation, with feelings of awe and respect, or we might feel intimidated and resentful, according to our associations. Equally, we might feel exposed, visible and vulnerable on the top of the cliff or relish the prospect, depending on our narratives and contexts (for a simple example, compare the contexts of the hunted with the hunter). The view from the cliff top might be structurally complex but we might find it diverse, intricate and interesting or we might find it confusing and illegible – and just selectively pick out what we can relate to. A woodland, for example, might be a confusing, intimidating tangle or equally a pleasant accessible refuge. Such reactions involving legibility depend upon prior knowledge and existing narratives. These narratives all influence what we are selectively looking at and sensing. In short, wherever we are, we all live in our minds and it is what is in our minds that gives any significance to where we are. As we introduced briefly in Section 1.1, Wordsworth wrote on this, expressed fully as:

How exquisitely the individual Mind
(And the progressive powers perhaps no less
Of the whole species) to the external world

Is fitted; and how exquisitely too –
Theme this too little heard of among men –
The external world is fitted to the Mind
(from 'Home in Grasmere', 1800)

Wordsworth's significance on environmental thinking is discussed by Bate (1991, 2020) and Roe (2002). A sense of association often also gives us a feeling of what is appropriate or incongruous to find and see in a particular setting. Such a sense of meaning of place is an under-acknowledged basis of many of our 'environmental issues'. The sense of being in the open air is one such meaning. One can cite Wordsworth's words from Bate (2020: 5) who feels that "the breeze was like an instrument carrying the music of nature to his inner self".

Oh there is a blessing from the gentle breeze
That blows from the green fields and from the clouds
And from the sky: it beats against my cheek
And seems half conscious of the joy it gives.
(*Prelude* I: 1–4)

It is how places make us feel – and the significance we find in landscapes, plants and animals – which is at the root of powerful emotions which drive our responses. These emotions may in turn underpin our representations and our actions.

Psychogeography, a Sense of Place and Planning Issues

The thesis is that what actually drives us is the coming together of these meanings and significances and our responses to them. Yet, when we consider, say the 'proposed by-pass through the ancient woodland' scenario, such relationships are rarely articulated; suppressed even as 'emotional'. Our emotional response is, in fact, fundamental to the means by which we relate to the environment (Milton, 2002; Trudgill, 2008) but we confuse feeling and the affective emotions with irrationality and 'being emotional'. The 'case against the road building' seems to have to rest on rarity of species or some other form of (often numerical) rationality. The non-rational, such as the way you feel about a place, is often dismissed as irrational and rarely legitimated. The 'protesters in the tree houses' are marginalised, along with their woolly hats, dyed hair and other indicators of 'fringe' values. But if emotion, feelings and meanings are fundamental, why do they get marginalised? Why do we have to have a 'scientific argument' if we want to preserve something? These questions are especially important because Burgess (1992) and Harrison and Burgess (1994) showed so elegantly that in a discussion of the future of an area to be developed such arguments only had institutional weight rather than public acceptance. In their studies, the general responses about the area belied a psychogeographic relationship of feelings and significances.

One can certainly conclude that what is important is how places make you feel. But if we walk with nature to feel peace, tranquillity, enjoyment and wonder, why is there a dominance of the 'rational' narrative in 'making the case for conserving nature'? Why do such narratives take over? There is a literature on the 'expert-lay divide' (e.g. Wynne, 1996) which, in its simplest form, can lament the lack of knowledge in lay people. This appears to be based on the assumption that the scientific arguments are cogent and 'right', with the inevitable conclusion from scientists that people who do not see them 'should be educated more'. Sensory responses can be dismissed as 'emotional' or at best ignored.

We could invert this and also examine the possibility that 'scientists should have more feeling'. However, the point is that they actually do have feelings, as anthropological writings such as those of Pang (1996) show (and see Trudgill, 2003b). What is actually going on is that one set of narratives, the scientific, is somehow seen as more 'valid' and therefore dominates. I would therefore like to look at the situation more fundamentally and consider the way we use narratives and discourses (Hajer, 1995), or are, indeed, used by them. Emotional responses are personal, deeper and possibly not so shareable as the rational narratives, but they can indeed be characterised and articulated, as shown, for example, by Milton's (2002) writings on the emotional response to nature and Cooper and Palmer (1998) on the spiritual engagement with nature.

This emotional response, revealed through narratives, matters critically when the environment changes around us or when we act directly to change the environment around us. If we propose an act of nature reserve management there has to be a justification: 'promoting rare species', 'removal of invaders', 'restoration' and so on abound, revealing fundamental motivational narratives such as appropriateness and naturalness (however manipulated and therefore putative). If we act on a garden it may be 'overrun', 'spreading', 'taking over', 'out of control' or we may relax and let nature take its course, but it is uncomfortable unless we give a narrative label of 'the wild garden'. Even the act of 'allowing' nature is deliberate. When, if through climate change or other reason, the environment changes around us we become distinctly uncomfortable. It is not what we are used to – and therefore somehow wrong. We may seek a target – find a reason, apportion blame, seek to act to mitigate or seek to counter a probable cause. Alternatively, if we are unable to mitigate the change and restore, we may become resigned and accept – but not without lamentation before we are resigned and accept. Fundamentally we place ourselves somewhere on the spectrum from one of control and 'we can't just stand by and let this happen' to one of not being able to counter 'the powers of nature' – so we adapt. But however we react, we have to have a justificatory narrative.

Within the topic of justificatory narratives I think we should try to separate analysis from advocacy. There is often an unthinking conflation of these. Analysis is about, for example, change with words such as 'increase' whereas advocacy is evident from words like 'overrun' or 'infest'. However, there is also a realisation that emotive arguments can stem equally from analytical statements as much as from statements of advocacy. Any denial of the emotions ignores the emotional processes which occur and these should be recognised.

While environmental management and conservation can be seen as 'rational' projects (Adams, 1997), it is our narratives with the associated deeper senses of meaning which are actually guiding us – and indeed also, I submit, limiting us. Making progress with environmental issues is limited by the basic assumptions we make about nature which depend on myth and deeply buried beliefs as Botkin (1990: 201) clearly felt when writing his book *Discordant Harmonies: A new ecology for the twenty-first century*: "[T]he guide to our action is our knowledge of living systems . . . and our willingness to recognize the limits of our actions, and to understanding the roles of metaphor and myths in our perceptions of our surroundings." Such metaphors and myths can enrich our view, as can be well seen in art, poetry and literature, but in other contexts they can limit our view, especially, I argue, in ecological science. It is therefore important to make these narratives recognised and to examine them carefully.

1.3 Ways of Seeing Nature

Necessity and Evidentiality

We see meanings and purposes in nature when there are none: that is to say that we find or see many meanings in nature – purpose and pattern – but these are all 'readings', rather than a 'discovery' of any kind of necessity. In this context, we can cite the following from Foucault:

> [W]e should not imagine that the world presents us with a legible face, leaving us merely to decipher it; it does not work hand in glove with what we already know; there is no prediscursive fate disposing the word in our favour. We must conceive discourse as a violence that we do to things, or, at all events, as a practice we impose upon them. (Foucault. 1971: 229)

Any sense of meaning and purpose in nature we may have thus tells us more about us than about nature. In this context, we can consider a saying attributed to Karl Marx: "Men can see nothing around them that is not their own image; everything speaks to them of themselves. Their very landscape is alive." We can also cite other similar viewpoints: "We mistakenly assimilate plants into human intentional life. We are really mirroring ourselves in describing plants" (Rolston, 1997: 362) and "To enroll [plants and animals] in the emerging collective, we first need grant them ... some of the social attributes necessary to integrate them" (Latour, 1994: 801; Latour, 1994b: 60).

These writings encapsulate, in different ways, the key characteristics of the human–nature relationship. As Whatmore and Boucher (1993: 167) write: "Nature cannot be (re)produced outside social relations." So, we can't even see, let alone replicate in any form, nature outside of our social relations. However, they also add: "neither is it reducible to them". This means that while we always construct in our minds something 'out there' which we call nature, this 'something' is independent of us and is more than just our construction.

It follows that while there is a constructionist view which can be seen as 'there is nothing in nature except that which we bring to it' and we realise that we have been positioned to look at nature through a particular cultural, contextual and perceptual lens, there is no necessity in seeing the way that we do.

This realisation about a lack of necessity in the view we have is crucial. In the everyday our assumptions derived from cultural, contextual and perceptual positioning normally remain totally unexamined. This is less the case in the world of art and literature, where part of the endeavour can be explicitly to challenge such things, but this total lack of self-awareness can be marked in scientific ecology. What is then worrying is that in ecological science the underlying beliefs are rarely examined but yet they continue to guide our thoughts and actions. This much is revealed by the use of the justificatory narratives which are rehearsed when actions are proposed. The beliefs may only be challenged evidentially when nature does not behave in the way we predicted and in this sense our relationship with nature can be reflexive, with experience acting to modify our narratives. In art, literature, poetry and music there is no such evidentiality – there is no visible 'come-back' as we are not physically engaged with doing something to nature and seeing how it works out. There is only a conceptual engagement with nature and we may construct it and represent it on canvas, in words or in musical notes as we wish.

In many senses, however, even in ecological science and management, nature may have so much latitude that we can still retain our notions of nature when physically engaged with it irrespective of any evidence. This is because the latitude means that we can probably find something somewhere which will support and provide a justification for an action – or that a belief alone may provide justification for action. Thus, if we are pursuing an action which is based on a belief that something is true, it may be that we have no need to find evidence to support an action, that is, we act without testing our belief. Equally, we may act despite any evidence which may contradict our belief by simply ignoring it or we might see the contradictory evidence but give greater weight to the evidence which does suit our purposes.

I am thinking here again of television programmes such as the one I saw on nature reserve management which we discussed at the start of the book about the narratives that "nature is so fragile that if you remove one species, the ecosystem collapses" (implying that we should physically cherish every species) followed only a few minutes later by "nature is so robust that if one species dies out on a site, another steps in to take its place" (implying that the preservation of ecosystem functions is more important than any one species). That these narratives can coexist illustrates the latitude of nature which permits contrasting readings. The first narrative justifies conservation effort for each species. The second helps to justify, post hoc, what was perhaps an inevitable loss but it also stems from the assumed relationship between high biodiversity and greater ecosystem stability, providing a justification for conserving as wide a range of biodiversity as possible.

Another example I found was a programme on gardening when one speaker celebrated the fact that "the garden is independent of me and it is doing its own thing" while another celebrated the fact that "gardens are so good because they are the one place I can feel in control". Pictures of the gardens showed them to be not very different from each other; both looked quite well ordered and tended but the perception of similar situations related to a personal meaning. Both gardens represented refuge and antidote: the first speaker had a job which was managerial but felt free of responsibility and therefore relaxed in an 'independent' garden; the second was subject to the instructions of others at work but could come home and organise things how he wished.

Even when the engagement is physical, with ample evidence for success or failure in the way a nature reserve or a garden develops relative to our criteria, our notions can vary with the viewer – and remain dominant and even intact, independently of any evidence. We may indeed choose the evidence selectively to fit our narratives. Thus, if it is these underlying narratives which dominate and guide our actions I maintain that, while they are often identifiable and discussed in art, poetry and literature, they should also be examined more in terms of their role in environmental management. Botkin's (1990: 16) conclusion is that: "We must break free of old assumptions and old myths about nature and ourselves, while building on the scientific and technical advances of the past." Though I do feel moved to add here that building on science and technology is not in itself a way of breaking free of assumptions and myths.

Biophilia, Duality and Other Ways of Viewing Nature

I would also like to give room to the point of view that relates to the 'Biophilia Hypothesis' (Kellert and Wilson, 1993). This includes an exploration of the atavistic, evolutionary basis of our responses to nature. The idea of the Biophilia Hypothesis is that there is considerable survival value in finding meanings in nature which have developed through our evolution. This can be exemplified by considering a rustle in the leaves – is it the wind or a predator: what does the rustle mean? Am I under threat? Clearly the automatic questions and interpretations have considerable survival value. This may provide a fundamental point about the response to the environment by humanity in general – inescapable rather than learnt – but as with any proposition about human responses, there is much more to consider in understanding our interpretations of nature than just that.

The question of 'how do we see nature' gives rise in my mind to two dualities: first, nature which is outside us and nature as constructed inside our minds; and second, the duality of the latter constructed in both positive and negative ways.

On the subject of the first duality, one of the most powerful concepts is a sense of independent 'other' – but it is an 'other' which is subject to our minds. This is not the Cartesian idea of the separation of mind and body, it is the separation of both from something external, albeit that Kant would ascribe the attributes of that externality as existing in the mind. This is the idea of something which is not ourselves but which reflects ourselves and which we can see as a metaphor for our own lives. Or as Shelley put it: "nothing exists but as it is perceived" (see Cooper, 1988, ch. 7). However, the important part of this is that nature is also essentially independent of us. McKibben (1989: 54) feels that "Nature's independence is its meaning", concluding that if we deprive nature of its independence then that is fatal to the meaning of nature. Additionally, as also cited elsewhere, Whatmore and Boucher (1993: 167–168) wrote: "Nature cannot be reproduced outside social relations, neither is it reducible to them", admitting both the constructivist view and the independence of nature. Without this autonomy we cannot draw upon it and without our sense of meaning we cannot relate to it. What is outside and what is inside merge reflexively. Truly, we make nature what it is to us.

Evernden (1992: 99) expresses the paradox of internalised externality and externalised internality well: "We must remember that nature itself was *our* creation [his emphasis]" and "Nature is simply the absorption of ourselves into ... our own conception of how it 'ought' to be." He continues that the dualism between nature and culture "cannot actually be resolved, because it never existed. The dualism we fret over only exists because of our own decision." So, we value nature as independent at the same time as projecting our values, including the attribute of independence, upon it.

The second positive – negative duality – arises from nature not being human. We see in nature something which we may both shun and value because of its non-human condition. Rolston (1997) sums this up as nature being both an assisting and resisting reality. Wilderness can readily be constructed as a non-human negation of civilisation. For some, such as those who trek in the wilderness and those who immerse themselves in nature, that is a positive construct – we rejoice in the sense of other, something greater than ourselves – we sense ourselves and our small existence all the more, surrounded by an independent, immanent (pervading the universe, inherent) nature – an assisting reality. Equally there are those who see wilderness as a denial of, and challenge to, all that we can achieve through our own ingenuity – a resisting reality, as is evidenced by the American pioneers' attitudes to wilderness (Nash, 1967). Non-human nature can thus be celebrated as independent and helpful or as independent and shunned for not yielding to our will.

Any scene of nature can be viewed in a number of ways and several writers have tried to classify our approaches to nature. Writing on landscape interpretation, Porteous (1996: 48–49) quotes Meinig's (1979) 'beholding eye' concept and cites at least ten modes of viewing the same scene, as discussed in Trudgill (2001b: 247–248). These modes include viewing a scene as nature, artefact, habitat, place and system as well as the more abstract problem, ideology, history and the artistic way of viewing. Porteous (1996: 49) also sees Thayer's (1976) notions of visual ecology useful, involving a number of levels of significance involving aesthetics, association and use, affective emotions (a scene may calm, frighten or interest us), symbolic and behavioural or activating – do you see yourself chopping a tree down or sitting under it?

Note how some of these narratives are evidential, some have an intentionality and some are celebratory – the 'reality' might be the same but the narratives of meaning differ. They tell us about the context of the viewer. The narratives need not be mutually exclusive and can move from colour and form to deeper association: when I ask a group of students for descriptors of a picture of a woodland, they usually start with the colour and form (green, leafy, branches) then, when pressed for more descriptors, they reach into their associations and memories, often of childhood, and come up with the more emotional attachments and meanings (family picnics, peace, quiet, tranquillity). It is these emotional points which are important – emotional responses and associated values prompt us into action, as in Thayer's behavioural or activating point 5, above, leading to contestations about meanings and uses.

Intentionality and the Pathetic Fallacy

Our intentionality is crucial to the construction of meanings. If we want to escape humankind, woods are wonderful; if not they might be seen as impenetrable. If we want to grow something, soil is yielding or unyielding, otherwise it is neutral and not really very significant (Trudgill, 2006). We have an idea of what we would like a garden to be like and struggle with the independent perversity of pests, diseases and uncooperative plants. Such is our intentionality, it is almost as though the plants too have an intentionality – they seem wilful, weeds sprouting out all over the place or reluctant, cherished plants not thriving, but it is us who have the will and we may characterise the plant as having a counter-will, when in fact it is just doing what it is doing. In a nature reserve we have an idea of what should be there, what is appropriate, and again we struggle to realise these ideas according to a variety of narratives like 'natural', 'controlling undesirable species', 'encouraging desirable species' or 'working with nature'. But even in the latter case, it is us who are doing the preferring – it is nature on our terms.

Critically, even when we do not propose to physically alter nature in some way, we still ascribe an intentionality to nature rather than just describe it. The tension between 'what is' and 'what things mean to individuals' is also writ large in the pathetic fallacy – the attribution of human feelings to objects, especially to nature discussed by Ruskin (1897: 161–177) and examined by Miles (1965) in *Pathetic Fallacy in the Nineteenth Century*. Ruskin understood the psychological importance of nature to us, attributing human characteristics to nature but baulked at an intentionality. Thus, a tree does not try to do something but it might be seen as fragile or the earth as timid. He essentially used a word-painting which involved not only the detail of description – "the lighted purple cloud . . . open sky of dull yellow above" – but objected to the "spendthrift crocus" as if the crocuses were being profligate with their blooms (Ruskin, 1897: 164).

However, the pathetic fallacy has never gone away – weather forecasters regularly describe rainy, low pressures systems as 'trying' to push in across the country but being blocked by areas of high pressure – with the hidden emotional associations that we can still enjoy the sun for a while till the depression 'wins'. Sports commentators who hope for good weather for an outdoor event say on a cloudy morning "the sun is trying to break through" which is no more than a transfer of our volitions to the weather. It does all seem very wilful of the weather systems and inescapably anthropomorphised. We do need and enjoy the stories about nature. This is very clear in nature programmes involving animal behaviour, which is so readily anthropomorphised rather than just observed. Television programmes abound with commentaries which refer obliquely or even very directly to human behaviour and morality, especially with respect to family relations and gendered activities. Out there on the African plains, the animals are doing what they are doing but interpret them we must: 'what is it doing and why is it doing it?'. We may see a programme focussed on lions, where the hyenas are robbers of their food, or we may be asked to identify with the hyenas, and the lions become a threat. The tensions between science, observation, the varied anthropomorphic portrayals of nature, the thrill of discovery and pure entertainment are well rehearsed by Davies (2000) in her study of post-war British natural history television: *Science, Observation and Entertainment*. In some senses there is nothing wrong with anthropomorphism as it engages our emotions in a way that identifies with other living creatures and when we can see that 'we all have something in common' there is great appeal which can only be good in terms of conservation motivation. The professional biologist has a hard job to study animals in a way that is unsentimental and detached from identification with the subject and the ready narratives. There is a good example of this in *Brazzaville Beach* by William Boyd (1991) which has an account of a zoologist who finds cannibalism in chimpanzees, which no one wants to believe – the independent reality clashes with our cherished narratives, the facts embarrass our values and are suppressed.

Here the language we use in our narratives is very revealing of our perceptions (Mühlhäusler, 1995, 2000). An intentionality is so often ascribed in terms such as 'invasive species' (Mooney and Hobbs, 2000) and 'aliens' when there is simply a conflict with our ideas of what things should be like. Our sense of 'what ought to be there' is as strong as our imperative need to interpret with a narrative. In this context I believe that the excellent book by Harré, Brockmeier and Mühlhäusler (1999) entitled *Greenspeak: A study of environmental discourse* should be compulsory reading for all biological scientists; only then would they become more self-aware both about the language they use and about the ways their science can be taken beyond their original intentions (see ch. 3 'Rhetorical Uses of Science' in Harré et al.).

As a further point, I would add to both Meinig's and Thayer's categories discussed above a final way of viewing and that is 'indifference'. This is actually a critical point to add since it implies a *lack* of motivation – something is not seen as significant at all and therefore there is no reason to interact with it in any way whatsoever. It provides a narrative nonetheless: 'conserve it, cut it down, whatever – it is of no matter to me'. We should not forget this aspect as it means that any attempt at motivation, in whatever direction, will 'fall on stony ground', as it were: the point or view may be received but it will be ignored or at least minimised and marginalised.

Where this gets us is that if our epithets and narratives tell us more about us than about nature, might we not be getting it wrong sometimes? But how do we tell that – and who is to judge? This matters if we propose to take some action, or even simply whether to care about nature or not. How do we tell what is an appropriate construct – and by what criteria? Is it just that actions might not give the results we expected – and so we have to change our ideas? But do we change them that readily? Narratives matter as they constrain and justify how we see and what we do. The study of the narratives of nature thus matters philosophically in the sense of how we are limiting our seeing and also in very real terms of how we treat the environment. The rest of this book is dedicated to exploring these questions. How we relate to nature in terms of ourselves, our sense of place and our psychogeographic perceptions lies at the heart of environmental meanings – and at the heart of environmental philosophies and the way we treat and purport to manage the environment and environmental change.

1.4 Chapter Summary

- Values and meanings give us reasons to want to cherish something. The meanings vary widely, but meanings there have to be. Hence the subtitle of the book: *Perspectives on Meanings and Motivations*. Meanings are the key to motivations.
- Nature is just doing what it is doing; things exist because they can. It is us who bring a sense of value and purpose: there are no meanings in nature other than those we bring to it.
- There are 'lenses' through which we are looking at nature, giving us our meanings of nature. We should realise that they are there, rather than just looking through them. Various authors have written about this:
  - '*Kulturbrille*': *Kultur* ('culture') and *brille* ('glasses' or 'spectacles') or 'culture-glasses' – a term used by Franz Uri Boas (1858–1942) to mean acquired cultural associations ("lenses") that shape an individual's perceptions.
  - Evernden (1992): 'conceptual imprisonment': referring to the transformations, inspirations and constraints which our ideas bring to nature.
  - Feyerabend (1999): 'Understanding a subject means transforming it.'
  - Foucault's question: 'How have I been situated to experience the real?'
- We emphasise the importance of stories – or narratives – in giving forms of understanding and meaning, including the imperative of the explanation. Marek Kohn (2004) encapsulates this in the title of his book on evolution: *A Reason for Everything*. There 'has to be a story' – and we emphasised the power of narratives in terms of the consequences which stem from holding them, such as seeing nature as 'robust' or as 'fragile'.

- The awareness of assumptions, constructs and narratives of meaning should mean that we do see that there are conceptual frameworks which might constrain us. This awareness should mean that we realise that not only are there consequences deriving from different conceptual frameworks, but also that we do have a choice of the conceptual frameworks which we hold.

2 · *Climate Change*

2.1 Setting the Scene

Introduction

The quotation "Civilization is in a race between education and catastrophe" is attributed to the writer H. G. Wells (1866–1946). While often quoted, the actual source of the quotation seems elusive, but I feel that it is relevant here. However, in the context of climate change, as in many other contexts, 'education' is much more than about being informed. It is also about 'education to be wary' – wary of the easy narrative, the received wisdom, the manufactured dissent and the fact that nothing enhances self-justification as much as a bogeyman – whether an actual person or an assumed problem. Further, I would add 'education to think carefully', to question, to realise that you might be being manipulated, to realise how you are being positioned, to read widely, to gain as many views as possible, to be open and to think for yourself. H. G. Wells continued, "Let us learn the truth and spread it as far and wide as our circumstances allow. For the truth is the greatest weapon we have."

However, having followed many Twitter feeds and other writings on climate change, one realises that 'the truth' can be whatever people want it to be in what are normative groupings engaged in confirmation bias. Many might argue that ignoring climate change is stupid while noting that climate change deniers seem impervious to reason. Those who take an opposite point of view are equally scathing of their opponents. In this context, it is useful to reflect on the writings of Bonhoeffer on stupidity.

> Stupidity is a more dangerous enemy of the good than malice. One may protest against evil; it can be exposed and, if need be, prevented by use of force. Evil always carries within itself the germ of its own subversion in that it leaves behind in human beings at least a sense of unease. Against stupidity we are defenceless; reasons fall on deaf ears; facts that contradict one's prejudgement simply need

> not be believed – in such moments the stupid person even becomes critical – and when facts are irrefutable they are just pushed aside as inconsequential, as incidental. In all this the stupid person, in contrast to the malicious one, is utterly self-satisfied and, being easily irritated, becomes dangerous by going on the attack. (Dietrich Bonhoeffer, Letters and Papers from Prison, 1943, www.goodreads.com/quotes/8616320-stupidity-is-a-more-dangerous-enemy-of-the-good-than)

This sounds all very familiar to those who look at climate change Twitter feeds. The difficulty is working out what is actually stupid. Indeed, we seem to be evolving into a 'click-protest' society without much dialogue, as observed by Charles (2020) in *Outraged: Why everyone is shouting and no one is talking*.

The aspect of imperviousness to opposing arguments is often related to belief superiority, as Toner Raimi and Leary (2014: 76) write in 'Belief superiority in the environmental domain': "This study examined belief superiority – the belief that one's own beliefs are more correct than other viewpoints. ... Those with high belief superiority thought they were better educated about energy than others, and [their] certainty about their beliefs tended to increase after reading the article, even when the article contradicted those beliefs."

What I find interesting is that there have existed for some time some really balanced appraisals of climate change, such as the book by Hulme (2009) and the Royal Society (2014) report with its easily accessible summaries. More recently, a very balanced and informative book was published, considering climate in a very wide context involving many environmental issues: Eisenstein's (2018) *Climate: A new story*. Eisenstein (2013: 49) also wrote one of my favourite climate change quotes: "Skeptical as I am about the conventional story of climate change, I am even more skeptical of climate change skepticism." In other words, while one might debate the details of climate change, it is clear that 'something is going on'. Most authoritative, and widely available, are the reports over a number of recent years from the Intergovernmental Panel on Climate Change (IPCC: www.ipcc.ch; 1990 onwards: www.ipcc.ch/reports). Yet one wonders what actual influence these carefully written volumes have on the public mind when such a great variety of competing narratives about climate change still exist both within and outside science. Even the putative game changer of Extinction Rebellion (XR; see www.facebook.com/

XRebellionUK/) and their book *This Is Not a Drill* (2019) have not stopped climate change–denier Twitter feeds. In his blog, Mike Hulme (https://mikehulme.org/author/mikehulme/page/3) felt that while many people certainly sympathised with the general aims of XR, they were not addressing the full heterogeneity of the public with their divergent values. To explore this diverse situation further, I think we might usefully start with a short historical perspective.

In their article 'Narratives of climate change: Introduction', Daniels and Endfield (2009) wrote about the papers in a themed issue of *Journal of Historical Geography*: "It is timely . . . to consider climate change narratives of all kinds in historical-geographical perspective, as forms of knowledge produced and distributed in particular periods and places, which propose powerful imaginative worlds in the form of past scenarios as well as future prospects" (Daniels and Endfield, 2009: 215).

They view the current narratives from the perspective of emphasising the power of past narratives, such as 'dust bowl'. These have been discussed with considerable insight by William Cronon (1992) in 'A place for stories: Nature, history, and narrative', and they also usefully refer to Denis Cosgrove's (2008) 'Images and imagination in 20th-century environmentalism', where narrative pictures are seen as both reflecting and influencing thought. They also cover the work of Gaard (2014), 'What's the story? Competing narratives of climate change and climate justice', which discusses the representations of climate change narratives in genres of literature. These historical perspectives are helpful as they show how environmental narratives are contextualised in particular historical situations and cultures and also within particular sets of knowledge prevalent at the time. They also stress the ways in which knowledge is perceived and understood by different sets of people over time. The reader can but conclude that powerful, but contested, environmental narratives are nothing new – and that they can be best understood by examining the widest possible range of cultural, social, anthropological and psychological perspectives. Indeed, to understand some of the depth and breadth of the issues which can be involved, the reader might usefully consult the book *Flight Behaviour* by Barbara Kingsolver (2012), which has a story of human psychology and meaning set in a context of climate change.

The literature shows that there is a long tradition of interpretative narratives of weather and climate, often involving personal diaries, including Daniels and Endfield's writings about:

> extraordinary 'meteoric' events, as well as normal, expected ones, and their actual or portentous bearing on livelihood, including such fundamentals as crop yields and dwelling, ... [bringing] weather and climate into the sphere of news, current affairs, as well as history, including a history that included the waters of the Noachian Flood and the fires of the Apocalypse. (2009: 220–221)

The authors add, "the magic of omens and prognostications ... persisted in popular culture, including mass circulation almanacs".

It is then hardly surprising that one of the major current areas of ecological and environmental discussion, climate change, is so endued with deeply rooted and often competing narratives (Trudgill, 2009; Trudgill, Jeffery and Parker, 2010), and their associated 'powerful imaginative worlds', which are now to be seen in many diverse representations and groupings in popular culture and associated media (see, e.g., Clay Shirky's (2008) *Here Comes Everybody*) as well as in the narratives of science. The narratives are much-rehearsed and almost used like weapons in a war of competing viewpoints (see, e.g., Hoffman (2011], 'Talking past each other? Cultural framing of skeptical and convinced logics in the climate change debate'). My aim here is a similar one to Hoffman's – not to judge the validity of competing arguments but to look at and try to understand the use of the narratives.

A Starting Point: An Initial Personal Assessment

I can find my interest in the narratives of climate change difficult to discuss with people because within seconds of me starting to talk someone says, "but surely ..." and they almost automatically come up with a judgemental statement on one of the narratives in order to counter what they think I am saying. Thus, I am confronted with what Hulme (2009: 353) in *Why We Disagree about Climate Change* calls "the inescapability of adopting ethical positions", and constantly being put in a position I am not in and then criticised for being there. The listener so often thinks I am promoting a point of view when actually what I find interesting is how people justify their points of view. It does show, however, how immediate and readily rehearsed many of the answers are and how quick people are to judge rather than to understand – even though they will claim that their judgement is based on a very defensible understanding.

So, bear with me, I shall now tiptoe down through what I would like to say about climate change. I am certain that you will scarcely be able to read my personal assessment without some critical thought occurring to you, but maybe I then address that point further down the page, but maybe I don't. This section will thus disappoint some readers, no doubt, but I venture it in the hope that it might increase some self-awareness of the use of narratives. I find that even in the circles of society where many people do carefully consider and weigh what they say, still the emotive clichés can be found. The media commentators and news reporters, as shown in Section 2.2, can show some subtlety, but as ever the easy, ready-wrapped, simplistic, emotive phrases dominate. We should thus look at climate change narratives in the media – and also at the psychology and history of the social, cultural and scientific narratives of climate change – and then reflect further. My attempt at an initial personal assessment is as follows.

The climate is changing. This is the one thing about which I have no doubt. It would be strange if it wasn't changing. The climate has always changed. Why would it suddenly stop changing?

Examination of the geological evidence back through the millions of years of earth history right through early human history to the present day shows that fluctuations, trends, cycles and relatively sudden changes have occurred. Many of the changes which have occurred through geological time have been far more drastic than those we are currently witnessing. For example, the carbon dioxide levels in the current atmosphere of the earth are nearing what they were fifteen million years ago (de la Vega et al., 2020). These climatic changes occurred when there were no humans present. They have also continued during the short recent history of the earth when humans have been present.

The climate is changing now. As ever, we can see cycles, fluctuations, trends and relatively sudden changes. There are discussions of causes, effects and consequences. When we consider the precise role of human activity in causing the current climate change, estimates of its significance vary, though many agree that our activity is significant. I can agree that human activity has some degree of effect on climate change. After careful consideration – and many people goading me with arguments that always seem to begin with "but surely you must agree that . . ." – I can manage to produce the following two rather obvious statements either side of the uncertainty about exactly how far we have caused the current climate change:

- We cannot say that we have caused all the current climate change.
- We cannot say that human activity has no role at all in changing climate.

We can thus justifiably act to mitigate our emissions and other activities which have an influence on climate, though there is still some uncertainty about the precise detail of the effectiveness of our actions. The general trend is, however, at least clear.

There often seems to be an assumption that climate change is bad. However, the concept that climate change is bad is, like any other simplistic statement, one which should be examined carefully. On the topic of judging how we should react to change, I feel that three different reactions can be identified: (1) in some ways, there are fights to keep things exactly as they are because change in itself is seen as bad; this is different from (2) a stance that changes are occurring, for whatever reason, so it is a good idea to adapt to and mitigate the effects; and this is different again from (3) trying to establish and tackle the causes. The first is indefensible and unfeasible, the second is prudent and the third is laudable.

Certainly, there are effects on human societies, for example through changes in water supply, effects on agriculture and sea-level changes. Many of these changes challenge the status quo. Whole societies and infrastructures are affected. There are questions as to the continued existence of some particular societies and their infrastructures in their current locations. The continued existence of particular types of plants and animals in particular places is affected, and indeed there are questions as to the continued existence of particular species (see, e.g., Usher (2005a), *Conserving European Biodiversity in the Context of Climate Change*). There are strong feelings that the ways forward include attempts at mitigation of climate change causes and effects together with adaptive strategies.

Climate change is normal, and inorganic and organic processes respond to change in a way that can feed back to influence that change. Life on earth has evolved in no small way in relation to climate change. This is first in terms of the organisms which actually exist and have survived and evolved during, and often in response to, drastic climate changes – and second in terms of their spatial distributions. Different types of organisms exist in a way which is not 'right' or 'good', which is often assumed, but in a way which happens to be the case in relation to the influences, including climate change, which have been acting upon them from the origins of life to the present day. Organisms are distributed where they are in a way which is not 'right' or 'good', as is often assumed, but in a way that is but a snapshot of their current position in what is a very mobile situation. The distributions of plants and animals are always changing in response to the influences in operation including climate change and associated migrations, extinctions and new evolutions. Indeed, humanity itself has also evolved socially and culturally as much as physically in relation to climate change and through migrations. If you look back through geological time, we are currently in an unusual cold era where there are ice caps on both poles; in previous times, there were higher temperatures and more widespread tropical conditions – as was the case about fifty-five million years ago when the first hominids were evolving.

What is different now is the prevalence of the idea that humans are to blame for current climate change, and that it is faster than ever. It follows that if it is our fault, we can and should do something about it. This idea is based on a set of narratives which stem from the guilt of the Edenic myth of a pristine nature destroyed by man (a narrative which is also discussed in the context of ecological science in Section 3.1). In the biblical story, Adam and Eve are cast out of Paradise in the Garden of Eden after eating the forbidden fruit. While Paradise is still there, behind the wall which surrounds the garden and we are out in the surrounding area, there is the notion of sin in Paradise. Although Bible scholars will see this as only one possible interpretation of the story of Genesis and one which is open to debate, whatever Bible scholars say, in the popular mind this has evolved over time to become a narrative for the way in which mankind has tainted a pristine creation. As also cited later in the book in the context of ecological thought, Glacken (1967) writes in *Traces on the Rhodian Shore* that he feels there has been a persistent question in Western thought, which was crystallised in George Perkins Marsh's (1864) *Man and Nature*: "In his long tenure of the earth, in what manner has man changed it from its hypothetical pristine state?". An entire chain of logic extends from this stance pervading the narratives of climate change and the 'guilt-laden' notion that human-induced changes have damaged a 'pristine' nature, with the attendant ideas of 'balance' or 'equilibrium' and the corresponding human 'disturbance'. These ideas are all firmly entrenched in Western culture. If, however, we classify climate change with volcanoes, earthquakes and tsunamis, this changes everything: we cannot blame ourselves. We can do nothing about the cause but we must work around what is happening and adapt. We blame those who do not predict, warn us or build capacity to resist. We do not have endless media columns saying that tsunamis and earthquakes are or are not caused by the tectonic shifts in the earth's crust; there is no vilification of the earthquake deniers. We just get on with coping with them as best we can.

It strikes me that the media coverage of guilt, blame, cause and effect, proposed action, avoidance of action, denial of trends, denial of causation, vilification, accusation and in fact the whole anger machine are all a tremendous waste of time and energy. I would rather that the column inches were focussed not on the hand-wringing but on discussing inventive strategies for coping with change.

If indeed the changes of climate are to be judged as detrimental, and if it is argued that our activity has a contributory significance, it seems prudent to examine our activities and take reasonable steps to modify those which we think are most likely to have an effect on climate change. However, there will be implications for taking such steps. The steps may or may not have the desired effect and may or may not be otherwise beneficial and could be otherwise detrimental. If you want this in shorthand: yes, cut CO_2 emissions, energy conservation is a good idea anyway and saves money – but don't let old people freeze by pricing energy too high. It is that kind of discussion which is important. We should also be careful to contextualise these attempts within other aspects of existence and to balance the likely benefits of attempting to modify climate with other attempts at improving the human condition. Climate change is but one aspect of global issues involving well-being, peace, equality, justice and health. We should also take care that attempts to limit harm do not themselves cause other harm. We should also consider the timescales of any ameliorative effects our actions may have. Meanwhile, we should be inventive about adaptation to changes, especially bearing in mind the paragraph above, that in many ways what we find in existence today is very much a response to past climate changes.

Returning to some prior condition is highly unlikely however much we try – it has never happened before in the history of the earth. This does not say that attempts at preservation or remedial actions are necessarily futile, but they should be thought through carefully and with due consideration to other aspects of existence. We must give ourselves conditions in which to be able to flourish and adapt and also give nature – organisms – conditions to be able to adapt, flourish and change.

If you want something shorter: climate change is happening, get used to it.

Discussion of an Initial Personal Assessment

In this initial 'starting point' statement, I have chosen my words carefully and written down what I have come to think, based on many years of reading and teaching about climate change and listening to narratives. If you find my attempt at a balanced, careful assessment above rather too convoluted, then it is perhaps no wonder that people prefer to deal with more simplistic polarised statements. However, I do then think that it is important to try to express my assessment simply; expression in simple terms being different from making simplistic, naïve statements. So, my interim headline would be that 'Our best shot is that it is wise to act to try to control the factors which we think can cause climate change while simultaneously taking care not to make further problems nor losing sight of other interrelated issues and meanwhile being adaptive and inventive in the face of changes' or, if you would prefer something more like a sound bite: 'Our best shot: act on climate change through amelioration and adaptation without losing sight of other related issues in the world.' That is simple but, to me, not naively simplistic.

I do not deny that there are those who will disagree with what I have written above, but having read extensively, discussed and taught about environmental change for many years these statements I have made are the nearest I can get to what I believe to be my best shot at assessing the situation (and it is interesting to note that I have just fallen into the same stance as columnists, who we discuss in Section 2.2, by having a set of justificatory credentials at my disposal). I also feel that a plea for subtlety may well fall on deaf ears.

The simplistic narratives inevitably tend to dominate the media presentations of climate change. There seem to me to be two particular sets of characteristics associated with climate change narratives: polarised dogmatic mantras and automatic assumptions of linkages. The first of these presents narratives, each of which quotes authoritative support in evidence and ridicules other points of view. The second of these makes links which, because they are automatic rather than reasoned, weaken the arguments. Arguments are much more powerful if linkages are not assumed a priori (or without any examination) but are defensibly made in succession.

The subtleties of the considerations involved and the conditionality of the links in the arguments are regrettably so often lost in the rehearsal of dogmatic mantras which have become polarised and therefore end up in competition with each other. There is no quarter between them; each argues that the other is right and will seemingly marshal almost any evidence while simultaneously vilifying the opposition in order to prove their point. If you think I am exaggerating then you cannot have seen many climate change Twitter postings.

A more subtle way forward is to consider carefully what is taken as evidence before making any argument. Analysis, interpretation and advocacy should be separated and the links between them carefully argued rather than conflating the three. This involves separating pattern analysis and interpretation into two distinct stages, where the latter is open to alternative explanations. Then taking the analysis and interpretations forward to a third stage of advocacy about action which takes into account wider contexts. This should be a separate stage and not necessarily predicated on the analyses and interpretations as many possible actions are still viable even given the analyses and interpretations. Thus, the links between 'this is happening', 'it must be caused by our actions' and 'we must do something' may actually be the case but the automatic assumption that the links follow weakens the case of making the argument. Only if you carefully examine the links in the chain of argument and defensibly make the links can you become convincing.

Meanwhile, as the arguments between polarised assumptions continue, it does seem prudent to take such steps as we can. These include reducing carbon emissions partly because there are arguments that we have reason to believe that carbon dioxide increases heat retention in the atmosphere. The issue is also tempered by the fact that we also know that there is absorption of CO_2 by the oceans and that plant growth that can be enhanced by elevated CO_2 and that there were also far higher CO_2 levels in previous geological eras like the Tertiary than there are now. Reducing carbon emissions is also a good idea, even if there were no effect on climate change, if it is achieved through the more efficient use of energy. Using alternative methods of power generation has to be thought through carefully, however, as they each can bring environmental impacts of their own.

These topics are well covered in David MacKay's book *Sustainable Energy – without the hot air* (MacKay, 2009) and his heartfelt last blog about energy use and thermal control in hospital: http://itila.blogspot.co.uk. An anonymous obituary in *The Telegraph* on 15 April 2016 covers some of his key points about increasing energy efficiency irrespective of climate change issues well: "[E]ven if some people do not care about climate change, with continued rapid depletion of North Sea oil and gas reserves (and because fossil fuels are a finite resource), a sharp reduction in Britain's fossil-fuel consumption would seem a wise move if we care about security of supply." Additionally: "Any substantial increase [in renewable power sources] would involve nationwide projects that would have significant effects on the environment." Some key points are then made:

Burning biomass (crops for fuel) would need about 75 per cent of Britain to be covered in biomass plantations to meet only 25 per cent of our current electricity demand. Wave power would need 500 km of Atlantic coastline to be filled with wave farms. For solar panels, covering between five and 10 per cent of the country with panels would provide less than half the daily electricity consumption of the average European. For wind power about the same amount of electricity would be produced by as an offshore wind farm filling an area of the sea twice the size of Wales.

The article concludes:

MacKay went on to point out that electricity generation accounts for only one-fifth of our total CO_2 emissions. So even if we managed to convert 80 per cent of our electricity to renewables (as some environmentalists say we should), Britain's total CO_2 emissions would be cut by only 16 per cent. The majority of emissions are created by transport, heating and food production. (Anonymous, 2016)

A companion volume to MacKay's book has now been produced concerning sustainable building materials (Allwood and Cullen, 2019 – *Sustainable Materials without the Hot Air).*

Additionally, while climate change is certain, it is not clear how far the term 'global warming' is helpful or appropriate as there are many other aspects of climate change, such as volcanic dust and emissions which can have a cooling effect (such as the 'year without a summer' in 1816 after the 1815 eruption of Tambora) as well as solar activity. And no, I did not write that I thought these latter aspects were necessarily involved or more or less significant than human activity. And no, I am not a climate change denier, nor am I a climate change sceptic nor an alarmist nor an environmentalist. I am just interested in what is going on in terms of narratives and social process.

What is then interesting is that there are many influences, interactions and feedbacks which are involved so that a complex situation allows a diversity of narratives to coexist. Such competing narratives are axiomatically contestable and indeed can be supported by a diversity of data which can be interpreted in a number of contestable ways. The interpretations especially include the nature and rate of current trends as much as the causes and effects of change. From the variety of justificatory narratives there then follow a range of actions proposed to alter climate change in a direction seen as more desirable and a varied prioritisation of these actions in relation to actions taken in pursuit of other goals.

I almost want to stop writing here as now we can but venture further into the minefield of contested narratives, but I will venture further as I think it is instructive to think carefully about the narratives we use. When we study the climate change narratives, as remarked above, it is possible to conclude that there is a persistent situation of the conflation of analysis and value judgement where a perceived pattern can be automatically judged in a variety of contexts by a variety of people.

Given the constant history of changing climate, one of the most inappropriate, but nonetheless strongest, judgemental narratives is the concept of 'normal' – sometimes expressed as 'a stable climate'. This one word 'normal' can be invested with the concepts of 'what we remember', 'what we are used to' and 'what has been the case' and there is widespread confusion between 'normal' and 'average'. We can think of people of average height when we know that a range of heights is perfectly normal.

This is not to deny that trends now exist; they do. This also is not to deny that the ranges of data distribution have changed; they have. But this is to warn that 'average' and 'normal' are not the same thing and that neither should be confused with 'good' and 'right', which they often are in, for example, the narrative of 'taking action to get back to a stable, normal climate'. Unprecedented is possibly better, but whatever is happening now, there are indeed some kinds of precedents; after all climate has changed rapidly before and there have been times of ice sheet cover and times of very little ice.

Additionally, this is not to argue that there may be multiple causes for these trends. Indeed, in a complex system it is very unlikely for there to be one single cause of the current trends. To repeat: this does not deny the role of human activity in changing climate; neither does it indicate that we have caused all the current climate change and neither can we say that we have not caused any climate change.

It is interesting to examine what is called The Little Ice Age, which was a period of cooling that occurred after the Medieval Warm Period from about 950 to about 1250 and is variously seen as covering a period from about 1300 to about 1850, particularly from the sixteenth century to 1850. There appears to have been a modest cooling of the Northern Hemisphere during the period. I like the Wikipedia entry (https://en.wikipedia.org/wiki/Little_Ice_Age) which reads that several causes have been proposed: cyclical lows in solar radiation, heightened volcanic activity, changes in the ocean circulation, an inherent variability in global climate or decreases in the human population. So, that is a noticeable cooling after a warmer period with narratives of human-induced change nested alongside other causes – and a fairly realistic assessment of the complexities which might be involved in any explanation.

It all has taken me quite some time to make only a beginning of a discussion of the climate change narratives in order to get somewhere near expressing the dimensions of what might be involved. No wonder we read the shorthand that the year 2016's Arctic ice melt is not normal, that it shows how rapid the change (we are causing) is and makes it more urgent to act (on curbing emissions). This linkage may indeed be defensible but the steps do not necessarily follow – though in the media they invariably do. All we really do know is that 2016's ice melt is rapid – and more rapid than previous observations. The rest depends on who is writing, and the apocalyptic narrative is an easy, obvious one while the sceptic counter-narrative rapidly flows in multitudinous form on Twitter and other media. Something quieter, considered and measured is pre-empted by the ready-made narratives.

People sometimes ask me what point am I trying to make and what is it precisely that I am objecting to, thinking that I wish to make counter-arguments against some theory, data or point of view. I'm not and I don't. The point I am trying to make is one of how monumentally unhelpful the ping-pong match of narratives is, with narrative and counter-narrative batted back and forth seemingly for ever to no great purpose.

In terms of the contextualisation of narratives in a social situation it is not just one of 'they would say that, wouldn't they' and of confirmation bias for those seeking to promote a point of view finding the evidence they want. That is of course present, but the underlying characteristic is the seduction offered by simplistic statements. A more fundamental understanding of what I am trying to say is very much in line with Feyerabend's (1999: 12) observations which we discussed in Chapter 1: "Anyone who tries to make sense of . . . events . . . is forced to introduce ideas that are not in the events themselves, but put them in perspective .... There is no escape: understanding a subject means transforming it, lifts it out of a natural habitat and inserts it into a model or a theory or a poetic account of it." And transform it, people do. My endeavour is to have a greater understanding that this is what is happening in general and to think more about the manifestations and implications.

To begin to sum up this section, and to try to end with a consideration of the permutations of the various arguments, a key point is that during transformative understanding, many people fail to distinguish between pattern and process and between pattern and value judgement and between pattern and advocacy. Trends are conflated with causes when, while the trends are readily observable, the processes involved may range in the number of causative factors. Trends are also conflated with value judgements about what is 'good' and what is 'bad', often revolving around the concept of departures from normal. It is so often unequivocally accepted that things being different automatically slot into the 'bad' category. For example, species distribution changes are often seen as 'bad' when in fact they are just 'different' – species distributions have always changed in relation to climate change but it so often becomes 'bad' if there is a layer of human guilt involved (and I am not passing judgement on that situation, it is merely an observation). There is the persistent narrative of a stable climate 'before we changed it'. Trends are then followed by prescriptions for actions which are often based on unspoken and implicitly (and unquestioningly) accepted assumptions about causes from which the remedies inevitably follow. Thus, we bounce back and forth from 'climate change is our fault therefore we can and must change it' to those who deny the change and/or the causes and/or the remedies, with every stage in between.

It is thus so interesting to consider how such a range of possible views can coexist and how they interact. For some, it is so often readily seen that global warming is all our fault. Here the Edenic story seems to prevail: we take the negative impacts of climate change upon ourselves as some kind of sin. We have caused global warming. The implication of this is, however, that we also have the comforting illusion that we could put it right. However, this can be in terms of the idealistic 'if only people would act out of long-term benefit rather than short-term self-interest'. Ah, if only they would. But I am going to act so I can feel good about it and worry about those who don't feel this way, and probably put posts on social media like Twitter and Facebook to boost my cause and find re-affirmation from like-minded people. In this context, the fact that climate has always changed throughout geological time and that there have been far more extreme climate changes in the past when there were no humans and no industry is hardly ever mentioned. The stance has the unspoken horror underneath it that if it is not all our fault then this is alarming as we could do nothing about it – and we hate that. Additionally, there is no cause to berate others with and nor is there a cause for the protagonists to feel desperate and virtuous about. Given the alternative view that climate change is not our fault and therefore we can do nothing about it, then we need not bother with it and we can carry on as we wish without further thought. This does seem to underpin some of the psychological justifications discussed in the next subsection. Meanwhile, we might think here of the 'categorical imperative' discussed by Immanuel Kant and it may be defined as a way of evaluating motivations for action. According to Kant, morality can be seen as an imperative, or ultimate commandment of reason, from which all duties and obligations derive. He defined an imperative as any proposition declaring a certain action (or inaction) to be necessary. We might then see how each climate change narrative leads to some kind of moral imperative for action (or inaction).

Consider the following narratives which can be espoused and consider what logically follows in terms of advocacy:

- Climate change does not exist. Carry on as usual.
- Climate change exists. We must adjust to it.
- Climate change has always existed. This is normal. We must adjust to it.
- Climate change exists and this is bad. We must adjust to it and try to act if we can on the causes.
- Climate change exists, this is good. Enjoy!
- Climate change exists; it is bad and our fault. We must act quickly (to keep things 'normal').
- Climate change exists; it is bad but we can't do anything about it. We must adjust.
- Climate change exists; it is our fault but not particularly good or bad. We must adjust and ameliorate both causes and effects as much as we can (but not to the detriment of other issues which may require more urgent attention).
- Climate change exists and can be seen to be having significant effects. The causes and interactions are complex but significantly involve human activity as a causative factor in the currently observable trends. It is therefore beholden upon us to do our best to minimise our impact on change and its effects.

What is interesting is that these statements, just because they are different, are not necessarily mutually exclusive and indeed can coexist. Equally, it is because they are different that they can be pitted against each other in a competitive way. Can we understand how and why the narratives are used?

Psychological Studies of Climate Change

The psychological framing of climate change narratives is not just one of considering positionality and vested interests; there is so much more involved than saying 'well, they would say that, wouldn't they'. Psychological studies seem to indicate that there is a complex range of indicative factors often involving a sense of self-identity. Aspects of self-identity are involved in both attitudes (preferences and intentions) and actual behaviour (Clayton, 2012; van der Werff, Steg and Keizer, 2013).

In a study of psychological research on 'Psychology and climate change: Beliefs, impacts, and human contributions', Swim, Markowitz and Bloodhart (2012) discuss the psychological sources of the beliefs about climate change. They write: "The complex interlocking causes and impacts of global climate change, time course of climate change impacts, and multiple solutions with unknown side effects contribute to uncertainty, ambiguity, feelings of threat, and inaction" (Swim, Markowitz and Bloodhart, 2012: 646). They make further successive points: "Climate change impacts are sometimes seemingly contradictory . . . which can potentially cause confusion about what climate change is and what is evidence of impacts" and "The scope of the impacts can be difficult to grasp, cope with and know how to respond to. Responding to climate change may require cultural shifts that challenge the status quo and therefore may meet with resistance" (Swim, Markowitz and Bloodhart, 2012: 646).

In their crucial section 'Who believes what and why?' (p. 650) the following summary points can be gleaned about demographic and psycho-social variables, though it should be stressed that these are 'head-lines', the validity of which are discussed in the paper (Swim, Markowitz and Bloodhart, 2012: 650). While women seem "more concerned about climate change than men" and are "more likely to underestimate their own knowledge", "men are likely to overestimate their own know-ledge". They found "no clear relationships between people's age and their climate change belief, concern or knowledge" but a weak, positive relationship "between educational attainment and increases in existence beliefs, concerns and preferences to confront climate change". Strikingly, they found that "beliefs about climate are strongly associated with political party identification and socioeconomic identity" with, in the USA, liberals, Democrats, moderates and Independents more likely to believe "that climate change is happening, that it is due to human actions and that it poses significant threats" than the conservatives and Republicans are.

Beliefs about climate change appear more powerfully shaped by our indirect experiences with the issue in media and social coverage than by direct experience such as the daily weather and extreme climatic events. This is, however, not to deny the considerable significance of direct experience but this latter relationship is highly likely to be related to awareness from the media in terms of the causal attribution. Thus 'a hot summer' might just be 'a hot summer' but with awareness from the media it can readily become 'global warming' and symptomatic of a perceived trend. The direct experience then in turn modifies the significance placed on the perceived trend.

The authors (Swim, Markowitz and Bloodhart, 2012: 656) feel that the social construction of the issue (Hulme, 2009) means that various opinion leaders can utilize "rhetoric and preferred scientific findings to either accentuate or discredit" various aspects of climate change (Hoffman, 2011). Individuals are likely to seek out information that allows them to "confirm pre-existing beliefs – and also to confirm their ideas about how the world works generally". There is also an element of finding a defence against the threats posed by information about climate change. In particular, there is resistance to ideas of climate change which challenge "deeply held beliefs about the world being a just, orderly and stable place".

Swim, Markowitz and Bloodhart (2012: 651) feel that at least some of the "political polarization in beliefs about global climate change may result from basic, underlying psychological differences between liberals and conservatives, including differences in values, system justification needs, and beliefs about how the world should operate". They make the point (Swim, Markowitz and Bloodhart, 2012: 651) that "the 'scariness' of the issue makes people cling to their group identities and values in a similar way that the terrorism threat does". In this process, the idea of climate change as causing significant harm to others is one which motivates liberals with "egalitarian and community-orientated" values. By contrast, people who hold what can be seen as "hierarchical and individualistic" values tend to reject the issue, especially if it requires change to the economic system. Such people tend to "support the status quo and justify the existing socioeconomic system" and are "are unwilling to respond behaviourally to the issue". They also make the point that climate change may be viewed as an overwhelming and unchangeable force, a problem with human solutions or no problem at all, with those who have their belief systems threatened by climate change choosing to reject the belief in its existence.

There are, however, many nuances which could be made about these kinds of conclusions about attitudes and behaviour and one of the pitfalls is arguing that behaviour necessarily indicates a particular attitude. Whitmarsh (2009) finds for example that energy saving, often taken as an indicator of a held attitude towards climate change, can be far more motivated by saving money. In a general context of overall environmental attitudes, but nonetheless relevant here, Duerden and Witt (2010) found that indirect experience led to a greater increase of knowledge than change of attitude whereas direct experience led to a more similar change in both. Greitemeyer (2013) found that participants watching a 'climate change skeptic' film had decreased concern whereas watching a "climate change affirming" film made little difference to concern. McDonald, Chai and Newell (2015) found that some studies suggest that personal experience reduced 'psychological distance' of climate change (i.e. brought it 'home' to people). It is, however, clear that the few illustrative examples of work on the psychology of climate change I have used here show the potential of the subject for the increased understanding of the issues involved.

2.2 Justifications for Action

Storylines in the Media and Recent Literature

There is a vast volume of column inches, opinions and popular articles as well as scientific research papers on climate change. Columnists are interesting to think about as they show several characteristics, one being the need for authority. They tend to quote an authority of years of experience together with their credentials. They also tend to promote a point of view while detracting from the arguments of others (see, e.g., Berger, 1997, *Narratives in Popular Culture, Media and Everyday Life*).

In *Narratives of Climate Change: Outline of a systematic approach to narrative analysis in cultural sociology* Arnold (2015: 7) elucidates: "The topics of these narratives are not just derived from a simple content analysis, but [involve] the interplay between ... content and ... the narratives [together with] setting . . . characters within the narrative (hero – villain – victim). The, sometimes highly emotional, discourse about a social phenomenon can [allow] analysis to uncover cultural meanings beneath these stories." Arnold concludes that "narrative analysis can 'help investigators think about "non-rational" characteristics of environmentally relevant situations' (Shanahan et al. 1999: 417)". Thus, the content is contextualised in what might be termed a social drama. Indeed, that term is used by Smith and Howe (2015: 51) in *Climate Change as Social Drama.* They write of the deep underlying structural similarities that underpin various narratives and that lead them to constitute a recognisable genre. They offer a systematic way of looking at the form and structure of story-telling and its consequences for human actions in a narrative genre model which involves a 'genre guess', that is, what sort of story the reader is becoming involved in. The genre guess fills in the gaps between isolated facts, actions and predictions by outlining what is at stake, for example a range of storylines from "Apocalypse!" to "Can climate change make us happy?" will readily give clues to genre from "disaster movie" to "a possible rosier future" scenario. They see uncertain events and real-world facts as "clues" which require a "genre guess" to have significance. They write: "This guess is vital for the reduction of information complexity, yet it carries with it deep implications for communication and opinion process." Thus, saying 'what type of thing is this' makes it easier to handle and simultaneously restricts the meaning: "[T]he genre guess works to close off alternative interpretative possibilities even as it makes the world more meaningful." So, the genre guess might be, for example, "romantic, tragic or apocalyptic".

Each then carries with it implications for powers of action, likely social outcomes, appropriate yardsticks for motivation and policy evaluation and the issues at stake (e.g. 'we can do something' vs 'we can't do anything' or 'we must act' vs 'business as usual'). There can be good or bad agents within our story or drama and the chosen genre determines how clues are put together into a more coherent picture. They write:

> Interested parties try to have their stories taken seriously or to falsify or eliminate the stories of others. The combat between frames and their sponsors for interpretative authority is a further important source of social drama. . . . The distribution or adoption of these frames over nations, over time, or over constituencies and interest groups in a civil discourse indirectly shapes political outcomes as well as their timing.

I have seen assertions, as discussed further below, that polar bear numbers are decreasing and this indicates that global warming is happening and is bad; then we find others have said that polar bears numbers are increasing and/or that they are thriving without ice so the alarmists are wrong and then, in turn, these people are vilified as deniers. How unhelpful is that? It might be more helpful to ignore the arguments about alarmists and deniers and say, OK, polar bears are adaptable and can probably survive in a number of situations with or without ice but as we have observed that they are associated with ice-covered areas which are changing in extent then there is a likelihood that their populations are going to be affected. And yes, I know that is far too subtle when what we are used to is columnists searching for support for their meta-theories with 'under threat' conflated with 'our fault' and 'we must act' versus 'they are fine', though some arguments can be more sophisticated.

Further, more detailed illustration of the ideological narratives can be readily found. Attempts to find balanced views can readily be ridiculed by those who espouse polarised dogmatic mantras. For example, some of the polarised dimensions of the debate are well summarised in a newspaper article in *The Times* of 28 September 2013 where columnist Matt Ridley comments: "In the climate debate, which side are you on? Do you think climate change is the most urgent crisis facing mankind requiring almost unlimited spending? Or that it's all a hoax, dreamt up to justify socialism, and nothing is happening anyway?" (Ridley, 2013). I do then like his stance which he published on 19 January 2015 in *The Times* (Ridley, 2015a) mainly because he appears to have been criticised by all 'sides' so this gives me the feeling that he is striving to be even-handed.

Some of the thoughts in his column are as follows:

> I am a climate lukewarmer. That means I think recent global warming is real, mostly man-made and will continue but I no longer think it is likely to be dangerous and I think its slow and erratic progress so far is what we should expect in the future. That last year was the warmest yet, in some data sets, but only by a smidgen more than 2005, is precisely in line with such lukewarm thinking.

He then follows this with:

> This view annoys some sceptics who think all climate change is natural or imaginary, but it is even more infuriating to most publicly funded scientists and politicians, who insist climate change is a big risk. My middle-of-the-road position is considered not just wrong, but disgraceful, shameful, verging on scandalous. I am subjected to torrents of online abuse for holding it, very little of it from sceptics. (Ridley, 2015a)

It is indeed difficult to see why this debate seems to have to be so fractious unless we understand that what is displayed in the media is a mingling of evidence and faith (the use of the phrase in the media:

'Climate Evangelists' tells us that much) and that people with differing views are accusing each other of confirmation bias – only seeing what they wish to see.

There is often a 'battle of authorities' concerning who appears to have the superior case in terms of being able to back something up. There is often little attempt at finding a balance but more a stance involving partisanship about differing viewpoints. Hample (2016: 247) makes the interesting point that the disputations by climate sceptics about the veracity of particular sets of data elevates the data sets to a position of prime importance. In trading in and deconstructing the science base of instrumental climate records the climate sceptics "have become the unlikely vanguards of the science-based politics of climate change they oppose".

In this context we can look at a column by Christopher Booker (Booker, 2015): 'The real "deniers" in the climate change debate are the warmists' which ran in the *Daily Telegraph* on 1 August 2016. The banner is: "Those who believe that the world faces a catastrophe from global warming dismiss anyone who dares question their beliefs." A claim conflates ice cover and polar bear numbers seamlessly: "Real evidence shows that not only is Arctic ice not vanishing as predicted, but polar bear numbers are rising, not falling." The use of the word 'real' is interesting, a claim made by many writers of differing opinions. The article continues, where we can see the themes of evidence, insults and quoted authority all mingled with emotive language:

> Among the more useful things psychologists have come up with in helping us to understand the world is what they call 'projection' – that tendency in people who are not seeing the world straight to 'project' on to others the very failings they suffer from themselves. One prominent example of this has been the contemptuous itch of those who passionately believe that the world faces a catastrophe from global warming to dismiss anyone daring to question their beliefs as a 'denier'. In fact, it has long been obvious that the only real 'deniers' on the climate front are those true believers themselves, who cannot face up to all the evidence which makes their scare story ever less convincing.

Again, there is a thread of superior argument which runs through into the next example. This is from Kerry Jackson (Jackson, 2016) in the *Investor's Business Daily* Politics column from 25 October 2016: 'When asked to show evidence of man-made warming, scientists can't do it.' The banner runs: "Dr. Patrick Moore, founder of Greenpeace: There 'is no scientific proof that human emissions of carbon dioxide are the dominant cause of the minor warming of the Earth's atmosphere over the past 100 years'." Within the article: "There's probably not a phrase that the global warming alarmists and dim celebrities trying to play the role of intellectuals use more than some variation of 'the science is settled'. It's a catchy phrase that's intended to shut down debate and shame skeptics. And it's simply not true." Later in the writing he asserts:

> What the alarmists call 'proof' and 'evidence' is nothing more than conjecture. They cannot prove that man's activities have warmed the planet, even if the next 100 years are twice as hot as they have predicted. They can lay out their 'evidence' as if in a courtroom and urge the jury to make the connection. But the fact they can't get around is that there is more than enough reasonable doubt to throw out their prosecution. Carbon dioxide simply isn't the only suspect. Earth's climate system has far too many influences for the inquisitors to settle on just one.

If you look on Twitter, it is the range of material available which is of interest here, with many sites saying the complete opposite to each other. To assist in assessing this range, some examples are given in Box 2.1.

The voices on social media are many but there are common themes so it is possible to give instances of the type of frequently occurring narratives about science, authority and 'the facts' such as are grouped and summarised in outline form in Boxes 2.2, 2.3 and 2.4.

Tweets commonly refer to websites, and two selected examples which illustrate common themes are shown in Box 2.5.

These illustrative examples make me feel that this is all beginning to look like the discussion earlier in this book, when we observed the two narratives 'if one species is removed then the ecosystem collapses' and 'if one species is removed then another steps in to take its place'. What was wrong with those is that there is no collapse, only a change, and not actually any kind of 'place' for a species that has to be filled by another

Box 2.1 *Examples of climate change Twitter sources (accessed July 2020)*

- Climate Alarmism (@ClimateAlarmism)
- Climate Realists (@ClimateRealists)
- hockey schtick (@hockeyschtick1)
- Pure Climate Skeptic (@Carbongate)

Box 2.2 *Examples of types of common narratives about the role of science*

- Authority: Science is referred to as 'proper' or 'real' when it supports a preferred argument of the writer and 'fake' or 'junk' science if it does not.
- Experience and gravitas: Professor [name] from [respected institution] says: . . .
- The science is settled . . .
- The science is not settled . . .
- This is true . . .
- This is utter nonsense . . .
- Models have clearly shown that . . .
- Model predictions are unreliable. The fact is that . . .
- Growing body of evidence that the climate has not changed . . .
- Current high temperatures are nothing new . . .

Box 2.3 *Example of narratives that increased CO_2 is not a problem*

- Oxygen which we breathe: 70 percent of it comes from phytoplankton which absorbs CO_2.
- Increasing CO_2 would increase plant growth, increase crop yield and reduce famine.

(Source: http://hockeyschtick.blogspot.com/2016/05/dr-willie-soon-takes-on-bill-nye.html)

Box 2.4 *Examples of types of common narratives about facts and theories*

- Facts are aggressively misrepresented . . .
- If the facts don't support the argument: ignore them/shout louder/attack your opponents using emotive language . . .
- Accusations: if facts don't fit a hypothesis people turn to criticism of others who hold an alternative theory . . .
- Climate change deniers are like the holocaust deniers . . .

Box 2.5 *Examples of narratives that nothing has changed (accessed November 2019)*

1. https://notrickszone.com/2016/12/22/the-hockey-stick-collapses-50-new-2016-scientific- papers-affirm-todays-warming-isnt-global-unprecedented-or-remarkable/
   - Nothing unusual about today's climate.
2. www.telegraph.co.uk/science/2016/11/24/scott-shackleton-log books-prove-antarctic-sea-ice-not-shrinking/
   - Scott and Shackleton logbooks prove Antarctic sea ice is not shrinking 100 years after expeditions.
   - Antarctic sea ice has barely changed from where it was 100 years ago, scientists have discovered, after poring over the logbooks of great polar explorers such as Robert Falcon Scott and Ernest Shackleton.
   - Experts were concerned that ice at the South Pole had declined significantly since the 1950s, which they feared was driven by man-made climate change.
   - New analysis suggests that conditions are now virtually identical to when the *Terra Nova* and *Endurance* sailed to the continent in the early 1900s, indicating that declines are part of a natural cycle and not the result of global warming.

but again just a changed situation. Both are romantic fictions which feed from and back into wider views of the world. The illustrative examples above show even more how different narratives can coexist and this I feel can relate both to the situation where evidence is interpretable in different ways but also possibly to a wider psychological and political context.

In 'Narratives of climate change: Introduction', Daniels and Endfield (2009) have this useful perspective:

> Climate change is a problem in which the stakes are high and political decisions may well be necessary, but in which facts are still very uncertain and values very much in dispute, so much so that 'traditional science is not always able to legitimize' – and governments unable or unwilling to take – the drastic steps that may in fact be needed to deal with the climate change 'problem'. (Daniels and Endfield, 2009: 219)

They continue that three narratives which have become embedded within climate change policies are identified:

- The need to avoid 'dangerous' climate change
- The common but differentiated responsibility for climate change
- Market-based solutions as a means of reducing the climate change problem.

This is quoting the work of Diana Liverman who, they write, traces

> the origins of these narratives . . . Liverman illustrates how the powerful rhetorical and representational strategies adopted by scientists, media and governments today masks the historical geographies of anthropogenic climate change, oversimplifying and generating largely ineffectual responses to the problem. Moreover, the visual imagery designed to alert policy and popular audiences has served to obscure the distinctive geographies of climate change. Two of the most powerful images which have been used to define and communicate ideas about 'dangerous' climate change, are the so called 'Burning Embers' image and the 'Tipping Points' map.

These are seen as masking geographical inequalities and offering only weak analyses of all-important spatial variations. They continue: "Market solutions to climate mitigation have, Liverman argues, done little to address this differential social vulnerability, but have fostered a new commodity in carbon reductions, which though a 'victory' for market environmentalism and neoliberalism, is of 'questionable value to the poor'" (Daniels and Endfield, 2009: 219).

They then make a summary of a keynote address which encapsulates much of the narrative of the narratives – or 'stories about stories': "In a keynote address on 'fables of climate change', Bill Cronon focussed on the history of global warming narratives, their currency in present scientific and policy discourses and implications for generating action in the public realm." Later they write:

> Cronon compared the diminishing public impact of some dramatic crisis narratives, such as the various sermons on Hurricane Katrina, when they enter a cycle of repetition in western news and media, falling on deafened ears, with the cumulative power of apparently minor anecdotes, from an account of an Inuit adjusting his daily hunting routine to garden talk about British butterflies, synecdochal stories about fellow humans figuring out impersonal forces in familiar places. (Daniels and Endfield, 2009, 217)

In 'Telling stories about global climate change', McComas and Shanahan (1999: 49–54) focussed on the news issue attention cycle in the USA. They saw an attention upswing phase, where often the coverage was dramatic and emphasised negative consequences, followed by a steadier maintenance phase, where scientific controversy tended to emerge more strongly, and then a phase of waning attention where the economic implications of actions became more apparent, political actions were proposed and often there was a realisation that the disasters foretold in the upswing phase may not be as immediate or as dramatic as were predicted. Interestingly, throughout such a cycle they observed that "average temperatures in the United States continued to set record highs throughout the sample years" and that "scientists' understanding of what might happen as a result of global climate change did not shift radically in that period" (McComas and Shanahan, 1999: 50).

Their overall assessment (p. 51) is that from a perspective of looking at the narratives, the dangers and consequences of global climate change first grabbed the attention; then scientific disagreements complicated the plot and sustained the drama as opposing interests sought to establish doubt about the certitude of the cases which others were asserting. Then there were parallel storylines about costs of resolution and political capital being made with the controversy among scientists being generally absent from those stressing the dangers and consequences of climate change but the controversy was played up by those who felt uneasy about the economic and political costs. Climate accords and international agreements tend to feed the narrative of problem resolution so there may be a "prolonged limbo – a twilight of lesser attention". More recently, one might add that that the situation may, however, change dramatically with denials of the accords and according to the increasingly competitive narratives about 'evidence' seen above when discussing the media.

McComas and Shanahan (1999: 54) refer to the idea from Berger's (1997) book on narratives in popular culture that we tend to derive meanings from themes in stories by relating them to, or contrasting them with, other themes present or absent in the stories. It is therefore interesting to see that the story-lines tended to be clustered, with controversy and current weather being mentioned together as were new evidence of research and the consequences of warming. However, these two clusters were separate from each other and covered almost entirely separately from economics and politics and also international relations. Thus, stories about new announcements contained very little about politics and in those on the dangers of climate change the efforts to solve them and counteract the problems tend to be absent; equally articles emphasising the dangers do so without emphasizing any uncertainties or controversies about the evidence. This is interesting as we can compare that with the current explosion of Twitter feeds about climate change which tend to cite evidence to prove that climate change is or isn't happening and that it matters but without explicitly mentioning any remedies or solutions other than the generalised 'we must act' or the implicit 'we don't need to'.

History Revisited and Perspectives on Evidence

Here I would like to cite Williamson's (1771) observations together with those of Oswald (1884) on climate change where both authors mention land use change and have scant mention of the topics we now regard as critical. Land use change does seem to be neglected in climate change science and indeed Slaymaker (2001) makes a very good point: 'Why so much concern about climate change and so little attention to land use change?' This includes the effect of climate change on land use and of land use change on climate. This is followed up to good effect by Spencer and Lane (2016) on their reflections on the IPCC involving landscape scale change. It is thus salutary to look back at these early examples of writing on climate change to compare what was emphasised then with what is emphasised now.

In 1771 the *Transactions of the American Philosophical Society*, Volume 1 (1 January 1769–1 January 1771) published a paper by a Hugh Williamson which was read before the Society on 17 August 1770 and entitled 'An attempt to account for the change of climate, which has been observed in the middle colonies in North-America'. Here we find the observations:

> Several members of our Society must have observed, that our North West Winds, during the winter season, are less frequent, less violent and of shorter continuance, than formerly they were. Seamen, who are deeply interested in this subject inform us, that in the winter season they have been beating off[1] the coast three, four, or five weeks, not able to put in, by reason of the North-Westers; they are now seldom kept off twice that number of days [i.e. only six, eight or ten days]. It is also agreed, that the hardness of our frosts, the quantity and continuance of our snows, are very unequal now, to what they have been, since the settlement of this Province. (Williamson, 1771: 275)

[1] By which we understand they were sailing backwards and forwards – so beating in the sense of 'beating back and forth' – because the sea was too rough. to negotiate the harbour entrance or 'put in'; nowadays we might say the ships were having to ride out the storm at sea as the seas were too rough

What precedes and follows these observations is a discussion of the effects of the sun, the roughness and reflectivity of the surface and the way this affects heat retention. There is also a discussion of the effect of cultivation with the conclusion that when previously wild land is converted to agriculture this ameliorates the climate. The example is given of the then contemporaneous climate of Italy as compared to classical Roman times, where there is evidence for that conclusion in the form of the two trends of a milder climate and increase in agriculture. Thus, it is said that cultivation makes the countryside more temperate. The writer also says that (p. 276), "I shall not say that a change of climate may not arise from other causes than the one I have described." But the writer asserts that, "It is not to be dissembled that their winters in Italy were extremely cold about seventeen hundred years ago" and that "Virgil described frost and snow meant that cattle had to be sheltered in winter" which is not the case in Italy at the timing of his writing. There is also an explanation given for the change in climate from beyond the local trend towards agriculture: "To account for this remarkable change, we must go beyond the narrow limits of Italy [to the north where the cold winds originate and where] the Germans have certainly made immense progress in population and agriculture" with the "wild and extensive forests" of Caesar's time "now little remaining". This is explained:

From the uncultivated deserts piercing North-Winds used to descend in torrents on the shivering Italian. Clearing and smoothing of the face of the country would promote the heat of the atmosphere and in many cases would prevent or mitigate those winter blasts, which are the general origin of cold whence the winters must become more temperate. Perhaps it may be apprehended that as clearing [of] the country will mitigate the cold of our winters it will also increase the heat of our summers. (Williamson, 1771: 277)

The mechanism of this process is only lightly alluded to and its operation somewhat obscure, but the conviction is clear. The advantages which accrue from this changing climate are also seen:

Every friend to humanity must rejoice in the more pleasing prospect of the advantages we may gain in the point of Health from the cultivation of the country. The general improvement of the colonies have already produced very desirable effects. While the face of this country was clad in woods and every valley afforded a swamp or stagnant marsh by a copious perspiration through the leaves of trees or plants and a general exhalation from the surface of ponds and marshes, the air was constantly changed with a gross putrescent fluid. Hence a series of irregular, nervous, bilious, remitting and intermitting fevers, which for many years have maintained a fatal reign through many parts of this country, but are now evidently in decline. Pleuritic and other inflammatory fevers, with the several diseases in cold seasons are also observed to remit their violence as our winters grow more temperate. (Williamson, 1771: 280)

Salutary? We can certainly learn that given a particular state of knowledge in 1771 about physics and of medicine, and a social context of colonisation, together with the observable trends in climate then the rest seems to follow. What else can you do but to reach for what you think you know about the world and how it works and place the working into a social context of your time?

Now we might find other explanations independently of clearance and cultivation. With such hindsight and a 'superior'(?) knowledge we can find other theories and derive our explanations in our current social context – but are we not just as limited, however we know it not? But then, indeed what else can we do? Truly I think this 1771 paper is a cautionary tale about inferences, cause and effect and human actions.

In 1884 there was a paper in similar vein in *The North American Review* by Felix L. Oswald on 'Changes in the climate of North America'. Again, there are multiple citations of evidence of climate change, citations of historical records from the Romans onwards and theories. The article starts with a clear indication that what one experiences becomes equated with what is normal (a theme which Hulme (2009) explores). He writes of what might be termed 'latitudinal norms' where what one might expect from a particular latitude in Europe is not the same in North America – the phrases "puzzled by the eccentricities of the weather" and "unnatural climate" are even used in this context (Oswald, 1884: 362). However, some 100 years on from Hugh Williamson's 1771 paper, instead of crediting tree removal with an 'improvement' in climate, Oswald is more modern, presaging the 'environmental' age by arguing that deforestation has led to more climate extremes, leading to winter floods, erosion and summer droughts. He advocates a system of reservoirs to ameliorate the floods and alleviate the drought, though fears that they may silt up. He writes of all climate changes in these contexts with no mention of any other possible factors. Both Williamson and Oswald focus on man-made impacts without mentioning any atmospheric or solar influences. In other words, all the discussion is (a) local and (b) made on short-term observations.

Hulme (2014) takes up the theme of short-term observations in a useful article entitled 'Attributing weather extremes to climate change: A review'.

He observes straightaway that when considering unusual events "the psychological need to attach blame to such events becomes overwhelming" (p. 499) and he cites works which have listed accusations and causal factors such as witches, moral deviancy of human behaviour and the gods, noting the complex human psychology of beliefs and perceptions summarised by Doyle (2011), Kerr (2013) and Rudiak-Gould (2014). He then poses the crux of the whole matter: "What does it mean for something to be caused by something else – especially in complex systems?" He then distinguishes between (a) deterministic (direct) causation and (b) randomness and probability, leading him to consider "in what ways are the answers to the questions of causation shaped by political or moral considerations rather than by scientific enquiry?" (Hulme, 2014: 500). He makes the fundamentally reasonable point that: "Knowing the cause of some adversity or personal affliction is often the first step towards living with it or overcoming it; it helps reconcile an undesirable lived reality with an alternative reality we might desire" (Hulme, 2014: 500). He concludes that climate adaptation is an "exercise in hedging against a variety of unknown and poorly known future events" and that the politics of vulnerability are involved (Hulme, 2014: 508).

Placing the current observable trends into a longer-term perspective is a further considerable endeavour. Out of the wide range of literature and websites one might pick some illustrative examples. These include Ljungqvist et al. (2016) who look at northern hemisphere hydroclimate variability using multi-proxy reconstruction (from many sources, e.g. tree rings and sediment cores) over the past twelve centuries and their conclusion is one of caution about the possible recent intensification of anomalies. In other words, when looking at the variability of the paleoclimate record the recent trends are not so clear-cut as some pundits claim. This paper is also reviewed by Jex (2016) under the heading 'No evidence of extreme drought and floods in the twentieth century', with a related commentary saying the worst drought occurred in medieval times and that water availability is not simply related to temperature.

Viewing *Watts Up With That* (WUWT), the self-styled "World's most viewed site on global warming and climate change" brings many a perspective but one post in particular charts the increase of plant growth with CO_2, something that scientific papers elsewhere have done, as seen in May (2016). This provides the historical perspective on carbon dioxide levels in geological times and shows graphic pictures of trees growing more in CO_2-rich atmospheres. The conclusion is that there is compelling evidence that the rising carbon dioxide concentration in the atmosphere is a primary cause of observed recent greening of the Earth.

Other data sites on carbon dioxide and temperatures include the recent changes in carbon dioxide in a longer perspective as shown in Box 2.6.

Box 2.6 *Recent changes in carbon dioxide in a longer perspective*

- Atmospheric carbon dioxide concentrations (1750 to present)

http://powerpoints.wri.org/climate/tsld001.htm

- Changes in atmospheric carbon dioxide, methane and nitrous oxide from 600,000 years ago to the present

https://archive.ipcc.ch/publications_and_data/ar4/wg1/en/tssts-2-1-1.html

- Recent greenhouse gas concentrations (2016)

http://cdiac.ornl.gov/pns/current_ghg.html

- What are the greenhouse gas changes since the Industrial Revolution?

www.acs.org/content/acs/en/climatescience/greenhousegases/industrialrevolution.html

- History of Earth's Climate 4 – Cenozoic I – Tertiary (concentrations were 750 ppm at the start of the Tertiary)

www.dandebat.dk/eng-klima4.htm

- Overview

https://en.wikipedia.org/wiki/Carbon_dioxide_in_Earth's_atmosphere

- This site plots changes in many factors and shows that recently CO_2 plots closely to temperature rise:

www.bloomberg.com/graphics/2015-whats-warming-the-world/

- This site presents fifty graphs of temperatures at various time scales and geographic locations:

http://notrickszone.com/2016/12/22/the-hockey-stick-collapses-50-new-2016-scientific-papers-affirm-todays-warming-isnt-global-unprecedented-or-remarkable

- Climate change denial is discussed here:

www.theguardian.com/environment/planet-oz/2016/dec/06/more-terrifying-than-trump-the-booming-conspiracy-culture-of-climate-science-denial?

From a trawl of this and the many other possible sites, one is left in no doubt that CO_2 is currently increasing. One is also left in no doubt that levels have been this high and higher before in geological time. However, some data give very little support for the latest warming being unusual, for example: https://notrickszone.com/2016/12/22/ the-hockey-stick-collapses-50-new-2016-scientific-papers-affirm-todays-warming-isnt-global-unprecedented-or-remarkable. As to actual effects there are useful reviews of the effects of climate change on hydrology by Watts, Hannah and Watkinson (2015a) and Watts et al. (2015b) as shown in Table 2.1 and Table 2.2.

Watts et al. (2015b) recommend that decision-makers should establish more explicitly how their decisions relate to projected changes and are sensitive to them as well as find ways to make plans which can accommodate the uncertainty in climate change projections. They feel: "If decision-makers expect research to support their work, they should engage actively from the outset, identifying clearly how research can contribute to their planning and decisions." They add that they cannot hope that research will solve all their problems and that "the expertise of decision makers themselves will be vital in understanding and adapting to the impacts of climate change" (Watts et al., 2015b: 18).

For researchers, they feel they should find ways to be clear about uncertainty and confidence (bearing in mind that the two are readily conflated by non-specialists trying to understand the relevance of research) and work to make sure that the main points of their work are accessible to non-specialists. Researchers should also work with decision-makers to understand their needs and identify how research can help to meet these needs: "Engagement from the beginning to the end of a project will yield results that are relevant and have genuine impact" observing that: "Researchers sometimes seem to disengage when the academic paper is submitted, but without continued involvement their research may never be embedded in practice" (Watts et al., 2015b: 20).

Watts et al. (2015b: 20–21) identify several future research needs including studies of evapotranspiration, hydrological response and system resilience to droughts, flooding in relation to intense rainfall and the impact of climate change on groundwater levels and quality. There should be an attempt to decrease the uncertainty in understanding the way in which aquatic ecosystems respond to climate change together with studies of change in the water environment at scales that help policy-makers and decision-makers. They comment: "Largescale, regional or countrywide assessments are perhaps inevitably compromised

Table 2.1 *Observed changes to water and the water environment in the UK*

Change	Confidence in the change*	Confidence in/ evidence for link to climate change*
Air temperature		
Increase of *c*.1°C in Central England temperature since 1980	High	Medium
Precipitation		
Little change in annual average rainfall over last 300 years	High	Insufficient
More winter rainfall as intense events over the last 30 years	Medium	Insufficient
Increased clustering of within-year extreme rainfall events	Medium	Insufficient
Evapotranspiration		
Possible increases since 1960s across the UK	Low	Insufficient
No systematic studies of change		
River flows		
Increase in winter runoff and high flows over last 40 years	Medium	Insufficient
No apparent trend in summer flows, low flows or drought	Low	Insufficient
Groundwater levels and recharge		
No systematic studies of change	Insufficient	
River water temperature		
Increase in river water temperature over recent decades	Medium	Low
Groundwater temperature		
Little is known. Insufficient evidence to understand changes		
River water quality		
Improved especially in lowlands in last 30 years	High	Low
Groundwater quality		
Increased diffuse pollution, especially from nitrates over the second half of the twentieth century	High	High confidence not linked
Freshwater ecosystems		
Some evidence of reductions in populations of invertebrates and fish that depend on cold conditions	Medium	Low

Source: Modified from Watts et al. (2015b: 13–14). Sources and supporting references given in the original paper.
Note: *Confidence statements are subjective and based on the quantity of information, its spatial coverage and the level of agreement between different studies.

Table 2.2 *Possible future changes to water in the UK*

Possible change	Confidence in the possibility*
Air temperature	
Increasing through the twenty-first century. Greater increases in summer than winter. Greater increases in the south than in the north.	High for increase Medium for range and pattern
Precipitation	
Little change in annual average precipitation through the twenty-first century	Medium for small change
Increase in winter rainfall, in much of the UK by the end of the twenty-first century; small decreases in Scotland	Medium for changes Low for patterns
Decrease in summer rainfall by the end of the twenty-first century, especially in the south, little change in summer rainfall in northern Scotland	Medium for changes Low for patterns
Increases in winter, spring and autumn extreme rainfall by the 2080s, summer extreme rainfall changes less clear	Medium for extreme Low for summer changes
Evapotranspiration	
Increases in all seasons through the twenty-first century and scale of increase	Low for increase
River flows	
Increases in average winter flows by the 2020s and 2050s	Medium
Reduced summer flows by the 2020s and the 2050s	Medium
Increased flood magnitude through the twenty-first century	Medium for increased magnitude
Low for scale of the increase	
Groundwater levels and recharge	
No clear picture	Low
River water temperature	
Increases in river water temperature through the twenty-first century	Medium for being in line with air temperature
Groundwater temperature	
No information available	Low
River water quality	
Many different possible responses: increased algal blooms, increased suspended solids, increased flushing after dry periods	Low for overall impact of different changes

Table 2.2 (*cont.*)

Possible change	Confidence in the possibility*
Groundwater quality	
Little information available	Low
Freshwater ecosystems	
Decline in species adapted to cold conditions, with increase in invasive species.	Low

Source: Modified from Watts et al. (2015b: 19–20). Sources and supporting references given in the original paper.
Note: *The confidence is the subjective view of the authors, based on the level of agreement of studies, their spatial coverage and the degree of quantification.

by their general nature, but these are the studies that provide the picture of change that decision makers find most useful."

'A review of recent developments in climate change science, Part I: Understanding of future change in the large-scale climate system' by Good et al. (2011: 291) presents a useful summary of key findings for each scientific sector from the IPCC Assessment Report 4 (AR4). This stresses both the uncertainties and the limits to modelling when looking at patterns of trends. The Panel observes the increased loss from Greenland and Antarctic ice sheets, with it being possible that they may not be able to recover once certain limits are reached. Arctic summer sea ice may disappear earlier than predicted by some models, with record losses in 2007 raising concerns about rapid loss of Arctic sea ice altogether within a few decades but subsequent ice recovery has reduced this concern.

Model uncertainty is also stressed in terms of ocean circulation, especially given the variability evident in actual circulation patterns. While tropical forests appear to be increasing the amount of carbon they store, the existing models may not accurately represent the ways in which drought can affect the forests. In terms of permafrost, while "model simulation of the permafrost can exhibit a potentially self-sustaining feedback, the likelihood, size and timescale of carbon release from permafrost and ocean hydrates are very uncertain" (Good et al., 2011: 291).

In terms of narrative framing, Hulme in *Why We Disagree about Climate Change* (2009: 342–364) refers to four concepts (the comments in parentheses are my own):

"Nostalgia – lamenting Eden. The concept of a pristine condition, now lost" (through human action).

"Fear – presaging apocalypse. The concept of the worst possible outcome" (and it is our fault).

"Pride – constructing babel. The delusion of self-confidence and the desire to dominate" (we caused it and we should fix it).

"Justice – celebrating jubilee. Concepts of justice, equality, freedom and celebration – climate change offers the chance to do the right thing" (for a change).

In terms of narrative framing in the media, Hulme (2009: 229) cites the paper of Shanahan (2007) on *Talking about a Revolution: Climate change and the media* where the author observes that: "Each frame is constructed to appeal to a particular audience." Thus, it seems that, for example, "Scientific Uncertainty" appeals to "Those who don't want to change", while the narrative of "Polar Bear under threat" appeals to wildlife lovers. Financial arguments tend to sway politicians and the private sector while "Catastrophe" and "Justice and Equity" tend to sway "Those who are worried about the future" and "Those with strong ethical leanings".

Hulme (2009: 186–188) also refers to his discussion of cultural theory where he cites a range of sources but focusses on the point that these stances may well relate to Hollings's (1986) four myths of nature:

1. Nature capricious – anything can happen. Nature is not receptive to our actions.
2. Nature perverse/tolerant where nature is uncontrollable but resilient if suitably managed: We can manage the risks with greater knowledge/appropriate technology.
3. Nature benign – even with humans altering the climate it will re-establish itself as tolerable for human beings.
4. Nature ephemeral. Nature is precarious and in a delicate state of balance. Human disturbance can lead to collapse; climate changes are frightening with the probable 'collapse of civilisation'.

(adapted from Figure 6.1 in Hulme, 2009: 186)

I have always found Hollings's categories difficult as I find that just because things are different it does not mean to say that they are mutually exclusive and indeed these four states can readily coexist in that you can find evidence for all of them if you are so minded. Hulme's own view is that nature is receptive to our actions but that it can take a very long time to achieve what we might see as a desired response. He feels that the headline indicators of climate change will resist our interventions for at least another generation if not longer, irrespective of our successes in slowing the growth of global gases. This is because of the three lags involved: between reducing emissions and reducing atmospheric CO_2; between reducing that and decreasing temperature; and between reducing that and reducing sea-level rise.

He says that: "One dimensional goal setting is bound to fail" and "Setting the overarching goal of humanity as the re-stabilisation of climate will, I believe, lead to disillusionment. Carbon dioxide concentrations will continue to rise, world temperature to warm, global sea level to rise and weather to wreak social havoc" (Hulme, 2009: 336). One could conclude from the above that the question "Is it worth actually acting then?" becomes legitimate. But the concern is more about the way we present the problem as one we can solve. Indeed, my own concern is what is done in the name of reducing CO_2. He writes of clumsy solutions and suggests that we tend to "construct the problems in relation to the way we think we can solve them" (Hulme, 2009: 336).

Surely, we should place the measures of tackling climate change with those of the general humanitarian projects including war, famine, disease, etc., and help to mitigate as much as we can. Why get outraged about polar bears when they may well adapt if we give them room; don't lament the end of nature, step back and let it get on with adjusting to climate change as it has in previous climate changes – not for everything to survive but making room for whatever happens to happen.

A Further Personal Assessment – Which Delusion?

I originally titled this whole section 'Narratives of Climate Change: Which Delusion Do You Want to Live Under?' I changed my mind in the face of lots of impassioned discussion where people said climate change is not a delusion, it is real. However, having been through the material of this chapter I have re-instated it here. This is not to say that climate change is not real but it is to say that the delusions are so powerful that they have become real in themselves.

Heartfelt rage on both sides and the narrative of stupidity from Dietrich Bonhoeffer which I started this chapter with become relevant if one tweaks some words and replaces the concept of stupidity with that of someone with a closed mind:

> Against a closed mind we are defenceless; reasons fall on deaf ears; facts that contradict one's prejudgement simply need not be believed – in such moments the person with the closed mind even becomes critical – and when facts are

irrefutable they are just pushed aside as inconsequential, as incidental. In all this the person with the closed mind, in contrast to the open minded one, is utterly self-satisfied and, being easily irritated, becomes dangerous by going on the attack.

But you might argue that you don't have a closed mind, that you have read a lot of information and you have made up your mind and now wish to argue a point.

I find it difficult to improve upon either what I see as the wisdom of Foucault that you have been situated to experience the real (much as you might argue against it) or upon the wisdom of Mike Hulme's writing about climate change, that we are deluded by framing it as a problem which can be solved, that we have to be inventive and we have to get climate change in proportion to all the other things which are involved in what the human endeavour is about. Just as Athanasiou (1996) argued in *Slow Reckoning: The ecology of a divided planet* that many people feel better about the environment by recycling when there are issues of global inequality and economic development which are more fundamental, climate change narratives are nested in the wider narratives of economy and nature, and the myths abound. This does not mean to say that we shouldn't recycle and feel good about it but we should realise there are also wider issues to tackle. However, we seem to continue to peddle simplistic truths, even the narrative of complexity is one of these too, and the 'answers' as ever depend on the way we frame the problem and the questions.

Such enlightenment is certainly to be found but it can be so readily drowned out by the noise of the politicisation of climate science. There ever seem to be people on all sides of any argument willing to denigrate anyone who disagrees with them.

Bailey (2017) writes in this context under the heading and byline: 'Georgia Tech climatologist Judith Curry resigns over "the CRAZINESS in the field of climate science": She is a prominent critic of the "consensus" that man-made climate change is an impending catastrophe'. He writes:

Climatologist and former chair of the School of Earth and Atmospheric Sciences at the Georgia Institute of Technology Judith Curry has announced her resignation effective immediately on her blog, Climate, Etc. I have long found Curry to be an honest researcher and a fair-minded disputant in the ongoing debates over man-made climate change. She excelled at pointing out the uncertainties and deficiencies of climate modeling. Given the thoroughly politicized nature of climate science her efforts to clarify what is known and unknown by climate science caused her to be pilloried as 'anti-science'.

The writer concludes:

The good news is that Curry is not bowing out [of] climate research and the climate change debate; she plans to continue and increase her blogging on climate research and climate policy. As she notes, "Once you detach from the academic mindset, publishing on the internet makes much more sense, and the peer review you can get on a technical blog is much more extensive. But peer review is not really the point; provoking people to think in new ways about something is really the point. In other words, science as process, rather than a collection of decreed 'truths'."

On a similar front, I did find it heartening to find Ridley (2017) writing against the politicisation of science which

embarrasses science journalists who have been chronicling the growing evidence of scientific misconduct in medicine, toxicology and psychology, but ignored the same about climate science because they approve of the cause, a habit known as noble-cause corruption. It is time for the many brilliant scientists who are discovering great insights into quasars and quarks, Alzheimer's and allergies, into neurons, fossils, telomeres and ice ages, to 'take a public stand and be counted' against the politicisation of some science within their own ranks. I have championed science all my adult life. It is humankind's greatest calling. That is why I deplore those who drag down its reputation by breaching its codes of conduct for political reasons.

However, if the reader does wish to gain a balanced insight into the science, one of the better websites about science, its uncertainty and what we think we do know is that by Tamsin Edwards from the Open University: https://allmodels.plos.org/author/models/.

Mike Hulme started his book by saying that he learnt from his father that disagreement is a form of learning. I can but also refer to the ending of his book (Hulme, 2009: 363–364), namely that "the world's climates will keep on changing, with human influences on these physical properties of climate now inextricably entangled with those of Nature".

Whatever a good answer is to the question 'is global warming/climate change man made or natural?', climate change surely "reveals our embeddedness in Nature". He adds: "the idea of climate change [will] keep changing. We will continue to create and tell new stories about climate change and mobilise these stories in support of our projects. ... [W]e must now come to terms with climate change operating as an overlying, but more fluid, imaginative condition of human existence." He concludes:

> If used wisely, this condition of climate change in which we are now embroiled may teach and empower us to embark on different projects from those which come easy to us. Even so we will disagree. But let us at least recognise that the sources of disagreement about climate change lie deep within us, in our values and in our sense of identity and purpose. ... Our engagement with climate change and the disagreement that it spawns should always be a form of enlightenment. (Hulme, 2009: 364)

Meanwhile, the literature continues to appear – at such a pace, one can only highlight a selection.

- Randall S. Abate (2019). *Climate Change and the Voiceless: Protecting future generations, wildlife and natural resources.*
- Mike Berners-Lee (2019). *There Is No Planet B: A handbook for the make or break years.*
- Malena Ernman, Greta Thunberg, Beata Ernman and Svante Thunberg (2020). *Our House Is on Fire: Scenes of a family and a planet in crisis.*
- Ruth Hobday and Geoff Blackwell (eds.) (2020). *I Know This to Be True: Greta Thunberg.*
- Mark Lynas (2020). *Our Final Warning: Six degrees of climate emergency.*
- Naomi Klein (2015). *This Changes Everything: Capitalism vs. the climate.*
- Naomi Klein (2019). *On Fire: The burning case for a green new deal.*
- Bjorn Lomborg (2020). *False Alarm: How climate change panic costs us trillions, hurts the poor, and fails to fix the planet.*
- George Marshall (2015). *Don't Even Think About It: Why our brains are wired to ignore climate change.*
- Nathaniel Rich (2020). *Losing Earth: The decade we could have stopped climate change.*
- Greta Thunberg (2019). *No One Is Too Small to Make a Difference.*
- David Wallace-Wells (2019) writes of *The Uninhabitable Earth: A story of the future* with its companion volume: Wider, J. (2019), *Summary of* The Uninhabitable Earth *by David Wallace-Wells: Life after warming – Conclusion: Adaptation as justification for action.*

Slaymaker (2001: 72) writes:

> The results of focussing the climate change debate exclusively on carbon emissions has led to a political impasse which scientific evidence cannot yet and may never be able to resolve (Sarewitz and Pielke 2000). It is argued that a totally different approach is needed, namely, a focus on vulnerability and an attempt to ameliorate the social and political conditions that lead people to behave in environmentally disruptive ways.

Sarewitz and Pielke (2006) have usefully written about science policy and the supply of and demand for science but Slaymaker is citing their paper Sarewitz and Pielke (2000) on 'Breaking the global-warming gridlock'. Here they write of the futility of pursuing data and science and of carbon reduction:

> Both sides on the issue of greenhouse gases frame their arguments in terms of science, but each new scientific finding only raises new questions – dooming the debate to be a pointless spiral. It's time . . . for a radically new approach: if we took practical steps to reduce our vulnerability to today's weather, we would go a long way toward solving the problem of tomorrow's climate.

They conclude: "In the global-warming debate the logic behind public discourse and political action has been precisely backwards. Environmental prospects for the coming century depend far less on our strategies for reducing carbon-dioxide emissions than on our determination and ability to reduce human vulnerability to weather and climate."

Furthermore, in Pielke et al. (2007: 598) the authors write on the importance of adaptation:

> [P]olicy-makers need to understand the limitations of mitigation for reducing vulnerabilities, and give more urgent consideration to broader adaptation policies – such as improved management of coastal zones and water resources – that will enhance societal resilience to future climate impacts regardless of their cause. To define adaptation as a cost of failed mitigation is to expose millions of poor people in compromised ecosystems to the very dangers that climate policy seeks to avoid. Until adaptation is institutionalized at a level of intensity and investment at least equal to those of the UNFCCC and Kyoto Protocol, climate impacts will continue to mount unabated, regardless of even the most effective cuts in greenhouse-gas emissions.

I'm quite sold on that narrative. Every type of living thing which exists today has no particular disadvantage in current climatic and environmental conditions otherwise it would not be here. We tend to see this as adaptation to change or see it in terms of advantages gained through evolution. However, whatever terms we use or however we see it, living things which were at a disadvantage during changes are now fossils. Indeed, of all the organisms which have ever existed on earth, most are now only found as fossils, while genetic mutations and behavioural changes have meant that other variants have survived. These variants have given rise to other variants and so it goes on. We tend to call this 'adapt or die' but whatever words or phrases we use, there is a lesson here. Observations in the UK by many thousands of people involved in a survey of timing of life history events of plants such as times of flowering have already given considerable insights into the ways in which plants are adept at adaptation (Tansey et al., 2017).

Investing in adaptation by people is likely to be far more useful than all the furious energy and spleen that goes into arguments using unhelpful words like 'normal' climate and the simplistic idea that climate change is due to CO_2 so if we curb that everything will be OK and 'back to normal' as matched by the equally strident view of those who deny either climate change and any human involvement in it or both. That is leading us nowhere except into further arguments. Research into human adaptation involving lives and livelihoods is the way ahead (see, e.g., Nightingale, 2016 and Spencer and Lane, 2016 on adaptive research and studies of the lived landscape in the geographic tradition).

Additionally, it will not be the case that 'wildlife will be OK' 'if only' we can reduce CO_2 emissions. Wildlife will be better off if it has places to be – spaces to move around in – and we have taken most of these away. Islands of isolated wildlife are particularly vulnerable when conditions change (see, e.g., Collingham and Huntley, 2000). So, while we are investing in adapting our lives to changing climate we should be allowing – or giving back, even – space for plants and animals to adjust, much as they ever have. Thinking about the way we use space – in terms of adaptive urban and rural planning and also of spaces for facilitating wildlife – is critical. For nature itself, it has always adapted to climate change by migration, changes in behaviour and distribution and, in the long term, evolution. However, the fragmented characteristics of many habitats mean that many species are rather tied to specific locations where appropriate habitats exist. The perceived rapid rate of change is also seen as presenting challenges. More use of wildlife corridors and, even better, greater re-wilding will enable nature to migrate and adapt to changing conditions. This also involves rethinking the concepts of 'what belongs where' as species move in relation to the geographical shift of climate zones.

Finally, in terms of escaping from what I can characterise as 'the battle of the rhetoric', I can but recommend the analysis of Rose (2014). He goes beyond the endeavours to increase the volume of evidence for climate change and its causes, and the drives to decrease uncertainty, and usefully writes of being informed by the evidence, telling good news stories and being policy-relevant. He recommends the endeavours to provide meaningful actions containing astutely framed practical solutions.

In the last analysis I can perhaps but recommend the idea of the provisionality of our knowledge – and of building adaptability in the face of uncertainty. We know the climate is changing, even if we are not sure by how much, in what way, where or when. The arguments as to why it is changing continue with a consequent confusion of remedies. Many remedies could lead down blind alleys while others would have consequences which, while purportedly being a solution to an assumed cause, could lead to considerable harm to aspects of the environment, culture and social-economic life without any discernible beneficial effect on climate change. For example, low-carbon 'solutions' such as tidal barrages can have widespread and far-reaching impacts on wildlife, both locally and in terms of migrating birds; solar farms can occupy large areas and, depending on the way they are laid out and structured may or may not be beneficial to local wildlife. As David MacKay wrote, as discussed in Section 2.1, there are many sides to the discussions about renewable energy including the impacts on a location and the questions over effects on overall carbon budgets.

On the topic of disagreements about narratives of climate change and how to tackle it, we might do well to remember the thoughts of Joseph Joubert (1754–1824) that: "The aim of an argument or discussion should not be victory, but progress." As Mike Hulme (2009: 330–364, as cited above) wrote, where we do think we know the causes of change, the remedies may well take generations to come to fruition. Hulme updates his ideas in *Contemporary Climate Change Debates* (Hulme, 2019) where he shows the complexities of the issues (and see also https://mikehulme.org/ for his blog). What is needed is a touch of epistemic humility, which refers to the value of suspending judgement, and recognizing that however much we (think we) know there will always be much more to learn. In terms of climate change, we will only learn more as time goes on; meanwhile, it would be prudent to invest in adaptability. It is most likely that, in any one place, this means getting used to dealing with a wider range of climatic conditions than we are used to – and to a wider ranging of narratives which allow for adapting to possible future scenarios.

2.3 Chapter Summary

- Powerful but contested environmental narratives are nothing new but can be understood by examining a wide range of cultural, social, anthropological and psychological perspectives.
- The subject of climate change is rather beset by belief superiority – the belief that one's own beliefs are more correct than other viewpoints. In this, the range of viewpoints held by people means that they can be variously termed 'warmists', 'alarmists' and 'climate change deniers', among other things. Polarised dogmatic mantras and automatic assumptions of linkages can characterise the narratives of climate change. Here pre-judgement tends to selectively emphasise or dismiss facts and evidence, which is unhelpful.
- A more dispassionate view is that the climate is changing. This is hardly surprising as climate has never done anything else throughout geological history. Nonetheless, the idea of a 'stable climate altered by human activity' is prevalent.
- There is a strong consensus that the human-induced loading of greenhouses gases into the atmosphere needs to be reduced drastically in order to counteract global temperature rise.
- The means and side effects of achieving this reduction continue to be a matter of debate – as is the extent to which they will be effective. The endeavour presents considerable opportunities, the success of which needs careful consideration. Parallel to this there should be a strong sense of being able to adapt to change.
- For nature itself, it has always adapted to climate change by migration, changes in behaviour and distribution and, in the long term, evolution. However, the fragmented characteristics of many habitats mean that many species are rather tied to specific locations where appropriate habitats exist. The perceived rapid rate of change is also seen as presenting challenges. More use of wildlife corridors and, even better, greater re-wilding will enable nature to migrate and adapt to changing conditions. This also involves re-thinking the concepts of 'what belongs where' as species move in relation to the geographical shift of climate zones.

Figure 1.5 Author's painting of a tree on a limestone pavement, Ingleborough, Yorkshire. Negative as the tree is partly dead or positive as the tree is surviving? (Photo: S. Trudgill)

Figure 3.1 Sea otter (*Enhydra lutris*) eating sea urchin (Noel Hendrickson / Photodisc / Getty Images)

Figure 4.1 Constable's *Hay Wain* (Art Images / Contributor / Hulton Fine Art Collection / Getty Images)

Figure 4.2 The current view. Preserving the landscape here refers to the iconic picture (Photo: S. Trudgill)

Figure 5.1 *Narcissus* by Caravaggio (DEA / G. NIMATALLAH / Contributor / De Agostini / Getty Images)

Figure 5.2 I'd like to introduce you to a wood in South Devon (Photo: S. Trudgill)

Figure 5.4 Ferns stand half uncurled, each new frond with a scroll of yet uncurled (Photo: S. Trudgill)

Figure 5.6 The bluebells keep their succulent showy secret here (Photo: S. Trudgill)

Figure 5.9 Finding yourself, being able to think (Photo: S. Trudgill)

Figure 6.1 Clearance of trees and shrubs at Wicken Fen to maintain the fen flora and fauna (Andrew Michaels/Universal Images Group / Getty Images)

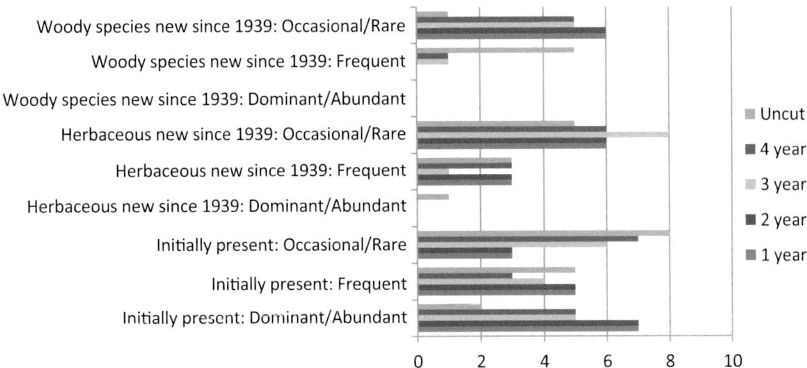

Figure 6.4 Data on loss of grassland and increase in tree species with less frequent cutting, from Godwin Plots 1955–1982 compared to 1939 baseline (mostly herbaceous) (Adapted from data in Friday and Harvey, 1997: 71)

Figure 7.1 *The Dreamer* by Caspar David Friedrich (Heritage Images / Contributor / Hulton Fine Art Collection / Getty Images)

Part II

Nature Imagined

3 · *Nature in Ecological Science*

Explanations, Emotions and Motivations

3.1 Psychological Terms in Ecology

Explanations, Judgements and Interpretations

How well do we know nature? We might start by considering the nature of our wisdom about and our intuitive understanding of nature. How far does our search for knowledge remove our intuitive knowledge? This question brings to mind the dialogue between Fuchsia and Steerpike in Mervyn Peake's *Titus Groan* (Peake, [1946]1968: 274) where Fuchsia feels she doesn't know anything about nature: "I don't understand it. I only look at it." Steerpike's reply is to the effect that you must understand what you love so much: "You look as though you understand." Fuchsia says she feels she doesn't understand wise things and the interesting reply from Steerpike is that is that her knowledge is intuitive: "You have no need of book learning and such like. You only have to gaze at a thing to *know* it." We might indeed ponder how the understanding of nature from 'books and learning' compares with and relates to our naïve knowing gaze – and how well they each serve us. In this chapter (Section 3.2), we enter a woodland with an ecologist – with all their books and learning – and, by contrast, in Section 5.4 we enter a woodland to gaze around without one.

One consideration which 'books and learning' tend to promote is that many of our ideas about nature contain not only observations but also explanations, judgements and justifications. Indeed, one could argue that observations can become secondary to saying why something is there, prescribing how we should react by saying, for example, what something should be like or 'what ought to be where'. Thus, we might readily categorise, dismiss and stop looking. For example, we might simply see an 'alien plant', a 'pioneering plant' or a 'predatory animal' when there are other aspects of the organisms which become overlooked. Such descriptions have to be learnt otherwise we tend to focus on things like colour and form rather than on given meanings. Tensions can thus arise in ecological science between on the one hand descriptive or explanatory ideas which are verifiable by observation and on the other judgemental narratives which are unverifiable, or at least less verifiable and often arguable, but which have a deep and pervasive psychological appeal. In either case, there can be a dialogue between 'facts' and 'values', as discussed in Chapter 1, and so an interest arises in studying this dialogue when, as so often, the former are clouded or confused by the latter (Harré, Brockmeier and Mühlhäusler, 1999; Trudgill, 2001a, 2001b). 'Values' become 'facts'.

A problem I have is with the 'why' question. To me in nature 'why' is the same as the 'how'. Thus, my narrative is that things exist the way they do because that state is possible, but that is not to say that just because it was possible, it happened – and it did not have to happen but some combination of prior states led to the happenstance of its existence. To me, the answer to the question 'why' is often erroneously predicated on a sense of necessity when in fact it doesn't have to be like it apparently is. Something happened because it was possible – but it didn't have to be like that; it could have been one of the many other possible states.

Thus, I am not such a fan of 'the survival of the fittest', more of 'the survival of the possible'. This frees me up from having to find an explanation for absolutely everything and leaves room for genetic randomness giving rise to a characteristic which had no particular disadvantage and which thus survived. Once a possibility comes into existence, Dawkins's (1989) extended phenotype ideas come into play which mean that behaviour then tends to maximise survival of the genes. But even so, any one state happens when others were possible in relation to what went before and what the other surrounding states happened to be. Say a type of bird evolved from a type of reptile. The only necessity is about what it could not have readily evolved from. While scales could become feathers it would take a stretch for a rose to become an elephant, so there was a need for some plausible precursor of the bird with the potential to evolve into a bird. This is what Richard Dawkins (1996) in *The Blind Watchmaker* calls 'evolvability'. Equally, it need not have evolved at all, but stayed a reptile – it evolved because it could but it didn't have to. Equally, other birds might have evolved from the same reptile but didn't because of the serendipity of genetic mutation and the surrounding circumstances of environment and other species.

Thus, there is no real 'why' something evolved, only a 'how': it evolved because it could and the conditions allowed it or did not militate against it. There is no 'function' – that is an imposition of our idea – there are only effects of something happening which, in turn, may affect something else – which we love to interpret as a 'cause'. There was no 'tight' pressure which meant something 'had' to evolve, it just did and survived because there was no great disadvantage or because it had some advantage. It wasn't adapted, it wasn't in balance, it wasn't fitting into a niche, indeed there is no such story as these – none of these stories exist. This is not the necessity of a narrative-free process, this is the narrative of a necessity-free process. There is no other necessity in nature than temporal dependency and spatial happenstance. Nature is a contingent state of conjunctions showing dependency but not necessity. Here I use the word 'contingent' in the sense of 'being true by virtue of the way things are' and not by logical necessity: something occurring or existing only if certain circumstances are the case. Contingent thus implies 'dependent on' with the concept also usefully having connotations of 'subject to chance' and of 'that which can be anticipated to arise if a particular event occurs'.

This is similar to the thesis of Stephen Jay Gould's (1989) book on the extraordinary fossil wealth found in the Burgess shale, a geologically early (Cambrian) deposit. In the book *Wonderful Life: The Burgess shale and the nature of history* Gould proposed that serendipity and contingency play as much a part in evolution as anything: outcomes arise from "an unpredictable sequence of antecedent states, where any change in the sequence alters the final result" (Gould, 1989: 283). Because "fitness for existing conditions does not guarantee long-term survival – particularly when conditions change catastrophically – the survival of many species depends more on luck than conventional features of anatomical superiority" (Gould, 2004: 97–98, 100). Gould maintains that, "traits that enhance survival during an extinction do so in ways that are incidental and unrelated to the causes of their evolution in the first place" (Gould, 1989: 307). He and co-author Elisabeth Vrba used the term 'exaptation' to describe fortuitously beneficial traits which do not result from natural selection (Gould and Vrba, 1982).

Our problem is then the one of the detective story 'body in the library' which was discussed in Chapter 1. We can't stand it if there is no story – no victim – they must be a murder victim so there must be a murderer – so we populate the murder novel with narratives and search for evidence to support one or the other. So, with nature, there is a species so we must have a causal, functional narrative. But there isn't one (and the concept of species is a fluid one anyway – at the very least debatable). But be sure that we will find causal, functional narratives, come what may: we have to have narratives all the same, and we have them in abundance. We ask why is that species there and what is its function and search for evidence – and we can find it. We search for order – and we can find it. What is there becomes what is right and what is right must be there for a reason and find it we must – and find it we will. This is a very striking and singular phenomenon. This much is not new – it is discussed extensively in Marek Kohn's (2004) book *A Reason for Everything: Natural selection and the English imagination.*

To try to understand what we are doing in this process involving narratives of rectitude let me give the example of the Church of England. If you were brought up in the tradition of that Church, there will be a tendency to feel that this Church is 'good' and 'right'. Many English people, while ignoring it for much of their daily lives, still reach for it automatically for important events such as weddings and funerals. But it doesn't have to be there and the fact that it is, doesn't of necessity make it right. Indeed, the Church of England, it can be argued, is only there because Henry VIII wanted to divorce his wife, not allowed then under the Catholic Church. Thus, he invented the Church of England in the sense that if his first wife had borne him a viable son, we might arguably still be a Catholic nation. This account of history is over-simplistic but the point is that the origin of the Church of England is dependent on a series of historical events. There is no necessity, only a dependency in history: it is a contingent state of conjunctions. The situation is how it is because that is how it is – and if it wasn't it would be in a different state. This does not make the Church of England any more or less worth defending but equally it doesn't mean that the Catholic Church is any more or less valid or invalid – it is just a different way of doing things. However, countless people have died defending either of these religions because they believed that one or the other religion is 'right' but often also for no reason other than tribalism. If you find that hard to accept, then your outlook can hardly be multicultural, liberal and fair. Such prejudice which makes one human being less valid than another because of what they believe is indefensible on both humanitarian and true Christian grounds. Equally, why is one animal or plant or state of nature more valid than other? Is this no more than a kind of ecological prejudice? Or is there something more – that we actually cherish the sense of history and we cherish what is there irrespective of how it came to be? However, cherishing the range of phenomena which exists is one thing, and seems laudable, but there seems to be a human trait for being partisan, for identifying with subsets of what exists and dwelling in a sense of 'other' which differentiates between phenomena in a way which expresses preference.

Furthermore, there still persists a sense of 'the way things should be' coupled with 'what we have done' to this putative order. I find it difficult to escape the conclusion that many of the psychological judgemental ecological narratives are, as with climate change (Section 2.1), some kind of allusion to an Edenic narrative. While the biblical story tells of how Adam and Eve were cast from the Garden of Eden, the narrative has evolved such that there is a putative natural, pristine, state – a 'natural order' – which has been disturbed in some way. This rests on the 'guilt-laden' notion that human-induced changes have damaged a pristine nature. As discussed in Chapter 2 under climate change, Glacken (1967: vii) writing in *Traces on the Rhodian Shore* feels that there has been a persistent question in Western thought which was crystallised in Marsh's (1864) *Man and Nature*: "In his long tenure of the earth, in what manner has man changed it from its hypothetical pristine state?" The ideas of 'balance' or 'equilibrium' in nature and the corresponding human 'disturbance' are firmly entrenched in Western culture (Stott, 1997; Worster, 1994). The paper by Lynne White on 'The historical roots of our ecological crisis' returned to this theme but also offered some redemption in the form of an appeal to St Francis (White, 1967). Horrell, Hunt and Southgate (2008) move on further from Lynn White's 1967 paper in a discussion of 'Appeals to the bible in ecotheology and environmental ethics'. The authors identify elements of 'recovery' and two types of 'resistance' – a resistance against a text given a particular perspective, and the contrasting resistance to a perspective given a particular commitment to a text. The authors develop a refreshing approach between these extremes which involves revision, reformation and reconfiguration. More recently Fred Pearce (2015) has expounded usefully on moving on from the "Myths of the Pristine" and argues against such "romantic illusions" (see also Section 7.3).

Those who seem to adopt the Edenic myth guilt seem to speak in a censorious and moralising way and I can see a sense of superiority over the foolish parts of mankind who do not care about nature (as much as one assumes the speaker does). I can think of many drastically and radically changed ecosystems such as for example the well-rehearsed loss of sea otters which eat sea urchins (Figure 3.1).

Without the otters, sea urchins thrive and kelp forests disappear (www.seaottersavvy.org/ecosystem-superheroes). This values kelp over sea urchins – there is no celebration of thriving sea urchins; the ecosystem is seen as degraded. Interesting, as ever, to compare this with the asteroid

Figure 3.1 Sea otter (*Enhydra lutris*) eating sea urchin (Noel Hendrickson / Photodisc / Getty Images). *A black and white version of this figure will appear in some formats. For the colour version, please refer to the plate section.*

that made the dinosaurs extinct, leading to new evolutionary opportunities. The key part of the story seems to me to be the people who have removed the otters for fur – it is the guilt argument and culpability that makes us reach for the 'house of cards' narrative. Bringing the otters back is so much more than the restoration of the previous situation – restoration removes the sense of guilt. Take the instance of the removal of wolves in the North American grazing ecosystem. Nothing actually stepped in to take their 'place'; the herbivores did increase in number and the trees don't grow so much as the saplings are eaten so you tend to get more grassland and some soil erosion especially round drinking areas – very much changed yes, very different certainly, collapsed only if you will. The herbivores are doing just fine and their numbers become limited by the amount of grazing available – if they eat too much grass they will die off and numbers will reduce. That, indeed, is something akin to the 'balance of nature' – whatever is there will always mutually adjust. The loss of trees and wolves doesn't upset the balance of nature – balance means that things shake down and find a new and different state of existence – the balance of nature is never upset – every reactive item tends to adjust to every other item which can influence it in some way (see Pimm, 1991: *The Balance of Nature? Ecological issues in the conservation of species and communities*). However, what many people love is to see the restoration of the wolf even as others argue against that. So, I think here that what we often mean by 'collapsed' or the 'balance of nature is disturbed' is actually 'not what we were used to' or think ought to be there. As Drury (1998) so eloquently points out, when a species is lost then it is just different, not better or worse – just as when the asteroid struck and the dinosaurs died out – meaning new species evolved. But so often there is the guilt element – we see it as worse because we feel culpable. This is a very strong motivation for conservation, then. Restoring nature restores so much more – it restores our self-respect. We can't shrug our shoulders and say 'Oh well, it's just like the dinosaurs' – we can't because this time we did it. Of course, the rub here is who 'we' are – some will feel the guilt, others will not see it – hence the importance of the stories – and the ones about sea otters as superheroes as they encourage kelp which soaks up carbon dioxide and increases biodiversity are both appealing and effective.

Doing without Emotive, Judgemental Terms?

In the context of being more clinical about nature – or at least attempting to envisage observation and emotive contexts as separate endeavours – I do like the observation Sir Arthur Tansley made in *Practical Plant Ecology* (1923): "It is not the ecologist's role to concern himself with hindering human activity – destructive or otherwise. If human activity destroys a large number of plant communities and plant habitats, and modifies, to a greater or lesser extent, many more, it also produces fresh habitats and fresh plant communities, and thus provides fresh opportunities for study on every hand" (quoted from Trudgill, 2007: 506). So, if, armed with this thought, we now feel it might be useful to separate terms of observation and emotive terms, we can attempt to do so, as in Box 3.1.

Box 3.1 *Emotive terms used in ecology (modified from Trudgill, 2001a)*

Observational terms	**Emotive terms**
Change, alteration	unstable, collapse, disturbance, succession
Unchanging	stable, equilibrium, undisturbed, pristine, natural, untouched
Decrease	deterioration, loss, impoverishment, paucity
Increase	outbreak, overrun, out of control, plague, infestation, augmentation, productive
New, introduction	invasion, alien
Diverse*	Diverse,* rich

Note: *This might be a numerical statement or a loaded term of preference.

What I want to argue is how unjustified the use of the emotive terms are and, paradoxically, simultaneously how effective they are as motivators. In the first column there are descriptors which can be verified by observation, often by counting species numbers or vegetation covers in an area over time. In the second column, the numerical observation is couched in terms of an emotive narrative. Unstable, collapse, disturbance, loss, overrun, invasion and similar terms have connotations on undesirability while stable, pristine, productive and rich have positive connotations. Succession can be more neutral, implying an observed change over time but this can readily be motivational in terms of conservation action, for example in arresting succession by clearing 'scrub' and tree growth to preserve open areas – the growth being seen as negatively invasive and open areas more desirable. The term 'scrub' itself is pejorative – when in fact a collection of bushes can form species-rich habitats – with an open grassy habitat with scattered small bushes being good habitat for many flowers, insects and birds. Succession can also be very positive, needing encouraging during land reclamation of, for example, mining spoil.

It seems evident that a clinical science, based on observation and verification, should thus use terms in the first column, above, rather than the second. Indeed, I have noted elsewhere (Trudgill, 2001a) that there are movements in philosophical ecological writings to separate out the curious occlusion of ecological science and judgemental cultural narratives. Here, when words such as 'alien' (Dunn, 1905) and 'invasive' are used to refer to plants they can, more dispassionately, be described as 'spreading'. Shrader-Frechette (2001) reviews the limitations of terms such as 'invasive species' in ecological explanation and Simberloff (2003a: 179) discusses our attitude towards introduced species and asks: "is this not a form of xenophobia?" Colautti and MacIsaac (2004) ask for a neutral terminology to define 'invasive' species. Richard Mabey (1998) tries for a non-judgemental descriptor and sees the new plants under the heading of 'Immigration'. However, this rewording is an immense task as the judgemental terms are historically firmly entrenched (see Fischedicks, 1995, in *Practices and Pluralism: Socio-historical analysis of early vegetation science, 1900–1950*). Notwithstanding that, there is already considerable re-writing of the narratives rather than the words, with Fred Pearce (2015) not attempting to change the language but making a case for invasive species being 'nature's salvation'.

Many psychological terms are applied to plants and vegetation ('dominance', 'disturbance' and 'recovery'). It is possible to study the use of these terms with respect to the contacts of the ecologist Sir Arthur Tansley with the psychologist Freud, as discussed by Cameron (1999), Cameron and Forrester (2000a, 2000b) and Trudgill (2007). Given that cherished historical narratives are currently challenged, it is of considerable interest to observe the evolution of ecological concepts and terms in the original works by Clements (1904, 1909, 1916, 1928, 1935, 1936; Clements and Shelford, 1939), Tansley (1920, 1923, 1929, 1935, 1939) and the accounts of them in Worster (1994). Revisiting the earlier papers reminds us of the scholarly logic and careful qualifications Tansley espoused. It seems that many of the terms discussed have been passed down through the last seventy to eighty or so years as if 'given', monolithic and unqualified. Many terms and concepts have been subject to criticism during that period but it seems from reading the original papers that their writers, by implication, might just have been put in a position which they were not in and then criticised for being there.

Sir Arthur Tansley was always careful to qualify the use of vegetational terms, especially in his classic 1935 paper on their use and abuse (Trudgill, 2007). The recent critiques of terminology seem to miss the subtleties and qualifications of the original writings. It seems that Tansley covered many of these points admirably some seventy years earlier. The reader of the 1935 paper might take issue with the points made but, far from resting his conceptual stance on faith – and being 'merely' a social product of his time, Tansley had a scholarly approach which is difficult to gainsay. He drew from logical argument and sought evidence from observation.

Interestingly, while Tansley was deeply interested in psychoanalysis, in terms of Cooper's (2001: 500) "a kind of psychotherapy for ecological practice" and "deep-seated beliefs about nature" and Botkin's (1990: 201) "myth and deep buried beliefs", Tansley (1935) warned explicitly of the "exposition of a creed" (p. 285). He was a critic of "a closed system of religious or philosophical dogma" (p. 285) and was against "a confession of a holistic faith" (p. 286) in ecology. He espoused scientific arguments. He considered that the concepts of succession "can be given useful scientific significance only if we can trace in the sequences of vegetation certain uniformities which we can make the subject of investigation, comparison, and the formulation of laws" (p. 286), adding that "many successions have been inferred rather than demonstrated" (p. 288).

He thus espoused scientific argument rather than anything teleological. He very much promoted empirical method and warned against making the facts fit the theory: "I plead for empirical method and terminology in all work on vegetation, and avoidance of generalised interpretation based on a theory of what *must* happen..." (p. 298). Perceptively, he commented: "a proposition obviously has different meanings according to the exact connotation of the words employed" (p. 290; Trudgill, 2007). It is difficult not to imagine that Tansley would have baulked at the accusation of 'ecological imperative' and would have relished the thought of convincing empirical evidence, whatever it showed or whichever theory it disproved. One can but conclude that, rather than Tansley's association with Freud, it is the Western penchant for the putative Edenic narrative of human disturbance which makes psychological terms so persuasively entrenched in ecology.

An alternative point of view concerns the merits of precisely that judgemental approach, so a duality is apparent. There is clearly an endeavour within ecological science about evidence and what can be verifiable – and seeing what is verifiable without judgementality. But alternatively, there are those who see clinical science as a loss of meaning.

Thus, some writers are actually dismissive of scientists trying to see 'what is' – Jonathan Dimbleby (1994) rejoices in an essay by John Fowles (2000; see also Aubrey, 1999) and cites from it the words:

> Keats' attitude towards the nightingale has arguably more scientific validity than that of the worthy gentlemen who pursued the bird with brass dividers and rulers. All the hard taxonomic facts in the world don't add up to the reality of the nightingale; and if a visitor from Outer Space wanted to know that reality, he would do much better with the *Ode* than the *Handbook of British Birds*. (Dimbleby, 1994: 67)

Science is, then, seen here as a reduction in and restriction of meanings.

In *The Social Creation of Nature*, Evernden (1992: 107) has a similar view:

> By eroding the old vocabulary, with its rich symbolic overtones, the naturalists [scientists] had completed their onslaught on the long established notion that nature was responsive to human affairs. This was the most important and most destructive way in which they shattered the assumptions of the past. In place of a natural world redolent with human analogy and symbolic meaning and sensitive to man's behaviour, they constructed a detached natural scene to be viewed and studied by the observer from the outside, as if by peering through a window, in the secure knowledge that the objects of contemplation inhabited a separate realm, offering no omens or signs [and] without human meaning or significance.

Thus, we appear to have, on the one hand, a call to have less emotional meaning in ecological terms in a verifiable ecological science and, on the other, a lament of a lack *of* meanings in a clinical approach.

I believe that these two are not incompatible. One is called science, the other cultural significance: these relate to each other, but need not, and I would argue should not compete or be conflated. They can have a complementary and beneficial coexistence as long as you realise where you stand when you reach for a narrative. You just have to ask yourself 'am I going to make a statement where I can also present the evidence?' or 'am I going to appeal to the senses and the emotions?' – or indeed 'I would like to do both, but I will do them in turn' as each should be discussed in different ways.

To examine these issues further, we might imagine a field trip with an ecologist. . .

3.2 In a Woodland: Enter an Ecological Scientist

'How Nature Works'

Now let me take you into a woodland with an ecologist (by which I mean an ecological scientist, rather than a 'Green'). My invented text below is constructed from experience of team-teaching with such ecologists.

'Here we have. . .' the ecologist starts, showing that they are going to use and impart a set of narratives with an authoritative given meaning. Thus, given meaning may usefully become a personal meaning and a motivator for conservation. However, I also wish to argue that it is not only authoritative, with which I have no trouble, but may also be authoritarian, with which I do have a problem if it precludes other possible personal meanings – or indeed precludes alternative scientific explanations. As Leopold (1949: 158) wrote: "Education, I fear, is learning to see one thing by going blind to another." A given meaning should be additional to personal meanings and act to enrich the experience of nature, not replace or compete with personal meanings which should always be seen as legitimate (as discussed further in Section 5.4 where we go into a woodland without an ecologist).

> Here we have . . . an ecosystem which is structured into the tree layer, the shrub layer and the ground flora. Notice the Dog's Mercury which adopts the strategy of vernalisation, that is, coming up in early spring and completing its life cycle before the canopy closes overhead. What we should do is to test the hypothesis that ground cover of the plant is inversely proportional to shade. Take quadrats at random and estimate the ground cover and a light meter and measure the incoming light beneath the canopy and draw a graph of percentage ground cover against light intensity.
>
> Notice the leaf litter; it falls in the autumn and then acts as a store of nutrients and energy so it can rot in the spring and release them ready for the growing season. The soil on the upper slope is freely draining, which leads to nutrient leaching and thus a rather more acid soil. This has less earthworm activity and less organic matter decay than the mid-slope. We can test this by measuring soil pH (acidity) and the depth of soil organic matter along a transect down the slope.

We can analyse this text in two ways – in terms of what is there in the taught set of narratives and also what is not there in terms of what it might preclude and omit.

Implicit in this teaching is, I think, something which is right and good – it is not all conscious, but note how everything 'works' beautifully. Note the purposefulness in the explanatory storylines and also that there will be measurement and verification. There is significance in that our attention is drawn to structure; functionality is implied – vernalisation gives a strong sense of logical narrative in terms of 'that is how it works'. This is all very agreeable. It makes sense. There is a sense of wonder in this. The test given is that there should be more ground cover where most light reaches the ground under the less dense parts of the canopy. In the second paragraph, there is again an elegant (and possibly unconsciously 'right') purposefulness in terms of a 'working ecosystem' cycle: leaf fall – storage – decay – nutrient release – nutrient uptake to new leaf growth. There is also a sense of spatially distributed function and the relationships between soils, earthworms and organic matter, which again can be measured. This is a really good story in the sense of a detective novel – there are things which we can observe and they are neatly inserted by the expert into explanations: what is taught here is a series of functional narratives which can be tested through the evidence of gathering data and plotting the relationships between the results. There is no hint of this in the text but it is such a small step to say that 'and it would be wrong to disturb it'. There is a store of energy in the leaves through the winter, released next spring. It is not quite giving the system a volition but the functioning is almost a morality narrative, even though the speaker would probably completely deny that this was the case. There is a strong sense of meaning in how the ecosystem works – there is a respect, awe almost, from a mechanistic view which we perhaps inherit from a learnt view of ecosystems (Anker, 2001). There is an imperative of the narrative – and mechanism is plausible, attractive, engaging and evidence can be found for it. I remain cautious, however, and bear in mind that Pollan (2002: 199) sees cherished ecological concepts as "little more than comforting narratives" (also see Trudgill, 2008). So explained might = comforting, and it remains arguable whether or not some apparently purposeful terms have a useful role in a verifiable science but their use should certainly be carefully examined. In itself, there is nothing wrong with explained = comforting, but if one is trying to understand what is happening, then one might demur that such attractive comfort can mean that other explanations and meanings might be excluded.

This includes the marginalisation of alternative scientific meanings and the exclusion of non-scientific meanings. So, where meanings are internal to the scientific endeavour, doubts might be raised when the data do not fit the hypotheses – and that is a real test of approach and openness to alternative scientific meanings. A common response is to doubt the misfit data as gathered but, if the data gathering can be checked, a better response is to ask 'so what else is happening to explain the data which depart from the expected?'. There can be a tendency to select sites where 'it works' – the data collected fit the expected hypotheses – but too often the conclusion is that 'unfortunately, this did not work' – and doubt the data – which is, frankly is not good science. Having an open mind to alternative explanations is an essential part of enquiry.

Just as alternative scientific explanations might be excluded or marginalised, all the other non-scientific (e.g. poetic, spiritual) aspects tend to be minimised. One might say 'so what?' as this is beyond the obvious teaching (syllabus) remit. However, I have taught classes where students have measured a topographical transect on the rocky shore and asked them to study the patterns they found and their possible interpretations. Next, I asked them to repeat their measurements at different sampling intervals and compare the – rather different – patterns and possible interpretations. But then I asked them to depict the surface by freehand drawing and to write some prose or poetry describing or suggested by the topography (Trudgill, 2003a: 26–29). It is notable that the artwork and written descriptions revealed many interesting and different ways of characterising the surface other than the transects and many meaningful personal associations. Indeed, new observations came to light as they were actually looking at the subject in different ways and not blinkered by the exercise of sampling on the transect and only seeing the sample points. Just as the scientific understanding increased their breadth of personal appreciation, the scientific understanding was actually enhanced by the non-scientific understanding. The aesthetic appreciation and personal meanings don't actually compete with the given scientific understanding – and not only can all the meanings coexist but they can each actually inform and illuminate one another.

There are thus two points to be made. First, we have a particular view of ecosystems derived from the history of ecological science and, as taught, this can exclude other scientific meanings. Second, scientific meanings and other meanings, such as the aesthetic, are usually excluded. When we are studying scientific narratives and gathering data relevant to them, we rarely engage with the poetic. If we are writing, drawing or just sensing the aesthetic, we are not necessarily engaging with the scientific. It is interesting that if we asked a scientist to engage with this they might argue that we shouldn't confuse the teaching with such non-scientific stuff. This is ironic when some of their teaching is unconsciously value-laden. This is a shame if on the one hand ecological science uses emotional value-laden terms but simultaneously can deny the utility of emotional non-scientific approaches when the use of non-emotive language could clarify the scientific endeavour and the parallel use of more intuitive, emotional approaches could be beneficial to a deeper understanding of nature.

I would muse as follows. Is it that it is a sense of the marginalisation of one aspect by the emphasis on another which is problematic? For example, how science might marginalise the aesthetic, or vice versa. I also can't help thinking that the ecology study group – the people crashing around with equipment, treading on plants – remind me of 'The Voice' by Rupert Brooke (see Chapter 5) where the intruder spoils the magic. The intentionality in the ecological narrative also bothers me. It is all worked out. Very cunning. This is adjusted to that, this works this way – the woodland becomes a mechanism. It might almost have been designed. It is all so logical. Does it not tell me more about the ecologist than the wood? I look at a tree just sitting there quietly. Are we not seeing through a lens of what 'ought to be' – reducing the variability to an ecological narrative and a couple of graphs, discarding what doesn't fit?

In Agatha Christie's Poirot stories (https://en.wikipedia.org/wiki/Agatha_Christie's_Poirot), the Scotland Yard detective always goes for the obvious suspect and arrests them, but he is always wrong. Poirot then finds the true murderer by looking at the detail; what is not obvious. It is that, like Poirot, I have the objection of going for the usual storyline, making everything fit into it because it is easier, ignoring anything else and not always looking and thinking. For the poetic, for me there is a reduction in significance, our education is compartmentalised, we look at one narrative and shut everything else off, excluding other meanings. Take a group of ten-year-olds into the woods and they will find all sorts of things and have all sorts of stories. Teach them and there is a danger that they will see only the given meaning as legitimate. It is the exclusivity I object to on both counts: the plausibility of the ecological narrative which stops you looking further and the exclusion of other meanings. What is worse is when they have to learn it and get it right in exams. That can easily be the end of creativity, maverick views and different ways of thinking.

I guess at this stage that I should confess how much I always hated debates at school – having to listen to biased accounts of either 'side' and then voting for one OR the other. I never could vote. Later in life I also hated role play involving 'the farmer' versus 'the environmentalist' – surely both had valid viewpoints. It readily follows that my difficulty with ecological science narratives can thus be the dissection, the partial view, the narrowed experience. A wood is an ecosystem if you want it to be and an ecosystem is a poem if you want to it to be. However, a scientist who wants verification and the poet who demands the freedom to be able to see things in terms of metaphors can surely coexist?

To sum up, I would say that just because things are different does not mean to say that they are mutually exclusive – but it should be absolutely clear that they are not only different but also complementary.

I am reminded of Proctor (1995: 269) who argues of the tautological folly that "we attempt to read moral and ethical tenets from the natural world when the natural world is a itself a construct based on our values, beliefs and perceptions" and as ever of Sheail (1995: 955) who deduced from Simmons' (1993c) book on environmental history that "we are simply projecting onto the world what the author wanted to believe anyway". I think that is fine if we realise what we are doing, but indeed, realise we should and examine the use of concepts carefully. Furthermore, in the context of poetry and woodland Bate (2000: 247) discusses the role of metaphor as "a way of understanding hidden connections and reunifying the world which scientific understanding has fragmented". In that I find support for a more dualistic approach in teaching.

My conclusions are that one should strive to focus less on the emotional judgements in ecological science (i.e. stick to the terms in the left-hand column of the list of psychological narratives discussed above in Box 3.1) while, however, recognising the importance of the emotions in human motivations, and to focus more on the highly significant role which metaphors and poetics in motivational narrative can play in the conservation and care of nature.

3.3 'Ecological Faith'

The Emotions, Species and Intentionality

While the call for removal of emotive, value-laden terms seems to imply that we can then be more rational, there is the point of view that we should indeed recognise the role of emotions more than we do (Trudgill, 2008: 'A requiem for the British flora? Emotional biogeographies and environmental change'). This latter is an entirely separate endeavour which does not contradict the former: on the one hand there is the call to remove, as far as possible, emotive terms from scientific ecology and on the other recognise the role of the emotions in motivation. Rather than competing, when both these views are recognised they can be complementary; the problems arise when they are unconsciously conflated rather than consciously considered as separate and equally important. It is indeed extremely useful to use neutral ecological descriptors so that an issue is not prejudged and it is important to recognise that the affective emotions are fundamental in our lives (see, e.g., Roberts, 2003: *Emotions: An essay in aid of moral psychology* and the critical review by Tappolet, 2006).

Anderson and Smith's (2001) 'Emotional geographies' draws attention to the importance of the emotions. They write (p. 7):

> We have been reflecting on the extent to which the human world is constructed and lived through the emotions. ... we have been forced to confront the glaringly obvious, yet intractable, silencing of emotion in both social research and public life. ... this suppression produces an incomplete understanding of the world's workings ... to neglect the emotions is to exclude a key set of relations through which our lives are lived.

They continue that it is usually implicit that emotion "impairs judgement" and that "good scholarship depends on keeping one's own emotions under control". They contest this and develop their theme in social contexts. Their conclusion is (p. 9) that: "[There is] a key area of human experience ... steeped in those feelings and emotions which make the world as we know and live it, yet which remains spectacularly unacknowledged in much of what we do, and in virtually every 'policy' that we recommend."

This is nonetheless so in ecological debates, as discussed by Milton (2002: i) in *Loving Nature: Towards an ecology of emotion.* She writes: "Emotion is a basic ecological mechanism which connects us to our environment"; "Emotional attachments are the products of learning – we learn what to feel about particular things" and "Our feelings then motivate our actions." She concludes that: "The conventional opposition between emotion and rationality in western culture is a myth. The myth ... excludes the kinds of emotional attachments which [would] support more environmentally sensitive ways of living" and "A better understanding of ourselves as fundamentally emotional beings is needed." So, can we address both aspects: being more neutral and dispassionate in terminology while still recognising the importance of the emotional?

The view that we should and can is promoted in 'The paradigm shift in ecology and its implications for conservation' by Fiedler, White and Leidy (1997). The authors (p. 90) quote Roszak (1972: 404) who felt that ecology was "capable of assimilating moral principle and visionary experience" and dealt with "the whole person", urging today's ecologists to become a "renaissance scholar" and "polymath", having the "clarity of a trained scientist" and "the clairvoyance of a poet". The authors allude to the Roman god Janus, who could look in two directions at once. They end their chapter on an emotive note, quoting from the poet Gary Snyder about "clouds of waterfowl, herds of bison, great whales in the ocean" and the "rich fabric to delight the mind". This is clearly a claim that we can and should cover both aspects, but, taking up the Janus allusion, perhaps we should be sure which way we are looking before speaking.

This call for a dualistic and parallel clarity of science + poetic emotion approach I think does not actually conflict with the calls to divorce the science from the judgements. This latter is the argument of 'sticking to our science' and leaving the value judgements up to others promoted by Robert Lackey, Senior Biologist of the United States Environmental Protection Agency, in 'Societal values and the proper role of restoration ecologists' (Lackey, 2004). He feels that [emotive] policy advocacy masquerades as science. He writes (p. 45): "Degradation, improvement, good, poor – do not use these words as they do not convey scientific information. They imply preferred states – this is not science but policy advocacy. Use alteration, change, increase or decrease." Lackey (2004) also strongly objects to the term the 'health' of ecosystems, such as might be evident in Holdgate and Woodman's (1978) *The Breakdown and Restoration of Ecosystems*. He argues (p. 45): "A 'healthy' ecosystem can be either a malaria-infested swamp or the same land converted to an intensively managed cornfield. Neither condition can be considered 'healthy' except through the lens of an individual's values and preferences. Science should be neutral, provide assessments of risks and probability but cannot make the decisions." To me this seems like a 'safe' stance, avoiding the 'difficult', more emotional, arena of value judgements. But does not the biogeographical scientist have a responsibility to become involved in value issues and decisions, given that they are the ones who are best informed? Just because the implementation of scientific methodology, in itself, can't make decisions, this does not mean to say that scientists cannot or should not.

Lackey's removal of emotive terms thus seems to lead to a 'retreat' into scientific verifiability and an explicit rejection of the emotive, leaving value judgement up to others. Equally, those who recognise the importance of the emotive make a call for an engagement with both, as Roszak (1972) did. I feel that Lackey's point is entirely valid but that Roszak's stance carries more weight in that it specifically encourages ecological scientists to *also* engage with the poetic.

I think it becomes problematic if science and the emotions are seen as mutually exclusive or somehow opposable. I feel that this is not the case and that they are separate, different and complementary endeavours which have much to offer to each other. I thus simultaneously hold the views that ecological science can be seen as a rational endeavour, albeit socially and culturally contextualised and relating to the positioning of the scientist, and that our engagement with nature can only be understood through an acknowledgement of the significance of the affective emotions.

Admittedly, such a dualistic stance is not easy in practice. In terms of the two approaches having much to offer to each other, an understanding of this stems from the relationship between facts and values discussed in Chapter 1. Concerned with the roles of evidence and experience, Kearns (1998) writes how values and experience interact, terming experience 'facts'. Values prioritise or relegate facts and the feedback is that facts can embarrass or endorse values (Figure 1.6). Thus a 'fact' can be endorsed as significant and taken as evidence to support the values or it can embarrass the value. We might then suppress the facts or, perhaps less likely, change our values. Physical 'reality' can thus be played up or down according to the selectivity of our values. I think that in saying this, there is a realisation of process – a recognition of the way things work and no sense of any advocacy in any direction.

In this context, Cooper (2001: 500) engages with the reality and values of the 'balance of nature'. He juggles issues which are matters of empirical fact with a "kind of psychotherapy for ecological practice" and concludes that "scientists cannot avoid making plausibility judgements ... such judgements are grounded in deep-seated beliefs about nature". This admits that we have a long way to go to reach anything like either of Lackey's or Roszak's advocacies. We can also remind ourselves here that Botkin (1990: 5) observed that: "The potential for us to make progress with environmental issues is limited by the basic assumptions we make about nature, – the unspoken, often unrecognised perspective from which we view our environment. This perspective, ironically in this scientific age, depends on myth and deep buried beliefs." This is a more hopeful statement than Cooper's, above, as it is more a call for recognition of process – which could be changed – rather than fatalistic about what scientists 'cannot avoid'. Botkin's stance leads us to now admit that science is never value free and argue that there should be common ground for discourse between science and the emotions in the sense that there are personal values held by ecological scientists and personal values held by the public.

As Lenoir (1997) argues, science is culturally produced and Fischedicks (1995), in *Practices and Pluralism: Socio-historical analysis of early vegetation science, 1900–1950*, is explicit that scientific knowledge is considered as a social construction rather than a description of reality. Pickett et al. (1997: 81), when discussing ecosystem science, write that it

> has a set of rarely recognised background assumptions. This set of assumptions suggests what things and relationships are important, the problems that are of high priority, the approaches that are trusted and the way solutions and applications are framed. Such assumptions, in essence, constitute the worldview shared by people engaged in an endeavour. … [such paradigms] are rarely clearly articulated and [can] touch on the deep personal values that attract people to a discipline or a profession in the first place.

'Facts' are thus contextualised and, as Pahl-Wostl (1995: 220) writes: "[S]cientific knowledge does not simply emerge in the brains of ingenious researchers enlightened to reveal the truth in nature. Knowledge must be seen from a relational perspective depending on the values, beliefs and perceptions of nature by society." While the scientific endeavour of verification might, and arguably should, attempt to marginalise sentiment, the people who practise ecological restoration are seen as motivated by values. These include concepts of appropriateness and what should be there in terms of plant and animal assemblages; 'natural' is often an uncontested justificatory narrative.

Maybe, despite laudable endeavours of finding a more neutral language, there is no escape from foundational beliefs? It seems apposite to say that if there is no escaping having some kind of foundational beliefs then we should indeed examine the ones we have and re-evaluate their appropriateness. Latour (2004) in *Politics of Nature* indeed critiques the distinction between fact and value and develops the idea of 'multinaturalism' where a complex collectivity is determined, not by experts with 'absolute reason', but by 'diplomats' who are flexible and open to experimentation.

If ecology can deal equally with what is actually scientifically verifiable and value judgements then we have to come clean that things like the integrity of healthy ecosystems, the 'rightness' of nature and concepts of equilibrium are actually beliefs and thus not necessarily in need of evidence to derive them (though of course evidence can be found to support them). The 'balance of nature' is, as Drury (1998) argues, untenable when faced with evidence but the *idea* is a strong article of faith. Indeed, Cuddington (2001) argues that the 'balance of nature' operates as a foundational metaphor in ecology. Such ideas are powerful and motivate the conservation effort, but they are beliefs. They amount to an ecological belief or constitute an ecological faith and should be seen as such.

Thus, if climate change means that if the arrival of migratory bird species in spring, the hatching out of insects and the emergence of foliage no longer coincide in the way which they have done in the UK in recent experience, this is not 'upsetting the balance of nature'. Such a balance is held as 'an article of faith' but in truth, the relationships between these three aspects will simply be different from what they were before. However, our 'ecological faith' tells us to lament – but we are doing no more than placing global warming into the idea of humans causing disharmony in the putative natural order of things. Such a natural order does not exist, though we like to think it does – and shoulder the guilt-laden notion that it is wrong and all our fault. It *is* just different, but we have to have a narrative and, in the West, we readily reach for a guilt one.

Botkin (1990: 75–89) in his discussion of the relationship between the mountain lion and the mule deer writes of 'Nature as Divine Order' – and of the balance between the mountain lion predator keeping in check the numbers of mule deer as if in some kind of order. He quotes Cicero about the "world marvellously ordered by divine providence and wisdom for safety and protection of us all .... Who cannot wonder at this harmony of things, at this symphony of nature which seems to will the well-being of the world (Cicero, *The Nature of the Gods*, 44BC)." Such myths prevail and order and purpose abound, he continues: "[T]here is a parallel and historical connection between the ancient, religious and metaphysical perspectives on nature and modern beliefs that have been accepted as scientific. What we learn from the mountain lion and the mule deer [i.e. from the studies discussed concerning 'balance' order and harmony in nature] is about what we believed not about what we know" (Botkin, 1990: 89).

Part of this 'ecological faith' seems to be some kind of teleological search for intentionality. There is a tension between 'what is' and 'what things mean to people' or 'how people feel that things ought to be'. 'What is', if such a thing can ever be assessed, is quite dispassionate. Here I am very much minded of Pahl-Wostl's (1995) book *The Dynamic Nature of Ecosystems: Chaos and order entwined* where the reader can only conclude, as I discuss elsewhere, that ecosystems are but contingent states of conjunction, showing dependency but not necessity. 'Contingent state of conjunctions' means that 'what is' occurs because it does. There are combinations of factors at a site which lead to the operation of processes. States of existence arise from those processes and so the state depends on the interactions of the components which are present.

However, it didn't actually have to be like it is because other factors and processes could have just as easily operated to produce different states. On the face of it, it is a bit like a crossword – it all fits together, but take one word out and you can put other words in which fit just as well – or the puzzle can be a different shape or have a different pattern. It fits together because it fits together but there is nothing given or sacred about the way it happens to work. But it is not even like that; in nature things don't actually have to fit or 'work' – 'fitting' and 'working' are our preferred ways of looking at things – we'd like it all to fit but that is our imposition; equally randomness, chaos, order, disorder and purpose are our delusions and are examples of the range of our preferred ways of seeing things. If we must have a description, and it seems that we must, then we might venture that there is a dependent nexus of entities which, because of historical events, are present and interacting together at a site.

It does almost seem like a kind of conceit to find order in nature but it seems clear that the search for order and purpose is nested in a sense of higher purpose, usually in a religious sense. Chaos and disorder are more postmodern ideas but using those terms just replaces one narrative of some kind of necessity with another. If we accept Feyerabend's (1999: 12) view (see Chapter 1) that "understanding a subject means transforming it", we can see that these narratives are still nonetheless transformative. Pahl-Wostl's 'chaos and order entwined' and Drury's 'comfortable disorder' are seductive but just as wide of the mark as any other emotive purposeful narrative. And while we still tend to abhor chaos (Kohn, 2004), even the narrative 'chaos' gives us a descriptor which is transformative and lessens insecurity. So, while we may move from cherished narratives involving balance and necessity to less comforting narratives, the new perceptions arising from a narrative of a 'contingent state of conjunctions' are just as transforming as a sense of order, a sense of divine purpose, Pahl-Wostl's 'chaos and order entwined' and Drury's 'comfortable disorder'. However, I feel that the dependency but not necessity is really the most crucial aspect of a 'contingent state of conjunctions'. There is no necessity for things to be the way they are but the way things are depends on what went before and what else is around at the time. Things can only get where they are when they are by the way they got there.

The promotion of the idea of 'stability' Adams (2003: 223) relates to the foundational ideas of George Perkins Marsh (1864): "Marsh's Theme was clear: nature established an equilibrium and humans disrupted it." Pollan (2002: 198–199) illustrates this by describing terms such as climax and stability, which to me are unverifiable illusions, as 'comforting narratives' and he very much promotes the idea of contingency:

> Nature may possess certain inherent tendencies, ones that theories of forest succession can describe, but chance events can divert her course into an almost infinite number of different channels. It is hard to square this fact with our strong sense that some kind of quasi-divine order inheres in nature's workings. But science lately has been finding that contingency plays nearly as big a role in natural history as it does in human history. ... Forest ecologists today will acknowledge that succession theories are little more than comforting narratives we impose on a surprisingly unpredictable process; even so-called climax forests are sometimes superseded.

He cites the example of mature stands of oak being invaded by maples: 'the skunk at the dinner party', as he puts it. "Many ecologists will now freely admit that even the concept of an ecosystem is only a metaphor, a human construct imposed upon a much more variable and precarious reality ... the process of evolution is not as logical or inexorable as we have thought."

As observed in Section 3.1, given that cherished ecological narratives are thus challenged, it is again interesting to actually read about their evolution in the original works by Clements (1904–1939) and Tansley (1920–1939) and the accounts of them in Worster (1994). Tansley, who indeed coined the term 'ecosystem', was always careful to qualify the use of vegetational terms. Clements, however, seems somewhat unselfconscious and uses the word 'is', never 'can be seen as', such as in: "each climax community [as though it were a verifiable entity] is able to reproduce itself, repeating with essential fidelity the stages of its development" (Clements, 1928: 3). The qualification is that while each "final community" seems "most homogeneous and uniform" there are swings of populations which can be "very considerable" (so Pollan's critique of maples in an oak forest is allowed for; Pollan 2002: 199). Both he and Tansley qualify that there is a *seeming* stability in which the observer would not necessarily notice change. It is pertinent to stress that those who have written recently criticising the idea of stability in ecosystems seem to have omitted to refer to Tansley's original writings which were indeed suitably cautious about this seeming stability (Trudgill, 2007). Thus, progression and particular states are not necessarily seen as inevitable but, for Tansley, disturbance followed by recovery is important.

Although the use of this psychological terminology in ecology may be attributable to Tansley in relation to his work with Freud (Cameron,

1999; Cameron and Forrester, 2000a, 2000b) the uses of human psychological terms in ecology were not new at the time. Clements (1928) cites earlier authors who laid the foundations for the idea of succession, including De Luc (1806) who uses phrases such as 'plants delight' in various conditions, 'restore' and 'progress' and we are straight to the intentionality of nature, the teleological order (see, e.g., Odum, 1971: *Environment, Power and Society*), perhaps finding the creator in nature – and Ruskin's pathetic fallacy (Ruskin, 1897).

As discussed in Chapter 1, Ruskin's pathetic fallacy is the attribution of human feelings and intentionality to objects, especially to nature (commonly expressed in school essays as 'hot air *tries* to rise'). Today we might write about the tension between 'what is' (ontology) and 'what things mean to individuals' (epistemology). Ruskin (1897) understood the psychological importance of nature to us, and the metaphorical attribution of human characteristics to nature, but he baulked at any implied intentionality. As mentioned in Section 1.4, he objected to the "spendthrift crocus" as if the crocuses were being profligate with their blooms. This poetic use can be metaphorical and thus subtly different from the ecological or other epithets we use for plants, but we still refer to plants as though they were purposeful in themselves and/or have a purpose relative to our purpose or for us (e.g. plants which are invasive, out of control or medicinal).

Ecological science has always seemed to have had a problem with intentionality which approaches the pathetic fallacy. A common approach was to talk of plant communities, strategies and functionality with plants clearly striving and attempting to reach some state or position. It is not unreasonable to see plants in human terms so we may empathise with them and wish to conserve them but when it is all worked out, very cunningly, this is adjusted to that, this works this way – and the woodland becomes a sociological mechanism, indeed the term plant sociology became commonly used (the term phytosociology was coined in 1896 by Józef Paczoski; Maycock, 1967) and this was consolidated in *Plant Sociology: The study of plant communities* by Braun-Blanquet, Fuller and Conard (1932). It all might almost have been designed. It is all so logical. My objection is about the unverifiability of the intentionality – it is seeing a purposefulness in plants with an exclusive persuasiveness of such a plausible narrative. I'm very happy with discernible patterns emerging for contingent reasons but not the intentionality. But then, as discussed in Section 1.1, Kohn (2004: 9) writes that "life is intolerable without a sense of purpose" and that Darwinian theory shows that "design may take place without a designer".

So, in short, nature has to be like it is or it wouldn't actually be like it is – it would be like something else. This is where Drury (1998), Pahl-Wostl (1995) and Pollan (2001, 2002) lead us. However, in attempting to understand what or how something is, our human notions tend to intervene in terms of 'why' which manifests itself as 'purpose' – as was discussed under 'vindictive traffic lights', in Section 1.1. "Nothing's free when it is explained", writes Les Murray (quoted by Bate, 2000: 93), but explain we must, so nothing *is* free.

Here, I think we could usefully return to and repeat Foucault's questions we asked earlier in the book: "how have my questions been produced?", "how has the path of my knowledge been determined?" and "how have I been situated to experience the real?" (from Bernauer, 1992 on Foucault as discussed in Darier, 1999: 224), admitting both that "personal experience is a form of knowledge" (Harding, 1986: 240) and that "Metaphor and image are conceived not as surface representations of a deeper truth but as a creative intervention in making truth" (Cosgrove, 1990: 345). Furthermore, it is precisely the psychological appeal of our explanations which provide motivational forces for individuals and their ecological identities (Thomashow, 1995).

However, it is when there is a tension between evidence and narratives which leads Drury to argue that existing narratives are inappropriate. He then replaces one narrative with another because 'seeing what is' simply involves changing your mind in the face of evidence. So, he replaces one set of 'ecological imperative' narratives with another set involving 'comfortable disorder'. This does demonstrate Feyerabend's necessity for a transforming narrative but it is undeniable that the replacement construct is rather freer than the one objected to. Are we convinced by anyone's ability to 'see what is', however? Drury allows that scientific method is fundamental in providing evidence where facts challenge the values and, moreover, he does not deny the cultural significance of "the delightful array of living things" (Drury, 1998: xix). But how selective is his vision? How do we deal with such positioning? What is clear is that motivation can come from a number of sources – verifiable evidence, metaphors, images and an emotive attachment to an array of living creatures. Ultimately, it seems to me that these should not compete but be seen as equal partners in the conservation endeavour. Each is useful and, it can be argued, each is necessary for a full and persuasive set of motivations.

Concluding Thoughts

What am I sure of so far?
Nature is out there doing whatever it is doing.
We have to have a narrative.
Narratives are a learned response.

Many of the ecological narratives are illusions, or at least only plausible constructs; however, evidence can be gathered to support many of them. However, many of them amount to an ecological faith rather than being something which is verifiable.

Narratives can be challenged by the evidence but simultaneously observations can also readily be prioritised or relegated to reinforce or challenge the narrative.

It is much more common to prioritise appropriate observations in order to reinforce the narrative, especially in teaching, relegating inappropriate ones, than it is to prioritise ones that 'don't fit' the narrative.

In ecological science we should 'free ourselves up' a bit and realise that we have been looking through a learned lens. We don't have to see it like that. 'It doesn't have to be seen like that.'

Seeing 'what is there' actually involves transforming what you are seeing. Often you just 'switch lenses'. As Vitebsky (2005: 89) wrote in *Reindeer People*, as he was sitting round a fire with the reindeer herders he noted that: "The sounds the fire was making were all given different meanings" [by the herders] and he recalls the conversation when he said: "They all sound the same to me. How do you tell what they mean?" and the reply came: "It depends what you are thinking about. . ." That sums up a lot for me.

We don't see what we don't want to see in nature and we do see what we want to see in nature. We discuss this in the contexts of poetic and artistic representation in Chapter 4. In ecological science we have to be clear that we are either trying to deal with what is verifiable or we are going to come clean and admit that the 'integrity' of ecosystems, the 'rightness' of nature and concepts of equilibrium are actually beliefs and thus beyond the judgement of right or wrong in terms of the evidence. However, while the two endeavours of verifiability and beliefs are separate ones, they are not opposable. They can coexist – the interesting question is how far the latter informs the former. It would seem to me to be in quite a substantial way. The 'balance of nature' is completely unverifiable (and, as Drury shows, untenable when faced with evidence) but the idea is a strong article of faith. In this sense, the ecologist is acting as a shaman. Thus, many papers have been written about the 'balance of nature' complete with mathematically elegant arguments and equally there are many writings questioning the concept (Cooper, 2001; Cuddington, 2001; Kricher, 2009; Pimm, 1991). In some sense, it doesn't actually matter very much whether it exists or not. The beliefs are powerful and motivate the conservation effort. However, they are beliefs. This amounts to an ecological faith and should be seen as such. Nature is just doing what it is doing; interpreting it is another story – and I mean that literally.

The critiques of cherished ecological ideas, such as climax forests, doesn't (or shouldn't) destroy – or even be opposable to – our belief that there is something good and wholesome in an old forest. We know that the climax community is only a construct; that it, and ecosystems, don't actually exist, but that they can provide important ways of seeing, especially in terms of interconnectedness. We can read thus a morality into nature which could be evidential or it could be faith-based – but we shouldn't confuse the two.

Ecosystems are a contingent state of conjunctions which show dependency but not necessity. This means that there is no 'hallowed state', there is no 'normal'. The 'balance of nature', if such exists, is a process of constant mutual readjustment. Plants and animals are not necessarily closely adapted to their conditions; some have no particular disadvantage. There is no vulnerable 'tottering edifice' about to collapse, there is no 'robustness'. Notwithstanding this, the powerful emotive narratives form very powerful motivators for conservation.

Anthropomorphism and emotional attachments are contested issues. It is clear that there is a call for dispassionate endeavours but also that motivation and empathy are strongly related to identification with the subject.

Nature is there for its own sake, and not for me, but I have made it what it is to me. Actually, it is not even there for its own sake. It is just there.

And just maybe things happened because they could.

As Laurens van der Post (1986: 62) wrote: "The real things in life have nothing to do with the question 'why', they are just 'so', they are just 'thus'."

3.4 Chapter Summary

- Nature is a contingent state of conjunctions showing dependency but not necessity.

- The language of ecosystem science is imbued with psychological terms which we project onto nature. Concepts involving value judgements are common such as balance, harmony, intact, stable, in equilibrium, undisturbed, pristine, natural, untouched, diverse, productive and rich on the one hand and disturbance, collapse, deterioration, loss, impoverishment, outbreak, overrun, out of control, plague, infestation, introduction, invasion and alien on the other.
- We can realise that we are looking through the lens of such emotive concepts and endeavour to make more dispassionate observations. We may then arrive at assessments of how and whether some things are changed or altered in some way separately from making value judgements about their desirability.
- Scientific observation and value judgements are not incompatible. Science and cultural significance relate to each other, but need not, and I would argue should not, compete nor should they be conflated. They can have a complementary and beneficial coexistence as long as you realise where you stand when you reach for a narrative.
- This is not to deny the importance and power of emotive judgements in providing motivations for conservation; it is to try to avoid the automatic pre-judgement of a situation by immediately reaching for the nearest emotive cliché. That situation sows doubt on the reliability of the observations if they are made from within an emotive context.
- It is surely far more effective to have a set of observations which are scientifically reliable and not clouded by emotive pre-judgements or expressed in emotive terms but then are subsequently discussed in a societal arena where emotional judgements on desirability can be made based on reliable evidence.
- Conservation motivation should come from a dialogue between the endeavours to gain reliable evidence which then feeds into spiritual, poetic and emotive engagement. Both sets of endeavours are important and necessary but the former should inform the latter without the latter clouding the former.

4 · *Nature in Literature and Art*

4.1 Imagery, Meanings and Metaphor

Imagery and Meanings

Cultural associations with nature can be readily found in literature and in art. For example, a poet may write about, or an artist may depict, 'dappled sunlight in woods', giving us a benign association of somewhere we may enjoy and perhaps thus cherish. On the other hand, there may be writing about 'tangled, impenetrable forest' and visual depictions of darkness and shadows under trees, giving more negative connotations. Such associations can be interpreted in terms of not only showing how we see nature but also as giving insights into how we treat it.

However, descriptions and depictions may not only reveal how we may feel about nature; they can also influence how we feel. There is a reflexive dialogue between representations and the emotions and this two-way relationship between the reader/viewer and the writer/artist is discussed lucidly and powerfully in Susan Owen's (2020) *Spirit of Place: Artists, writers & the British landscape*. Her thesis is that artists and writers do not just describe the landscape; they, in turn, can influence how we see it. In this way, meanings derived from writings and artworks are not dissimilar to given meanings derived from ecological narratives in their influence on us, as discussed in Chapter 3. However, the relationships between literature, art, ecological science and personal meanings of nature are far from simple. What is difficult to say is whether and to what extent personal meanings can be over-ridden, replaced, reinforced, enhanced or enriched by the meanings derived from either literary and artistic depictions or from the given meanings from ecology – and whether the influences of these sources differ. One tends to suspect that given meanings from a didactic ecological context are more persuasive and less open to discussion than they are from what could be seen as the more optional, contested and individualistic meanings which may be derived from literature and art. However, this is an interesting area, worthy of further thought, not least because ecological science is not immune to the influence of cultural imagery in literature and art – and this is notwithstanding the influence of ecological concepts on literature and art.

In his writings on 'Images and imagination in 20th-century environmentalism' Denis Cosgrove (2008) discusses how environmental meanings are shaped by the dialogue between the landscape and the viewer with their memories of constructed and presented images. He writes about pictorial images: "[T]he affective responses they generate are complex. An examination of iconic images of key 20th-century environmental crises . . . reveals both continuities in image making and presentation, and the evolving roles of physical nature itself in shaping their composition and meaning" (Cosgrove, 2008: 1862). This again confirms a complex reflexivity between the mental constructs of the viewer and the viewed.

When viewing art in a gallery, there are both the viewer's own meaning and the given narrative of the explanatory label. The label can challenge, confirm, enrich or deny our meaning, and we react accordingly. We usually have in mind the question: 'How are images to be interpreted?' See Box 4.1 for an example of a discussion in an art gallery.

We may readily consider the role of the imagination in image construction, as described by Delacroix: "Even when we look at nature, our imagination constructs the picture" (Eugène Delacroix, September 1859; quotation displayed in a Delacroix exhibition in the National Gallery, UK, visited March 2016). We also realise the importance of prior images in perception – as with this from Cezanne: "Today our sight is a little weary, burdened by the memory of a thousand images. We no longer see nature; we see pictures over and over again" (Cézanne in conversation, 1902; quoted from ch. 8 in Andrews, 1999). Equally, we readily construct our ideas of nature when we look at a picture.

Written images are no less complex. Bill Adams (2014) wrote that 'conservation' poems could be bio-centric, offering a view from other lives (or making an attempt to tell truths about nature from the perspective of other species); bio-nostalgic, of lament for lost places or naturalness and accounts of the costs of human consumption; and bio-regional, encompassing poetry of place and landscape ecology. In all these cases the identification with an organism, the lament of loss of naturalness and the sense of place, so often written with a deep-held motivational emotion, can be highly motivational to the reader according to how these touch

Box 4.1 *A day at Tate Modern – some years ago, author (ST) with a friend (AK)*

ST: Salvador Dali! Here it is! Look at the *Narcissus* painting! The daffodil is such a significant flower for us, symbolising how we mirror ourselves in nature, projecting our own image onto everything and then falling in love with it because it speaks to us of ourselves.
AK: The book says something about revealing "the weakness of the hold of reason and logic over the human consciousness".
ST: But there is reason and logic, just of a different sort. I'm entitled to my interpretation.
AK: OK, so the everyday is turned upside down, back to front and inside out. So what?
ST: Even incongruity has a logic.
AK: OK, so Art challenges our preconceptions. Then what?
ST: Look at that Hannah Collins. I immediately saw trees growing out of gravestones as nature triumphing over 'eternal' remembrance which is actually ephemeral.
AK: The book says: "This is a poignant image of absence and loss, reminding us that history is an artificial concept extracted from the experience of individuals."
AK: You'll like this one. *Self-burial*, Keith Arnatt.
ST: Wow! [laughing]. The man gradually disappears. Must read the note. Oh, yes; "he gradually disappears into the earth". It's the inverse of Man's impact on the Earth. Great!
AK: But he leaves a scar. Shouldn't it be all healed over when he's gone?
AK: Map of Britain with everything in the wrong place! Layla Curtis!
ST: Can't get near, there's so many people crowded round.
AK: Loch Ness just should be actually there, it looks so right. Fantastic.
ST: It's so very engaging, thinking of places in the wrong place. It's like that discussion of what Britain would be like if the Scottish mountains were in the south and the chalk downland in the north. Would there still be 'soft Southerners' and 'gritty Northerners'?
AK: We can't tell. The concepts are so ingrained in us.
ST: Look at these stones. Reminds me of a mountaintop. The book says, "each with a kind of 'eye' ... linking with ... myths ... slumbering warriors awaiting the call to arms ... spent fuel rods".

on our prior personal experience but, by the same token, can also become part of our future personal experience.

It is interesting to think rather more about the differences and similarities between the relationship between people and nature in literature and art and the same relationship in ecological science. The former does seem more exploratory and self-aware while the latter could be seen as influenced by a sense of authoritativeness in ecological concepts. However, it also becomes clear that in either case, images, metaphors and narratives not only reflect but also influence the way we think. In *Metaphor and Thought*, Ortony (1993) and other authors discuss how the language we use acts as a 'conduit' between people for conveying meanings, feelings and thoughts. Indeed, cultural values which are imbued in language can also become closely related to scientific evaluations, but there is possibly little awareness of this in scientific circles. For example, in *The New Wild* Fred Pearce (2015: 163) writes of the "Myths of the Pristine", arguing that: "The idea of the tropics largely comprising a pristine wilderness seems to go back to the 19th century romantic writers and painters. For a long time, scientists bought into it too." The concept seemed to be accepted as axiomatic in scientific writings. Such a term as "pristine" can usefully lead us to a wider discussion of the use of such metaphors which can be further illustrated by the themes of "naturalness" and "equilibrium".

Stott (1997: 207) shows how such metaphors can be highly motivational but erroneous, arguing that: "The idea that most of the world's 'natural' forests are essentially climatic climax communities in equilibrium with a given climate has probably been one of the most persistent, yet pernicious, concepts in world ecology." He cites the overwhelming evidence for past changes and dynamism in forest ecosystems (e.g. Bormann and Likens, 1979), concluding that the notion of stability is "plain wrong". However, such a notion is so deeply entrenched in many ecological writings, for example all the discussions about the relationship between diversity and stability which tend to see stability as an uncontested axiom and as somehow right and good, when in fact it is completely illusory. This is strange as mutability in nature is not a new idea – the Roman emperor and philosopher Marcus Aurelius (AD 121–180) is attributed with the saying "Observe always that everything is a result of change, and get used to thinking that there is nothing Nature loves so well as to change existing forms and make new ones like them." But Stott sees ecological scientists as "unable to let go of the 'prop' of equilibrium", arguing (p. 209) that they are thus tricking "an honourable, moral and well-meaning populace". But how pernicious actually is the (deeply rooted) notion of a pristine forest damaged by mankind? Myth it may be, but is it a good myth to have? One wonders, given the publicity about how indigenous peoples have been involved in the tropical rainforest since prehistoric times: Levis et al. (2017: 925) in 'Persistent effects of pre-Columbian plant domestication on Amazonian forest composition' conclude that "modern-day Amazonian tree communities across the basin remain largely structured by historical human use".

The narrative of inevitable change is hardly a motivator for conservation. Contrast this with the deep emotional feeling of moral outrage which can be evoked as a reaction to the idea that a pristine forest is being destroyed. Indeed, it can be concluded that metaphors and their associated narratives have to be carefully examined – and we can surely ask is it not possible to have scientifically defensible and powerfully motivating conservation metaphors in our narratives? This can mean that the conservation argument should not be one so much of conserving states but more of conserving processes, often seen as the processes aiding renewal – even aiding change. But that is easy to say but less easy to define what it means. When we are looking at ancient woodland which has been consistently on the same site for many hundreds of years, the current state and the long-term historical processes are deeply embedded in each other in a heritage which is irreplaceable. There, we need to conserve the state to conserve the processes of renewal that, for example, might rely on viable seed banks present in the soil from times past. Maybe emotive metaphors do indeed serve us well? Certainly, the cultural associations of nature in literature and art can usefully be examined and considered further as part of thinking about the significance of the meanings of nature for conservation motivation.

Meanings and Metaphor

Analysis of the abounding meanings of nature in literature and art is challenging as there is such a huge range. Additionally, the fascinating book by Potter and Sargent (1973) about 'words from nature' shows how our very language is deeply imbued with nature. For example, we talk of 'to lionise' a person who is the centre of attention or people as 'foxy' or 'bullish'; we have robust from *robur*, oak-like in Latin.

A bibliographic list of writings on the narrative meanings of nature could take up all the pages of the rest of this book but a short list of examples will illustrate some of the range of sources available, as shown in Box 4.2.

However, while at first sight the range of meanings of nature can be difficult to make sense of, one approach is to think about how literal

Box 4.2 *Examples of sources on nature in literature*

- Beinart, Middleton and Pooley (2013): *Wild Things: Nature and the social imagination*. Good global coverage of imagined landscape, appropriation and imageries of nature.
- Bramwell (1989a), *The Literary Ecologist* and Bramwell (1989b), *Ecology in the 20th Century* provide useful summaries of earlier works.
- Ferber (1999): *A Dictionary of Literary Symbols* is a useful compendium.
- Impelluso (2004): *Nature and Its Symbols* is a good coverage.
- Maitland (2012): *Gossip from the Forest: The tangled roots of our forest and fairytales* looks at the origin of some of our earliest stories.
- Murphy (1998): *Literature of Nature* provides interesting discussions.
- Owens (2020): *Spirit of Place: Artists, writers & the British landscape*. A 'tour de force' of the two-way relationship between the reader/ viewer and the depicted.
- Philippon (2004): *Conserving Words: How American nature writers shaped the environmental movement* is extremely interesting and a worthwhile read.
- Smyth provides critical review in 'Plashy fens: The limitations of nature writing' in the *Times Literary Supplement* (Smyth, 2015).
- Westling (2014): *The Cambridge Companion to Literature and Environment*. A comprehensive survey of key points.
- There are a wide range of papers in the journal *ISLE: Interdisciplinary Studies in Literature and Environment* (www.asle.org/research-write/ isle-journal/).

meanings and associative meanings might differ. Finding unambiguous terms for the distinctions between 'descriptions of essence' and 'associations' and 'associative meanings' is not necessarily simple as different authors have different contexts and different ways of using the same words. However, in *The Poet as Botanist*, Mahood (2008), when discussing the poetry of John Clare (p. 133), usefully uses the words "denotative" and "figurative". Denotative can be taken as the surface or literal meaning of a signifier as distinct from the associated connotations. A common example often given is the distinction between the denotation of a red rose with a green stem – the simple description – while association or connotation is that a rose is a symbol of passion and love – this is what the red rose can represent. The figurative departs from the literal use of words and is metaphorical – a figurative expression which is non-literal and can be symbolic, allegorical, representational or emblematic. We find different uses of words to express what is tangible and what we associate but whichever words are used we can understand the difference between them – and also begin to appreciate the significance of the wider associative meanings for how we may view, value and treat the object of nature in question.

Mahood gives the example of denotative in John Clare's writings as involving yellow petals, purple stamens and so on while the figurative included comparing flower spikes to the dashing plumes of an army officer and being "as thick as they can stand by each other" (p. 133), suggesting the pride of the flower show exhibitor. Mahood (2008: 133–134) writes that: "Clare's nature poetry everywhere displays this blend of the exact and the evocative." She talks of his descriptions of shape, colour and pattern with 'vivid green', 'barbed leaf' 'gashed leaves' and 'pied beauty'. She writes of this "sensory precision" which goes alongside "the grassroots familiarity that, for the poet, endows every plant with its aura of associations". She gives the example of aconites with 'green leaf frilling round their cups of gold/ Like tender maiden muffled from the cold.' Mahood's writings are invaluable in helping us think about nature writings and this duality of writing from description to association.

In addition to the distinction between denotative and figurative, Boer (2012: 38–39) in *The Earthy Nature of the Bible: Fleshly readings of sex, masculinity, and carnality* makes a distinction in the Bible between explicit anthropocentric metaphors ('your eyes are doves') and implicit metaphors ('the flowers appear upon the earth') – which make "no explicit connections with human beings yet in some way they are drafted in to do the work of anthropocentric metaphors".

In David Leary's edited book *Metaphors in the History of Psychology* (1990), Averill (1990) writes in ch. 3 on 'Inner feelings, works of the flesh, the beast within, diseases of the mind, driving force, and putting on a show: Six metaphors of emotion and their theoretical extension'. Here, he makes the useful distinction between the targets of metaphor and the source of the metaphor and then also he recognises categories of explanatory metaphors and evaluative metaphors. He quotes Lakoff and Johnson's book (1980) *Metaphors We Live By* in that targets of metaphors are often aspects of experience which are poorly delineated, such as physical objects which lack clear boundaries or orientation, abstract concepts such as time, many social practices and mental activities –

especially the emotions, and he includes fear, anger and love. Sources of metaphors are some other aspects of experience which help to clarify the meanings and significance of the targets including anatomical structure, spatial direction and colour.

He feels that the emotions can serve as both target and source. For example, 'the storm unleashed its fury' and 'his fury was a storm' has 'fury' as the source clarifying the target 'storm' in the former and then the source 'storm' clarifying the target 'fury' in the latter. Additionally, explanatory metaphors are concerned primarily with knowledge and evaluative metaphors with attitude or mood. Emotions as a term have tended to involve both explanation and evaluation, and the example of 'diseases of the mind' is cited as involving both. This is explanatory since emotions can be seen as disturbing the mind just as a disease disturbs the body but also as evaluative since diseases are unhealthy. Emotion is also seen as important as it can be used as a generic term for such specific states as anger, fear, grief and love but also (Averill, 1990: 104–106) "a broad and diffuse matrix of experience" from which "more delineated thoughts and feelings arise". What is then interesting is that he also makes the key point that: "Unfortunately, it is not always easy to distinguish explanatory from evaluative uses of metaphor. And when the two are confused, value judgements may masquerade as objective explanations." He sees this as a vexing problem for research in the psychology of emotion. However, I see this as particularly insightful as this fusion is very common in metaphors about nature. Such fusion seems particularly vivid when people cannot ascribe a reason for a phenomenon and attribute nature with human characteristics, such as when thunder is attributed to the anger of a god. There is an explanation and a negative evaluation. Such is writ large in the pathetic fallacy, discussed elsewhere in the book. This fusion of explanation and evaluation is also writ large in many terms such as 'invasive species' and 'alien plants' in ecology. Here the metaphor leads us straight to a value judgement in a way that 'new species in the area' does not. Thus, the metaphor can cloud our view and lead us readily from judgement to motivation for action.

A different perspective is provided by Jozef Keulartz (2007: 27–28). When writing on 'Using metaphors in restoring nature' he sees metaphors as indispensable conceptual tools in thinking, talking and acting. He writes that metaphors perform important cognitive functions especially when we meet something new and can compare it with something we already know: metaphors as "devices crucial for creating and conceptualizing novel ideas and new knowledge". He also says that they are "important discursive tools that enable communication and negotiation with others". Moreover, "metaphors also have a clear normative function. They not only determine our thinking but also our acting." This is crucial to the discussions in this book as metaphors enable us to "mostly automatically and unconsciously make a 'normative' leap from data to recommendation, from facts to values, from 'is' to 'ought'". The example given is that of an area of slum dwellings which, if the metaphor 'blight' is used, recommends removal but if 'natural community' is used this recommends protection or enhancement.

Keulartz then admits that: "Once it is acknowledged that the use of metaphor is inescapable, however, we are confronted with the sheer multiplicity of metaphors" about nature. He quotes Philippon's (2004) list of such metaphors which range as in Box 4.3. It is small wonder that explanation and evaluation become merged.

In his book *The Song of the* Earth Bate (2000: 246–251) wrote about Paul Ricoeur (Valdés, 1991) and his "representative illusion" and the relationship between "the interiority of mental image and the exteriority of something real". He discusses Gary Snyder's poetic and ecological writings and draws the parallel between poetry and scientific knowledge. There is a comparison between the decomposition process on the forest floor and the recycling of energy and nutrients with the remaking of human consciousness. Bate takes this up in terms of how reading a poem recycles its energy back into our cultural environment. He develops the theme in terms of Snyder's Zen beliefs and the

Box 4.3 *Metaphors in nature*

Nature as:

Place: frontier, garden, park, wilderness, utopia.
Person: self, mother, father, sister, brother, wife, husband, partner.
Agency: god or goddess, minister, monarch, teacher, enemy.
Connectivity: web, community, tapestry.
Machine: clock, engine, computer, spaceship.
State: pristine, virgin, harmony, balance.
Message: book to read.
Object: bank, sink, storehouse, pharmacy, lifeboat, home.
Contested: battlefield, commons.

(Modified from Keulartz (2007) quoting Philippon (2004))

interconnectedness of all things which "means that he does not have to worry that the recycling analogy is merely a metaphor". He goes on that "he [Snyder] would reply that metaphor is a way of understanding hidden connections and reunifying the world". Here, then, metaphors are seen positively.

Metaphors are certainly worthy of our attention as they may direct our thoughts in particular directions. We should realise that they are there and how they function – and indeed endeavour to seek explanations of how metaphors work to influence us separately from our evaluations of that influence.

4.2 Nature in Literature

The Range of Ideas and the Duality of Nature

A definitive coverage of books written by naturalists is offered by Allen (2010) in *Books and Naturalists*. Here the observations and ideas are charted historically showing how our knowledge has burgeoned, often through fieldwork as chronicled by Trudgill (2020) in 'Pioneering fieldwork heroes in the life sciences'. Parallel to that more scientific genre there are the closely allied genres of the more imaginative fictional writing and a more experiential genre of what is commonly called nature writing. There are many debates about narratives of the pastoral, the rural, the idyll and the savage, wild and untameable, most notably recently encompassed by the works of Macfarlane (2003): *Mountains of the Mind*, his (2007) *Wild Places* together with (2012) *The Old Ways*, (2014) *Introduction to the Old Straight Track* and (2015) *Landmarks*. One of the foremost recent nature writers has been Roger Deakin with (1999) *Waterlog*, (2007) *Wildwood* and (2008) *Notes from Walnut Tree Farm*. In this context it is interesting to cite a discussion in the media. In 2013 *The Guardian* newspaper ran two columns. The first is by Steven Poole, a writer on English whose works include *Unspeak* on how words become weapons (Poole, 2007). His *Guardian* column is entitled 'Is our love of nature writing bourgeois escapism?' (Poole, 2013). He has a trenchant critique of the nature writing genre and includes the sentence: "[N]ature writers do tend to whitewash the non-human world as a place of eternal sun-dappled peace and harmony." He continues: "Some of us, then, become all the more nostalgic for an imaginary Edenic life in which we were welcome in nature's bountiful embrace. Today's back-to-nature revival is a response to corporations and the financial crisis: the global machine of mass 'productivity' is broken, so we should retreat to our gardens and tend our organic carrots." He is also critical of nature as a 'prescription', though one example, www.nature-rx.org/, is imbued with levity rather than being serious and self-regarding.

The second column is by the nature writer Richard Mabey (2013), 'In defence of nature writing'. Mabey (2013) accepts that "somewhere in Poole's essay there is a legitimate questioning of the way that nature has been commercialised and commodified, as day-trip redemption, off-prescription Prozac". He continues: "Writing about [nature] is difficult and skiddy work, prone to anthropomorphism. Fortunately, there has been a strong strain of self-interrogation in much recent nature writing." He asks whether "language (and therefore our writing) is complicit in humans' supposed alienation from nature" and he "warm[s] towards the concept of neighbourliness as a template with which to approach and write about our relations with our fellow organisms. It permits concern, shared circumstance, even love from afar, but demands no reciprocity." He feels that "'new' nature writing was not new at all, but embedded in a long tradition" observing that "Ronald Blythe (no mean nature writer himself) has lauded the poet John Clare's 'indigenous eye'" and "his extraordinary ability to see furthest when the view was strictly limited". Mabey therefore sees a continuity with the past but, rather than a harking back to a non-existent idyll lambasted by Poole, sees a genre of empathic writing about those who share our space. In this context Robert Macfarlane (2019) writing of the rise of a new animism extends this to consider 'Should this tree have the same rights as you?'. Another useful paper in this context is Wallach et al. (2020), 'Recognizing personhood in compassionate conservation'.

Many theorists have attempted to find rationales in human approaches to nature as expressed in poetry, literature and paintings. In *Poetry, Space, Landscape: Towards a new theory* Fitter (1995) suggests that our landscape consciousness is always generated from multiple bases of awareness which he sees as contextualised in historicity. Fitter (1995: 15) feels that all typologies are inadequate and that a complete theory of landscape perception is elusive as the processes involved are "wider, richer and less stable" than any scheme which purports to explain them. He espouses the idea of four matrices of perception: Ecological (subsistence and security), Cosmographic (agency and structure), Analogical (similarity and symbolicity) and Technoptic (visual codes of appearance learned in art).

The Technoptic relates to the concept of 'landskip' which is a representation of form lacking in Palaeolithic art but evolves through the use of line and notions of framing vertically and horizontally. Fitter also proposes the rise of Managerial Spaces from the agricultural revolution, giving us a dualism of ordered world and outer wilderness; Comparative Space, deriving from travel; Quotidian Space – the everyday; Possessive Space – celebrating homeland and ownership; and Rational Space – close material definition of nature. There is also a range of relationships with structural elemental aspects – sky, earth, sun, moon, water, rock and vegetation.

Further possible categories of explanation range from the atavistic to the aesthetic. Some theorists have sought notions which relate to human biological evolution while others have been more mythical and cultural. A fundamental evolutionary approach is adopted by the idea of *The Biophilia Hypothesis* promoted by E. O. Wilson (Kellert and Wilson, 1993). This relates to early human evolution on the open savannahs and our deep affinity with other forms of life. This atavistic view also relates to the interpretations of views and their artistic representations in terms of 'prospect and refuge' (Appleton, 1975, 1996). Here, we are seen as preferring an open view (so that we can see both threats and potential food sources) and a place of personal safety.

Duality also imbues our representational relationship with nature in so many ways, especially the notions of assisting and resisting realities (Rolston, 1979). The assisting relationship with nature is compensatory, contextual, a setting, a place to be and exist. It is a refuge and a restoration, as with Hardy's poem seen at the start of Chapter 5, and a metaphor for the human spirit, emotions and feelings. The resisting aspect is expressed by Rolston (1979: 29) as: "Environmental life, including human life, is nursed in struggle" and he refers to our relationship with nature as: "We cannot succeed unless it can defeat us."

I see this as saying that the relationship with nature is characterised by the way in which nature can facilitate our will, without which we would not cherish it, combined with the possibility of defeat, without which it would not engage us.

Nature in Poetry

In terms of trying to reveal our cultural constructs of nature, I have turned to poetry in the light of *The Song of the* Earth by Bate (2000), who feels that: "The poet's way of articulating the relationship between human-kind and the environment, person and place, is peculiar because it is experiential, not descriptive. Whereas the biologist, the geographer and the Green activist have narratives of dwelling, a poem may be a revelation of dwelling" (Bate, 2000: 267). The literature online website http://literature.proquest.com/ contains transcripts of all major works of Western literature and the texts can be selected using any keywords. Hence, I use this database (originally accessed as http://lion.chadwyck.co.uk/) to ask specifically whether a study of the cultural constructs of soil in poetry can shed any light on deeply held notions about soil which have evolved since early history. Accessing the poetry database I searched for perceptions of forests, woods, woodlands, wilderness, gardens and birds through the epithets attached to them (Table 4.1).

The engagement through the duality of assisting and resisting can be readily seen. Forests and woods seem essentially dark, deep with shade and a feeling of mystery. Epithets such as 'sweet' or 'summer' appear but scarcely. They can be metaphorically puzzling, tangled and seemingly hiding something – certainly a resisting reality: resisting ease of passage and comprehension. Impenetrability leads to fear in terms of being lost and what might be 'lurking' in there, as is not uncommon with wolves, ogres and witches in fairy stories and folk myths. The lack of visibility has a contextualised duality, however: not only a place of threat but also a place to hide from threat. Here, you can flee from a threat – often from other humans – disappear and hide in the woods. Thus, there is an assisting reality as you can hide safely and not be easily seen or found – Robin Hood, outlaws and the refuge of the Greenwood readily spring to mind.

German narratives of forest (*Wald*) have a special significance in metaphor and in German landscape poetry, fairy tales and legends as well as in art and culture. The Battle of the Teutoburg Forest in AD 9 has particular resonance in the German psyche. In this battle, Roman legions were ambushed and defeated by an alliance of Germanic peoples (see Schama, 1995, *Landscape and Memory*, especially ch. 2, 'Der Holzweg: The track through the woods'; Wilson, 2012, *The German Forest: Nature, Identity, and the Contestation of a National Symbol, 1871–1914*; and Zechner, 2013, 'From poetry to politics: The Romantic roots of the "German Forest"').

Gardens, by contrast, are seen as places of accessibility – walking, sitting in; shady rather than shadowy, they can be owned, they can be private places – where you can kiss, an expression of the self, and are, of course, productive. Gardens are thus an independent assisting reality, but

Table 4.1 *Nature in poetry*

Forests
(12,736)

barbarian
bowers
damp
deep
depth
depths
echoing
glade
glades
glimmer
great
green abyss
murmuring
native
old
puzzling
rejoices
roots
shade
shades
shadows
shadows of
shaggy
silvered
solitude
tall
tangled
troubled
wild

also
disappears into the
fled into the
(safety)

ripping the
scalps the
slash the

Wood
(18,040)

ancient
bluebell
breathless
bushy
damp
dark
darksome
dismal
echoing
echoing
embosomed
enchanted
gloomy
gruesome
haunted
infested
listening
moonlit
moss-hung
mournful
night-locked
painful
parched
phantomed
rotten
shady
shy depths of
soggy
summer
sweet
thick
venerable
yonder
young

Woodland
depths
lonely
maze
silent
wild

Wilderness
(4,049)

barren
bones
craggy
desolate
grey
lovely
parched
shattered

Garden
(14,020)
beauty
blossoming
bower
breathing
cocooned in
cool
fruits
gate
green
growing
hoeing
kissed in the
little
lost
my
my own
neat
neglected
odorous
planted
pleasure
quiet
shady
sheltered
sitting in
still
sunshine in
tree-filled
trim
walk in
walks
walled
walled
weeding

Bird
(19,840)

bouyant
careless glee
happy
little
sea
singing
soaring
song
wild
wounded

simultaneously weeding and other vigorous activities are needed and often used phrases like 'getting out of control' and 'needs pruning back' show that gardens are also an independent resisting reality. Gardens really are at the heart of the man–nature relationship because we physically and tangibly create an otherwise independent nature in relation to the mental images we have (gardens, and the closely related activity of creating nature reserves, are discussed in Chapter 6).

4.3 The Soil

Assisting or Resisting

The dual notions of assisting and resisting seem especially writ large in our notions of 'soil' in poetry (Trudgill, 2006), positive and negative descriptors almost equally balanced. It is clear that soil is cherished when it 'plays our game' and is dark, rich, crumbly, productive, but not when it doesn't – it is then churlish, cold, unwilling and joyless. The essence of an assisting and resisting reality is clear. Part of the construction is to do with the nature of the soil itself and part of it depends on what we are trying to achieve. Part of the construction is evidential, relating to the characteristics of the soil, and part is to do with our intentionality despite the evidence. Take a 'poor' soil (however defined but probably by the evidence of a poor crop) – we can go with the evidence and give up growing crops or we can say that it is soil, so it should grow crops – and we will make it do so even though the prospects are not good, adding organic matter and fertiliser, for example. The soil is the same but we can construct it differently, both mentally and physically. Our intentionality collides with an independent nature and we may reconstruct it physically and certainly we construct it in our minds. It is the interaction between the nature of nature and our will which matters.

There are also many notions of attachment, patriotism and nationality, as expressed in the term 'native soil'. One of the most powerful examples of this is the concept of *Blut und Boden* (Blood and Soil), the slogan of Nazi agrarian romanticism. The essential elements of this are "settlement, and aggression in defence of settlement" which link "the mythical dark powers of the earth [with] the irresistible force of inherited blood" (Ritchie, 1983: 15).

Is it also the case that the dismissive, negative notion of 'dirt' prevails in our cultures? Indeed, in a review of why soil matters – or should matter – to society, Yaalon (2000) simply asks: "Is soil just dirt?". We can find quite a range of responses to these questions throughout history, revealing both positive and negative attributes of soil. The Greek botanist and philosopher Theophrastus (327–287 BC) wrote that soil is the source of plant nutrition. Vergil (70–19 BC), the Roman poet and farmer, made what might be regarded as the first recorded observation in soil science in that he recorded that if you dig a pit and attempt to replace the soil back in the hole, the soil which would not all easily fit back in would be the best type for crops (being heavier, i.e. clay-rich, and more retentive of moisture and nutrients). Culturally, the terms 'soil', 'land' and 'the earth' can be imbued with notions of yield and fertility: 'mother nature', provision and abundance as in "The earth shall endure and blossom forth in spring" (*Das Lied von der Erde*, German translation of Chinese folk poetry, *Die Chinesische Floete*, by Bethge and set to music by Mahler).

Other notable writings about the soil include the novel *The Growth of Soil* by Knut Hamsun ([1935]1980) described in the publisher's blurb as "the story of Isak, 'the tiller of the ground, body and soul' [which] sinks its roots into man's deepest myths about his struggle to cultivate the land and make it fertile". It describes how he worked on the land: "there were stones and roots to be dug up and cleared away, and the meadow to be levelled ready for next year" and of the pleasure when the fields and meadows were looking well. Here, the notions of struggle, mastery and productivity are embedded in the text.

In *La Terre*, the writer Émile Zola (1880) has a central character very attached to the land – and land ownership forms a central theme in the novel. On revisiting his land, once lost and now regained, the text is:

> [He] stood for a long time contemplating [the field]: it was still there and seemed to be in good heart, nobody had harmed it. His heart overflowed with joy at the thought that it was his again, and forever. He stooped and picked up a lump of earth in both hands, crumbled it, sniffed it and let it trickle through his fingers. It was his own good earth, and he went home humming a tune, as though intoxicated by its smell. (Zola, [1880]1980: 465)

These narratives of positive attachment to the soil contrast markedly with narratives associated with the history of agriculture in the United States. Whitney (1994, ch. 10) readily cites the 'Dust Bowl' and the descriptive epithets of 'earth butchery', 'predatory agriculture', 'spoilation' and 'exhaustion' in what is seen as the "most rapid rate of wasteful land use in the history of the world" (pp. 227–228). This approach to the land seems nested in the early construct of North America as a wilderness to be conquered and of unlimited productivity, as described in the book on *Wilderness and the American Mind* (Nash, [1967]2014), together with the assumption that there were always new fertile lands to the west.

Indeed, it is instructive to look at the post-Dust Bowl era literature on soil conservation which still appealed to the pioneering spirit and the need for toughness of approach (Trudgill, 2001b: 155).

If we are asking why a contrast should exist between a positive attitude to soil resources and our abuse of them, there is a relevant observation from the North American literature about the role of mechanisation over time. In Steinbeck's (1939) novel *The Grapes of Wrath* a farmer climbs aboard a tractor and loses contact with the earth:

> He [the farmer climbing into the tractor rather than walking behind a horse-drawn plough] could not see the land as it was, he could not smell the land as it smelled; his feet did not stamp the clods or feel the warmth and power of the earth. He sat in an iron seat and stepped on iron pedals. . . . The land bore under iron, and under iron gradually died; for it was not loved or hated, it had no prayers or curses. (Steinbeck, [1939]1995: 39)

However, given that soil erosion and degradation can occur without mechanisation, what there seems to be in common to these writings appears to be an underlying unwritten assumption that the soil is an infinite resource and bountiful and thus perhaps needs no special care. A central point is that 'soil' and 'earth' are celebrated in literature and folklore as part of 'mother nature', yielding and bountiful, but also as something which can be taken for granted – and indeed dismissed as dirt. This much might be confirmed by reference to mentions of soil in literary writings.

There were 7,412 hits for the word 'soil' when selecting texts using the keyword 'soil' in poetry from a literature online website (http://literature.proquest.com/, originally accessed for Trudgill, 2006 on soils in poetry as http://lion.chadwyck.co.uk/). Any epithets, such as 'fertile' soil, were noted. Taking a sample of the first 300 entries of poetry, by which stage few new epithets were beginning to appear, the results were as follows (Table 4.2). Soil as in 'dirt' or 'soiled' (dirty) gave a score of 11 per cent and, while the classification is my own, 26 per cent of the attributes I could see as 'negative' and 22 per cent as 'positive'. 'Native soil' scored 14 per cent and references to plant/crop growth/agriculture 13 per cent.

Negative notions record a sense of obduracy, perhaps a resistance to our will (e.g. during attempts at cultivation), with the use of negative epithets. The positive notions record a bountiful, celebrated nature and can show a sense of ownership. The neutral ones see soil as a passive receptacle. There is scant reference to the origin or loss of soils.

Table 4.2 *'Soil' in poetry (modified from Trudgill, 2006): sample of 300 entries of poetry with the word 'soil' revealing a duality*

Attribute	Number	%
Positive	67	22
Native soil	45	14
Growing	41	13
Ownership	21	13
Negative (of which 'dirt' was 35 or 11%)	82	26
Passive	32	10
Colour/neutral	16	5
Loss of soil	3	1
Creation of soil	3	1
POSITIVE DESCRIPTIONS	kindly	
abiding	known	bitter
as melody	mulched	churlish
beautifying	poetic	cold and pestilential
Christian	praise the	dry-blown
crumbled	repaying	dull
crumbly	rich (4)	dust (5)
dark rich	rich brown	fear of
dearer (as	richness	hated
in valued)	sacred (4)	hard
deep (2)	Saviour's	hardened
delightful	soft	harder
Elysian	soil where pretty women	haunted
embroidered	grow	heavy (2)
envied	strong	hottest
fair	sublime	joyless
faithful	sweet (2)	mouldering
fat	sweetness from	naked
firm	sylvan	neglected
genial (3)	teeming	parched
glad	thankful	rugged (2)
glorious	verdant	sluggish (2)
glory	warm	sodden
gorgeous-tinted	warm dry	sterile (2)
grateful	wholesome	stubborn (2)
green-vested	willing	sultry
healthy		swarthy
Heaven's	NEGATIVE DESCRIPTIONS	the killings
holy (3)	acid	thin
human	ashes	thirsty
humid	bare	ungrateful
kinder	barren (4)	unwilling

Soil is, it seems, seen as either unhelpful or bounteous, with reference to our endeavours, basic in terms of identity and ownership and perhaps also as something rather inert. Cultural geographers tell me that this is a gendered narrative, displaying a male attitude to soil which is akin to women. It is true that the majority of the authors cited are male, but be that as it may, what strikes me is the attribute of passivity and the lack of a notion of any dynamics or vulnerability.

I would maintain first that the negative notions of obduracy and the like prevail; second, that dismissive notions of 'dirt' seem widespread and third that while there are many positive associations of cherishing a growth medium and an expression of identity, there does seem to be a pervading blind spot in the cultural constructions of soil in terms of origins, the time taken for soil to form and of vulnerability. Knut Hamsun does write of the 'growth of soil' but this is more about making what is already there become productive through human toil, and it is also used as a metaphor for the human condition, but there are not even many references to the fragility or vulnerability of the soil, which is actually quite revealing.

In terms of vulnerability, one might observe that soil occupies a conceptual space between the more inert, more durable entities like rock and the more vulnerable, living entities such as vegetation and animals. A literature search for epithets for 'forests' and 'woods' reveals that a conception of vulnerability to loss does exist, with such phrases as 'lose', 'ripping', 'scalp' and 'slash' the forest being not uncommon. King's (2003) book on the botanical vernacular in the English novel abounds with metaphorical references to floral vulnerability. By contrast, in the *Faber Book of Landscape Poetry* (Baker, 2000) references to rocks often use the word 'endure' or 'enduring'.

However, we tend to see solid inanimate objects as being able to provide reassurance through their immutability. As Eagleton (2000: 105) observes, "to compensate for our fragility, we do need to construct forms of solidity in our cultures". In poetry the 'endurance' and solidity of rock seem to perform this function.

Wordsworth does, however, seem to see rock as less enduring. He was geologically aware through his association with the geologist Adam Sedgwick (Park, 2017), acknowledging the forces of nature and the process of weathering: "summits ... are in a rapid process of dissolution ... would in time become levelled with the plains" (Roe, 2002; Wyatt, 1995: 45). W. H. Auden clearly acknowledges that limestone dissolves in water (Baker, 2000: 119). However, in Table 4.2 the epithets for soil which might be grouped under the terms 'unyielding', 'productive' or 'passive' dominate over the few conceptions of fragility and being washed away. It does seem that in general the more 'solid' concepts of soil prevail, with associations of durability rather than any vulnerability.

One might conclude that the conception of soil as an almost inert solid entity means that it can be taken for granted, neglected even, and does not need our care: why worry about conserving soil? Is it not surely durable, infinite – and thus reassuring? This seems to lie at the heart of the paradox that soil is certainly valued but also thereby neglected because it is just 'there'.

However, there is also another paradox involved – in that if the concept of soil formation exists it can give rise to the notion, present in some academic texts, that it is a renewable resource – and therefore just as easily neglected, as perhaps it just re-forms anyway. What seems to be missing here is a clear assessment of the relative timescale of soil formation, which is perhaps unsurprising because, given that soils involve both inorganic and organic components, renewability is a hybrid notion.

The idea that a resource can be viewed as renewable does usually depend upon the timescale over which it might be renewed. A 'geological' resource, such as oil or coal, might be viewed as renewable but only if we wait for several millions of years for new deposits to form, so obviously from a human perspective these are regarded as non-renewable. On the other hand, a biological resource such as grassland can grow back within a few weeks of cutting and thus is regarded as a renewable resource.

Soil erosion can remove several centimetres in one day whereas weathering might provide something of the order of a few millimetres over a timescale involving decades. Paradoxically, what does seem to fool us is that many soils formed so long ago in human terms that to us they do actually seem solid, durable and infinite on a human timescale.

There was also 'Stony Grey Soil' by Patrick Kavanagh (1947: 26) in which "soil" is in part being used metaphorically for his origins and early days, but in which the stony, grey soil "clogged the foot of my boyhood" and "burgled the bank of my youth". Hardly sentiments which display cultural constructs leading to an attitude of cherishing the soil.

It seems somewhat understandable, then, that we do not cherish the soil as much as we should. It is something taken too much for granted, as aspects of our literature show. In truth, in many areas, soil is degraded, either through erosion or by loss of organic matter and hence loss of soil organisms which act to maintain the structure and fertility of the soil, as discussed more extensively in Trudgill (2001b: 151–197). Given that literature shows how we regard soil both as assisting and resisting, it would behove us to dwell more on the former and cherish it – we do rather depend upon it.

4.4 Birds

The way we have looked at birds through time brings to mind the thoughts of the French naturalist Buffon (Georges-Louis Leclerc, Comte de Buffon, 1707–1788) who wrote that an important point in scientific studies is "to know how to distinguish well what there is of the real in a subject and that which we add to it arbitrarily as we consider it; to recognise clearly which properties belong to the subject and which properties we only imagine it to have" (Buffon, 1749; see Lyon and Buffon, 1976: 177). It is important here to note, first, that it can be difficult to tell the difference between the two and, second, that both can provide an emotional response of wonder and a conservation motivation of a sense of care. Scientific study is a powerful tool for understanding and it is also the imagined properties which can provide a sense of engagement. Thus, the understanding of bird behaviour, especially for example migration, can evoke a strong emotive response of awe and there can be just as strong an emotional response about a creature's assumed attributes without scientific understanding being necessary. In Section 3.1 there were examples of the emotions evoked by the song of the nightingale with the many cultural signifiers in Keats's 'Ode to a Nightingale'. However, while Dimbleby (1994) rejoiced in an essay by John Fowles (2000) and cites from it the argument that the poem was more telling than the *Handbook of British Birds*, a competition as to the relative validity of the cultural and the scientific is not helpful because both are significant motivators for conservation.

In trying to distinguish between real and imaginary attributes, it is useful to think about some of the early discussions of the migration of birds as discussed by Bircham (2007) in *A History of Ornithology*. Bircham clearly shows how in the 1800s onwards ornithologists had largely accepted that birds moved with the seasons. However, the observation of swallows flying low over water in the autumn and then disappearing over winter led to a hibernation theory. This even included a search for dormant birds asleep in the mud of ponds or elsewhere in winter. Indeed, in 1769 the naturalist Gilbert White (1720–1793) refers to this in his account of *The Natural History and Antiquities of Selborne* and he spent some considerable time in the field trying to find swallows hibernating (White, 1789). We now know better – and can marvel at migration – and we realise that to protect the bird we have to look at their entire life cycle and address issues in all locations involved. This involves protecting areas in Africa where the swallows migrate to – rather than protecting the mud of ponds where they were putatively hibernating. This understanding is vital to a conservation motivation. The cultural significance then lies in the emotional response of the swallow, especially the first swallow seen, as a harbinger of spring and summer, irrespective of the degree of understanding about migration – and that too is a powerful conservation motivator.

If we think about songbirds such as the nightingale and the skylark, we can know that their songs are proclamations of territory and part of pair-bonding so we can be motivated by thinking about breeding success and the continuation of the species. But it is as much the emotions that the beauty of the sounds brings which are also the conservation motivators. Writing about Keats's 'Nightingale' and Shelley's 'Skylark' in *The Song of the Earth* Jonathan Bate (2000: 93) writes of how a biologist will indeed be able to explain why a lark rises but he talks about the freedom of the lark in his imagination – and how his "heart leaps up" – and his spirit rises, rejoicing as the lark rises. He feels that the freedom of birds is a necessary imagining. Without that rising of spirit as we hear a lark, we would be all the poorer. We need both the scientific understanding and the emotional engagement and the former can be wielded all the more powerfully when enriched with the latter.

'They Speak for Us': Birds and Our Emotions

The engaging thing about birds is that they don't have to be where they are. They can so easily fly away. So, if you see one in a particular place there seems to be some special sense of purpose and significance. Unlike plants which stay where they are as you walk past them, birds are liable to move and tend to fly away – and so if they don't there is an added sense of privilege; they could so easily have moved but they didn't. The fact that they could have so easily been somewhere else readily gives us a sense that somehow they have had a choice and that they are exhibiting some kind of volition. It is thus not a particularly large step to find some kind of omen or other meaning in their presence, as is amply and richly described in Peter Tate's book *Flights of Fancy: Birds in myth, legend and superstition* (Tate, 2007). In *The Value of Birds* (Diamond and Filion,

1987), the wide range of social, economic and cultural valuations is apparent, including food resources, hunting for sport, birds as pest controllers, indicators of the wider ecosystem, aviculture and birds as pets, ornamentation, birds in religion and mythology, the arts and literature. There is also a joy expressed in being with birds and creating and cherishing places for them as, for example, amply expressed in H. J. Massingham's (1924) *Sanctuaries for Birds and How to Make Them.*

There seems to be a bird – or a bird attribute – for a wide range of human moods and emotions. We can think of nest building, protection, security ('nest egg' for savings) and the home; then 'hawkish', 'watchful', 'vigilant' and 'eagle-eyed'. Then there is musical, sweet and light bird song, colourful golden and iridescent plumage, and also birds seen as sacred. In Table 4.1, above, we had 'happy, singing, buoyant, careless glee, soaring, wild, little and wounded' giving ideas of uplifting emotions, freedom and vulnerability. There is also what Simon Barnes (2018: 10) in his book *The Meaning of Birds* calls "flight envy" – wishing we could soar above, as they do. So, we can identify with their activities, share attributes and be influenced by their sounds and activities.

In *The Poetry of Birds* by Armitage and Dee (2009) Simon Armitage in his 'Afterword' (p. 285) writes that

> poets have written about birds from the very beginning; why they have done so is another matter, and probably a matter for speculation rather than certainty. One reason ... is their apparentness. Birds are, for most people, the most frequently seen of all creatures, and it would be virtually impossible to spend a day on Earth without seeing or hearing a bird, no matter what corner of the planet. But the relationship between poetry and birds is more than a function of familiarity. Poets, I believe, seek and find in the world of birds unlimited and unequalled reflections of their own world.

Armitage then goes on to our relationship in more detail. I have grouped his thoughts into fairly direct attributes of birds and then the wider contexts and metaphors (Box 4.4). Any one of these would suffice to engage us but taken together they emphasise our many-faceted commitment.

In order to expand on these themes, using the literature online website as a source (http://literature.proquest.com/) I interrogated the poetry held on that site from 1550 to 2015 for the word 'bird' which gave 19,660 hits, rather proving Armitage's point about poets writing about birds (contrasting with 7,412 for 'soil', as discussed above). From this wealth of sources one can scan through and find such epithets as 'bird

Box 4.4 *Our relationships with birds – groupings derived from the writings of Simon Armitage (Armitage and Dee, 2009)*

Attributes

- Habits and behaviour – mirror certain human tendencies.
- Colours and costumes – a cast of characters.
- Talons and beaks – phobias and fears.

Contexts and metaphors

- Icons – for example, of environmentalism.
- Narratives.
- Shapes and silhouettes.
- Representative of our obsessions and compulsions.

Additionally

- Perhaps at some subconscious level they are also our souls.
- We find in them a sense of 'soaring otherness'. 'Maybe that's how poets think of birds: as poems.'

quick', 'arrow' and 'messenger' for birds and 'bird-brained' and 'hawk-nosed' for people.

Surely most powerful writings on birds are about cages – or the denial of Armitage's 'sense of soaring otherness'. Blake's "A robin redbreast in a cage/ Puts all heaven in a rage" (from 'Auguries of Innocence', published in 1863) hardly needs adding to but the theme is ever rehearsed. Several poems mention many attributes of birds in relation to freedom and metaphorical associations, for example William Lisle Bowles's (1762–1850) 'The Caged Bird': "Oh, who would keep a little bird confined,/ . . . In his cold wiry prison? Let him fly,/ And hear him sing: How sweet is liberty!" (from *The Poetical Works* of 1855).

'The Caged Bird' has both empathy with the encaged and the contrast of human joy at 'free' birdsong with the 'cold, wiry prison' within which the bird is kept – presumably also for human entertainment. Implicit in 'who would keep' is the answer that only a human who is similarly caged, presumably in cities, could keep a bird caged to hear the poor substitute for free birdsong – but a poor substitute is nonetheless welcome as better than nothing in an enclosed man-made environment. The double encagement of the caged man as cager and the caged bird is thus encapsulated. It is thus a commentary on the human condition as well as empathising with nature.

'The Bird Uncaged' contrasts the security of domesticity with the state of liberty, propounding that whatever kindness the human showed was no substitute for the 'natural' state. How we comfort ourselves with domesticated nature which, the poet imagines, will be far happier free. Thus, we contemplate both our needs and the perceived needs of nature. In both these poems mankind has placed itself above nature and controls it, but the poet demurs, speaking for a nature which has no voice. This thus alludes to the human condition, but more, it celebrates nature. Hannah Flagg Gould (1789–1865) wrote 'The Bird Uncaged' and the poem starts with the lines where she empathises with the bird: "She opened the cage, and away there flew/ A bright little bird, as a short adieu/ It hastily whistled, and passed the door,/ And felt that its sorrowful hours were o'er" and the poem ends in a celebration of flight: "'Earth for the wingless! but air for me!'"

'The Flown Bird' by Richard Henry Stoddard (1825–1903) uses the idea of a flown bird to express loss, emotion and grief. Here, the human condition is illustrated through the use of bird characteristics: "My wandering feet ... Through the lone woods, and by the sea,/ To find the bird that fled from me" and then: "The empty nest, if that remains/ And leave me in the long, long rains./ My sleeves with tears are always wet,/ I have forgotten to forget" (from *The Poems*, 1880).

Then we can move to the paradoxical presentation of innocence, evil and corruption which in many places uses aspects of nature in allegorical and metaphorical illustrations. In Blake's 'Auguries of Innocence' (1863) many people know the first six lines:

To see a world in a grain of sand
And a heaven in a wild flower,
Hold infinity in the palm of your hand
And eternity in an hour.
A robin redbreast in a cage
Puts all heaven in a rage.

But equally expressive are:

Each outcry of the hunted hare
A fibre from the brain does tear.
A skylark wounded in the wing,
A cherubim does cease to sing.
The game-cock clipped and armed for fight
Does the rising sun affright.

Birds can speak for us – and indeed we can speak for them.

The Emblematic and Evocative Curlew

Few birds evoke such an emotional response as the curlew. Mary Colwell (2018: 1–4) expresses it in her tribute to the bird and she analyses what it means to us: "There is a wildlife spectacle that can transport the soul to a place of yearning and beauty, to an experience that has inspired generations of thinkers and dreamers." She then describes the curlew – and how it can be seen feeding on the mudflats of estuaries and coasts. "A plump body sits atop stilty legs. The long neck arcs into a small head, which tapers further into an extended curved bill. The smooth, convex outlines of this curlew are alluring." She continues: "But it is not the sight which is astonishing, it is the sound." As well as a bubbling, trilling call there are long, pure notes: "The air is cleaved by a piercing, soul-aching cry – 'curlee, curlee' – that spreads over land and water. It is at once sweet and painful to hear." Colwell cites the poetry of Norman MacCaig's 1987 'Curlew' and Alan McClure's 2011 'Schrodinger's Curlew' which allude to music which is both desolate and beautiful and how the heart leaps and simultaneously breaks.

The title of Colwell's book comes from the scientific name for the curlew *Numenius arquata*. She writes how *Numenius* is the Latinised version of the Greek *neos* for new and *mene* for moon while *arquata* is for the archer's bow, curved as its beak is (Colwell, 2018: 5). The book charts the literary associations with the curlew and its secure place in human emotions and writings; the word 'evocative' might almost have been coined for the associations of its call with moorlands, wild places and winter sea shores. The cultural rationale for the protection of this bird is clear. However, her chapter 10 on 'Curlews and controversy' wrestles with some of the difficulties of conservation in practice, especially in terms of the uses of moorland for walking, recreation, farming and grouse shooting. The book is a tour de force of answers to 'why conserve nature', showing the meanings and motivations which spur the efforts to action.

4.5 Animal Stories

Nature's Independence and the Interchange of Human and Animal Attributes

Our relationship with animals appears to be quite complex. In terms of their actual presence, we seem to value their independence from us but we also domesticate and seek to control them. In metaphorical terms, we see human attributes in animals and we appropriate animal characteristics to describe humans and human conditions. We give them significance and characteristics which tell us as much about ourselves as about the animals. I especially like the quotation from Thoreau about owls. As far I am aware, they hoot as part of their own communication system, but he observed: "I rejoice that there are owls. Let them do the idiotic and maniacal hooting for men. It is a sound admirably suited to swamps and twilight woods which no day illustrates, suggesting a vast and undeveloped nature which men have not recognized. They represent the stark twilight and unsatisfied thoughts which we all have" (Thoreau, *Walden*, [1854]1981: 114).

One of the best papers I have read which makes a lot of sense about this complexity is that of Jamie Lorimer on 'Nonhuman charisma' (2006, 2007). He provides a three-part typology of non-human charisma, comprising ecological, aesthetic and corporeal charisma. This to my mind incorporates both the sense of difference from and identification with animals. It contains the reflexive relationship between the sense of other and a sense of ourselves. He describes how there is another creature, independent from us and which we react to in some way, where not only is its independence valued, there is also our identification with some of its attributes, recognising both ours in them and theirs in us. This sharpens and focusses our understanding of the creature in terms of both similarities and differences. There is also a tension between wildness and domestication/obedience to our will. Again, there is a duality where we greatly value the freedom and wildness of a creature, often tinged with fear and awe, while also keeping selected animals in domestic situations either as pets or as a resource for food or some other product. Here, while we may value performance and provision there may be a special sense of privilege when something which is putatively wild actually comes to us. We can easily think of a pack animal such as a dog which may follow us readily and contrast this with the more independent cat; the latter seems to bestow some kind of privilege upon us when it comes to us and sits on our lap. Equally, a close contact with something wild seems to bestow a sense of privilege (see, e.g., Fisher, 1998, on the aesthetics of rare experiences).

There are nature writers who have attempted to 'get into the mind of' a variety of animals while others are anthropomorphic and anthropocentric, though the divisions are not clear-cut. The endeavour of attempting to see things from the animal's point of view brings to mind J. A. Baker's *The Peregrine* (1967, 2005), Williamson's *Tarka the Otter* (1927), *The*

Peregrine's Saga (1923) and *Salar the Salmon* (1935). To name but a few others in the animal stories genre, there is the more recent *River Singers* (Moorhouse, 2014), which is in the English nature writing tradition, and in the USA Batten's (1924) *Dramas of the Wild Folk*, Jack London's *White Fang* and companion story *The Call of the Wild* (London, 1903, 1939). These are in contrast to the more anthropomorphic *Wind in the Willows* by Kenneth Graham (1908) and Beatrix Potter's (1902) *Peter Rabbit* tales and the more anthropocentric Ernest Thompson Seton's (1906) *Wild Animals I Have Known* and Arthur H. Beavan's (1905) *Animals I Have Known*.

For Beavan, both wild and domesticated animals are covered and those from different countries. Extraordinarily from our modern perspective, one of the main endeavours throughout the book is to shoot the animals he finds "for the purpose of securing specimens" (Beavan, 1905: 249) – and our museums with their stuffed animals are testament to that era. There is some anthropomorphism but little empathy, except perhaps for some more pitiful sights of younger creatures which were orphaned by the shootings. Nevertheless, there is a respect and tenderness of observation towards the animals in question – and the practice of shooting for specimens was unquestioned and axiomatic at the time of writing.

Seton's book relates stories based on experience and actual events and includes people and so this is one stage back from an immersive writing. It sees animals from a human point of view and tends to the anthropomorphic. Nevertheless, he writes: "How many of us have ever got to know a wild animal? I do not mean merely to meet with one once or twice, or to have one in a cage, but to really know it for a long time while it is wild, and to get an insight into its life history" (Seton, 1906: 59). He continues that we have an advantage in this endeavour if an animal has a distinctive mark or characteristic so that we can recognise it. He then narrates and muses on myriad observations which have been made and understands the animals through interpreting their behaviour. The narratives are graphic and involve the words 'proud', 'handsome', 'the crows know', 'ever wise' 'the younger birds begin to really love' [the older, wiser bird]. To balance this, Mark Cocker's (2007) *Crow Country* chronicles not only the crow but also the contribution of the crow to a sense of place, with assiduous observations and a great understanding of both the bird's biology and also its significance to us.

In his 'Introduction' to *The Peregrine* (Baker, 1967, 2005) Robert Macfarlane (2005: vii) writes that "as an account of a human obsession with a creature, it is peerless". He sees it as "not a book about watching a bird, it is a book about becoming a bird" and notes that "Baker hopes that, through a fierce, prolonged, and 'purified' concentration upon the peregrine, he will somehow be able to escape from human form and abscond into the 'brilliant' wildness of the bird." Throughout the book, however, Baker is present as 'I' the narrator. In Williamson's writings the narrator is not present as such. You, the reader, walk with the otter, hunt with the peregrine and swim with the salmon and thus you feel the water around you and can see the land down there before you as you fly, and sense the currents in which you swim. Similarly, the *River Singers* has no narrator.

In a review of Tom Moorhouse's *The River Singers* Linda Buckley-Archer (2014) highlights the remarkable achievement of the author – to be scientifically accurate, to empathise with the animals, to see things from their point of view – and even succeed in giving them dialogue without deserting their essential animality and without "putting the voles in waistcoats". The review continues: "Tom Moorhouse is an Oxford-based ecologist and expert on water voles, something that, in itself, makes this novel noteworthy. Moorhouse's love of nature and the countryside shines through in many of the lyrical passages devoted to the water vole's habitat." Most interestingly, the reviewer feels that: "Moorhouse combines a scientist's approach with that of a storyteller who is not afraid of a little anthropomorphism. ... In fact, Moorhouse succeeds in informing with a light touch ... [he does not] shy away from painting nature in her true colours." Indeed, reading the book myself, I well sensed the terror of a vole as the heron, with its dagger-like beak, was overhead, looking for something to eat.

In *The Call of the Wild* (London, 1903) the central character of the novel is a dog named Buck. The story opens at a ranch in the Santa Clara Valley of California when Buck is stolen from his home and sold into service as a sled dog in Alaska. He progressively reverts to a wild state in the harsh climate, where he is forced to fight to dominate other dogs. By the end, he sheds the veneer of civilization and relies on primordial instinct and learned experience to emerge as a leader in the wild. The story of *White Fang* is mostly written from the viewpoint of the animal and takes place in Yukon Territory, Canada, during the 1890s Klondike Gold Rush. It details White Fang's journey to domestication and thus can be seen as a 'mirror' to *Call of the Wild*. By reversing the story in the two accounts, these books provide thoughtful insights into the nature of our relationship with domesticated animals and the dialogue between their instincts and learned experiences.

A book published in 2016 by Charles Foster – *Being a Beast* – has chapters where he empathises successively with a badger, otter, fox, red deer and swift. He does this by living, in so far as this is possible, like the animals in question – for example, living in a hole in the earth and eating earthworms or catching and eating fish with his teeth. He critiques anthropocentrism and anthropomorphism and has a whole chapter devoted to the pitfalls of his approach in that he is irrevocably limited by being a man. Nonetheless, the result is a very interesting exercise in gaining insights from trying to see the world from the animals' perspectives.

In terms of the reflexivity between human and animal attributes, we may usefully turn to the poetic writings of the Californian poet Robinson Jeffers. Here we find the metaphorical technique in the attribution of animal characteristics to human perverse drives, as in the 1937 poem 'Sinverguenza' (shameless/brazen rogue/scoundrel/villain) from the volume *Such Counsels You Gave to Me and Other Poems* (Jeffers, 1989). Here, Jeffers speaks of the Spanish Civil War in such ways as: "They snarl over Spain like cur-dogs over a bone" and "wolf-fierce, cobra-deadly and monkey-shameless" (p. 458; Brøgger, 2009: 145), thus giving powerful animal imagery to the protagonists he is describing. In the paper 'The cultural contamination of the language of nature: Dos Passos's *Manhattan Transfer* and Jeffers' nature poems' by Brøgger (2009: 145) the author writes: "Thus, in his poetry Jeffers does not only attribute anthropomorphic qualities to animals, he attributes animalistic qualities to human beings. … [He] ends up affirming the human-oriented position that it [the poetry] appears to reject." Brøgger adds that "Jeffers' inhumanism [manifests itself as a] passionate balancing of the inanimate world and the animating mind" (as described by Rothman, 1995: 51).

Robinson Jeffers also wrote 'Orca', which, to me, celebrates the nature of orcas (the killer whale or orca: *Orcinus orca*), also writing of the 'flying vipers' as an evocation of human war: "Silently like a shadow into the sea-gorge./ It had the shape, the size, and it seemed the speed/ Of one of those flying vipers with which the Germans lashed London." However, he continues detaching the orca from human motivations in saying that while there was death and terror, it was "clean and bright, it was beautiful" because "there was nothing human involved … / no lies, no smirk and no malice". He thus sees the animal with a kind of purity he obviously feels we lack, saying that it was all "strict and decent; the will of man had nothing to do here" (see https://robinsonjeffersassociation.org/his-writing/poetry/orca).

The New Zealand poet Chris Orsman also writes about orcas in his poem 'He Gazes into the Depths' (Orsman, 1999: 47). He uses the word 'infested', with its negative connotations but, to me, the poem is neither celebratory nor judgemental in any way; more questioning of the relationship between himself and the animals and is thus an appropriately poised equivocation: "The orca-infested sea/ he gazes into and is gazed at" and then: "a killer-whale surfaces its head/ and leans on the ice-foot, its right eye/ steady on the stranger."

In recent times the killer whale or orca, also referred to as the orca whale or blackfish, has been the focus of much media attention and discussion. It is a toothed oceanic predatory organism and the largest member of the dolphin family. Its high intelligence is valued and as such has been kept and trained as a performing animal seen as a spectacle by many, notably for example in 'Sea World' in San Diego, California and elsewhere. Films such as *Free Willy* and *Blackfish* have made 'performing' orcas in 'captivity' controversial with moves to ban their continuation as such. This kind of situation pretty much sums up our ambiguous relationship with such a creature and encapsulates the contrasting values which different people may simultaneously hold about the same creature. Without the 'performance' aspect many people who do not otherwise 'visit nature' would not see and appreciate them; others see the human-induced 'performance' as degrading. Yet others spend hours on boat trips just to see the orca in the wild – but even here there can be a sense of performance: if these are not seen to breach – jump above the surface – and just their fins show, there is a sense of disappointment and, crucially, the lack of a photograph which is now expected as evidence of an authentic experience. What, in fact, is being celebrated? It is a curious mixture of wildness, freedom, performance and privilege. The 'best' aspect is often seen as an 'authentic' experience, with photograph, of a free, wild animal, performing. An experience of a free, wild animal not performing is good and a valued privilege but may be somewhat disappointing, especially if photographic evidence is deficient. The experience of performing animals in a Seaworld situation is endearing and entertaining with narratives abounding such as 'isn't marvellous how they do that' or 'they get them to do that'. But there is an unease for some people thinking in terms of narratives of captivity and loss of freedom. And so still, in this complex relationship, people flocked to the cinema to see the film of, or otherwise watch the DVD of, *Free Willy* and *Blackfish* about orcas going free while others have flocked to Seaworld.

Box 4.5 *Modes of engagement with animals, derived from Beardsworth and Bryman (2001)*

- *Encounter* – actual physical proximity to a distant glimpse. This may be commonplace, unusual or specifically sought, such as on an animal safari.
- *Representation* – from the depiction in art to the wildlife documentary. Human values may well influence the type and impact of the mediated image.
- *Presentation* – the captivity of an animal which is subject to a high level of human scrutiny, such as in a zoo.
- *Quasification* – animal as artifice such as stuffed animals in natural history museums, animatronic animals in theme parks and soft toys.

There is a strong modern theme of what might be called the 'Disneyisation' of nature following the success of the Walt Disney cartoon films; see, for example, Whitley (2008, 2012) on *The Idea of Nature in Disney Animation*. This then filters through into how we treat real nature. Beardsworth and Bryman (2001) write of 'The wild animal in late modernity: The case of the Disneyization of zoos'. They have four principal 'modes of engagement' between humans and animals: encounter, representation, presentation and quasification (Box 4.5):

These modes are not seen as mutually exclusive and indeed interact but provide useful ways in which we may think of human–animal relationships. Often the 'commodification' of animals can be involved and the authors engage with 'Disneyisation', stemmed from idealised cartoon characters (see also Whitley, 2008, 2012) to the theme park where there are four trends: (1) theming with a master narrative – for example, 'jungle', 'sea world' 'penguin', 'tropical' and so on; (2) de-differentiation of consumption where the animal theme is undifferentiated from other themes and experiences of consumption and entertainment; (3) merchandising; and (4) what they term 'emotional labour' which refers to "the worker's control of the self which is geared to expressing socially desired emotions in the course of service transactions". The paper cites the "smiling, ever helpful 'cast members'". They conclude with a discussion of 'wild' as a theme where wildness is "re-invented and reformulated, rendered playful and engaging . . . it becomes available for safe and easy consumption" (Beardsworth and Bryman, 2001: 96–98). Even the dangerous and threatening aspects of 'wildness' are themselves sanitized and rendered harmless and entertaining.

It seems to me that the key elements become the entertainment orientation with an associated desire to promote conservation – the reservation is, however, not of wildness but as a 'fun day out' where nature is presented packaged and commodified.

The obverse of animals as entertainment is the rejection of animals with the use of such terms as vermin or, more recently, *Trash Animals*. This is the title of a book edited by Kelsi Nagy and Phillip David Johnson II with a subtitle of *How we live with nature's filthy, feral, invasive, and unwanted species* (Nagy and Johnson, 2013). The list of species includes pigeons, prairie dogs, gulls, wolves, coyotes, carp, cockroaches, magpies, rats and spiders. The associative emotions seem fairly clear – many species are scavengers, without which there might be far more carrion lying around, and beyond that there are attributes of competition with humans and qualities seen as less than admirable such as furtiveness, shuffling, unpredictability rather than the, say, soaring qualities of an eagle. Here it seems to me that the transfer of negative human qualities to animals which may otherwise be performing useful functions is clear and writ rather large.

4.6 Plants

Associations and Meanings

Many of the associations attached to individual plants involve a given symbolism and some have become significant eponymously. Geoffrey 'Plantagenet', who married King Henry I of England's daughter Matilda, received his nickname from the yellow sprig of broom blossom he wore in his hat, *genêt* being the French name for the broom plant or *planta genista*.

The rose is one of the objects in nature that has perhaps had one of the longest histories of varied associative meanings including luxury, seduction, romantic love, secrecy, death, rebirth, sexuality (both same sex and male–female), Christianity, power – see Table 4.3, below and, for example: https://en.wikipedia.org/wiki/Rose_(symbolism) and www.pinpush.com/symbols/artSymbol-Rose.htm.

In Sarah Maguire's (2003: xxv) *Flora Poetica: The Chatto book of botanical verse* the author writes of "flowers as metaphors of femininity because the cultural associations linking flowers and women were, and are, so

Table 4.3 *Epithets of flowers (modified from Pickston, 1968)*

ANEMONE – Forsaken
BLUEBELL – Humility
CROCUS – Cheerfulness
DAFFODIL – Regard; Unrequited Love; You're the Only One; The Sun Is Always Shining When I'm with You
DAISY – Innocence; Loyal Love; I'll Never Tell; Purity
DANDELION – Faithfulness; Happiness
FORGET-ME-NOT – True Love; Memories
HEATHER Purple – Admiration; Solitude
HEATHER White – Protection; Wishes Will Come True
IRIS – Your Friendship Means So Much to Me; Faith; Hope; Wisdom and Valour; My Compliments
LILY-OF-THE-VALLEY – Sweetness; Tears of the Virgin Mary; Return to Happiness; Humility; You've Made My Life Complete
MISTLETOE – Kiss Me; Affection; To Surmount Difficulties; Sacred Plant of India; Magic Plant of the Druids
MONKSHOOD – Beware; A Deadly Foe Is Near
NARCISSUS – Egotism; Formality; Stay as Sweet as You Are
ORCHID – Love; Beauty; Refinement; Beautiful Lady
POPPY General – Eternal Sleep; Oblivion; Imagination
PRIMROSE – I Can't Live Without You
ROSE (according to colour) – Happy Love; Ambassador of Love; Mourning; Thankfulness; Enchantment; Modesty; Grace; Joy; Love; Respect; I Love You; I Still Love You; Remember; Always; Love at First Sight; Innocence and Secrecy; England; Joy; Friendship
ROSEBUD – Beauty and Youth; A Heart Innocent of Love; Confessions of Love; Pure and Lovely; Girlhood
VIOLET- Modesty; Watchfulness; Faithfulness; I'll Always Be True, Let's Take a Chance on Happiness

deep-seated as to be almost unquestioned". Gendered narratives abound but mostly in poems written by men about women – the bloom delicate, fragile, transient – the beautiful rose famously accompanied by cruel prickles, petals soon to fade, profligate, sweetest, perfumed, fragrant, and so on are all very well rehearsed. The 'petals soon to fade' aspect is writ large in Robert Herrick's 'To the Virgins, to Make Much of Time' ('Gather Ye Rosebuds') of 1648:

Gather ye rosebuds while ye may,
Old time is still a-flying:
And this same flower that smiles to-day
To-morrow will be dying.

Trees by comparison are often masculine – "prickly, hairy, phallic or imposingly large" writes Maguire (2003: xxviii). Aside from these more obvious connotations, Maguire also cites the ways in which "poets use plants to articulate issues of power other than those of gender". She cites the Irish poet Tom Paulin writing about juniper as the tree of freedom, admiring the way it ducks its head down and "skirts/ the warped politics of other trees/ bent in the Atlantic wind". Lynching is remembered in the form of a haunted oak by Afro-American poets while the seeds of the jacaranda tree, which "explode when trodden underfoot", are used by two African poets as metaphors of political violence following suppression. Maguire also cites the powerful metaphors associated with colonialism: transplantation, uprooting, replanting, roots – and so not only plants native to the European colonists planted abroad but also the individual qualities of the native species in colonised areas assume symbolic significance. Plants transported to Europe and especially England from the colonies also assume a significance – the exotic, perfumed and the sensuous narratives associated with the larger showy blooms – such as camellias and orchids – become conflated with femininity, allure and desirability – but not without a hint of treachery. This is also curiously at odds with the narratives of aliens and invasive – presumably if these 'wanton' species have escaped from the confines – maybe the hothouse/ greenhouse – or is it the harem – and run wild over our British countryside. This is an interesting possible insight into the narratives of invasive species.

In *The Poet as Botanist* Mahood (2008) explores the botanical poetic themes especially associated with Wordsworth, Crabbe, John Clare, Ruskin and D. H. Lawrence. Reading through Mahood's book it becomes progressively astonishing how plants became endowed with associations but in part it makes more sense if we remember the 'doctrine of signatures' – the idea that plants were placed on this earth for human use and that God had left a sign to us to show what they were to be used for. Thus, lungwort has leaves which look like the blotchiness of lungs so clearly that this plant was designed to cure lung disease; there is also eyebright, woundwort, liverwort, spleenwort and toothwort (see, e.g., the discussion by Court (1985) in 'The doctrine of signatures or similitudes'). The idea of plants having signs relating to their use was recorded when the Ancient Greek Dioscorides (*c.* AD 40–90), a physician, pharmacologist and botanist wrote *De Materia Medica* on herbal medicine. Galen (AD 129–*c.* 200/216), well known for laying many foundational principles of the medicine of the time, also acknowledged the idea. Paracelsus (1491–1541) developed the concept, writing that "Nature marks each growth ... according to its curative benefit." The writings of Jakob Böhme (1575–1624) spread the doctrine of signatures and that God marked objects with a sign, or 'signature', for their purpose. It was his 1621 book *The Signature of All Things* that gave its name to the doctrine. A later reinforcement of the idea was by botanists like William Coles (1626–1662) asserting that God would have wanted to show men what plants would be useful for.

It is therefore no particular surprise that plants should become imbued with a plethora of metaphors, associations and literary allusions. Apart from medical and abundant poetic allusions, the associations actually became codified in Edwardian and Victorian times as is recorded in books, for example *The Language of Flowers* (Pickston, 1968; see also http://thelanguageofflowers.com/). Epithets vary with the sources used but it is notable how the characteristics of the plant do in many cases suggest an attached symbolism, for example prickly holly being about defence, though the Pickston book has 'foresight' for holly. In all sources it is the rose which is easily the most diverse, the epithet often varying markedly with the colour of the rose. For English wild flowers the epithets are shown in Table 4.3.

The folklore and local names of plants abound, quite apart from the Doctrine of Signatures, as recorded in 1958 by Geoffrey Grigson and the several editions since (e.g. Grigson, [1958]1975, *The Englishman's Flora*). Grigson quotes widely from *Culpepper's* [*sic*] *Herbal*. Nicholas Culpeper (1616–1654) was an English botanist, herbalist, physician and astrologer who wrote the *Complete Herbal* in 1653, now widely available in numerous editions. Many of the local names refer to physical attributes such as colour or similarities with other objects, such as bonnets or indeed some kind of suggested function – as with the lesser celandine which was hung in cow's byres to increase milk yield – its roots resembling cows' udders: "clusters of four bulbs like the four teats of a cow" (Grigson, [1958]1975: 51) and the associated names involving butter, cream and cheese, though these are also suggested by the yellow colour.

Margaret Baker's (1971: 24) *Discovering the Folklore of Plants* rehearses, inter alia, how elder is considered "an unlucky tree in the house, perhaps because it was the wood from which the Cross" was made for the Crucifixion of Jesus; this is interesting as biblical scholars tell me that the wood used is not given in the Bible, though there are some traditions that involve cedar, pine and cypress and also dogwood (though both elder and dogwood seem unlikely candidates to me as they are rather shrubby in habit and possibly unlikely to yield significant timbers). Even more whimsically, the elm was associated with elves, hawthorn is a magical tree and smoke from a juniper wood fire kept off demons. There is a more recent book with updated information by Roy Vickery (2019): *Vickery's Folk Flora: An A–Z of the folklore and uses of British and Irish plants*. Jonathan Silvertown's (2009) *An Orchard Invisible: A natural history of seeds* also provides useful insights into stories involving seeds as well as discussing our scientific knowledge of seeds. Paul Evans's (2014) *Herbaceous* has sections on each plant with poetic associations. The books by Richard Mabey provide extensive information including his volume of *Flora Britannica* (Mabey, 1998) together with his *Weeds: How vagabond plants gatecrashed civilisation and changed the way we think about nature* (Mabey, 2010) and *The Cabaret of Plants: Botany and the imagination* (Mabey, 2015).

We have rehearsed earlier in the book the observation by Evernden (1992: 107) of how the Enlightenment seemingly destroyed a lot of earlier superstitions, but yet in a sense I feel we have replaced one set of superstitions with another. Let us examine Evernden's words again: "By eroding the old vocabulary, with its rich symbolic overtones, the naturalists had completed their onslaught on the long established notion that nature was responsive to human affairs. This was the most important and most destructive way in which they shattered the assumptions of the past." Yes, the old assumptions were shattered but the new assumptions were just as strong – the balance of nature, diversity, stability and all the other mantras. He continued:

> In place of a natural world redolent with human analogy and symbolic meaning and sensitive to man's behaviour, they constructed a detached natural scene to

be viewed and studied by the observer from the outside, as if by peering through a window, in the secure knowledge that the objects of contemplation inhabited a separate realm, offering no omens or signs [and] without human meaning or significance.

One just has to think of current nature narratives to realise that human analogy, symbolic meaning and sensitivity to man's behaviour are still dominant today – if not so much in terms of flowers, then just think of the climate change narratives.

4.7 Seas and Oceans

Cultural Associations: Awesome, Infinite, Threatening and Bountiful – But Not Vulnerable

As with any part of nature, an understanding of how we see the sea helps us to understand how we treat it. Of all the deeply held cultural associations of the sea, the 'sea as vulnerable' does not spring to mind – and so it is unsurprising if we do not treat it as such. The 'sea under threat' has only arisen through contemporary awareness of, for example, oil and plastic pollution and of coral bleaching rather than through cultural associations which have tended to stress the power and infinity of the sea. Indeed, it could be argued that our cultural associations have not only hindered our protection of the seas but have also actively helped in causing pollution and harm to wildlife.

So, what do we understand about how we see the sea – and thus how we treat it? 'Endless', 'boundless' and 'infinite' certainly seem to feature highly, so we can already see how this assists the idea of disposal of waste at sea – which will surely disappear in this limitless place. We also have 'gaze out to sea', 'the open sea' and 'the call of the sea'. So, there is also mystery, wonder and allure. And then we also have threat, confusion and unknowingness. In an introduction to Conrad's *Sea Stories* the human struggle against the sea is seen by Carabine (1998: vii) as about "seamen whose solidarity and endurance are tested by the sea and all its works". The phrase 'the cruel sea' is well known, not least from Nicholas Monsarrat's (1951) novel of that title, as is 'lost at sea'. The *Encyclopedia of the Oceans* (Stow, 2004: 10) uses the descriptors: "savage and powerful, serene and beautiful"; the hostile environment is seen as populated by monsters, such as Leviathan in the Bible and the Kraken of Norse mythology. We also have 'unfathomable'; indeed, psychiatrist Carl

Jung saw the sea in dreams as symbolising the personal and the collective unconscious. 'All at sea', 'a sea of faces', 'sea change', 'ebb and flow' and 'going against the tide' all extend the ideas derived from the sea to human situations. In *The Sea: A cultural history* (Mack, 2011: 72–104) the author has a very useful chapter on 'Concepts of the sea' which covers the range of 'barbaric' sea as "unwelcome and unwelcoming wilderness" as contrasted with a more Pacific Island view of sea as "entirely familiar and unthreatening". These are the two extremes but he says "conceptions are multiple" and include the "ancestral sea", "the sea will provide", "the sea as territory" and the sea being endued with remoteness as part of the "uttermost ends of the earth".

This combination of threat and allure shows that, throughout history, as with many aspects of nature, humans have seen the sea as both assisting and resisting. The sea enables travel to distant lands and also affords strategic protection. It provides resources like food and salt. However, it resists our will through storms and shipwrecks and in terms of the erosion of coasts we value. We have 'the threat of rising sea levels' and 'coastal retreat' – retreat implying inevitable loss in the face of an impalpable enemy. There is thus an ambiguous, almost confusing and contradictory, view of ocean and seas.

In literature, we have well-known examples such as the familiar "Water, water, everywhere ... Nor any drop to drink" from Samuel Taylor Coleridge's 1798 poem 'The Rime of the Ancient Mariner'. John Masefield's poem 'Sea Fever' begins: "I must go down to the seas again, to the lonely sea and the sky" and in his 1902 poem 'The Sea and the Hills', Rudyard Kipling wrote of desire for the sea – "the sight of salt water unbounded/ The heave and the halt and the hurl and the crash of the comber wind-hounded". In *Poems of The Sea* (McClatchy, 2001) the items are grouped under the headings: 'Sea Fever' (with John Masefield's poem of that title); The Call of the Deep' (where John Keats writes of "eternal whisperings"); 'Storm and Calm'; 'Ballads'; 'Songs and Chanteys'; 'Anthem, Prayer, Hymn'; 'Seafarers'; 'Wrecks'; 'Legends'; 'Above and Beyond'; and 'Reading the Waves' including 'Neither Out Far Nor in Deep' by Robert Frost and Stevie Smith's 'Not Waving but Drowning'. The duality of allure and threat is very evident.

In art we have the same themes. The Japanese artist Katsushika Hokusai's *The Great Wave off Kanagawa* shows the destructive force of the sea as well as its majesty and beauty, as described by Clark (2011). The art critic John Ruskin described the strengths of J. M. W. Turner's sea paintings as "terror and repose". Indeed, in *Turner and the Sea*

(Riding, 2013) Christine Riding writes that "the juxtaposition of 'storm' and 'calm' have a long tradition in marine painting". She also observes that the wide and diverse range of paintings which Turner produced was derived from the nature of the sea itself "given its supreme changeability and elusiveness". In a cultural study of the sea Mentz (2009: 1001) recognises that the ocean is "a space of abundance and recovery", with phrases such as 'the provident sea' and 'full of fishes' but he argues that "many ancient texts define the sea through its basic inhospitability to human life, especially in traditions that link the sea to primeval chaos". Early visions of paradise "hail a utopian future when 'there will be no more sea'". Thus, the seas are places of tranquillity, provision and abundance while also being unfathomable places of change, death, threat and terror.

At the shore we experience a special relationship between being in one world on the edge of another and being able to sense it in all its changeability – tidal ebb and flow, waves lapping, edge of the sea, 'at the seaside', 'beside the sea' – contemplating something greater than ourselves while literally having our feet safely on the ground. In Victor Hugo's (1866: 213) *Toilers of The Sea* the central character, Gilliatt, contemplates the sea. The text is that "nothing is more disturbing to the mind than the contemplation of the diffusion of forces at work in the unfathomable and illimitable space of the ocean". He writes of how the mind seeks to understand the "unceasing movement" and "vast prodigality of effort" and how the "ebb and flow of these questionings is eternal, as the flux and reflux of the sea itself". All this occurs amidst the "terrible ... perpetual recommencement" in the "Infinite Unknown". Mentz (2009: 1003) argues that "the oceans ... figure the boundaries of human transgression; they function symbolically as places in the world into which mortal bodies cannot safely go". The sea as representing the boundaries of our knowledge and influence, but not the boundaries of our imaginings, is well expressed in a book on the literary and historical imaginings of the North Sea (Ritson, 2019: 27). The boundaries of our influence are discussed by reference to *The Rider on the White Horse* by Theodor Storm (*Der Schimmelreiter*, 1888; trans. Wright, 1964) where the central character Hauke takes pride in implementing the construction of dykes to protect the land from the sea. Later, in a storm surge, some dykes break and his wife and daughter are swept away. Driven to despair, he rides on his white horse into the sea and is himself lost. Later, there are associated stories of a ghostly rider on a white horse haunting the area. While many of the dykes stand firm and protect many people this is an evocative story of hubris, resistance and loss in the face of an implacable sea. Ritson also focusses on the metaphorical significance of the story of King Canute, unable to hold back the tide: "humans on the edge of the shore, at the limits of their agency" – and the power which this imagery has in our imagination.

The lack of our agency appears in Shakespeare's *The Winter's Tale* in the line often quoted in writings on the sea: "To unpath'd waters, undream'd shores" (Act 4, Scene 3; first performance 1611; first folio 1623). The context epitomises the metaphor of 'being all at sea', in this case emotionally:

CAMILLO: A course more promising
Than a wild dedication of yourselves
To unpath'd waters, undream'd shores, most certain
To miseries enough; no hope to help you.

There is a modern version (www.sparknotes.com/nofear/shakespeare/winterstale/page_204) which may be more accessible, and while this loses the classic 'unpathed waters' has the equally explicit 'unmarked waters':

CAMILLO: It's a much more promising way of doing things than simply throwing yourself on unmarked waters and strange shores, which will certainly lead you to plenty of misery.

A sense of sea as 'other' is identifiable. Mentz (2009: 1001) discusses citations in Raban's (1992) *Oxford Book of the Sea* and asserts that Ariel's song in Shakespeare's *The Tempest* "captures this early modern understanding of sea as pure alterity". Mentz also cites *Richard III* where "Clarence's vision of submarine opulence" – gold, pearls and jewels – is presented along with: "Methought what pain it was to drown!" Mentz concludes that: "Seeing the sea as simultaneously wealth and death highlights two early modern patterns of maritime symbology: the sea is a highway to commercial prosperity and also a vision of God's torment." Others have seen the sea as symbolic of the self: Shalini Sharma (2002: 31) in *George Eliot's Novels: Language and meaning* writes of the sea as "Eternal and Uncharitable" and that the "the sea is part of the iconography of the self" with the sea as a representation of the self and "death by drowning is indicative of self-destruction."

The sense of other and the identification with the unfathomable ocean as a metaphor for the human condition is admirably summed up by Longfellow in 'The Sound of the Sea' (1920):

So comes to us at times, from the unknown
And inaccessible solitudes of being,
The rushing of the sea-tides of the soul;
And inspirations, that we deem our own,
Are some divine foreshadowing and foreseeing
Of things beyond our reason or control.

Purification and Pollution

These cultural associations give evidence of the sea as something very much beyond us and bigger than us and something detached from our sphere of influence; something to be held in awe. The sense of infinity is beguiling. If, however, you combine the idea of 'infinity' with the idea of the irretrievable 'lost at sea', one begins to understand our human tendency to regard the sea as a 'dumping ground' for our waste – once lost, never to be seen again. It is small wonder, then, that we have taken time to realise that the apparent infinity and resilience of the seas are indeed illusory. Our deep-rooted cultural associations of the unfathomably deep and infinite sea have indeed hindered our appreciation of the vulnerability of the seas. It is only in relatively recent decades that there has been a growing realisation that they have a finite capacity to absorb the results of our activity, not least our waste products, and mighty and fearful as storms are, that the seas contain life forms vulnerable to our influence.

Mack's (2011) book *The Sea: A cultural history* includes a section on 'polluting, cleaning and transforming the sea'. Here, the author provides further useful insights from the past. "For the Ancient Greeks the sea had, as Semonides [an early Greek poet] described it, two faces. . . . On the one hand polluting and polluted aspects, on the other it had cleansing properties" (Mack, 2011: 91–92). The sea could indeed be seen as a kind of 'sewer'. The polluting aspect was seen as "teeming with low-life born of its rotting substance and accompanying stench". One calls to mind rotting seaweed cast up on the shore after a storm. As polluted "it was a place to dispose of corrupted substances". The example cited is of bronze statues of people no longer valued and cast into the waters – and thus erased from public memory. So, the sea is part of purification – of purging from the memory.

The Greek mythology of the sea also involves powerful gods and the notion of changeability. The god of the sea, Poseidon, seems to epitomise the shifting character of the sea, presiding not only over the sea, but also earthquakes, storms and horses. Another Greek sea-god, Proteus, embodies sea change; "protean" meaning able to assume many forms. Shakespeare picks up on these stories and in *Henry VI, Part 3*, Richard III says: "I can add colours to the chameleon,/ Change shapes with Proteus for advantages". Ariel's Song in Act 1, Scene 2 of Shakespeare's *The Tempest* is also often quoted in this context of change:

Full fathom five thy father lies;
Of his bones are coral made;
Those are pearls that were his eyes;
Nothing of him that doth fade,
But doth suffer a sea-change
Into something rich and strange.

Moreover, Mack maintains that the sea is a place of "deeper waters" and "places of no return". The sea can also be "a space of forgetting" – there is a sense that the sea has no history as it "lacks archaeological remains and accessible monuments". So, we have understandably built our sewers to discharge out to sea and chucked all sorts of things overboard, never to be seen again. It also possibly accounts for a sense of denial when items thought to be 'disposed of' are found on the tide line. It has taken plastic, not least the plastic ducks lost overboard and then found scattered globally (Ebbesmeyer, 2006; Ebbesmeyer and Ingraham, 1994; Hohn, 2012) and David Attenborough's TV programmes (BBC, 2018) to alert us to a truer situation.

Before the 1970s many widely available scientific writings did not seem to see the sea as vulnerable. One might think that Rachel Carson, who did so much to alert the world to the dangers of pesticides in her book *Silent Spring* (Carson, 1962), might have written about such an idea. However, the concept hardly features – and is certainly not prominent – in her writings on the sea from 1941 to 1955 as, for example, published in a compendium volume: *The Sea* (Carson, 1964). Equally, the books on the sea in the renowned New Naturalist Series show little such awareness. In Hardy's (1958) *The Open Sea: Part I – The world of plankton* and his (1959) *The Open Sea: Part II – Fish and fisheries* the former sounds no warning bells and the latter focusses on food chains and fisheries and looks ahead to fisheries development in relation to new research and technology. In Yonge's (1949) book *The Sea Shore* debris might afford an interesting habitat on a sandy shore but human concerns seem confined to the economy of the shore and shellfish. More obviously, Steer's (1962) *The Sea Coast* is more about the vulnerability of the land to the sea.

Marine pollution did feature in the United Nations' Conventions on the Law of the Sea from the 1950s onwards but the conventional wisdom was that the seas were so vast that they had an infinite capacity to dilute and thus render pollutants harmless. However, some events created global headlines, such as the wreck of the oil tanker the *Torrey Canyon* in 1967 (Smith, 1968) but legislation about dumping of waste at sea only realistically began to develop in the early 1970s. The Royal Commission on Environmental Pollution was formed in 1970 (Owens, 2015) the same year which saw the first volume of the *Marine Pollution Bulletin* published, covering oil pollution, effects on fisheries and pesticide pollution.

A key event was a conference at The Royal Society in London on 'Pollution at Sea' (Cole, 1971), a conference which I well remember attending where there was a growing awareness of the idea that the sea was indeed not an infinite dumping ground. There was interest in the capacity of the sea to absorb pollution and the awareness that organic material can decompose, and indeed provide a stimulus to food chains, but it is the more persistent chemical elements and man-made substances which do not decompose which present the biggest threats. Cole (1971: 227–228) wrote that "it is difficult to reach a balanced appreciation of the extent to which it is reasonable to use the sea for waste disposal" and that "we need to know a great deal more than we do at present about the waste reaching the sea, where it is coming from, what is happening to it and what effects it is producing". There is, however, the central idea that: "The sea fortunately has a great capacity to dilute and disperse wastes." A follow-up paper on dispersal of organic matter but persistence of chemicals followed (Cole, 1979).

In the context of oil pollution, hindsight tells us that the type of oil spilled varies considerably in its effects and that oil, especially the lighter oils, will disperse and that greater damage may indeed be caused to marine life if dispersants are applied to rocky shores in an attempt to clean the oil up (*Coastal and Deep Ocean Pollution*; Arias and Botté, 2020). A very interesting consideration of both cultural and scientific aspects was given by Kornberg (1982). Referring to the study of oil pollution of the sea by the Royal Commission on Environmental Pollution (1981) he notes that (p. 429):

> Oil spills appear to generate wider concern than do most other forms of pollution, even among people whose interests are not directly affected. The environmental insult of a large spillage of black oil is so apparent that emotions

are deeply stirred; these emotions are aroused especially by the distress caused to seabirds. The strength of feeling here reflects not only a civilized revulsion, that animals deserving our protection should be wantonly destroyed, but perhaps also reflects a collective guilt that a substance on which our way of life so much depends should cause such havoc. At any rate, the public's response to oil spills is a real factor that must be recognized in considering policies for control.

These scientific assessments speak of the way we value the sea, its resources and wildlife – but also continue to stress the capacity to absorb and disperse many waste products. This seems to match the generalised cultural construction of the sea through history, with only more recent analyses showing the persistence of harmful substances.

It seems that we might rely upon the Greek idea of transformation by the sea maybe too much. The story of Polykrates' ring from classical times, as told by Herodotus is, however, an interesting one for current times. Polykrates threw his ring into the sea, never to be seen again. However, that evening it was found in the belly of a fish being served for supper. "How was this shocking and unexpected return to be understood?" asks Mack (2011: 93). There was an ambiguity. Things which float to the surface and refuse to disappear are generally regarded as omens of misfortune. However, Herodotus asserts that Polykrates had immunity from this bad luck and he argued that those who get things back, despite having thrown them in the sea, have access to "an unquenchable well of good fortune". For current times the latter seems wide of the mark as it is clear that the plastics we throw in the sea not only float to the surface and refuse to disappear, it is also our misfortunate that micro-plastics enter the food chain and thus can appear in the fish we are eating for supper.

4.8 Seeing Pictures: Nature in Art

Imagery and Landscape

As with literature (Section 4.1) there can be literal, descriptive and denotative depictions and also non-literal, associative, figurative, metaphorical, symbolic, allegorical, representational or emblematic connotations and meanings. Many of the latter to be found in older paintings are not immediately now apparent to present-day society as they would have been at the time of painting and have to be explained to the modern viewer by art historians and exhibition curators. In this latter context some of the useful books are Lucia Impelluso's (2004) *Nature and Its Symbols* together with her *Gardens in Art* (Impelluso, 2007), Battistini's (2005) *Symbols and Allegories in Art* and Hall's (1996) *Dictionary of Subjects and Symbols in Art*. Impelluso (2004: 9) writes that "what looks like a simple still life [picture] can hide an extraordinarily rich language, where every single fruit, flower or animal is charged with a specific, characteristic significance" – which of course is true if you can read the code.

Tim Barringer's chapter, 'Poetry', in *Rubens and His Legacy* (2015: 262–264), gives the impression that paintings with allegorical meanings dominated early paintings and when non-allegorical more literal paintings were exhibited they were rather looked down upon. Barringer notes Sir Joshua Reynold's writings which articulated his theory of art and where Reynolds lauded the 'grand style' of Raphael and Michelangelo but was ambivalent about Rubens. "Rubens' work was, for Reynolds, marked by a 'careless, loose and inaccurate style'" while Rubens's landscapes were

> damned by association with the Dutch school because of their 'locality' (meaning their interest in local topographic features): each, to Reynold's eye, was merely a 'representation of an individual spot, and each in its kind a very faithful but confined portrait'. For Reynolds the Dutch insistence on the particular details rendered painting a 'mechanical' exercise in representation, in contrast to the quest for universal truths that distinguished the liberal arts.

Barringer (2015: 264) also writes that: "Superbly fresh and textured with myriad details, Gainsborough's early landscapes transgressed the desire for generalisation and abstraction demanded by academic theory. Horace Walpole found in such work 'the drudging mimicry of nature's most uncomely coarseness'." Nowadays it seems that many find literal landscapes very accessible, for example those from Jacob van Ruisdael, Constable and Rubens's *A View of Het Steen in the Early Morning*, while the meanings of earlier allegorical paintings elude us.

Writing on British landscape art Charlotte Klonk (1996: 1–3) shows how changes in scientific outlook changed the perception of nature and thus influenced art. She begins by discussing how Gainsborough painted an idealised landscape while Constable painted more what he actually saw, seemingly reflecting changes in natural philosophy and science. Indeed, in Heidegger's *The Origin of the Work of Art* (1950) art is seen as a means of creating truth by being not merely representational, but actually producing a community's shared understanding, with the attendant observation that each work of art changes the meaning of existence for the observer. Thus, art reflects but can also change the culture of a society. A further interesting point is that while art reflects the landscape, there is the possibility that landscape imagery can have an effect upon the designed landscape. This is a point not often made but there could be an unconscious process of image reinforcement or a very conscious one, as with the practice of landscape architecture.

In *The Picturesque* and *Landscape and Western Art* Malcolm Andrews (1994, 1999) asks the question of how the mind of the artist influences the subject and mode of depiction. Thus, genres, movements and styles can be traced, placed within cultural contexts and the lurches and progressions of styles induced by mavericks are seen. He does then move on to say how having mental images of artworks then can influence what we see and, as discussed earlier in this book, starts his chapter on nature as picture or process with the Cézanne quotation: "Today our sight is a little weary, burdened by the memory of a thousand images .... We longer see nature; we see pictures over and over again" (Cézanne in conversation, 1902 from Andrews, 1999: 177) and he writes (p. 131) how travellers in Europe might refer to the names of artists when they came to particular views "according to whether the subjects before our eyes reminded us of the manner and choice of one or other of the masters [artists] named".

My question is, then: to what extent does such imagery have such a hold on us that we consciously or unconsciously refer to it when we wish to make a case for conserving a particular state of landscape? Susan Owens (2020: 7) has this reciprocal idea very much in mind in the Introduction to her book *Spirit of Place: Artists, writers & the British landscape*. Here, she records how, when attempting to depict an oak tree, Samuel Palmer very much felt that the oak he chose did not measure up to the image he had in mind from a description by John Milton of a monumental oak. She writes that what he felt is something that "affects many of us as we go about our daily lives. Artists and writers do not just describe our landscape, they make it too. The pictures we see and the stories we read seep deeply into our minds, forever changing the way we perceive the world around us." I thus wonder about extending the loop of landscape artists' mind-imagery not only to landscape artists' mind-imagery-viewing landscape but also to closing it with landscape artists' mind-imagery-viewing-producing/conserving landscape. As such, I think that this may well often be unconscious rather than explicit and also it may be more obvious when attempting to protect landscapes than when producing them. The classic case of imagery invoked during protection is a painting like Constable's *Hay Wain* (Figure 4.1,

Figure 4.1 Constable's *Hay Wain* (Art Images / Contributor / Hulton Fine Art Collection / Getty Images). *A black and white version of this figure will appear in some formats. For the colour version, please refer to the plate section.*

Figure 4.2). Andrews (1999, 171–175) refers to Constable's landscapes as providing 'portable icons', but also Dutch and French landscape artists have contributed very much to Western consciousness of the countryside. Andrews (p. 175) refers to "a . . . contribution to the construction of English national identity as fecund, domesticated and profoundly stable" and Helsinger (1997) in *Rural Scenes and National Representation* writes of the political instrumentality of art. Depictions such as the 'heroic' and the 'pastoral' are seen as ways of reinforcement in our cultures, as discussed for Dutch landscapes (Shawe-Taylor, 2010), English landscapes by Kriz (1997) in *The Idea of the English Landscape Painter* and in a much wider context of changing ideas by Potts and Meyers (2009) in *Endless Forms: Charles Darwin, natural science and the visual arts.*

While the production of landscape is always going to be very strongly influenced by economic, technological and political factors, it seems likely that if we are discussing the relationship between art and landscape then it is likely to be a reflexive relationship – involving both the way landscape influences art and the way art images influence landscape design and production. This relationship between landscape, art, artists, gardeners and landscape designers is admirably discussed by Harman (2009) in *The Culture of Nature in Britain 1680–1860.* I also sensed this

Figure 4.2 The current view. Preserving the landscape here refers to the iconic picture (Photo: S. Trudgill). *A black and white version of this figure will appear in some formats. For the colour version, please refer to the plate section.*

relationship when reading George Mather's book *The Psychology of Visual Art: Eye, brain and art* (Mather, 2014). When writing about landscape art in chapter 8 on 'Visual aesthetics and art', chapter 9 on 'Visual aesthetics and nature' and chapter 10 on 'Evolution and art' he stresses that we seem to have innate preferences for types of landscape even across a range of cultures and that this has some kind of biological and evolutionary basis. Although the weighting varied from country to country (ranging from the USA, Germany to Kenya and China) the dominant preferences were for visual representation of the lakes/rivers/oceans category and the fields/rural areas category (Mather, 2014: 129). He shows how in Europe there was a northern tendency to represent dense forests, mountains and vast horizons such as in the landscapes of Cranach the Younger, Altdorfer, Durer and Brueghel while in the south of Europe "the predominant motif was rolling countryside, a cultivated landscape dotted with ancient ruins or farm buildings" (Mather, 2014: 138). He continues:

> By the seventeenth century, painters such as Claude had developed a set of conventions for depicting idealised or classical landscape scenes. . . . Some of these elements recur in landscape art of the nineteenth century, such as paintings by Constable and Corot. By this time 'a peaceful scene, with water in the foreground reflecting a luminous sky and set off by dark trees, was something which everyone agreed was beautiful'. (Clark 1976: 147)

In terms of the origin of these preferences Mather (chs. 9 and 10) refers to our evolution on the savannahs of Africa and the related idea that this gives us a preference for open landscapes (p. 138). He argues that this is a limited hypothesis as the archaeological evidence shows that early hominid evolution was in a range of habitats including woodland and brushland. He relates the importance of what may be hidden (a sense of mystery) and the associated exploratory behaviours as well as the refuge-prospect theory of Appleton (1975, 1996). Here, preferred scenes offer both shelter and a good view – both for viewing possible resources and also potential threats. He develops the theme that aesthetic preferences reflect some kind of advantage in order to have survived and developed during evolution and these may involve fitness and location of resources, though he observes that aesthetics may not necessarily be focussed explicitly on utility.

Mather also observes (pp. 128–129) that the most consistent responses to the question 'which type of outdoor scene appeals the most?' were for a preference for "open, rural scenes containing water, rather than forest or manufactured landscapes". Mather is citing here a discussion of the work of two Russian-born American conceptualist artists: Vitaly Komar (born 1943) and Alexander Melamid (born 1945) from the book on a scientific guide to art edited by JoAnn Wypijewski (1997). Mather continues that: "It is remarkable how often the world's most popular paintings contain all the elements highlighted in Komar and Melamid's work – predominantly open rural scenes containing both animals and humans." The telling finding is that while these elements are so prevalent in Claude's landscape and those of so many other artists, it is "unlikely to reflect culturally transmitted standards based [solely] on Western art": these preferences were expressed strongly in all populations surveyed including African and Asian respondents and are also common themes in Chinese art.

Landscape architects such as Lancelot 'Capability' Brown were adept at catering for these universal preferences in creating garden designs that contain undulating open spaces broken up by clumps and belts of trees, incorporating water features such as lakes and streams. Such has become oft-rehearsed in books and garden columns. *The Times* columnist Matt Ridley (2015b) summarises the arguments well in an article entitled 'Why we love a bit of Africa in our parkland', quoting from Orians's (2014) book *Snakes, Sunrises and Shakespeare: How evolution shapes our loves and fears* where he develops his earlier ideas from his 'An ecological and evolutionary approach to landscape aesthetics' (Orians, 1986).

The simple thesis in Ridley (2015b) is that "Capability Brown's designs reflect our ancestral wish for open grasslands, clumps of trees, animals and distant water". This attractive theory, which relates to what can be called the 'savanna theory' of evolution and which is a focus of E. O. Wilson's biophilia writings (see, e.g., Kahn, 2001, ch. 1; Kellert and Wilson, 1993 for discussions) should also be placed alongside discussions of human evolution in relation to water, popularly known as the 'aquatic ape' hypothesis (see, e.g., https://en.wikipedia.org/wiki/Aquatic_ape_hypothesis).

Ridley (2015b) writes: "There is something deeply pleasing about a view of rolling grassland punctuated with clumps of low-branching trees and glimpses of distant water." He then muses:

> When I first saw an African savanna at the age of ten, something stirred within me. The great open grassland, the flat-topped fever trees by the distant lake, the herd of grazing antelope – did it feel like a Stone Age ancestral home? . . . It is our natural habitat as a species and it would almost be odd if, somewhere deep in our natures, there were not an evolved tendency to feel at home in it, as monkeys do in trees and fish in water.

Ridley then observes: "Gordon Orians, an ecologist, has congealed this idea as the 'savanna hypothesis'; that people's preferred landscapes bear an uncanny similarity to the most welcoming parts of East Africa's savanna, where humanity arose." This atavistic narrative is further expounded:

> In a Claude painting or a Brown landscape there is a pleasing combination of what the geographer Jay Appleton [1975, 1996] called 'prospect and refuge': you can see a long way, but you can also hide. There is a long view over grassland, but there are clumps of low-branching trees to hide among (and up), and to supply your needs there are bodies of water and herds of game.

Thus, the creation of landscape and the creation of artworks have narratives in common which belie our origins which thus make landscape and artworks both coincide and also appear reflexive. Thus, saying that we would like to conserve a landscape because it appears in a painting makes the work of art an intermediary because of the way art both reflects and reinforces our preferences in landscape.

4.9 Chapter Summary

- Cultural associations with nature can be readily found in literature and in art. Such associations can be interpreted in terms of not only showing how we see nature but also as giving insights into how we treat it.

- Descriptions and depictions may not only reveal how we may feel about nature, they can also influence how we feel.
- There are explanatory and evaluative uses of metaphor. When the two are confused, value judgements may masquerade as objective explanations. This fusion is very common in metaphors about nature.
- Metaphors may direct our thoughts in particular directions. We should realise that they are there and how they function – and evaluate their influence.
- The relationship with nature can be characterised by the way in which it can facilitate our will, without which we would not cherish it, combined with the possibility of defeat, without which it would not engage us.
- Such duality imbues our representational relationship with nature in so many ways, especially the notions of assisting and resisting realities (Rolston, 1979).
- Literature shows how we regard soil both as assisting and resisting. Narratives of cherishing the soil are present, leading to conservation motivation, but soil is often taken for granted rather than cherished.
- There seems to be a bird – or a bird attribute – for a wide range of human moods and emotions. Plants, too, are attributed with a wide range of associations and animal stories reveal an interchange of human and animal qualities. Positive cultural attitudes, which can lead to conservation motivation, seem to rest on a sense of identification with these organisms.
- Cultural associations of the seas and oceans show little idea of vulnerability – awesome, threatening, bountiful and infinite are concepts deeply embedded but do not serve us well considering the pollution and over-fishing of the waters.
- Saying that we would like to conserve a landscape because it appears in a painting makes the work of art an intermediary because of the way art both reflects and reinforces our preferences in landscape.

Part III

Nature, Self and Place

5 · *Personal Meanings of Nature*

5.1 Reflexivity and Spirituality

Personal Significance and Meaning

The relationships between nature, self and place are often expressed in the context of solitude, where nature is a receptacle of personal meanings. In this chapter we discuss these personal meanings of nature and extend it to explore aspects of environmental psychology.

We may see ourselves in nature, much as Narcissus falls in love with his own reflection (Figure 5.1).

We may also escape to nature, as in Hardy's poem 'In a Wood'. The poem encapsulates a human relationship with nature. The writer is, and the reader can become, located in a place where the self can exist. The wood is opposed to the city. It offers a home, a location, a sense of being. In nature we can cherish ourselves. Cherishing nature should, then, be part of our endeavours because of what it can give us, as much as for its own sake.

Heart-halt and spirit-lame
City-opprest
Unto this wood I came
As to a nest
dreaming that sylvan peace
Offered the harrowed ease-
Nature as soft release
From men's unrest
(from 'In a Wood' by Thomas Hardy, 1898)

When my mother died, one of her carers re-visited the house where she had been tending her for a number of years. It was late in the season and she saw a single clematis flower blooming. "Ah", she said, "that is a sign from your mother that all is well with her now." The fact that this species of clematis only normally flowers in the spring made her even more sure that this was a 'sign'.

Figure 5.1 *Narcissus* by Caravaggio (DEA / G. NIMATALLAH / Contributor / De Agostini / Getty Images). *A black and white version of this figure will appear in some formats. For the colour version, please refer to the plate section.*

That example of a personal meaning encapsulates what I wish to explore in this chapter. On the one hand it was a warm autumn and it is not unusual for spring flowers of many types to have a second flowering in such conditions – for example, the wisteria in my garden often does and was in bloom at the same time. So, we can take a rationalist, Enlightenment view of the carer's inference and dismiss it as superstitious. But then, for all the Enlightenment and how it is meant to have made us into rational beings, we still look for – and find – signs in nature.

As described elsewhere in this book, Evernden (1992: 107) lamented the way rational enlightenment leads to a loss of the significance of nature, observing that "the objects of contemplation inhabited a separate realm, offering no omens or signs [and] without human meaning or significance". Similarly, Eagleton (2000: 104) writes that "we degut ourselves of instinct in the struggle for civility". I see what they mean but I feel that they are mistaken. Romanticism, along with spirituality, is alive and well in modern times: powerful ideas about nature persist and influence us completely irrespective of scientific rationality. Emerson's (1836) view of the 'transcendental spirituality' which can be found in nature is still with us.

What has really happened is that romanticism has just become rather hidden and stays covert until something, like the death of a loved one, allows us to express it. Thus, legitimised by sensitivity the spiritual part of us which is suppressed by the everyday can appear unafraid – and only a churl would challenge a grieving person about their beliefs. The carer thought that the clematis flowering was a sign so indeed it was, to her, a sign without doubt or question.

This reflexivity between nature and the self is a projection that is both self-reinforcing and selfless. Narcissus, who in Greek mythology fell in love with his own reflection (Figure 5.1), can be seen as a metaphor for one relationship with nature where we project our self-love onto what we are viewing. Conversely, it can be said that 'hug a tree' is the projection of our values onto something outside ourselves. The former is more inward looking, finding something of ourselves in nature, while the latter is more outward looking, finding something intrinsic in nature which is valued because it is independent. The first is more egotistical while the second is more empathic with nature though still through our lens of values.

I am thus making a subtle distinction between: "Men can see nothing around them that is not their own image; everything speaks to them of themselves" (Karl Marx[1]) together with: "We are really mirroring ourselves in describing plants" (Holmes Rolston III, 1997: 362) as distinct from: "To enrol [plants and animals] in the emerging collective, we first need grant them . . . some of the social attributes necessary to integrate them" (Latour, 1994: 801). Both are forms which reinforce the identity of the self through an identity with nature, but the former is a mirroring of ourselves while the latter is seeing nature more for itself, though still on our terms.

These are, in turn, distinct from an identification of nature. To illustrate my view of these topics, I have here an extract from one of my youthful diaries:

[1] This attribution by Debord (1956) to Marx is widely cited (without reference) but seems not to be in any of Marx's authenticated writings: https://enwikiquoteorg/wiki/Karl_Marx/.

In the afternoon, we went to a nature reserve. I could see some places where bulldozers had cut out ponds and ditches and where nature reserve people had carefully made different habitats. There were wooden walkways and wooden huts for hides where you could sit and watch birds without getting your feet wet. People sat there with their bird books, discussing which bird they could identify. In the hide they sat in comfort and got excellent views through powerful telescopes and I'm sure they would go away with the feeling that they had experienced nature. They all seemed to be enjoying it thoroughly, but I felt that I couldn't dream while they were there.

It wasn't the same as spending a day away from everybody with my binoculars and boots, chancing on some bird or discovering a skulking waterfowl in some lost and hidden ditch. Do I want to sit in an organised hide and listen to people talk with each other about what they could identify? Well, I did love these outings in many ways, and I learnt a lot from them, but I'd rather curl round tree stumps in the sun and daydream, merging with the soil and bracken, feeling like a tree root myself, searching in the soil, dreaming. I couldn't help thinking, why can't they go away and leave it all alone?

I went down over the sloping beach with its soft, warm, dry, yielding sand in the upper parts, over the crusty strand of black, dried and twisted knobbly seaweed to the flatter, wetter, firmer shore where the large sand ripples, rocks and pools were. I paused to watch a seagull float in its freedom. (S. Trudgill, 1960s diary)

There are two sorts of engagement with nature here, one a 'viewing', a cataloguing – an identification of. The other an 'immersion', a relationship – an identification with. Everyone is in the same place, but they are in different places of meaning. Some people loved it, with the ease of walking and of viewing; I clearly questioned the contrivance of organised nature and, for me, an associated loss of personal meaning.

In another of my teenage writings, I recalled cycling round Norfolk and visiting a church:

I walked to the far end of the church. Gold, red, blue and green rays of sunlight streamed in through the pictures of an immanent Christ in the window, the rays picking out the flecks of dust in the air before me. The altar stood in front of me in the cold stone end chapel. The altar itself was covered with a white cloth and on either side cold white lilies stood poised impassively between sprightly dark green box sprigs and sad laurel branches. In the centre stood the plain, cold, gold cross, burning in the sunlight. I wondered if God was really in a cold place like this, or in the warm woods outside. I had never dared to go up to an altar before. Not quite sure what I was doing, or why I was doing it, I went right up to the altar, half kneeled and then stood up again self-consciously and looked round behind me, but no one was there. I stood and bowed my head.

I whispered to myself: "I want It All To Be Pure. I want Nature to be Pure. The Woods. The Sea. The Mountains. The Flowers. The Birds. Please let them leave it all alone. I want it all to be pure."

Visions of leaves and sunlight filled my mind as my eyes blurred with tears; I felt a bit dizzy. Birds cried on unsullied shores. I leant forward to the cross and pressed my lips to it. The steel coldness of the cross stung and frightened me and burnt my lips as I kissed it. I could see the moist breath caught on the cross where my lips had been. I turned furtively and fled, scared, away from the Cross, down the aisle, past Sir Archibald glaring at me, past the ashes buried in the wall and over the slabs of the trodden-on dead and out of the cold church and away from the cold, pure cross into the sunlight and out to a warm God where the sparrows cheeped feebly in the rush of sunlight and where the air smelt faintly of distant manure and leaves danced in the sun. (S. Trudgill, 1960s diary)

Small wonder then that I found great joy when I did my PhD on the island of Aldabra in the Indian Ocean (see, e.g., Beamish, 1970 in *Aldabra Alone*) and where for reading I had Steinbeck's ([1951]1960) *Log from the Sea of Cortez* about his marine biology expedition with Ed Ricketts. I wrote:

A quiet moment of unsurpassed peace, sitting on the beach, amongst the Casuarina pines, a small fire going, glowing red in the dark, throwing a pale glimmer over the sand. Looking out over the still pool of the sea in which a bright star shone a reflection. Listening to the surge of the waves on the reef in the dark beyond and feeling the warm breath of wind under the vast sky and millions of stars. (S. Trudgill, Aldabra diary, 1969)

And then:
There is much that man does love
that does not much love man.
The vast blue inhumanity
of boundless sea and sky.
Vast inhumanity, of elements of sky, of sea
makes my light my spark of life shine brighter.
(Trudgill, 2001b: 106; also Trudgill, 2003b: 273–274)

Aldabra did indeed seem a very 'pure' place when I was there in 1969 and 1971 with a group of geologists and biologists, especially when birds, like the flightless rail, came out to see what you were doing rather than running away, and other creatures seemed quite fearless. Such experiences are foundational for an individual.

The relationship between the individual self and nature can be seen to have many dimensions but individual experiences can be put into a more accessible context by thinking of the types of experience. On this topic I am very much minded of the analysis by Van Matre (1974, 1979, 1983) of deriving meaning from outdoor experience. His codification of what can be involved when viewing nature is shown in Box 5.1. This seems to me to take the ways of the (solitary) naturalist with their gaze directed outwards to nature and promotes the idea that we can simultaneously 'let nature in' and find our own fresh autobiographical meanings. Van Matre feels that our experiences shape our perceptions and that (1974: 74) "our eyes focus unconsciously but persistently on objects which we already know". He proposes that we tend to "gather light images on the basis of past receptions" (p. 31) and that "to change our perception we must

Box 5.1 *Deriving meaning from the outdoor experience*

Derived from section headings in the text of Van Matre (1974: 23–57).

- **Touching**
- **Tasting**
- **Hearing**
- **Smelling**
- **Seeing –** how does what you are viewing make you feel?
- **Feeling**
- **Focusing –** asks us to focus on the usual.
- **Framing** – enclosing scenes we want to examine using fingers/hands.
- **Grouping** – find the major elements in the scene.
- **Expanding** – make a conscious effort to avoid looking at familiar objects.
- **Filling** – look at spaces between solid objects.
- **Surveying** – "the familiar is unfamiliar from a different vantage point".
- **Observing** – relax and let the natural world engulf you.
- **Orchestrating** – fuse all the facets of awareness.
- **Scrutinising** – looking at small things.
- **Empathising** – identify with what you are observing.
- **Silencing** – forget about making sense of things, let meanings seep away.
- **Waiting** – let whatever occurs next happen.

change our past" (p. 31), and he stresses the importance of gaining impressions "undimmed by our recollections or verbalisations" (p. 37). He proposes that we can see anew by persistently looking for what is there rather than by just recognising what we know.

One of Van Matre's courses which I went on personally I found very revealing – to me he was saying nothing more than something about the way I had grown up, immersed as I was in nature writing and being outdoors by myself or with other naturalists. However, others on the course, with a more urban upbringing, found it all a revolutionary revelation. It is also interesting to note that in parallel to Van Matre, Macnaghten and Urry (1998: 119) use the words "sustained immersion and sense of . . . the auratic landscape" to describe one's relationships with nature. Thus, an immersion is recognised as possible and develops the idea of *being in* rather than *watching*. Most importantly, in terms of finding the self, Van Matre (1974: 53) stresses that "you are what you feel. One way to get outside yourself is to get inside something else. By giving your whole self to the [nature] experience it will fill your world." There are elements of both losing yourself and finding yourself here. A personalised empathic identification with meanings in nature becomes self-validating.

5.2 "Inspired by Nature but Destroyed by the World"

Finding the Self in Nature

The contextual self, located in nature, has a long literary tradition (see, e.g., Bate, 1991 on *Romantic Ecology: Wordsworth and the environmental tradition*; Bate, 2020 on *Radical Wordsworth: The poet who changed the world* and Hall, 2014 on *Romantic Naturalists, Early Environmentalists: An ecocritical study, 1789–1912*). "Inspired by Nature but destroyed by the world" is a quote cited by Jonathan Bate in his book on John Clare (Bate, 2003: 509). The observation comes from Eliza Cook, a poet and journalist, writing in *Eliza Cook's Journal*, her weekly paper. For me it is a convenient, pithy shorthand for the content and purpose of this section: the relationship between nature and the – possibly damaged – self in specific places. A simplistic starting point is that for Clare you could say that he found himself in nature first and then was subsequently at odds with society; we might then add that for many in modern society it seems that damaged people can (re-)find themselves in nature. We can find the subtleties and nuances in this nature–self–place relationship by examining further writings.

For Turner (1992) writing about the poet Rupert Brooke in terms of *The Splendour and the Pain*, there is a context of the meaning and detail of the place and the connection between these and the imagination: "Often he would pause at one particular open space. . . . Here Rupert sat superbly suspended along serene depth and shadowed height. . . . He came to know each curve of the course of the river, each tree-clump that marked it with uncanny intimacy. . ." (extracts from Turner, 1992: 71–72).

To me, one of the best writings on solitude which the intrusion of others can destroy can be found in Brooke's 'The Voice' (1909, seen in full at www.rupertbrooke.com/poems/1908-1911/the_voice/). He describes being: "Safe in the magic of my woods" while "birds were hushed; and peace was growing;/ And quietness crept up the hill;/ And no wind was blowing." Here, we are taken to a great depth of tranquillity with nature, and then even with a sense of an imagined other (and we think here also of Brooke's ambiguous sexuality):

And the night and the woods and you
Were one together, and I should find
Soon in the silence the hidden key
Of all that had hurt and puzzled me –
Why you were you, and the night was kind,
And the woods were part of the heart of me.

And then we share the outrage of shattering intrusion – and disdain for the intruder (and note the sense of possession in 'my' woods) – with the ". . . uproar in my woods,/ . . . Crashing and laughing and blindly going,/ Of ignorant feet and a swishing dress,/ And a Voice profaning the solitudes."

And then follows the exclamations about nature, ironically celebrating being alone with nature, together with the trite observations and platitudes which shattered Brooke's personal meanings to the extent of him uttering his final malediction:

You said, 'The view from here is very good!'
You said, 'It's nice to be alone a bit!'
And, 'How the days are drawing out!' you said.
You said, 'The sunset's pretty, isn't it?'
. . . By God! I wish – I wish that you were dead!

There is a real engagement with nature in solitude here – a magic and a knowledge and, as with so many nature writings, a profound sense of self – and this together with the sense of identity and ownership in 'my' woods which had brought him so much peace. This then followed by the utter resentment of the crassness of humankind purporting to share the experience.

The diminishing of personal cares and the sense of identity which nature can bring is exemplified by John Clare in a poem 'I Am', written probably around 1844 or 1845 after he had been committed to an asylum for the second time. While obviously feeling bereft, he reaffirms existence and a place in nature in this poem, which is one of the last things he wrote:

I long for scenes where man has never trod;
A place where woman never smil'd or wept;
There to abide with my creator, God,
And sleep as I in childhood sweetly slept:
Untroubling and untroubled where I lie;
The grass below – above the vaulted sky.
(from 'I Am' by John Clare, 1844/1845)

Further back in time, Sir Philip Sidney (1554–1586) wrote 'O sweet woods the delight of solitarines!' (Sidney, 1593), where he celebrates the lack of treason, flatterers, usury, duty, arrogance, vanity, slander or abuse and delights in the creator and heavenly order. He writes of the woods where he feels in touch with the creator: "Where mans mind hath a freed consideration/ Of goodnes to receive lovely direction" and "and wise thoughts do behold what the creator is:/ Contemplation here holdeth his only seate."

Finding fulfilment through experiencing nature in comparative isolation independent of interpersonal relationships is interesting because rather than occurring through a sense of social rejection or alienation this may refer to more solitary individuals who may be solitary through positive choice. It can also refer to well-balanced and socially adjusted individuals with many friends who may or may not be like-minded about nature. So, there is a wide spectrum of experience, though the solitary experience of nature as a counterpoint to social experience is a theme which receives much attention. So, Brooke is safe in his woods, Clare is ultimately untroubled amid his mental turmoil, Sidney is secure from human threat and finding a higher meaning. In his nature writings Thoreau was refreshed and felt the "need to witness our own limits transgressed". His thought that: "There are from time to time mornings . . . when especially the world seems to begin anew" encapsulates this (Box 5.2). Whatever the range of experiences and motivations,

Box 5.2 *Thoreau on mornings*

There are from time to time mornings, both in summer and in winter, when especially the world seems to begin anew, beyond which memory need not go, for not behind them is yesterday and our past life; when, as in the morning of a hoar frost, there are visible effects as of a certain creative energy. . . . The world has visibly been recreated in the night. Mornings of creation, I call them. In the midst of these marks of a creative energy recently active, while the sun is rising with more than usual splendor, I look back . . . for the era of this creation, not into the night, but to a dawn for which no man ever rose early enough. A morning which carries us back beyond the Mosaic creation, where crystallizations are fresh and un-melted. It is the poet's hour. Mornings when men are new-born, men who have the seeds of life in them. (Henry David Thoreau, *Walden*, 26 January 1853)

there is thus an interesting combination of simultaneously sensing connections with something much greater than us in nature together with a sense of experience – ownership and possession even – which is self-validating.

A further point in the nature–self relationship is that nature may well be very therapeutic but it is also indifferent to us and so often people bring their own problems with them rather than necessarily escape them; hence a duality of the wilderness experience where the counterpoint is both the essence and pitfall of the experience. Thoreau certainly is recorded as opining that there were few companions with whom he could enjoy a nature walk and with many it was the companion who occupied the attention, rather than nature, with the walk "degenerating into the mere vigorous use of the legs". It seems from the writings of Thoreau that the benefits of nature are perhaps less debatable than the benefits of a companion.

However, I am minded here to go back to the writings of Bill Bryson on Thoreau in his book *A Walk in the Woods* (Bryson, 1997: 66) who charts his own experience in the Appalachian Woods where he is deriving a pleasurable feeling of grittiness and determination to see "one of the world's great hardwood forests – a relic of the richest, most diverse sweep of woodland ever to grace the temperate world". Bryson writes that while the "inestimably priggish and tiresome" Thoreau "found nature splendid" this was "so long as he could stroll to town for cakes and barley wine" and that when Thoreau actually experienced real wilderness "he was unnerved to the core". The experience apparently left Thoreau, in the words of one biographer, "nearly hysterical". "This wasn't the tame world of overgrown orchards and sun-dappled paths that passed for wilderness in Thoreau's Concorde, Massachusetts, but a forbidding, grim, oppressive, primeval place that was [and here he quotes Thoreau] 'grim and wild ... savage and dreary', fit only for 'men nearer of kin to the rocks and wild animals than we'." He also records Daniel Boone's description as "so wild and horrid that is impossible to behold ... without terror".

This charts extremely well the duality of wilderness as something dark and threatening needing conquering or avoiding; yet, as civilisation progresses, something of release, freedom and wandering (presumably when we feel safe and have a working satnav or a map?).

In a study of wilderness and the search for solitude, Krakauer ([1996] 1998: 25) in *Into the Wild* writes of the personality type that can find solace in wilderness, quoting Paul Shepard (1967) from his *Man and the Landscape: An historic view of the esthetics of nature*: "To the desert go prophets and hermits; through deserts go pilgrims and exiles. Here the leaders of the great religions have sought the therapeutic and spiritual values of retreat, not to escape but to find reality." Krakauer ([1996]1998: 62) also quotes from Anthony Storr's ([1989]1997: 75) *Solitude: A return to the self*:

> It is true that many creative people fail to make mature personal relationships, and some are extremely isolated. It is also true that, in some instances, trauma, in the shape of early separation or bereavement, has steered the potentially creative person toward developing aspects of his personality which can find fulfilment in comparative isolation. But this does not mean that solitary creative pursuits are themselves pathological.

Krakauer also cites: "Avoidance behaviour is a response designed to protect the infant from behavioural disorganisation. If we transfer this concept to adult life, we can see that an avoidant infant might very well develop into a person whose principal need was to find some kind of meaning and order in life which was not entirely, or even chiefly, dependent upon interpersonal relationships" (Storr, [1989]1997: 146–147).

The subject of Krakauer's book had family problems and turned his back on civilisation. He writes ([1996]1998: 142) how many people find release through the wilderness experience: "The accumulated clutter of day to day existence – the lapses of conscience, the unpaid bills, the bungled opportunities, the dust under the couch, the inescapable prison of your genes – all of it is temporarily forgotten." So, here we have the counterpoint of nature as an escape.

However, he relates the true story of "an idealistic 22 year old . . . who in 1992 walked deep into the Alaskan wilderness and whose SOS note and emaciated corpse were found four months later". The subject had been inspired by wilderness stories in American literature and Krakauer writes (p. 4) how "people think the unsullied enormity of the Last Frontier will patch all the holes in their lives. The bush is an unforgiving place, however, that cares nothing for hope or longing." He continues more positively, though, that the wilderness experience is one where "the accumulated clutter" is "crowded from your thoughts by the overpowering clarity of purpose and the seriousness of the task in hand" (p. 142). Also, as when rock climbing/mountaineering: "you get used to rubbing shoulders with doom, you come to believe in the reliability of your hands and your feet and your head. You learn to trust your self-control" (p. 142). Such attributes are clearly worth developing, even though the author also admits that the problems do not actually go away but are often merely suspended, though they may be put into perspective: "I thought that climbing . . . would fix all that was wrong with my life. In the end, of course, it changed nothing" (p. 154).

The therapy of the nature experience as a counterpoint to society and escaping from one's problems is thus not a straightforward topic to espouse. Notwithstanding this, the sense of refuge from society and the sense of personal refreshment are recurring themes in both nature writing (Section 5.3) and in environmental psychology (Section 5.5).

5.3 Naturalists and Nature Writers

The Personal, the Universal and the Writings of Henry Williamson

In a study of autobiography *Metaphors of Self: The meaning of autobiography* James Olney (1972) shows how the creative process can transform individual experience into something universally apprehensible and significant. In a study of T. S. Eliot (Olney, 1972: 261) he writes that he "treats his own experience as representative and symbolic . . .. The individual self – a self-belonging indistinguishably to poet, reader and poem – that is realized by the process of a work like *Four Quartets* stands for the whole integrated psyche of mankind." Olney (1972: 262–263) then quotes Stephen Spender (see Spender, 1997):

> [T]he autobiographical is transformed. It is no longer the writer's experience: it becomes everyone's. He is no longer writing about himself: he is writing about life. He creates it, not as an object which is already familiar and observed, as he is observed by others, but as a new a revealing object, growing out of and beyond observation.

This indeed may be lifted into a prescriptive mantra where the autobiographical meanings which can be derived from the literature are turned round and become a way for individuals to alter their future autobiographies. Nature writers like Henry Williamson (1895–1977), who made his own personal experience of nature accessible to the reader, indeed help the reader to have a sensitivity to nature in their lives which they might otherwise not have had. Indeed, not only does he transform his individual experience into something universally apprehensible and significant, he also enables that universality to transform the reader's individual experience.

As noted above, Brooke wrote: 'my woods'; similarly Henry Williamson (1945: 164) recalls how: "My fatigue passed, and hope came into my heart" when he saw what he called "my Barn Owl" in London. This personalised narrative shows what something means to sense of self of a person and displays a form of ownership of nature which is part of an individual's autobiography. Williamson (1921, 1922a, 1922b, 1923, 1924a, 1924b, 1927, 1928, 1935, 1945) indeed wrote several stories which are autobiographical where he draws on his own experience of nature: *The Flax of Dream* – a tetralogy following the life of Willie Maddison: *The Beautiful Years* (1921); *Dandelion Days* (1922a); *The Dream of Fair Women* (1924a) and *The Pathway* (1928) together with *A Chronicle of Ancient Sunlight* (1951–1969) – a series of fifteen novels based loosely on Williamson's own life (see www.henrywilliamson.co.uk/bibliography/booksbyhw). In these, nature is never very far away and a counterpoise to the difficulties of coming to terms with aspects of his life involving other people, as described by Anne Williamson (1995) in her biography of Henry: *Henry Williamson: Tarka and the last romantic*. She sees Henry as (1995: ix) "complicated, eccentric and controversial . . . soldier, naturalist, broadcaster, journalist, farmer, visionary and, above all, writer". As a writer, he could create the character of Willie Maddison and she writes (1995: 198) that "Williamson was Maddison and Maddison was a dreamer, a lover of beauty, of birds and animals, and a sensitive youth". She encapsulates the juxtaposition of his imaginative inner life and society by citing a letter where he wrote that (1995: 89): "The mob spirit always goes to torture & crush the solitary spirits who have risen above it." While the 'tortured soul finding solace in nature' is the easy trope to reach for, we find from Anne Williamson's book that Henry was far more complex than that. Certainly, however, as we roam with the otter and swim with the salmon, his writings do indeed take the reader deep inside what we can imagine to be their lives.

Wilderness, Identity, Gender, Sexuality and the Self

I begin by wanting to be both cautious and open-minded about accounts of the human–nature relationship which involve gender and sexuality. There are deep pits of stereotypes waiting to trap the unwary. Moreover, there are easy divisions, fences, categories, labels: straight, gay, bisexual or AC/DC which are no more than cop-outs for a fluid situation. I also wonder if there is not a core of the human–nature relationship which is gender-free, free of sexuality?

This questioning is thus not one of easy labels and pigeonholes – it requires more poise, more balance, more effort, thought and intelligence. It is not so easy as a dismissive comment, not so comforting as the roles and categories we pretend we're in (or have been positioned in), not so secure as: here is a fence, I'm safely on one side or the other.

I have before me two books: *Women Who Run with the Wolves* by Clarissa Pinkola Estés (1992) and *Iron John: Men and masculinity* by Robert Bly (1990). One is about wild women and the other about wild men, both gendered but have the same theme – the importance of nature to the human soul. Estés (1992: 1) writes that "the pristine wilderness of our planet disappears as the understanding of our own inner wild nature fades". Bly (1990: ix) does not "make a big distinction between homosexual and heterosexual men" and addresses "the masculine depth of feeling" which "does not constitute a challenge to the women's movement". Bly's book and the associated concepts discussed by Bonnett (1996) on the mythopoetic men's movement, together with the not unrelated *Manhood* by Steve Biddulph (1994) are counterblasts to the stereotypes. Estés especially stresses the endurance and strength of women in their wildness. In *Sex, Ecology and Spirituality*, Ken Wilber (2000) moves from observing Foucault's description of obsessive sexuality to the conclusion that: "Sexuality [has been] invested with a force, a power, a mystique, an aura, an authority . . .

out of [all] proportion" (2000: 503; the pointless stereotyping is discussed further at pp. 761–762).

I think that when considering another person, whether in person or in written word, there is always another person out there in front of you and a separate representation of that person in your mind. The latter is always a representation to you and for yourself and we can readily and lazily jump for the easy categories. But the person in front of you is always much richer, more diverse, wider, deeper, more complex, more surprising than you can possibly imagine or represent to yourself. It is also liable to be the same with any categories about the relationship between any individual and nature when nature itself is always much richer, more diverse, wider, deeper, more complex, more surprising than you can possibly imagine or represent to yourself. Thus, to say that people relate to nature in a way that is automatically and necessarily gendered or related to sexuality is to me a non-starter.

However, this does not mean to say that gender and sexuality may not play a key role in our relationship with nature – indeed, gender and sexuality may well play a key role in nature writing especially in terms of a society's attitude to these characteristics. This in turn is also not to say that there is not a high degree of common ground in the human–nature relationship irrespective of individual differences in characteristics.

In this general context let's do something rather obvious and ask you, the reader, how many pioneering women nature writers and naturalists you can name. There is a North American website (Lew, 2017) on ten women who changed the way we see nature:

The website author writes: "These women expanded our understanding of the natural world. They don't always get a proportional place in the history books, but women have played a vital role in wilderness exploration, conservation and our understanding of nature and wildlife." The women listed are: Florence A. Merriam Bailey, an ornithologist, nature writer and early advocate for the protection of wildlife in the late nineteenth and early twentieth century; Rachel Carson of *The Sea Around Us* and of *Silent Spring* fame; Herma Albertson Baggley, who was the first full-time female naturalist of the US National Park Service; Margaret Murie, who pushed for passage of the Wilderness Act and the creation of the Arctic National Wildlife Refuge; Caroline Dormon, who campaigned for a national forest; Annie Montague Alexander, who has more than a dozen plants and animal species and Alaska's Lake Alexander named after her; Anna Botsford Comstock, who promoted nature field trips in schools; Ynes Mexia, an exploration botanist; Celia Hunter, who campaigned to protect nature in Alaska; and Hallie Daggett, the first woman Forest Service field officer. The website emphasises how fundamentally important they were to writing, science and campaigns: "They thrived on being in the wilderness and brought us a new level of understanding about the natural world. Not only were they interesting characters with compelling life stories, many were also writers who crafted exciting accounts of their exploits or wrote eloquent arguments for the preservation of the environment."

I only recognised one of them, Rachel Carson. The point that 'women . . . don't always get a proportional place' is well made. Many people are able to refer to Thoreau's thoughts, Ralph Waldo Emerson's writings and Aldo Leopold's *A Sand County Almanac* but few can cite equivalent female figures though indeed they are all there, equally foundational but unsung. One might surmise that if observers conclude that natural history is imbued with masculine writing then this displays a bias in recognition rather than the necessity of an actual bias.

I began by wanting to be both cautious and open-minded about the roles of gender and sexuality in the human–nature relationship and I am now perhaps thinking more of a communality of the human experience involving the relationship between nature and any individual irrespective of gender. At the core of this there is often a sense of love of nature and this may or may not be in lieu of a specific love for other humans or stem from a generalised lack of love for humanity. While a love of nature can be expressed by anyone, it can often be found in literature as a manifestation of a love for other people which either may be denied or otherwise cannot be expressed.

Themes which are related to this can be found in Helen Macdonald's powerful book *H Is for Hawk* (Macdonald, 2014). She discusses the life and writings of T. H. White, who wrote *The Once and Future King* (White, 1958), as well as a book on the goshawk she is specifically referring to (White, 1951). She writes, citing the words of him: "One of the saddest sentences I have ever read: 'falling in love is a desolating experience, but not when it is with a countryside.' He could not imagine a human love returned. He had to displace his desires onto the landscape, that great, blank green field that cannot love you back, but cannot hurt you either" (Macdonald, 2014: 39). To me this resonates with the writings of the poet W. S. Landor (written in 1849 on his seventy-fourth birthday): "I strove with none, [i.e. no one] for none was worth my strife:/ Nature I loved and, next to Nature, Art" (Landor, 1849).

Macdonald develops her thoughts further (2014: 39–45). She notes that White reveals himself while writing about his county: "When White goes on to explain how Buckinghamshire 'concealed its individuality in order to preserve it' but is 'secretly exuberant in its private way' you realise that he is writing about his own character." She feels that: "When White is writing about a love for the countryside, at heart he is writing about a hope that he might be able to love himself" and that "But the countryside wasn't just something that was safe for White to love: it was a love that was safe to write about." Macdonald then makes an interesting point about sexuality and the way homosexuality was marginalised, supressed and repressed by society and the legal system during many writers' lives: "It took me a long time to realise how many of our classic books on animals were by gay writers who wrote of their relationships with animals in lieu of human loves of which they could not speak."

She then cites the writings of Gavin Maxwell (1960) who wrote of his life with an otter in *Ring of Bright Water* and of a BBC radio naturalist Maxwell Knight, also a former M15 spymaster, whom she describes as a "closet queen . . . doubly disallowed to speak of his allegiances" and who became obsessed with hand-rearing a cuckoo (Knight, 1955). She finds the description of this endeavour in Knight's book on the subject terribly moving: "[T]his small, greedy, feathery, parasitic bird . . . it was a species made of all the hidden elements of Knight's life: subterfuge, deceit, passing oneself off as something one is not."

She continues that White is part of this "poignant literary tradition". He had dispiriting romances with younger women, was frightened of grown women and found their shape unpleasant. He fell in love with a younger man but this was unreciprocated. "But there were always animals" in his life and books: "dogs, owls, hawks, snakes, badgers, hedgehogs, even ants". Apart from his dog he insisted that his animals were never pets. He likened the relationship with a pet as that of a mother and child: "They [pets] are ruined by the owners the same way that 'mothers ruin their children, choke them like ivy'. Pets mean dependency and he had a terror of it." He much preferred hawks because of their independence. In short, "He'd decided he hated people. He much preferred animals" (Macdonald, 2014: 43). There is an evolution of this tradition to be seen in Luke Turner's (2019) *Out of the Woods* where the author finds Epping Forest a place of comfort as he struggles with concepts of masculinity and sexuality. Here, it is the concept of being away from society that enables him to reconcile the expectations of others with his own way of being.

The 'poignant literary tradition' of supressed gay writers brings to mind a series of questions where one is forced to confront the nature of the relationship between emotional torment and the solace of nature. Immediately one can see that this is not a necessary relationship: one neither has to be a supressed gay to love and write about nature nor do you have to love and write about nature if you are a supressed gay; these are not exclusive preserves. Equally, widening the argument, one does not have to be emotionally damaged to be a naturalist and emotionally damaged people don't have to be naturalists. However, there is such a genre of tradition where under stress of some kind people find solace in nature in some form, there must be something fundamental operating here.

In an introduction to a recent edition of the renowned and powerful *The Peregrine* (Baker, 1967) Robert Macfarlane (2005) writes that "it is . . . made clear that the narrator is suffering from some deep wound, mental or physical, which tinges his perception with 'dimness' and 'desolation' as well as sharpening his awareness of [natural] beauty" (pp. ix–xi). He continues: "[T]o abolish yourself through intense focus on another creature is [akin to] Keats's famous doctrine of 'negative capability' and the 'poetical' capacity to empty yourself so totally into another being that you do not merely think like that being, but *are* that being." Apparently Keats, on seeing a sparrow, started picking about in the gravel as the sparrow so "'that I am in a very little time annihilated'". Macfarlane feels that: "This self-obliteration was precisely what Baker sought" (p. x). Sections of the book describe how Baker more or less mimics the behaviour of the bird, sitting over the remains of a recent kill as if mantling the prey and looking around him sharply as the bird does.

There are insights into Kenneth Grahame's *Wind in the Willows* (1908) provided by Mathew Dennison's biography of the author: *Eternal Boy: The life of Kenneth Grahame* (Dennison, 2018). While much has been written on representations of society and the metaphors of the 'Wild Wood' in the book, for me the most moving part of it is in the chapter 'The Piper at the Gates of Dawn' where Mole and Rat meet the god Pan. Mole felt "a great Awe [in] some august Presence [and] he looked into the eyes of the Friend and helper . . . kindly eyes . . . were looking down at him . . . all this he saw, for one moment breathless and intense, vivid on the morning sky; and still as he looked, he lived; and still, as he lived, he wondered. . . . the two animals, crouching to the earth, bowed their heads and did worship" (Grahame, [1908]1963: 234–236). This intense personal relationship with nature which Grahame felt comes,

Dennison feels, from the way in which "he lived . . . in his imagination, this eternal boy . . .. In imagination, if not in life, he was frequently alone" (Dennison, 2018: 243).

We may be able to further understand what is happening in such experiences and writings by thinking about the creative writing process together with some psychological insights. In terms of analysis, on the one hand there is our innate affinity for nature as espoused by followers of E. O. Wilson's Biophilia Hypothesis who will not find this strange, as discussed elsewhere in this book. On the other hand, there is some kind of psychological profile which Anthony Storr ([1989]1997) explores in *Solitude*. In chapter 8 which he entitles 'Separation, isolation and the growth of the imagination', Storr ([1989]1997: 106–107) writes that "imaginative capacity tends to become particularly highly developed in gifted individuals who, for one reason or another, have passed rather solitary childhoods". Storr espouses the idea that "absence of, or partial deprivation of, interpersonal relationships encourages imagination to flourish". He can but conclude from his studies that "an imaginary world can sometimes serve as a retreat from unhappiness, a compensation for loss, and a basis for later creative achievement". Storr ([1989]1997: 111–112) then relates the isolated childhoods of a variety of creative writers including Anthony Trollope and Beatrix Potter – the latter of whom had many animals as friends but few human friends as a child. However, he refers to criticism of such analyses of "supposed . . . lonely, withdrawn and introverted individuals" and records his dislike of stereotypes but admits that there can be much truth in the case of writers.

He cites the case of Edward Lear, separated from many of his siblings and his family and parents at an early age and who "grew up to be a lonely adult, predominantly homosexual, but probably never consummated his desires" (Storr, [1989]1997: 112). He quotes Vivien Noakes's 1985 book on Edward Lear that: "His search was not for a physical love, but for someone who would want him as a person in the way that his parents had not . . . real spiritual involvement with another person." Storr (pp. 113–122) also discusses the writings of Kipling, H. H. Munro and P. G. Wodehouse in similar contexts. In this context, Pulkkinen (1990) usefully has a broad psychological discussion of the relationships between childhood experiences and adult lives, including 'loners' and childhood precursors but rightly cautions about the dangers of simplistic assumptions about the relationships. Storr indeed is cautious that "what began as compensation for deprivation became a rewarding way of life". He feels that: "All these writers were successful; in spite of the emotional scars they bore. . . . What began as compensation ended as a way of life which is as valid as any other . . . there is no reason to suppose that their lives were unfulfilled" (Storr, ([1989]1997: 122).

In this context, there is one particular poem by Ronald Wallace (1983) entitled 'Bird Study' which stood out for me as it seemed to capture the essence of a socially inept birdwatcher, having both an obsession and a compulsion. Through the eyes of the poet, the birdwatcher, Clark, himself becomes an object of study. The line "hawknosed and friendless" perhaps captures the idea of someone who relates to nature better than to other people. The birdwatcher is undoubtedly very human and his inner world is revealed, but the poet is somewhat unsympathetic in his portrayal though nonetheless vivid in the way in which the birdwatcher is living his life through the fantasy(?) of bird watching. Wallace also alludes to a possibly lonely, wounded person relating to birds more than other people.

In the poem Wallace (1983) starts with a telling quotation which sets the scene for the poem: "'One of the penalties of an ecological education is that one lives alone in a world of wounds' – Aldo Leopold." In it he characterises the birdwatcher named Clark as "gawky with binoculars, all elbows and awkwardness" and proceeds to the species list endeavour: "He's got 58 kinds by breakfast." He then places the birdwatcher socially using avian metaphors:

I think as a child he must have been
'bird-brained', 'for the birds,'
. . . hawknosed and friendless, wrens
nesting in the crofts of his arms,
inept and furtive, fluttering
on the edge of anybody's attention.

But then he ends by alluding to the kind of release and freedom that birdwatching gives to the birdwatcher:

I see Clark flying high beyond me,
beyond all showy display,
beyond any call or cry,
there with the wounded great blue heron,
his slow wings echoing
over the hills from sky to sky!

'Bird Watching' by R. S. Thomas (1995) writes also about the avian passion of those with binoculars. These poems are about people immersed in nature who are being viewed by an outsider and they can be interpreted as the reader wishes. However, it is possible that further insights may also be gained from the psychological literature including the identification of avoidant personality disorder (AvPD). This is manifest in the avoidance of social interaction and the use of fantasy as a form of escapism, often with a causal factor of childhood emotional neglect.

Bringing into play all the usual caveats about using internet sources and the pitfalls of extracting the headlines from a complex and contentious subject from the proper context of the discussions within its discipline, the following extract from https://en.wikipedia.org/wiki/Avoidant_personality_disorder is of interest: "*Avoidant Personality Disorder* (AvPD, also known as anxious personality disorder) . . . People with avoidant personality disorder often . . . avoid social interaction for fear of being ridiculed, humiliated, rejected, or disliked." Clearly, one is tempted to immediately argue that it follows that a relationship with nature is going to be so much safer than with people as the possibility of rejection is not paramount. However, in our discussions of solitude above, I quoted Storr that there is no necessity between any kind of psychological state and attachment to, and writing about, nature. Similarly, of course the discussion of AvPD does not imply that all 'loner' nature writers have some kind of 'disorder' nor that people who might be thought of as displaying such a condition are necessarily dysfunctional. AvPD is a matter of clinical diagnosis to be undertaken by an expert (and as is often rehearsed by trained psychotherapists, self-diagnoses of such disorders are often wrong) but I think for the general reader it is useful to be able to see it as perhaps an end-member of a spectrum. In terms of understanding how the use of narratives works, however, the study of the psychological literature is extremely useful as it illuminates the ways in which the non-psychologist readily adopts psychological explanations and jargon and explanations as mediated by the popular media outlets.

Thus, however tempting it is to use the AvPD label, this is too easy. 'Loner' naturalists are often very happy and fulfilled people. Our 'hawknosed and friendless' subject in the poem above may well be perfectly happy and the assessment of him tells us as much about the poet as the birdwatcher. Birdwatchers indeed are often quite sociable in terms of being willing to share their common enthusiasm. I think that one can hazard some tentative conclusions that it is possible to discern a range of relationships between aspects of nature and a great variety of different people. That is to say that many such relationships can be found but none of them have any necessity. There are a range of loners who may or may not be dysfunctional socially, and who can find solace and fulfilment in nature, but you don't have to be a loner to find solace and fulfilment in nature. Many nature writers can be seen as socially limited in some way in terms of interpersonal relations but equally such limitations are not a prerequisite for nature writing.

Earlier in this chapter we discussed the value of being both cautious and open-minded when thinking about gender and sexuality – this clearly applies to any relationship we might perceive between human characteristics and the human–nature interaction. We may find patterns and trends but association does not imply necessity.

It is thus useful to think of specific psychological analyses and terms alongside more generalised understandings of 'loner' together with notions of 'suppression' and 'wilderness therapy' – and, as one observer said to me when talking of the genre of English nature writers, 'eccentricity'. Somewhat random, elusive characteristics such as eccentricity do allow for a very wide range of traits which are not necessarily readily explained by a rational analysis. Such analyses seem somehow to me to define, categorise and thereby somehow limit human conditions. The subtleties are to my mind more discernible through the study of poetry and literature than necessarily illuminated by psychological analysis. The studies of creative writings and of psychology, however, are not in a competition for superiority – both usefully illustrate the human condition – and deepen our understanding of the human–nature relationship – in different but equally valuable ways. Equally, it should be realised that understanding and explanation are not necessarily the same thing: there can be an intuitive understanding which is beyond categorisation, analysis and explanation, and it is this elusive but very real understanding which can be found in poetic writings. They and their revelations of personal meanings in which can be found some universal meanings should surely be included in the pantheon of reasons to be considered when trying to answer the question: 'why conserve nature?'. Personal meanings about nature are very real and powerful but somehow we seem to have to reach for a list of species and emphasise rarity when justifying nature conservation. We should take more heed of what places and their wildlife mean to people.

I would like to end with a few thoughts on poetry by citing some quotations (source: www.brainyquote.com/topics/poetry-quotes):

- 'All bad poetry springs from genuine feeling' (Oscar Wilde)
- 'You campaign in poetry. You govern in prose' (Mario Cuomo, American Democratic politician and Governor of New York; www.brainyquote.com/quotes/mario_cuomo_111605)
- 'Poetry is the spontaneous overflow of powerful feelings: it takes its origin from emotion recollected in tranquillity' (William Wordsworth)
- 'Poetry is when an emotion has found its thought and the thought has found words' (Robert Frost)
- 'Poetry is not a turning loose of emotion, but an escape from emotion; it is not the expression of personality, but an escape from personality. But, of course, only those who have personality and emotions know what it means to want to escape from these things' (T. S. Eliot)
- 'I decided that it was not wisdom that enabled poets to write their poetry, but a kind of instinct or inspiration, such as you find in seers and prophets who deliver all their sublime messages without knowing in the least what they mean' (Socrates)
- 'Poetry is finer and more philosophical than history; for poetry expresses the universal, and history only the particular' (Aristotle)
- 'When power leads man toward arrogance, poetry reminds him of his limitations. When power narrows the area of man's concern, poetry reminds him of the richness and diversity of existence. When power corrupts, poetry cleanses' (John F. Kennedy)

5.4 A Woodland, without an Ecological Scientist

These Are My Meanings, What Are Yours?

Turning more to creative writing now, it is obvious that the self as an object of study is fraught with pitfalls one need not rehearse. However, as a further insight into the inner personal world of nature, I can, of course, turn to my own experience. I would first like to make a complete contrast about the experience of being in a woodland with an ecologist and their drowning narratives as discussed in Section 3.2. Here, I don't want to impose scientific narratives, perfectly valid as they may be, but wish to be more experiential and deferential to nature.

I'd like to introduce you to a wood in South Devon (Figure 5.2), without an ecological scientist telling me where to look, what to see and how it all works. Can you see what I meant in Section 3.2 when I baulked at the ecological scientist saying "Here we have..." and explaining everything? I must admit that I have done this many times

Figure 5.2 I'd like to introduce you to a wood in South Devon (Photo: S. Trudgill). *A black and white version of this figure will appear in some formats. For the colour version, please refer to the plate section.*

myself when teaching but I shall always be grateful to the Field Studies Council who allowed me to run family natural history courses at Slapton Ley Field Centre where we could engender a sense of wonder in all ages of people by writing descriptions and poems and by drawing and painting. Thus, people not only listened to me at some stage and found a given meaning – a meaning given to them by me – they also found their own meanings – personal meanings – which are much more important in providing motivations. There is no reason why teaching ecology should not impart a sense of wonder, and in fact in many ways it should, but somehow the syllabus militates against this. Here, I go into Slapton Ley Nature Reserve in Devon, UK, free from didactic ecology and can dwell in a poetic sense of wonder and associations with nature.

Make of these writings what you will. I may cite again here the quote: 'All bad poetry springs from genuine feeling' from Oscar Wilde. So, however flawed you might think these poems are, that is not the point, they are mine – and they express what nature means to me and why I would wish to conserve it. It wouldn't necessarily be the rational case of the rare species, the biodiversity count, the trophic structure, it can be all that but it is more the associations which give me the meanings. It would be the way nature makes me feel.

Woodland Associations and Meanings

Around, patches of the woodland floor are sunlit.
The sun shines too on flaky, cracked red-warmed glow of bark.
The wind in the leaves makes a soothing yearning sound
and Bracken dances below in rusty jerkiness.
Grasses hang in delicate plumes
in subtle infinities of light and shade (Figure 5.3).

Small Wood Sorrel flowers with delicate veining inviting the bees
bending down to touch them, cupped between my tentative fingers.
Wood Anemones pulse gently in the breeze
pure white within with blushing purple on the backs of petals.

Ferns stand half uncurled, each new frond (Figure 5.4)
with a scroll of yet uncurled at end
pale green against the ivy-laden Chestnuts.

Figure 5.3 Subtle infinities of light and shade (Photo: S. Trudgill)

Figure 5.4 Ferns stand half uncurled, each new frond with a scroll of yet uncurled (Photo: S. Trudgill). *A black and white version of this figure will appear in some formats. For the colour version, please refer to the plate section.*

The grey-green Beech trunks lean
grappling their roots into the soil.
New leaves quiver in the wind with sun through silver-haired edges.
Sun shafts spread out in dust-speckled rays
over tumbled grass-tussocked mounds and curled leaves.

Dapples of moving light wander as I watch.
Twigs and old beech mast crackle in the sun,
green stains seep from cup-jointed boughs
where brown water collects with leaves.
Ferns uncurl yet more, their feathery edges catching the sunlight and the sea air is blue beyond (Figure 5.5).

Figure 5.5 Ferns uncurl yet more, their feathery edges catching the sunlight (Photo: S. Trudgill)

Pale petals of woodland flowers
pale cheeks and deep eyes, gentle hair, sunlight in leaves and wood floor
bluebells, dazzling, crushed slightly
nature unfurls,

Brave is the Campion in the Bluebell's sheet of light
brave is the verve of the sun in the new veined leaf
and brave and deep is the love I have for woods
Courage is not men's bravado, yelling and roaring;
Courage is to have the quiet vulnerable thought
like the fleeting sun in the new-veined leaf
new wrought
new thought
new wonder

The bluebells keep their succulent showy secret here (Figure 5.6)
and their haze is not the sky reflected – as might be glimpsed
but their own light floating in the grasses
where the badger might make his home.

Figure 5.6 The bluebells keep their succulent showy secret here (Photo: S. Trudgill). *A black and white version of this figure will appear in some formats. For the colour version, please refer to the plate section.*

Trees, Their Associations and Meanings

I remember how in 1968, when I was 21 and on a student field trip and meant to be studying some historical monument out of the coach window, I had actually been writing:

When I see them, I feel as if there is nothing
that can move me as much
as black silhouetted pine trees,
black against the sunset sky or lurking in the sunset murk,
east glow and moon tears of lighter cloud from the edge of the night
and, that Oh so moving gaunt black silhouette.
Nothing can express the movement within,
stirred by that black primeval shape
and form of black sunset pine
in the blue white red sky.

I did ask myself if, when I wrote that, it was because I had read Brooke's 1907 'Pine Trees and the Sky: Evening' only for it to emerge from my subconscious again as my less worthy but nonetheless strongly personally felt poem? A fragment of a Brooke biography comes to me and I ask myself if I too should be banished from the Presence of the Almighty? – "for thy song was not thine own", as was the derivative poet in Brooke's Fable (in *The Venture*, January 1906; from Hassall, 1964: 82). But, from whatever source or inspiration I had written my poems, I have always felt so close to Rupert Brooke, especially when I was younger. I sometimes felt then that he was the only person I could relate to. He made me feel that I was not alone in my relationship with nature. Others have said that my poems are influenced by Wordsworth, Gerald Manley Hopkins or Hermann Hesse. However, to me they are mine even if somewhat derivative. It is my expression of myself.

Meaning about Me as a Transient Human Being

See the dead tree in the sky.
See how its torture
and its twists speak screaming
and below along the path come I
to listen for a while and now
to a tale of death
not told, a feeling, no cry
but a semblance, an emotion
from within its crusty trunk,
dusty, cracked, split and dry
which tells so much of me
that I am here just now,
here to pass along and die.
But I did not mind
if to die is to be like the dead tree in the sky
and to live was to be passing by.

All Summer Long; by a River with Like-Minded Friends

The Kingfisher draws his dart across the scene.
Tall, whispering lushness grows by the river (Figure 5.7)

as I wonder at the fleeting flash of colour
above the tea brown blue reflected ripples
and, turning round in the specked sunshaft,
at the soft green roundness of the trees
embracing my soul in gentleness and in depth.

Figure 5.7 Tall, whispering lushness grows by the river (Photo: S. Trudgill)

I feel that there is something else here with me, a presence.
Much greater than me.
Much older than me.
A chill breath tingles the back of my neck.
It is a poet's moment, a reverend dream.

The leaves proclaim their green
and mists gather dewy in the meadow dawn.
Flights of birds chorus in the sun-ripe wood
while I walk in wonder at the joy.
Glory in flowers and grasses
and relive and live again.
And I may wander
by the immensity of the sea
where salt-laden legs are crusty,
with feet on sand-ribs by the rock and weed
and sea birds pipe and call.

All summer long.
Recalling the meal in the shade,
dappled with memories,
laughing with wine and friends.

Figure 5.8 The white umbels comforted the hedges (Photo: S. Trudgill)

Filled with an undying love in the sun.

A picture painted, framed and gone, yet never leaving me.

A June Evening – Associations of Time and Place

A quiet music seemed to play in the evening's depth,
gently lifting up to the fingered sky-cut chestnut leaves
and caressing down over the swallow-dashed meadows
where the white umbels comforted the hedges (Figure 5.8)
and the hawthorn spilled her blossoms to the grasses.

Quietly, the flowers gently lilted in the shade
and the low sun warmed the scented herbs.
The wind flowed through the lime trees,
taking the leaves to one side

in a gentle rippling confidence
between the refreshing cloud-washed air
and the gaunt, earth-bound trees.

Softly, out on the moors beyond,
the heather and bilberry dappled in a mystique of greens and earthy hues
and whispered rustlings.
Gently, the river flowed in lush corners of rippling stones
and the soaking bank sprouted its yellow irises
while the lazy trout flocks sank in the sun-lost weed and gloom.

Bluebells gracefully fade to leave their green purses proud
and bracken uncurled yet more;
oak is now a manly green
and the ash has softened its grey branches
in the velvet air warbled by the sound of blackbirds,
to say the embrace of night,
though scarce begun,
will lift again so soon.

Over the farmland, the dusk-laden evening wore on
the sun sank towards the reddening horizon.
A lapwing cried from the dusk-bound soil.
The land heaved in corn-breasted rises,
as if the earth was trying to breathe
stretch and shake off domestication.
Neat, the squared fields yielded and grew
woods and hedges, trimmed and accounted for,
glowed in the lowering sun.
A star appeared above the farmhouse
a badger sniffed the air in the wood.
I saw an otter stir from her holt
slide into the river in search of food,
the ghost of Henry Williamson going with her
as she sniffed her sensitive way along the path.
Lapwings cried and rose from the soil,
evoking the ghosts, tearing and tumbling into the air
the old forgotten wild forest souls stirred a little.
Was there a small clank of horse metal in the woodland ride
as some spectral horseman kept a tryst?
The old tree trunks stood in dark quiet solidity over the land
the land where grandfathers had sat under harvest hedges
and village lads had courted blouse-girt breasts
in the shy straw stacks.

The lapwing cried one last time
a white owl swam in silence over the darkened fields.
It was the poet's hour.
Souls and the soul of nature mingled in my soul.

Nature Metaphors for Human Relationships

Love should be like a flower
it should grow; in the dark room at night
  it should wave its showy head
Flaunt its petals in the beery smoke choke at a party
wave its colours like mayweed in a tarmac crack
send its arms round shoulders, tenderly tendrils
and kiss the lips with unafraid open petals.
It should wave its stamens and sepals in the breeze
Be bright, red or yellow or delicate and white
as flowers are.

It should stand up like a daisy in the breeze
stutter and bend and wave like a dandelion on the verge
stand out in the sweaty room like a bluebell in the park
and cling and flaunt its elements as the raging weed
willowherb covers the bare ground. It should
Thunder and Roar with the cotton grass wind on the mountain
and be not afraid to show its head.
And, having bloomed its best
be faded by morning
. . . maybe to grow from the root . . .
. . . next time?

Do not lose the root, despite the hurt
This most precious thing.
Nurture the root well in the soil of your soul
Remember, you, like the flower
cannot bloom all the time and
the flower will come again
Be gone by morning
and flower again, again.

Being with a Friend in Nature

The Last Human

I want to write a poem
and I don't know what it is

but it has something to do with
being
and that there really are not any answers
it has something to do with eyelashes, face, cheeks and a smile
no, something closer. Arms thin from your shirt
being next to you,
seeing your eyes
sensing you and your being
reading you
like your shirt and arms and you being you
and your eyes finding mine
sensing the difference
between you and me
and the 'I am there for you' feeling
and that you sense my 'I am there for you' feeling
the tirade against all the crap disappears
the rant is dissolved
I am with you, another human being
it is the
unconditionality
the devotion to the chance
that you might be you
and that I might be me
and that we shall smile to
at
and for
each other
the poise
between
you
me
and us
sensed separately
on our islands
together and alone
where you are and me
are the most important
and where 'us' is just a way of you being you and me being me

Nature

Nature is
an analogy,
a comparison of feelings,

Figure 5.9 Finding yourself, being able to think (Photo: S. Trudgill). *A black and white version of this figure will appear in some formats. For the colour version, please refer to the plate section.*

a wholeness,
a hard thing, callous and indifferent,
a contrast,
comfort, a human source of warmth, a sympathy,
finding yourself, being able to think, (Figure 5.9)
a vigorous force, participation, joy, sweeping emotion,
hope, individual, inspiration.

Meanings and Associations

So, if it is proposed to build a road though these places, concrete it over, build houses, dump rubbish in it, what do you lose? Yes, you lose biodiversity, interesting and rare species, ecosystems. Yes, you lose capacity to absorb carbon dioxide. Yes, these can all be costed. Yes, a rational case can be made. But with one sweep of the bulldozers and chainsaws, you lose associations and meaning. As in the quotation attributed to the writer John Muir: "In every walk with nature one receives far more than he seeks." You lose places to be. There is ecological damage but, I submit, also psychological damage. The Lakeland writer Alfred Wainwright (1992: 210) has observed that: "We should all of us have a treasury of happy memories to sustain us when life is unbearably cruel, to brighten the gloom a little, to be stars shining through the darkness." If these memories are associated with places, then we treasure the thought of these places to sustain us even when we are not in these places.

For ancient woodland, the sites have been stable for many hundreds of years and often, it can be reasonably estimated, for much longer. The Woodland Trust website www.woodlandtrust.org.uk/trees-woods-and-wildlife/habitats/ancient-woodland/ defines UK ancient woods as areas of woodland that have persisted since 1600. They feel that they "are our richest and most complex terrestrial habitat" with "centuries of undisturbed soils and accumulated decaying wood" which means that "ancient woods are irreplaceable" because "we can't replace the complex biodiversity of ancient woods which has accumulated over hundreds of years". They point out that "all ancient woodlands are unique, and are distinctive of their locality. Once what little we have left is gone, it's gone for good." For those who propose to destroy an ancient woodland and replace it with a modern plantation and assume that this will be fine, I would point out that this is akin to demolishing St Paul's Cathedral, Stonehenge or the Giant's Causeway and building a replacement in modern materials. The deep history has gone for ever.

Yet there are limitations. When I walk somewhere I am referring all the time to associations – to what I know, to ecological knowledge, to literary knowledge: if I see a river I might well be thinking of otters and Henry Williamson's *Tarka the Otter* book. But if I do not know any of these things, then there are no such associations. Thus, no such loss if the scene I contemplate is gone. The conservation endeavour then becomes one of engendering such association as, for example, promoted by Action for Conservation (www.actionforconservation.org/about-us) which was born of a vision that every young person in the UK is moved and empowered to protect the natural world. And here there is a crucial difference between a given meaning, from someone else, and the discovery of your own meanings. The latter are always more telling, deeper and more affective. Additionally, environmental psychology tells us that there are benefits to us even if we are not necessarily conscious of them.

5.5 Environmental Psychology, Nature and Solitude

Useful Overviews

In a paper in the first volume of the *Journal of Happiness Studies*, the role of our affinity with nature is discussed in relation to contemporary mental health (Gullone, 2000). Here, the interesting thesis is that we have well-developed valuable responses to natural stimuli of evolutionary significance but few such responses to more recent potentially dangerous human-made stimuli. It can thus be argued that there is a general benefit of increased psychological well-being upon exposure to natural features and environments to which the human psyche has become attuned through human evolution.

However, psychological well-being on exposure to nature does not necessarily seem automatic. Nor is it simple. Many writings in environmental psychology attempt to assess the varied relationships between people's attitudes to the environment and their actual behaviour towards it, including the study of how the relationships might be explained and predicted. Other discussions concern the putative positive aspects of nature therapy and the wilderness experience. I say 'putative positive' as Davis-Berman and Berman (1993) point out that a wilderness experience is not automatically positive. In their paper on therapeutic wilderness programs they write that some kind of directional focus may be essential for a positive experience because, as they put it, "the mountains do not speak for themselves" (p. 131). They thus feel that the positive narrative may have to be facilitated. This is reinforced by Long et al. (2003) who stress that solitude experiences in nature can be both negative and positive, ranging from a "feeling that drains you of positivity" to a comforting "blanket of mental warmth" (Long et al., 2003: 583). It is evident that the type of nature experience is important. This can range from an encounter with an engaging bird in a safe setting like a garden to a riskier – but possibly more rewarding – wilderness immersion. The reward is often related to preparedness – the saying that 'there is no such thing as bad weather, only bad clothing' is an example of this aspect. The experience is also moderated by the social and personal context of the person involved and whether or not companions are present.

One particularly useful paper which caught my attention because it synthesised several other papers is by McMahan and Este (2015) on 'The effect of contact with natural environments on positive and negative affect: A meta-analysis'. Their main conclusion from an analysis of

Box 5.3 *Selected environmental psychology writings*

- Some of the earliest papers which were by Wohlwill (1970) on 'The emerging discipline of environmental psychology' and Craik (1970) on environmental psychology, with the *Journal of Environment and Behaviour* starting up in 1969.
- Proshansky, Ittelson and Rivlin (1970): *Environmental Psychology: Man and his physical setting.*
- A classic and oft-quoted book: *The Experience of Nature* by Kaplan and Kaplan (1989).
- A series of edited books on different psychological aspects of people and the environment involving Irwin Altman and Joachim Wohlwill, especially *Human Behavior and Environment* (e.g. Altman and Wohlwill, 1977, 1983).
- The edited book by Altman and Low (1992) on *Place Attachment.*
- Bell et al. (1996) on *Environmental Psychology.*
- The edited volume by Clayton and Opotow (2003) on *Identity and the Natural Environment: The psychological significance of nature.*
- The *Oxford Handbook of Environmental Psychology* edited by Susan Clayton (2012) and the introduction to environmental and conservation psychology by Clayton and Saunders (2012) who cite Proshansky, Ittelson and Rivlin (1970) as the first core text on environmental psychology.

32 studies, with a total of 2,356 participants, is that even given all the variation in attitudes and experience, overall the exposure to natural environments was on balance associated with a moderate increase in what they call 'positive affect', which is another way of saying 'emotional well-being'. Other relevant environmental psychology writings which I have found especially useful include those in Box 5.3. In terms of the psychology of the care of nature and the restorative benefits of nature important books and papers, to my mind, include those in Box 5.4.

Of particular note in the context of nature in the urban environment is the work of the OPENspace centre at Edinburgh (www.geography-matters.org/; www.openspace.eca.ed.ac.uk/) on the connection between nature experience and well-being with a focus on urban green space. Selected publications include: Braubach et al. (2017) on 'Effects of urban green space on environmental health, equity and resilience'; Ward Thompson (2002) on *Urban Open Space in the 21st Century*; Ward

Box 5.4 *Selected writings on the psychology of the care of nature and the restorative benefits of nature*

- Blewett (2018): *Medicine for Contemporary Ills: A 'dose of nature'?*.
- Clayton and Myers (2015). *Conservation Psychology: Understanding and promoting human care for nature.*
- Kaplan (1995): 'The restorative benefits of nature: Towards an integrative framework'.
- Lewicka (2011): 'Place attachment: How far have we come in the last 40 years?'.
- Mancha and Yoder (2015) on 'Cultural antecedents of green behavioural intent: An environmental theory of planned behaviour'.
- Robbins (2020): 'Ecopsychology: How immersion in nature benefits your health'.
- Roszak, Gomes and Kanner (1995): *Ecopsychology: Restoring the earth/healing the mind.*
- Saunders (2003: 138): 'The emerging field of conservation psychology', who defined conservation psychology as: "The scientific study of the reciprocal relationships between humans and the rest of nature, with a particular focus on how to encourage conservation of the natural world."

Thompson's overview (2016) editorial on landscape and health; and Ward Thompson et al. (2019) in 'Enhancing health through access to nature' on the effectiveness of woodlands in deprived urban communities.

Further literature abounds but particularly interesting aspects include the role of solitude in psychological well-being, especially in the context of solitude in nature and the general restorative effects of nature.

Solitude

There is a clear distinction to be made between loneliness, seen as generally negative, and solitude, often positive but not necessarily so. Indeed, it is cited above that Long et al. (2003: 578) mentioned both negative and positive aspects of solitude. They begin their article by discussing the relationships between creativity, solitude and nature, noting that the sentiments of many creative people were expressed by Thoreau ([1854] 1981: 205) when he observed: "I never found the companion that was so

Box 5.5 *Nine types of solitude, modified from Long et al. (2003: 579)*

1. *Anonymity*. Free from the constraints of society. P
2. *Creativity*. Self-expression helped by being alone. P
3. *Diversion*. Distracting activities. Neu
4. *Inner peace*. Relaxation, calmness, freedom from pressures. P
5. *Intimacy*. You can feel close to someone you care about. P
6. *Loneliness*. Longing for contact with other people. Neg
7. *Problem-solving*. A chance to think things through. P
8. *Self-discovery*. Gaining insight into your own being. P
9. *Spirituality*. A sense of something greater than yourself (e.g. God or nature). P

companionable as solitude." The authors then note that the Wilderness Act of 1964 (US Public Law 88-577) mandated congressionally designated wilderness areas "to preserve natural conditions, to provide opportunities for solitude, and to provide a primitive and unconfined type of recreation" (Shafer and Hammitt, 1995: 266). They then note that recently psychologists "have become interested in the positive aspects of solitude, particularly the opportunity it provides to engage in self-selected activities, relatively free of social encumbrances and expectations".

Long et al. (2003: 578) stress the work of Larson (1990) which suggested that "the ability to profit from solitude requires a sense of self that can survive in the absence of immediate social reinforcement", noting that this point is derived from Winnicott's (1958) influential article 'The capacity to be alone'. They write (p. 579) that Winnicott "posited that people who as infants were free to explore and independently occupy themselves in the security of their mothers' presence are best able to benefit from solitude" and that: "A closely related conceptualization of solitude by Modell (1993) suggests that such securely attached people are free to surrender themselves in solitude to some passionate commitment outside the self, whether it be God, an ideology, a lover, or a creative muse." In their own research with undergraduates Long et al. (2003: 579) proposed nine types of solitude, where P = Positive, Neg = Negative, Neu = Neutral as shown in Box 5.5. They then asked 320 psychology undergraduate volunteers (80 per cent female, median age 20, range 18–56) to complete a questionnaire. They were tasked to rate the importance of the solitude types listed. The aspect of being alone to 'think things through' (problem-solving)

Table 5.1 *Mean rankings of importance for nine varieties of solitude on a scale of 1–7 (7 = highest) (modified from Long et al., 2003)*

Solitude Type	*Ranked Mean Importance Score*
Problem-solving	5.4
Inner peace	5.2
Self-discovery	5.1
Diversion	5.0
Creativity	4.4
Anonymity	4.2
Intimacy	4.0
Spirituality	3.6
Loneliness	2.8

Table 5.2 *Physical setting in which each type of solitude is likely to be experienced: percentage endorsing ranked by 'in nature' (modified from Long et al., 2003)*

	Percentage Experienced		
Solitude Type	In nature	At home	In a public place
Spirituality	67	23	10
Inner peace	42	53	6
Self-discovery	26	62	12
Creativity	20	61	19
Problem-solving	18	72	11
Intimacy	17	70	13
Anonymity	5	83	13
Loneliness	2	70	28
Diversion	1	95	4

came top next to tranquillity (inner peace), thinking about yourself (self-discovery) and getting away from pressures (diversion) (Table 5.1).

In terms of the setting there are relationships between the type and the location of the solitude (Table 5.2), with 'spirituality' featuring highly in the 'in nature' category. The negative category 'loneliness' features highly in the 'at home' category but is very small in nature. While the authors note that participants overwhelmingly reported that solitude was most likely to occur in their own home, they feel that this is hardly surprising for undergraduate respondents, many of whom have their own individual study bedrooms, so the authors feel that this is a trivial finding.

They feel that it is significant that spirituality, when it did occur, was far more likely to occur in nature (67 per cent) than at home (23 per cent). A sizable minority of participants also indicated that inner peace, self-discovery and creativity were likely to occur in nature (42 per cent, 26 per cent and 20 per cent for the three types, respectively).

The authors' insights on their results include Long et al. (2003: 582): "nature ... was considered conducive to both inner-and outer-directed types of solitude, especially to spirituality and inner peace. Few participants considered nature to be a place of loneliness. This may be due, in part, to the fact that people seldom find themselves alone in nature except by choice." Specifically on the positive aspects of the nature experience they concluded: "Volition [wanting to be there] is a major determinant that tips the balance between positive and negative experiences of solitude. But the aesthetic and awe-inspiring qualities of the natural environment undoubtedly also play a role in contributing to positive experiences (Hammitt and Madden, 1989)." The respondents were also all asked about their own psychological profile including indices of depression, emotional creativity, close relationships, introversion-extroversion and neuroticism, life satisfaction, preferences for solitude, self-esteem, loneliness (Wood, 1986) and values. They conclude that: "People who are securely attached (low avoidance and low anxiety towards close relationships) would experience solitude positively, whereas people who are insecurely attached (high avoidance and high anxiety toward close relationships) would experience solitude negatively."

A particularly useful insight in these contexts can be gained from the work of Staats and Hartig (2004) reported in a paper entitled 'Alone or with a friend: A social context for psychological restoration and environmental preferences'. Their overall conclusion is that personal restoration in nature settings was enabled by solitude provided the lone person felt safe. In a city, the company of another enhanced personal restoration while in the wilderness the effect of company was ambiguous unless the researchers allowed for the feeling of how safe the subject felt: "The absence of a general effect of company in the natural environment owes to two opposed effects: company enabled restoration through its effect on safety, while solitude enhanced restoration when safety was controlled for in the analysis" (Staats and Hartig, 2004: 199). They found that in a city "being in company enhances the pleasure of walking in an urban environment, but not because it enhances restoration .... the social nature of the city evokes a desire to share this experience with others, especially intimates" (Staats and Hartig, 2004: 209). For walking in nature they found that if the participants felt safe, then there was a preference for solitude in terms of restoration benefit: "company enables restoration by providing safety, but, when safety is not a concern, restoration is enhanced by the absence of company" (Staats and Hartig, 2004: 209).

A conclusion that the experiences of solitude in nature and elsewhere will vary with the person, the context and the setting will hardly surprise a scientifically trained psychologist but it does give us insights which promote a sense of questioning about the automatic assumption of the benefit of the wilderness experience. We can thus think about the exact kind of 'therapy' which nature and wilderness can provide and also raise questions about whether any benefits are greatest for solitary individuals or in some kind of social groupings, be they small or large.

Restorative Nature

In terms of the restorative effects of nature, there are debates as to precisely what this might mean or entail. In an article on 'Natural resistance: Exposure to nature and self-regulation, mood, and physiology after ego-depletion' Beute and de Kort (2014) examine Kaplan's (1995) Attention Restoration Theory and Kaplan and Berman's (2010) discussion of executive functioning and self-regulation. They stress the importance of exposure to nature in our daily lives for "numerous health outcomes" in relation to the strengthening of self-regulation capacity (Beute and de Kort, 2014: 177). These authors refer to the work of Terry Hartig (Hartig et al., 1997, 2003, 2014; Hartig, Mang and Evans, 1991) and they stress what he calls instorative effects (Hartig, 2007: 164) and he writes thus:

> Restoration involves beneficial changes, but not every benefit warrants description as 'restorative'. Some benefits realised in a particular environment involve deepening or strengthening capabilities for meeting everyday demands. A person may for example become more self-reliant or self-confident, acquire new skills or gain in physical fitness. I have used the word 'instorative' to distinguish this other family of benefits from restorative benefits. (Hartig et al., 1996)

In this context, the paper by McMahan and Este (2015), mentioned above, is worth exploring in more detail. Their study posited that: "A growing body of empirical research suggests that brief contact with natural environments improves emotional wellbeing." They concluded that "exposure to natural environments was associated with a moderate increase in positive affect and a smaller, yet consistent, decrease in negative affect relative to comparison conditions".

In terms of the study of the psychology of the benefits of nature, Bratman et al. (2015) again compared the responses of sixty participants in a fifty-minute walk in either a natural or an urban environment in terms of affective and cognitive functioning. Compared to the urban walk, the walk in a natural environment was found to have marked affective benefits in terms of decreased anxiety, rumination and positive affect and preservation of positive affect as well as cognitive benefits in terms of increased working memory performance.

On the affective impact of nature experience Bratman et al. (2015: 42) write: "Stress reduction theory (SRT) provides an explanation for the impact of nature experience on affect. This theory posits that natural environments have a restorative advantage over artificial environments due to the role that they played in our evolution as a species (Ulrich, 1981)". Specifically,

> nature scenes activate our parasympathetic nervous system in ways that reduce stress and autonomic arousal, because of our innate connection to the natural world. Particular natural landscapes (especially grasslands with clusters of trees) tended to provide human beings with 'opportunities' for gain, and places of 'refuge' for safety. According to Ulrich et al. (1991), viewing these types of landscapes activates our physiology in affectively beneficial ways, as we have evolved to have an innate preference for these types of environments. (Bratman et al., 2015: 42)

On cognitive functioning they ask:

> Why might nature experience influence cognition? According to Attention Restoration Theory (ART), . . . urban environments deplete this cognitive resource, and can thereby worsen performance on tasks that rely on this focused, directed attention (Hartig et al., 1991 and Kaplan and Kaplan, 1989). According to ART, natural environments invoke a different sort of attention from people – a sense of 'fascination', 'being away', 'extent', and 'compatibility'. This, in turn, may lead to improved performance on tests that measure memory and attention. (Bratman et al., 2015: 42)

They give examples of benefits from a number of authors and sources:

- students who had views of nature through their windows performed better on tasks that require concentration (the Necker Cube pattern test – cognition of the possible patterns from the outline of a drawing of a cube, as described by Necker, 1832) than students without such views;

- the restorative influence of nature on sustained attention showed that participants who viewed nature photographs performed better on the task than those who saw images of urban environments; and
- similarly, walking through a natural greenspace, compared to walking through an urban environment, yields benefits for verbal working memory, cognitive control and concentration (the Necker Cube pattern test).

It seems apparent that the reasons why people can feel an engagement with nature are not easy to encompass in any simplistic way. Attempts at such an analysis have found associations with a variety of psychological profiles and social and cultural contexts. However, what is somewhat clearer is that whatever a person's psychological profile and social and cultural contexts, the evidence is that contact with nature can be seen as beneficial in a range of ways. So, while this range of effects obviously varies with the individual and the context, there do seem to be a range of positive benefits ranging from the cognitive, the affective as well as the physical. Thus, as McMahan and Este (2015) concluded in their meta-analysis there is a general 'positive affect' but we now have some greater awareness of the dimensions of the issues and variations which can be involved. This section has discussed a partial and selective review of the literature, but nonetheless, some conclusions can now be afforded.

Solitude and Nature: A Conclusion

Long et al. (2003: 582) felt that:

> As human beings, we are social by nature. An isolated person, with few means of natural defense, would not survive for long 'in the wild'. Not surprisingly, then, we seek and enjoy the company of others, and we may go to great lengths to avoid being alone. But too much sociality can be oppressive. We need time alone as a relief from social stressors, an opportunity for reflection and insight, and a chance for personal, spiritual, and creative development. (e.g. Burger, 1998; Koch, 1994)

Long et al.'s (2003) study was about solitude per se in a number of settings and for a range of people and it is clearly one thing to come to conclusions about their findings in these contexts but yet another to extrapolate from them to reach conclusions about the benefit of nature as experienced by the solitary person.

One can but conclude that beneficial solitude is not solely to be found in nature settings, as some more romantic writers would have us believe, and if solitude is not necessarily a positive experience then the benefits or otherwise of solitude are related to the personality and psychological profile of the individual as much as to setting and context. What is suggested, however, is that nature can provide benefits for the solitary person in terms of both the more reflective aspects of the experience and the outgoing aspects, with a higher, more spiritual experience and experience of some 'other' being writ largest in nature.

It also might be salutary to ponder on the implications of the idea that:

> We are all alone, born alone, die alone, and – in spite of True Romance magazines – we shall all someday look back on our lives and see that, in spite of our company, we were alone the whole way. I do not say lonely – at least, not all the time – but essentially, and finally, alone. This is what makes your self-respect so important, and I don't see how you can respect yourself if you must look in the hearts and minds of others for your happiness. (Hunter S. Thompson, 1997: 182)

It occurs to me that being alone in nature – and enjoying it and surviving it, thriving even – is one way to greatly increase one's self-respect. We simultaneously can find ourselves and also find within us a higher spiritual experience of nature. Most significantly, neither the self-respect nor the spirituality is dependent on anyone else.

5.6 Chapter Summary

- Personal meanings of nature may be more inward looking – finding something of ourselves in nature, or more outward looking – finding something intrinsic in nature which is valued because it is independent of us.
- Engagements with nature may be a 'viewing', a cataloguing – an identification of – or an 'immersion', a relationship – an identification with.
- There is a significant idea of immersion in nature, being in nature rather than watching nature. By giving yourself to the nature experience, there are elements of both losing yourself and finding yourself. A personalised empathic identification with meanings in nature and simultaneously sensing connections with something much greater than us, often with a sense of ownership, possession even, is self-validating.
- Finding fulfilment through experiencing nature in comparative isolation independent of interpersonal relationships can occur though a sense of social rejection and alienation or it may be found in individuals who may be solitary through positive choice and indeed may be socially adjusted individuals.

- There is a wide spectrum of experience, though the solitary experience of nature as a counterpoint to social experience is a theme which receives much attention. Here, the person involved tends to be one whose principal need is to find some kind of meaning and order in life which is not entirely, or even chiefly, dependent upon interpersonal relationships.
- Nature may well be very therapeutic but it is also indifferent to us. People may bring their own problems with them rather than necessarily escape them. There can be a duality of the wilderness experience where the counterpoint to everyday life is both the essence and pitfall of the experience.
- In nature writing, the creative process can transform individual experience into something universally apprehensible and significant. Gender and sexuality may not play a key role in our relationship with nature but gender and sexuality may well play a key role in nature writing especially in terms of a society's attitude to these characteristics.
- A sense of love of nature may be in lieu of a specific love for other humans or stem from a generalised lack of love for humanity. While a love of nature can be expressed by anyone, it can often be found in literature as a manifestation of a love for other people which either may be denied or otherwise cannot be expressed.
- Personal meanings about nature are very real and powerful but somehow we seem to have to reach for a list of species and emphasise rarity when justifying nature conservation. We should take more heed of what places and their wildlife mean to people. Loss of nature means that you not only lose wildness and species but you lose places to be. There is thus ecological damage but also psychological damage.
- In the study of human–nature relationships, it seems apparent that there are associations with a variety of psychological profiles and social and cultural contexts. However, what is somewhat clearer is that whatever a person's psychological profile and social and cultural contexts, the evidence is that contact with nature can be seen as beneficial in a range of ways.
- This range of effects obviously varies with the individual and the context but there do seem to be a range of positive benefits ranging from the cognitive, the affective as well as the physical. There is a general 'positive affect' of being alone in nature. Enjoying it and surviving it, thriving even, greatly increase one's self-respect. We simultaneously can find ourselves and also find within us a higher spiritual experience of nature.

6 · *Places for Nature*

6.1 Places and Nature: From the 'Domestic' to the 'Wild'

The State of Nature and the 'Biodiversity Crisis': Global

It seems that there is a decreasing place for nature. World wildlife populations 'fall by 58% in 40 years' runs the BBC News headline for 26 October 2016 at www.bbc.co.uk/news/science-environment-37775622. The assessment from the Intergovernmental Science-Policy Platform on Biodiversity and Ecosystem Services (IPBES, meeting 29 April–4 May 2019 in Paris) showed a widespread global loss of habitats and species (UN, 2019: www.un.org/sustainabledevelopment/blog/2019/05/nature-decline-unprecedented-report). The report is the most comprehensive ever completed and draws from scientists and indigenous and local knowledge. Key conclusions are that current efforts to conserve the earth's resources are likely to fail without radical action and about one million species are at risk of extinction – one in four of the existing species. Crop security is threatened long-term. Marine pollution has increased tenfold since 1980 (https://news.un.org/en/story/2019/05/1037941). Many of these points are also endorsed in the World Wildlife Fund (WWF)'s *Living Planet Report 2020*: https://livingplanet.panda.org/en-gb. Selected, summarised key points are shown in Box 6.1.

A key finding is:

> Recognition of the knowledge, innovations and practices, institutions and values of Indigenous Peoples and Local Communities and their inclusion and participation in environmental governance often enhances their quality of life, as well as nature conservation, restoration and sustainable use. Their positive contributions to sustainability can be facilitated through national recognition of land tenure, access and resource rights in accordance with national legislation, the application of free, prior and informed consent, and improved collaboration, fair and equitable sharing of benefits arising from the use, and co-management arrangements with local communities.

Box 6.1 *Selected key points from UN (2019) Global Assessment Report of the state of nature*

- Nature is declining globally at rates unprecedented in human history; around one million animal and plant species are now threatened with extinction.
- Abundance of native species' land-based habitats has fallen. Amphibian species, reef-forming corals, marine mammals and insects are specially cited.
- The five global drivers of change in nature are, in descending order: (1) changes in land and sea use; (2) direct exploitation of organisms; (3) climate change; (4) pollution; and (5) invasive alien species.
- Decline in soil organic carbon and pollinator diversity, with land degradation leading to reduced agricultural productivity.
- There is an increased risk of floods and hurricanes because of loss of coastal habitats and protection.
- Many fish stocks are being harvested at unsustainable levels.
- Pollution has increased, by plastic tenfold since 1980, with heavy metals, solvents, toxic sludge and other wastes dumped and fertilisers producing ocean 'dead zones'.
- Key issues are cattle ranching in Latin America and palm oil plantations in South-East Asia.
- Loss of biodiversity is related to people's poverty, hunger, health, water supply and welfare and is a developmental, economic, security, social and moral issue as well as environmental.

The State of Nature and the 'Biodiversity Crisis': UK

The UK Wildlife Trusts cite the figure of "60% of wild life lost in the last 40 years" and see their aim as to "restore 30% of land and sea for nature by 2030" (www.wildlifetrusts.org). The report by the National Biodiversity Network *State of Nature 2019* (https://nbn.org.uk/stateofnature2019) presented an overview of UK wildlife, using fifty years of monitoring the pressures on wildlife and the responses to them. It concludes that "statistics demonstrate that the abundance and distribution of the UK's species has, on average, declined since 1970 and many metrics suggest this decline has continued in the most recent decade" (p. 6). The report highlights agricultural management, climate change, hydrological change, urbanisation, pollution, woodland management and invasive non-native species as among the most significant of pressures acting upon terrestrial and freshwater wildlife. At sea, climate change and fishing are having the most significant impact upon marine biodiversity. The report covers a wide range of conservation initiatives including effective partnerships. Key points are shown in Box 6.2.

Box 6.2 *Key points of the UK State of Nature 2019 report*

- Since 1970, 41% of species have decreased and 26% have increased in abundance, with the remaining 33% showing little change. Over the past ten years, 44% of species have decreased and 36% have increased in abundance, with 20% showing little change.
- Long-term decreases in average abundance in butterflies since 1976 (16%) and moths since 1970 (25%) have not slowed.
- The mammal indicator shows little change since 1994.
- An increase of 43% in the bird indicator has been driven by recovery of some species from very low numbers, conservation successes and colonising species, as well as increasing numbers of wintering waterbirds.
- These increases mask abundance declines in common and widespread breeding species; the total number of breeding birds in the UK fell by forty-four million between 1967 and 2009.
- Widespread losses of habitats such as heathland, wetlands and ancient woodland.
- Some 5,000 individual nature reserves have a combined area over five times the size of Greater London.
- Increase in the area of designated inshore and offshore Marine Protected Areas (MPAs) since 2013, although designation, of itself, does not ensure effective conservation.
- Few habitats are stable and most require management of grazing levels, woodlands or hydrology.
- Reserves should welcome in people with a balance between the needs of visitors and the wildlife they come to experience.
- Need to reduce fragmentation by creating corridors between sites for wildlife to flow through to help species jump across.
- The management of large areas of potentially wildlife-rich semi-natural habitat, such as in the UK's uplands, is unsympathetic to biodiversity.

- Conservation action targeted at one species can help others – for example, reed beds for bitterns benefit other aquatic species and agri-environment options for birds benefit plants.
- Invertebrates and plants are receiving less attention than mammals and birds.
- Insects are showing rates of decline that may be greater than other taxonomic groups.
- Financial investment is crucial, as are government policy and legislation.
- The most successful conservation action arises from partnerships, across governments, charities, business, landowners and individuals.

It seems there may be a way to go in improving this situation. As an example, consider the following case made for saving Treloyhan Woods, Cornwall from development, modified from online postings from Rachael Levine's campaign on the 38 Degrees Campaigns by You website: www.youtube.com/watch?v=KWyxR2gsrIs (30 November 2014) and www.youtube.com/watch?v=nu5KKEf5kUQ (19 May 2015).

- The mature woodland at Treloyhan is unique in that it contains 34 species of trees, consisting of deciduous, coniferous and evergreen trees; the majority of trees are over 120 years old; 62 of the trees have Tree Preservation Orders (TPOs) on them; and 93 per cent are over 60 years old.
- The diversity of trees has enabled 86 species of bird to be recorded here, as well as 7 species of bats, which feed on the myriad of moths and beetles.
- Many species of birds feed exclusively in the various types of trees, for example woodpeckers, tawny owls, flycatchers and many species of warbler feed exclusively on deciduous trees while the rare firecrests and goldcrests feed on the conifers and the evergreens are nesting sites and roosting sites for the wintering visitors.
- Some of the breeding birds are catalogued as Nationally Declining species and Category 1 birds which have the highest level of protection such as the two pairs of spotted flycatchers which breed here. The population has crashed by 87 per cent and so the loss of this species not only affects Cornwall but also the population nationally.
- Local and visiting ornithologists visit this particular woodland because of the large number of bird species either resident or migrant.

This stance was not successful despite the considerable weight given to statistics like this.

Land, Cities and Sea: Domesticated, Permitted and Wild Nature

We can see that it is a conventional wisdom that we have left isolated habitats, fragmented in precious relics of nature in a small percentage of the world. For example, in the report by Professor Sir John Lawton (2010) *Making Space for Nature*, there was call for "more, bigger, better, joined" wildlife sites, extending conservation thinking beyond reserves. One response to this is that to help nature to flourish, we should be thinking of corridors which link such islands of nature. Others say that rather than focussing on the isolated places we have restricted nature to and how to link them, we have to think of whole landscapes and beyond countries if species are going to survive where they will.

Implementation ideas range from excluding people from some areas so that nature can thrive while others argue for integration of nature and human activities. Many different people have many different priorities – some of which marginalise nature and others which prioritise it and so the problem is seen in different ways and therefore the solutions differ. There are good discussions of the issues in the papers by Sandbrook et al. (2019) 'The global conservation movement is diverse but not divided' and Schleicher et al. (2019) 'Protecting half the planet could directly affect over one billion people'. There are useful insights in these writings about shared views, social representation, environmental justice and the multiple views people ascribe to nature in the contexts of the economic and prediction drivers of biodiversity loss.

In truth, it is certain aspects of nature which have become isolated: nature is everywhere, as it ever was and will be. The differences between the aspects of nature involve the spectrum of nature from the domesticated through to the wild. The spectrum is admirably discussed by Harman (2009) *The Culture of Nature in Britain 1680–1860*, together with the origins and evolution of the concepts of nature and landscape.

The aspects of domesticated or permitted nature – that which is allowed or indeed encouraged – are to be found in highly managed landscapes such as farmland, gardens, parks and smaller managed nature reserves. The relationship between domestication of the landscape and human culture as reflected in poetry is admirably described by Crawford (2002) in *Poetry, Enclosure and the Vernacular Landscape 1700–1830*. In such landscapes, there is some form of control and management ranging from cultivation through to cutting and the selection of which species to encourage or eradicate. This involves the species we tend to value like crops, flowers and some birds and animals, though the criteria for 'being of value' can vary. These situations can be found quite widely spread – and the species are present because of our decisions to foster them and their presence is on our terms. This results in the prevalence of preferred species and productive varieties developed by human agency to the detriment of others, such as is documented by an earlier compendium of such awareness by Mellanby (1981) in *Farming and Wildlife*. Additional perspectives can be found in the contemporaneous *The Common Ground: A place for nature in Britain's future?* (Mabey, 1980) and *Nature's Place* (Adams, 1986). The species may be domesticated but, however, the environmental constituents upon which the preferred organisms depend, such as soils and climate, are not there on our terms; we cannot generate them, though we can modify their effects.

Then there are aspects of wild nature – that which is not there on our terms – such as moorland, mountains, forests and the coast. This independence is core to its appeal (Mellor, 2014, 'The lure of wilderness') but it is nevertheless often managed to a greater or lesser extent and is therefore often only putatively wild. Our relationship with wild nature is more contested and ambivalent in that our attitudes can range from ones of cherishment to indifference or hostility. The latter the more so if it comes into conflict with domesticated nature. Thus, we see that we can have isolated islands of wild nature, for example woodlands (Rackham, 1986, 1990, 2003, 2006), in a contested landscape which is dominated by domesticated nature. There is also an evolving relationship with the city (MacLean, Landry and Ward, 1999; Williams, 1973) and with identity (Readman, 2018). However, we can now observe that the tide can be turned the other way, making domesticated nature a haven for wildlife, as seen in the book by Isabella Tree (2018): *Wilding: The return of nature to a British farm*. There are indeed now widespread efforts to enhance wildlife on agricultural land, for example those by the UK Wildlife Trusts: www.wildlifetrusts.org/farming.

The writer Wendell Berry (2017, 2018), seen as one of America's most powerful and radical voices about life on the land, has an interesting chapter called 'Getting along with nature' (Berry, 2017: 160). He writes that "people cannot live apart from nature, that is the first principle of conservationists. And yet, people cannot live in nature without changing it. But that is true of all creatures: they depend upon nature, and they change it." This is such an interesting observation – we can't live without nature, but we tend to modify it to our advantage if we can. He continues with two further interesting statements. The first is: "Pure nature is not good for humans to live in, and humans do not want to live in it – or not for very long. At least not without realising the desirability of basic human amenities [such as] clothing, shelter, cooked food . . ." He is here talking about an extension of his first statement – we modify nature and also mitigate its effects. His second is: "It is equally true that that a condition that is purely human is not good for people to live in, and people do not want to live for very long in it. . . . The more artificial a human environment becomes, the more the word 'natural' becomes a term of value."

So, we have trees and parks in our cities and other dwelling areas and bring nature into our dwellings in the form of houseplants or pets. We build shopping malls to protect us from the weather but then fill them with plant pots; albeit some of them plastic. And so, if we follow his reasoning, the circle is complete – we depend on nature, but we alter it; we alter it to our advantage but the more we create artificial conditions, the more we value it. I am not sure of the universality of this chain of reasoning – do urban dwellers value nature more than country dwellers; perhaps not, but certainly in *Restorative Commons: Creating health and well-being through urban landscapes* Campbell and Wiesen (2011) stress the critical interaction of planned urban structures and nature in the way the whole urban ecosystem influences human well-being.

Nature in Cities

There has been growing interest in nature in cities. One of the earliest compendiums in the UK was Fitter's (1945) *London's Natural History* in the Collins New Naturalist Series. This had a historical format from the early beginnings through to the bombings in the Second World War. The latter was notable for the considerable interest in the way in which, post war, the black redstart colonised bomb-damaged urban areas as an ideal habitat, as documented by Fitter (1971). This was recorded in *Birds of Our Country* by Finn and Robinson (n.d. but commonly cited as *c.*1920: 289) as a scarce winter visitor from the continent. Ironically, there is a report from the British Trust for Ornithology (Holloway and Glue, 1999) on the decline of the black redstart and how it could be encouraged given the restoration of buildings. However, Oliver (1997) in 'The breeding birds of inner London, 1966–94' actually showed an increase in breeding numbers from the 1968–1972 to the 1988–1994

Table 6.1 *Birds breeding or present in inner London 1968–1994*

Little Grebe *Tachybaptus ruficollis*
Great Crested Grebe *Podiceps cristatus*
Great Cormorant *Phalacrocorax carbo*
Grey Heron *Ardea cinerea*
Mute Swan *Cygnus olor*
Greylag Goose *Anser anser*
Canada Goose *Branta canadensis*
Mandarin Duck *Aix galericulata*
Mallard *Anas platyrhynchos*
Garganey *Anas querquedula*
Common Pochard *Aythya ferina*
Tufted Duck *Aythya fuligula*
Ruddy Duck *Oxyura jamaicensis*
Eurasian Sparrowhawk *Accipiter nisus*
Common Kestrel *Falco tinnunculus*
Moorhen *Gallinula chloropus*
Common Coot *Fulica atra*
Little Ringed Plover *Charadrius dubius*
Great Ringed Plover *Charadrius hiaticula*
Black-headed Gull *Larus ridibundus*
Common Gull *Larus canus*
Lesser Black-backed Gull *Larus fuscus*
Herring Gull *Larus argentatus*
Common Tern *Sterna hirundo*
Rock Dove *Columba livia*
Stock Dove *Columba oenas*
Wood Pigeon *Columba palumbus*
Collared Dove *Streptopelia decaocto*
Rose-ringed Parakeet *Psittacula krameri*
Tawny Owl *Strix aluco*
Common Swift *Apus apus*
Green Woodpecker *Picus viridis*
Great Spotted Woodpecker *Dendrocopos major*
Lesser Spotted Woodpecker *Dendrocopos minor*
Sky Lark *Alauda arvensis*
Sand Martin *Riparia riparia*
Barn Swallow *Hirundo rustica*
House Martin *Delichon urbica*
Meadow Pipit *Anthus pratensis*
Yellow Wagtail *Motacilla flava*
Grey Wagtail *Motacilla cinerea*
Pied Wagtail *Motacilla alba*
Wren *Troglodytes troglodytes*
Hedge Accentor [Dunnock] *Prunella modularis*
Robin *Erithacus rubecula*
Black Redstart *Phoenicurus ochruros*
Blackbird *Turdus merula*
Song Thrush *Turdus philomelos*

Source: Adapted from Oliver (1997). Reproduced by permission, British Trust for Ornithology

periods. This paper records the wide variety of habitats in inner London and lists the bird species breeding or present between 1968 and 1994 (Table 6.1).

In *Birds Britannica* Cocker and Mabey (2005: 343–345) record how "at least three pairs bred 1926–1941" at Wembley but how the blitz left "swathes of the capital in a state of ruin – perfect conditions for a rock-haunting species". The black redstart then spread widely first as a 'bomb-site' bird but then as a 'power-station' bird. The bird seems to flourish even in some polluted areas feeding on midges attracted to sewage discharge sites. This is certainly a bird which makes an interesting comparison with what Cocker and Mabey refer to as 'prescribed' nature reserves, instead thriving on uncared for and unmanaged sites – as they put it, like finding "a jewel on a rubbish dump". Notwithstanding the fears of Holloway and Glue above and the loss of nesting sites through re-development, the *Bird Atlas 2007–2011* (British Trust for Ornithology, 2013: 584) does record not only numbers of winter sightings but also a small but sustained distribution of breeding birds, numbering between nineteen and forty-four pairs in the city and also some coastal sites.

The New Naturalist Series published a more widely cast book by Goode (2014) on *Nature in Towns and Cities*. This chronicles how even more species have adapted to life in cities, with, for example, urban foxes and peregrine falcons nested on ledges becoming regular features. The latter is admirably in Macdonald's (2006: 173–198) *Falcon* where she refers to Henry Williamson's (1923) *The Peregrine's Saga*.

In a more general sense, green spaces have become something of a cause célèbre in planning and in urban ecological thinking. Some notable writings include Louafi (2013) on *Green Islands in the City*, which espouses ideas for urban gardens and the more integrated approach of Armour and Tempany (2020) in *Nature of the City: Green infrastructure from the ground up* where green ideas are part of the integral design of cities. The University of Sheffield Department of Landscape Architecture has done extensive work on planting in urban areas, including the work of Hitchmough and Dunnett (2004) on naturalistic planting in urban landscapes; Hitchmough (2008) on ecologically based, designed urban plant communities and Jorgensen, Hitchmough and Dunnett (2007) on urban woodland as a contribution to residential satisfaction and place identity. There is also much discussion of grassland in urban areas and how it could be made more biodiverse. The waste of water and use of fertilisers on lawns is an all too prevalent part of the urban – or at least suburban – ecosystem (Trudgill, Jeffery and Parker, 2010: 'Climate change and the resilience of the domestic lawn') not least because it lowers the resistance of the lawn to drought let alone decreasing biodiversity.

The dialogue between the intended and the spontaneous elements of nature in cities is discussed by Matthew Gandy (2002) in *Concrete and Clay: Reworking nature in New York City*; (2013), 'Marginalia: Aesthetics, ecology and urban wastelands' and in Gandy and Jasper (2020) *The Botanical City*. The topics discussed show that we can begin to understand the dimensions of an interactive relationship, with a dynamic cultural fusion of nature and human activity – a kind of reflexive dialogue involving allowing, permitting, encouraging, controlling, cherishing, celebrating, despoiling, removing or otherwise transforming nature.

Landscape and Psychogeography

This interaction has been discussed by the author David Matless (2014: 5) who has written on cultural geography, nature and landscape. He feels that while "non-human life shapes cultures" this is "subject to human attention, care and exploitation". The relationship between nature and culture is one of how "non-human objects and subjects" act "in according with or across human expectations". In more specific terms the variation of this relationship is well described by Dymond (1990: 258) when writing of the Norfolk agricultural landscape. "You can pass from a barren landscape, ecologically impoverished ... to the land of a farmer who has found a compromise ... [farming] efficiently and ... profitably but yet still manages to leave the landscape rich and stimulating." It shows that finding a place for wildlife is an individual decision and not necessarily related to a particular land use.

This involvement with the landscape gives us a sense of belonging to it. Landscapes have meanings, as well documented by Hoskins (1955) and Schama (1996) and especially by Arntzen and Brady (2008) in *Humans in the Land* and Oliver Rackham (1991) in *Landscape and the Conservation of Meaning*. The involvement can be very physical in that we actually alter the landscape or it can be psychological in terms of the way we relate to something we do not – or cannot – alter. Both the physical and the psychological may be involved, but the former tends to be more true of landscapes, the latter more so for wilderness and seascapes. Where both are involved it is often the psychological which predicates the physical, the actions being based on the psychological feelings. This idea of relating to the landscape in the sense of belonging to it is cognate with the idea of psychogeography (as discussed in Chapter 1) which addresses the way which people relate to and feel about the place they are in. There are the generalised notions such as 'heart of the country', 'mouth of the river' (Stein, 1987) but, more specifically, psychogeography developed in relation to the writings of Debord (1956, 1977; Marcus, 1989) about the urban environment and the ways you might feel about and relate to what is around you (see also Pinder, 2001). It is this 'feeling' aspect which I took in my 'psychobiogeography' paper (Trudgill, 2001a) and developed, and especially in relation to Sack's (1990) 'realm of meaning' which he sees as all important to human–nature theory. Everything springs from ideas and feelings, as stressed by Blackburn (1998: 200) in his philosophy book *Ruling Passions* where he writes of "the sentiments that actually motivate us".

If we use the concept of ownership not to refer to material rights of possession but to refer to a place which we not only feel to be ours, in the sense of belonging to it, and a place where we have our identity but also, crucially, a place subject to our influence, we own the city because we built it and somehow we can readily feel that we own the land but do we feel the same about the sea? In Mentz's (2009) cultural study of the sea, whereas a garden symbolised happy coexistence with nature, life was threatened at sea.

We might feel we own the city, at least in part where we are familiar with it. We only own wilderness in the sense of being there on its own terms, not on ours. We own a city or a dwelling in the sense that it is there on our terms, less so to individuals the city which is subject to planners, more so a dwelling which we can alter. A garden is there partly on our terms and partly on its own terms. However, while it might seem that we own the land because it is quite passive and we can alter it, this is an illusion, a fateful illusion – it too has terms of its own. Steinbeck wrote movingly of the American Dust Bowl and Wendell Berry has, among many others, written on the perils of treating the land and the soil like dirt. Wendell Berry would argue that if we think the land is there on our terms, we do so at our peril. Yet when we think of Rembrandt's painting *Het Steen* – a lovely domesticated landscape – we can feel we own it. Evidence of human influence is everywhere – we have planted, nurtured or otherwise allowed everything. Yet, as a saying goes, 'I may plant a tree but I do not grow it'. So, we have this curious 'detached ownership' where the relationship is ambiguous.

Seascapes

When we see a Turner seascape we feel the awe – in no way is it there on our terms. However, we can still feel a sense of 'ownership' of the sea in the sense of feeling that we 'belong' to it. In *The Boundless Sea* David Abulafia (2019) charts how, for most of human history, the seas and oceans have been the main means of long-distance trade and communication between peoples – for the spread of ideas and religion as well as commerce. The author shows how seafaring societies such as the Polynesians of the Pacific indeed feel 'at home' in the sea. It is the land-based traders, perhaps, who stood to lose so much at sea, that saw it as more hostile.

It has taken more recent years for people to appreciate and articulate the therapeutic aspects of the sea as Deborah Cracknell (2019) has done in *By The Sea: The therapeutic benefits of being in, on and by the water*. Interestingly, the book does indeed focus on the seas, and especially the coast, as a place for us – for human beings – to find restoration. In chapter 3 'The mental and emotional benefits of the sea' the words 'restorative', 'calm and relaxed' feature together with 'refreshed and revitalized'. More specifically, the benefits were seen as 'achieving' – especially through exercise – and 'social' – providing spaces to meet, especially for families. The 'immersive' nature of the experience was stressed – not necessarily meaning literally in the water but immersed in multi-sensory experiences of sight and sound, especially listening to and watching the breaking of waves. Fine weather and gently lapping waves are seen as soothing while watching stormy seas and wind – rain even – can be invigorating. Highly featured was something less tangible but very powerful which the author cites as 'symbolic'. The sea can be seen as 'cleansing' and 'purifying' – people could lose themselves watching the sea and the waves 'wash away' their emotions making them feel calmer. People are recorded as saying that they 'stopped and paused', forgetting the smaller things of life, finding a bigger picture and feeling 'rooted' when they were at the sea. There is reference to Heraclites who observed that 'all things are in motion like streams' – by which he meant ever changing: 'All things are passing, and nothing abides; nothing ever is, everything is becoming.' While he seems to have meant this to apply to impermanence, his thoughts on motion have led to the use of the term 'Heraclitean motion' to refer to a form of movement that is 'always changing but always remaining the same'. Repetitive, predictable patterns which always change but always stay the same are soothing – like grass blowing in the wind – whereas erratic and sudden movements put us on the alert, as discussed by Campbell and Wiesen (2011) on health and landscape and Katcher and Wilkins (1993) on nature and culture.

The Cracknell book sums up with the positive effects which the sea has on our physical and mental well-being – how it provides food and medicines, supports livelihoods, enables trade, commerce, exercise, social interaction, relaxation, contemplation, helps to alleviate stress and – as a place of beauty and inspiration – is culturally and spiritually important.

Hardly surprising, then, when looking at the sea as 'a place for nature', the book sees it very much as a space where these benefits to humankind should be enhanced and certainly preserved. Equally emphatically, the negative effects of human activity on the seas are seen not only in terms of the loss of wildlife and environmental quality per se but also as a lament on the loss it represents to us in terms of detraction from the positive benefits listed above. The title of chapter 6 is 'Taking care of the oceans so they take care of us'.

Thus, the sections on the negative effect of human activity include climate change, overfishing and destructive fishing (such as bottom trawling and by-catches) – and some of the problematic side effects of fish farming are also included (such as poor water quality, disease and escape of exotic species – though many who espouse this practice will counter that these are not necessary effects in a well-managed situation). Pollution includes chemical pollution, sewage, oil, light and noise pollution and litter – especially plastics; added to the list are aggregate and mineral extraction.

On the land we seem to be able to tell ourselves that if we fence off an area, we can save it for nature, which in many ways can be true, if only for selected species. However, the promotion of wildlife corridors and a whole landscape approach admits that the preservation in isolation can only go so far. It may work for some plants (provided we manage and control competitive species) but for more mobile species isolated reserves are not enough, albeit that they can act as centres of regeneration from which species may be able to spread. Certainly, airborne and waterborne pollutants are not good at observing boundaries and can be all-pervasive. If this is the case for land, and the nuances are debatable, is it true for the sea? Again, protected zones should be encouraged as these can readily help to restock adjacent areas of depletion. However, it seems clear that as a place for nature the interconnectedness seems more evident – everything is in or on water through which substances can move. Fish spawn in one area and move around seas and oceans during their life cycle. Currents and tides carry whatever they have from place to place; what is dumped at sea on an outgoing tide may well reappear in a similar location on the incoming tide. It seems inescapable that we should think not only of land and marine reserves but of whole landscapes and seascapes – and that a good place for nature cannot but be a good place for us.

6.2 Gardens and Nature Reserves

Gardens

Gardens are special: "Gardens are simultaneously real places and representations. They bring together, in one place, nature and our ideas about nature" (Pollan, 2002: 263). They constitute nature on our terms – a sort of controlled freedom. David Cooper (2006: 42) in *A Philosophy of Gardens* notes that a common Japanese word for garden is '*teien*' which he maintains is derived from the two words 'wildness' and 'control'. Although this is an attractive idea, on further research (Peter Kornicki, pers. comm.) I learn that the normal word for garden commonly in use in Japan is '*niwa*' and that '*teien*' refers more to a grander garden as one might expect in an aristocratic house. The word '*teien*' is in fact a Sino-Japanese compound and a combination of two characters: the first, pronounced '*tei*' in Japanese but '*yuan*' in Chinese, means the space between the gate and the house proper. The second character, pronounced '*en*' in Japanese, means an enclosed pleasure space with trees surrounded by a hedge. This etymology seems equally satisfactory, however, as it implies a managed space of nature. In *The Penguin Book of Garden Writing* (edited by David Wheeler, 1998: 21–22) Mirabel Osler (1990) is quoted as having written: "Gardens ... reflect their owners; they are totally dependent; and yet in no time at all they are breathing with their own lungs, growing at their own pace, behaving with either wilful disregard or subjugation." She calls this a paradox but rather I would call this a dialogue between the owner and nature – a relationship. There is an old story, told in a variety of forms, about the vicar complementing a gardener on his garden: "You and God have done a good job", the vicar said. "Ah well", the gardener said, "you should have seen the mess when he had it all to himself." This controlling, this very engagement with nature is itself a crucial aspect. Although it can be seen as wilful disregard or subjugation it is of course neither because plants have no volition, they are just doing what they are doing. However, we are trying to incorporate nature into our volition, so any setback can appear as an opposition which does indeed have volition. Thus, the narratives of control and loss of control abound.

Central to this is the observation quoted in Kahn's (2001: 57) *The Human Relationship with Nature* from Holmes Rolston III: "Environmental life, including human life, is nursed in struggle. ... If nature is good, it must be both an assisting and resisting reality. We cannot succeed unless it can defeat us" (Rolston, 1979: 29). This seems to me to be quite profound, or conversely, once you think about it, completely obvious – and at the heart of the psychology of gardening. Nature in gardens is neither 'inert' nor cosmologically overwhelming. On the one hand, take a brick or even a patio plank – we can build with it and we can succeed and we can fail, but whatever we achieve, or don't achieve, is entirely up to us and our expertise. On the other hand, when we go out 'in the wilderness' we can see a nature of some ferocity which can easily defeat us. So, to me, in the halfway position of gardens, the engagement comes from the possibility of defeat, without which it would not engage us so much. Just think of the language we use in our narratives: terms such as 'out of control', 'overrun' and 'out of hand' give us away; and even the 'wild patch' or 'wild garden' is there and allowed or nurtured on our terms. To me this possibility of defeat is the central element between our engagement with nature on the one hand and our creativity on the other – it's the interaction which counts. In gardens, our intentions are dominant and we value and judge everything in terms of how much something (plant, soil, animals) 'plays our game' or not.

The history of gardens is covered by various sources. A readily available one is Wikipedia: https://en.wikipedia.org/wiki/History_of_gardening. The website claims that:

> The enclosure of outdoor space began in 10,000 BC ... historians imagine the first enclosure was a type of barrier for the purpose of keeping out animals and marauders. ... The modern words of 'garden' and 'yard' are descendants of the Old English term 'geard', which denotes a fence or enclosure. ... Vitruvius, a Roman author and engineer, wrote ... a ... design manual in 27 BC. ... wealthy individuals began to create gardens for purely aesthetic purposes.

Box 6.3 shows some of the salient points from the website as a timeline:

Box 6.3 *Timeline of the evolution of gardens*

- Ancient Egypt herbs and flowers.
- Roman developments in horticulture and botany. Seeds and plants were widely shared.
- Byzantium monastery vineyards, vegetables and fruit trees.
- Medieval monastery kitchen and infirmary gardens with herbs and vegetables.
- *Vegetabilibus* of Albertus Magnus *c.*1260, grass plots, fruit trees.
- Middle Ages. Gardens seen as uniting the earthly and divine. Enclosed garden an allegory for paradise – '*hortus conclusus*' often depicted with the Virgin Mary, a fountain, a unicorn and roses.
- Renaissance. French Classical style, André Le Nôtre. Italian Renaissance garden. Descartes's coordinate system.
- 1790s: the picturesque; also architectural follies: castles, Gothic ruins, rustic cottages.

- Humphrey Repton: the garden harmonizing with surrounding landforms.
- The English 'gardenesque'. Trees and shrubs positioned so each plant can be displayed. Artificial mounds and island beds.
- 1890s: William Robinson 'wild' gardening. Mixed herbaceous borders: Gertrude Jekyll with Edwin Lutyens. Vita Sackville-West: Sissinghurst romantic style.
- Last quarter of the twentieth century: less structured. Wildlife gardening, ecological gardens using native plants.

(Modified from https://en.wikipedia.org/wiki/History_of_gardening)

Literature on gardens abound but, for me, one highly perceptive book stands out. In *Nature Displaced, Nature Displayed: Order and beauty in botanical gardens* Nuala Johnson (2011: 1) writes of "the subtle relationship we have with nature as we engage with it through abstract reason and embodied practice". She writes of senses of proportion and harmony, displays of knowledge, the colonial dimension and the linkages between the world and the botanic garden together with the prevailing sense of order with classification and themes. To me this is all about nature under our control – and it is the same with nature reserves.

Nature Reserves

If you think about the text on gardens I started this section with, substitute the words 'nature reserve' for 'gardens' and it works just as effectively: "Gardens [nature reserves] are simultaneously real places and representations. They bring together, in one place, nature and our ideas about nature" (Pollan, 2002: 263).

I was once talking to a nature reserve manager who on the one hand was waxing lyrical about conserving nature in its natural state but on the other was busy showing me his management plan where every square metre of a quite large nature reserve had an action plan. This included rotational cutting, some planting, some removal and many, many other interventions including boardwalks for access. After a while I said: "Go on, admit it: you are gardening, aren't you." He demurred for a while and then I said: "Otherwise, why can't you just put a fence round it and put up a Keep Out notice and leave it alone – and let nature take its course?" His first reply was that he would not get any funding without a management plan. His second answer was that there was indeed a core sanctuary area from which people were excluded, especially in the bird breeding season. "What, nobody?", I said. "Well", he admitted, "we go in for monitoring and ringing the birds and some management but on a strictly limited basis." When I reminded him about the rotational cutting and the way in which it arrests succession from grassland to woodland to keep a diversity of insects, his third reply was "Oh, OK, I am gardening there." I never minded that, having been brought up reading a book which my godfather had left me by H. J. Massingham (1924) on *Sanctuaries for Birds and How to Make Them*. I had duly enhanced my parents' garden wherever I could with plants suitable for birds in one way or another (happily my parents were in full agreement with this).

What is really significant is the history of Wicken Fen, one of the UK's first nature reserves (Box 6.4). It reveals that here nature can indeed be very man-made – this is in the sense that the most valued habitats for the greatest diversity of species relate at that site to the history of human management, especially reed and sedge cutting for thatch and peat digging for fuel.

Box 6.4 *Wicken Fen Nature Reserve*

Acquired in 1899, Wicken Fen in Cambridgeshire is the National Trust's oldest nature reserve, with over 9,000 species recorded, notably of plants, birds and dragonflies associated with wetlands. There are over 800 hectares covering waterways, woodlands, flowering meadows, sedge and reedbeds supporting water voles (*Arvicola amphibius*), hen harriers (*Circus cyaneus*) and bitterns (*Botaurus stellaris*).

The reserve is designated as a National Nature Reserve, Site of Special Scientific Interest (national designations), a Special Area of Conservation (European designation) and a Ramsar Site (an international wetland designation).

On reserve management, the National Trust writes:

> The historic heart of the reserve is managed much as it has been for hundreds of years, using traditional principles but modern techniques. The annual work programme includes harvesting sedge, litter cutting (marsh hay) and scrub management. It would not be possible to manage newer areas of the reserve in such an intensive manner. On these areas we are adopting a less prescriptive approach to its management, using extensive grazing to control the growth and spread of vegetation. Highland cattle and Konik ponies are helping to create a diverse range of new habitats. (www.nationaltrust.org.uk/wicken-fen-nature-reserve)

The conservation of nature here contains at least two aspects. First, 'allowing' nature – letting nature take its course, preserving wilderness and preserving the integrity of natural processes. Second, 'managing' nature in some preferred state through intervention – scrub clearance to preserve grassland and creating suitable habitats for species seen as of value (Figure 6.1, Figure 6.2). As recorded by Lock et al. in Friday (1997: 216) at Wicken Fen, "the early intention to preserve nature was soon followed by the realisation of the loss of desired habitats and the need for intervention". I find this the most telling sentence in the whole of nature conservation. In 1899 there was a general idea that the Fen should be allowed to "run wild and return to its original state". Areas were "set aside as a sanctuary for insects and birds with the result that some large areas were never cut [and] the resulting lack of active management inevitably led to a deterioration in the birds' preferred open, grassy nesting habitat". Plots were established by the botanist Harry Godwin and have been studied since 1939. The different cutting regimes show that the less frequent the cutting, the greater the establishment of tree

Figure 6.1 Clearance of trees and shrubs at Wicken Fen to maintain the fen flora and fauna (Andrew Michaels/Universal Images Group / Getty Images). *A black and white version of this figure will appear in some formats. For the colour version, please refer to the plate section.*

Figure 6.2 Konik ponies grazing on Wicken Fen to maintain biodiversity (Dave Porter / 500px / 500px / Getty Images)

species (Figure 6.3, Figure 6.4). Thus, at Wicken Fen it seemed that the desire to keep the diversity of insects and birds was dominant.

There are thus two sets of arguments – a generalised one which refers to the ethic of leaving nature alone and a more detailed management discussion of precisely what state is important and which involves the preferences of the stakeholders. In many senses the former is readily grasped by the non-specialist but the latter might be less accessible, especially if detailed identification skills are involved. A generalised conservation ethic (the fact of the existence of a conservation area) is not the same as a guide to the implementation of the details of conservation management and it is evident that there can be wider participation in the former than the latter.

In terms of the detailed management, it becomes clear that in practice the manifestations of the conservation ethic resolve into struggles between differing experts – in other words it is to do with preferred states and cultural constructs rather than about allowing nature to exist. In this way, conservation becomes a cultural activity about arresting succession, preserving what are seen as fragile ecosystems, keeping rare species and enhancing biodiversity. Thus, rarity, collapse, guilt and threat mingle with stability and function to justify the being of each individual conservationist. The rationalisation of competing claims comes down, as

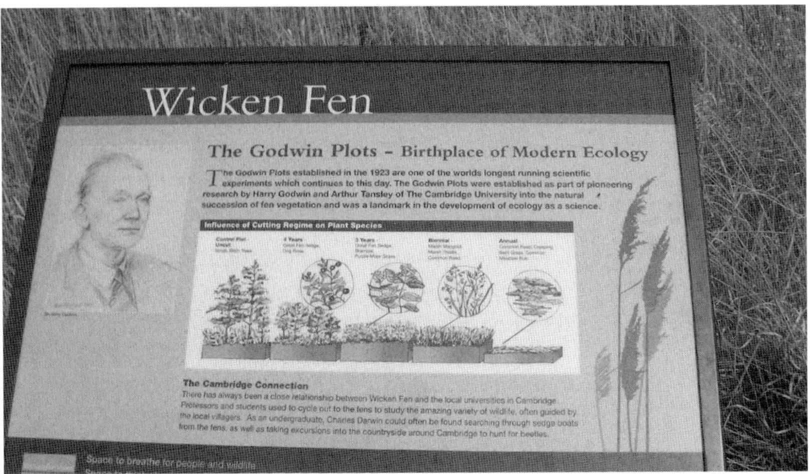

Figure 6.3 Godwin Plots in *c.*2005 (more frequently cut plot to the right) (Photo: S. Trudgill)

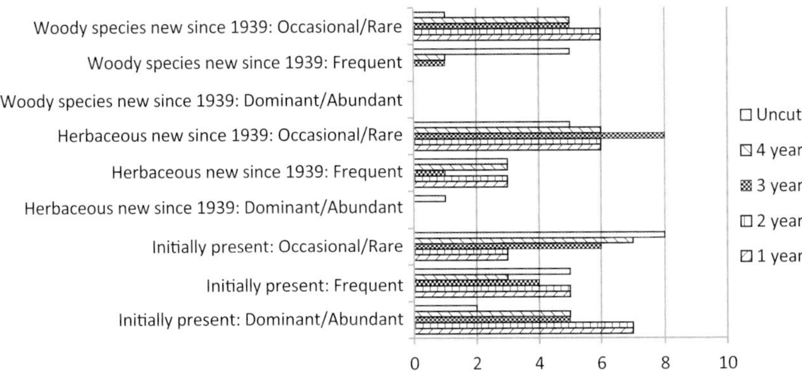

Figure 6.4 Data on loss of grassland and increase in tree species with less frequent cutting, from Godwin Plots 1955–1982 compared to 1939 baseline (mostly herbaceous) (Adapted from data in Friday and Harvey, 1997: 71). *A black and white version of this figure will appear in some formats. For the colour version, please refer to the plate section.*

ever, to a form of pluralism where different spatial areas are managed differently for different purposes, thus allowing the agendas of different voices. Any liberal-minded thinker will eventually conclude that pluralism is the answer in such a context. However, while specialists might argue over preferences for particular species or groups of species, and while the specialised knowledge involved in this cannot be shared with the public, there is also an evident deeply held passion which characterises the specialists which is valued.

If Lefebvre (1991) argues in the *Production of Space* that "space is produced and reproduced through human activity and it thus represents a site of struggle and contestation" (from Macnaghten and Urry, 1998: 105) then what do nature reserves as spaces represent? I go here to Harrison and Burgess (1994: 300) and their conclusion that while the general public have a "common-sense understanding of how nature is organised", nature reserves are often managed in terms of "a rhetoric that extols the intrinsic worth of organisms" and that this is "based on the assumed universal authority of scientific 'experts'". I am sure that the scientific notion of ecosystem complexity is quite genuine, but such notions can make the ecologist's arguments somewhat unshareable. Similarly, while birds are a great conservation motivation currently, neither 'birds as objects to be ticked on a list' nor 'birds as components of an ecosystem' is something shared by everybody. However, 'birds as songsters' is, as is 'birds as indicators of spring'. However, such embodied cultural constructs, while widely held, are perhaps seen by scientists as something rather lesser in terms of an argument. Indeed, when I presented the results of my survey of the public views as to the value of a nature reserve, based on the findings of Harrison and Burgess (details in Section 6.4), there were groans from specialists that number 1 came out as 'a haven of peace and tranquillity' rather than the specialised rarities the area was renowned for – that is to say, renowned among biologists.

The democratisation of the conservation ethic is not, however, that difficult – let the specialists have their piece of land and let the place be putatively wild with at least some access, like in a nature trail, and most people will be happy. Both the specialists and the public will have their emotive engagements.

6.3 Emotional Biogeographies

What Is – and What Ought (Not) To Be – Where

A prime mover in gardening and the activities of nature conservation is dissatisfaction: an existing situation does not suit and we will not rest until it does. What is interesting is the dimensions of the dissatisfaction and what forms a judgement of suitable. This is perhaps epitomised by an item on an East Anglian television programme: "This region is famous for its Nature Reserves . . . and it takes a lot of hard work to keep them looking like nature intended" (Susie Fowler-Watt and Stuart White, presenters on BBC *Look East* TV News Bulletin on 2 February 2016 at 18.54). Where we have a strong sense of 'what should be where', as discussed, for example, by Shirley (2019)in 'Nature's place – what should live where?', this is matched by a sense of what does not belong where. The proclivities vary but the attachment to appropriateness is always through the emotions. In this section we look at the rational case for considering the emotions as key factors – and I don't mean 'being emotional', I mean studying how we feel and what nature means to us.

A key aspect of emotional ecologies concerns the study of the spatial distribution of plants and animals: biogeography. It seems particularly timely to explore our emotional attachments to biogeographical distributions in the context of the way changing climate can result in changing biogeographies (Trudgill, 2008: 'A requiem for the British flora? Emotional biogeographies and environmental change'). While we can have a strong, and understandable, sense of 'what should be where', this sense of appropriateness to a particular place may now be seen as unhelpful. While the causes and predictions of climate change are subject to scientific and political debate, it would seem that scientific analysis offers little guidance on how we might react culturally to consequential changes in plant and animal distributions. In essence, it seems that cultural constructs tend to persist despite new evidence. For example, plants change their distributions yet people still seem to cling to the idea of 'national' floras, or, at least, what 'ought to be there', despite exhortations to facilitate migrations in order to help plants and animals survive in the face of change (Jongman and Pungetti, 2004).

The presence of particular plants and animals at a particular place seems to contribute to our sense of place of that location. In the UK, we appear to have a powerful emotional attachment to the notion of 'British flora' such that it could seem that species have a right to exist – but not just anywhere. However, we might question the idea of a plant 'belonging' somewhere. If plants are adapted to their environment and thus have particularly biogeographical distributions, how come they survive elsewhere when introduced? Clearly, the relationship between plant and environment has some latitude. True, some plants are killed by frost or drought while others survive and there are physiological mechanisms to enable plants to thrive in acid and alkaline soils, as gardeners well know. It could thus be said that plants 'belong' in cold or temperate regions and in deserts and indeed 'belong' on acid or alkaline soils. It is the notion of 'belonging' to a country which is more problematic.

Notions of a 'British flora' evolved before 1800 (Henrey, 1975) and were consolidated in the nineteenth century (as recorded, for example, by Anker, 2001 and Fara, 2003a, 2003b, 2003c). The associated concept of alien plants was consolidated by Dunn (1905) and Salisbury (1961). In Britain, these concepts form powerful cultural constructs concerning the presence of particular plants in particular locations and contribute to a sense of place (Mabey, 1998; Short, 2005). In particular, Dunn (1905: 2) enshrined the concept in *The Alien Flora of Britain*, defining an alien plant as "any species which . . . originated in Britain through human agency". The cultural concept of 'belonging' is clearly nested in a sense of nationalism. It thus seems evident to me that we have here a situation which can only be understood by the realisation that our engagement with biogeographical distributions is fundamentally emotional. Interestingly, in considering introduced species in New Zealand, Steer (2015: iv) writes of "a positioning of humans as 'moral predators' against a foreign invasion of introduced species [which] reconciles people's own place in nature." Hitchmough (2005) simply asks the question: 'What value exotic plant species?' feeling that ecologists and conservationists who regard exotics as vermin need to consider why so many people have transferred their traditional relationships with native plants to exotics.

Our problem is that we so readily read purpose and necessity into situations so that they somehow become imbued with 'rightness'. For example, oak trees are somehow 'right' in Britain – native, emblematic, a ready metaphor for strength and nationhood. We thus might defend oak trees at the expense of other species. I recently saw a Local Council tree grant scheme – it was stated that money was available for tree planting, especially if they were oaks. There was no need for an explanation and none was given. It is just axiomatic that oaks are good and British. By contrast, rhododendrons are rarely encouraged outside formal gardens and indeed they can often be eradicated in the wild. The justification is that they are alien and invasive and their damp, acid, sour leaves kill off other (native) species. The 'alien' label sticks despite the fact that species of rhododendron were present in Britain in the last interglacial (Godwin, 1975; Trudgill, 2001a). They just missed out in the recolonisation of the UK after the last glaciation, rather like the snake failing to reach Ireland. My point is that the oak is not somehow 'right' and 'good' while the rhododendron is somehow 'wrong' and 'bad'. If you make the point that the oak need not be here but did recolonise after glaciation and the

Table 6.2 *Percentage of British flora which are now present and also were present at differing post-glacial stages from the immediately post-glacial about 11,500 years ago*

Post-glacial Stage	Years	% Current British Flora Present
Middle Weichselian	11500–9000	21
Late Weichselian	9000–8500	30
IV	8500–7000	32
V + V1 Boreal	7000–5500	43
VIIa Atlantic	5500–3000	35
VIIb Sub-Boreal	3000–1000	38
VIII Sub-Atlantic	1000	52

Source: 1970 data; modified from Godwin (1975).

rhododendron was and could have been again but didn't make it back, then this gives us the realisation that in biogeographical distributions there is dependency but no necessity.

If we look at the post-glacial history of the British flora we see a successive increase in post-glacial times (Table 6.2).

What then is British flora? While these stages in Table 6.2 have now been revised and the data with them, we might argue, if we so wished, that there was a small percentage of our current flora immediately post-glacially and all the rest have been 'aliens' and 'invaders' as the ice melted northwards.

Similarly, in response to current environmental change, some species in the UK spread northwards and are lost from the south, others arrive in the south, extending their range northwards (see, e.g., Huntley's 1998 discussion of this for butterflies). Do we lament the losses at a particular location and resent new arrivals or do we take a more European, if not global, view, that at least the species survive somewhere? Do we not try to promote the survival of species but stumble over the locationally specific attachment which has arisen historically?

Changes in ecosystem function and distribution now challenge our values of how things should work and appropriateness to a place. Drury (1998) asks us to accept new situations rather than being nostalgic and mystical. Can we rise to this challenge?

Calls for a greater objectivity might seem futile especially when a treasured plant is lost from a specific location and another arrives and is 'not kept in check' and 'overruns' an area. Yet, while we might usefully employ a more neutral terminology to describe the distributions of species, value judgements still seem inescapable. It seems that if our narratives and values become inappropriate, the only way ahead is to call for a changed philosophical approach – one based not on any territorial imperative but on the acceptance of the need for species to migrate to survive.

We might regard this with a stance akin to the negative reception afforded to Linnaeus's 'objective' system of plant classification in relation to the positioning of floral reproductive parts (Fara, 2003a, 2003b, 2003c). Here, the establishment fulminated against a 'loathsome harlotry', 'gross prurience', 'shocking to female modesty' and 'such immorality'. With hindsight, we may smile at this, but I think people have been almost as shocked by the appearance of non-British species in the UK.

Objectively, we have to remember that the Quaternary history of the British flora is indeed one of invasion (Godwin, 1975; Table 6.2). The difference now is the more rapid timescale but we should realise that we have been positioned by nineteenth-century botanists to think of a 'British flora' and realise how inappropriate this now is before we can move on to new ways of thinking. I suspect I am not alone in regretting a certain loss of a sense of place, but I realise that I have been positioned to think like this. One might regret, but that's tough – get used to it.

One could almost argue that anything could be anywhere. Indeed, Pearce (2015) writes on why invasive species will be nature's salvation and argues that if you wish for ecosystem services, then we should look to the successful species which flourish and that this increasingly means looking to plants hitherto classified as aliens and invaders (see Section 2.3).

Meanwhile, nature is quietly doing it itself – spreading around without our help. Egrets are a well-known example in the UK – spreading in a human generation from limited numbers of the south coast to becoming quite widespread. Compare a 1998 article with a 2012 website. Lock and Cook (1998) in 'The Little Egret in Britain: A successful colonist' show the data as in Table 6.3.

Compare this situation with the 2012 report on the British Trust for Ornithology (BTO) website (Appleton, n.d.) in Figure 6.5 and the data shown in Balmer et al. (2013): *Bird Atlas 2007–11* published by the BTO. In the latter, the maps show the little egret to have the greatest range of wintering species of any bird in the atlas and in the breeding season was recorded as present or with breeding evidence in 1,214 ten-kilometre squares distributed widely in southern UK with sporadic instances further north. On the website on the little egret (https://app

Table 6.3 *Northwest European records of breeding little egrets (*Egretta garzetta*)*

Location	Year of First Confirmed Breeding	1997 Breeding Pairs (Colonies)
Brittany	1960	500+ (18)
Normandy	1993	120 (4)
Picardie	1996	42 (2)
Britain	1996	7 (2)
Ireland	1997	12 (1)

Source: Adapted from Lock and Cook (1998). Reproduced by permission, British Trust for Ornithology.

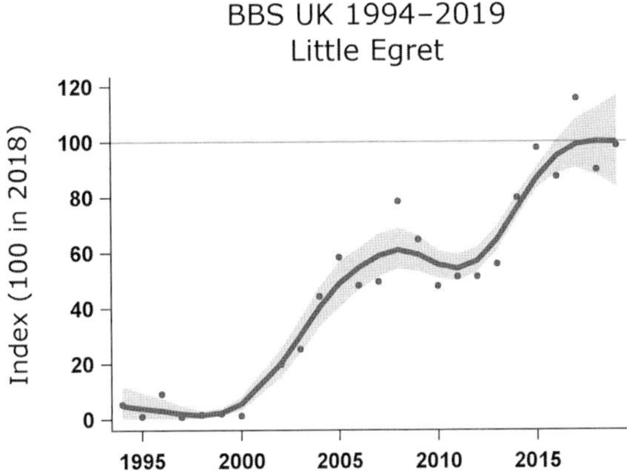

Figure 6.5 UK breeding expansion of little egret based on Rare Breeding Birds Panel figures (from www.bto.org/about-birds/species-focus/little-egret © British Trust for Ornithology, BTO, The Nunnery, Thetford, Norfolk IP24 2PU. Reproduced by permission, British Trust for Ornithology)

.bto.org/birdfacts/results/bob1190.htm) it is recorded that from the earliest record in East Yorkshire in 1826 and the first confirmed successful breeding record in recent times in Dorset in 1996 there were summer populations of 1,100 pairs in 2013–2017 and winter populations of 12,000 individuals in 2012–2017 (Woodward et al., 2020). Little egrets are now accepted as part of our fauna. However, maybe that has to do with their appeal and acceptable characteristics?

The notion of 'acceptability' does seem curiously relevant when it comes to the characteristics of species. In an article on teaching biogeography to a multicultural class Job (1999) focusses on the writings of

Agyeman (1995, 1998) who discussed the relative merits of the oak (*Quercus*) and the sycamore (*Acer pseudoplatanus*). Conventionally, the oak is seen as native and the sycamore is believed to have been introduced by the Romans so the latter can be seen as worth less. The argument then goes that introduced species don't belong so therefore they can readily be eradicated in conservation management. A further rationalist scientific justification seems to make this 'acceptable' and can be based on the identification of 284 invertebrate species which are found on the oak and only 43 on the sycamore: 'oak good, sycamore bad'. This appeal is to the weight of numbers based on the assumed superiority of biodiversity arguments about species: more species = good. However, Agyeman is writing from a multicultural educational point of view and does not wish to teach nationalist biogeography about native British plants and unacceptable aliens to a class of mixed ethnic origin, so he reaches for a different argument.

Agyeman (1998) writes: "Later research showed that other native trees supported insect species similar in number to those found on sycamore, and that what matters is the (larger) biomass of invertebrate fauna rather than species diversity" (cited from Job, 1999: 75). His argument is that the number of species does not matter, it is the weight of biomass of invertebrates which can, after all, feed more birds and other species – thus providing a 'vote for sycamore' stance. Aliens are thus of equal, but different, value to native trees – and just as acceptable.

However, hidden within all these narratives are many uncontested and automatic narratives. Numerical biodiversity is an uncontested axiom as is the 'what matters is the biomass'. The fact that there are more invertebrate species on oak than sycamore and more biomass of invertebrates on sycamore than oak could be the end of the story, but it isn't, because somehow such statements are conflated with values. But why? Why on earth should numerical biodiversity be somehow 'better'? Why is more biomass 'good'? Why, indeed, do we need these value judgements at all? Viewed more dispassionately – and separating analysis from advocacy – we can (a) list the different attributes and characteristics of each tree (species found on them; biomass of insects) and then completely separately (b) ask why do we have to choose between them? And then if a choice has to be made (and why should it be?), then might not the choice be context dependent and carefully argued in specific situations rather than an automatic – and all too easy – narrative of 'native versus alien'. Instead of 'more species = good', it should be 'more species – good?'.

There is no automatic reason why there should be a particular number of number of species which is seen as good. As Perlman and Adelson (1997: 25) so elegantly argue, "If biodiversity is good, is more biodiversity always better than less biodiversity?". Apart from intelligently saying that it depends on which the species are and where they are, they can't come up with a good automatic general reason because there isn't one. In many situations there is a human psychological preference for diversity which we sense as more interesting but we are constantly reaching for functional arguments when, in truth, cultural prejudices and preferences creep in. There is also the common automatic argument that greater diversity leads to greater stability. But this begs some other questions – is that indeed the case and why is stability important? The answer is that stability is a preference (it is what we are used to) and function can be conflated with preference for a state.

In 'Nature's place – what should live where?', Shirley (2019) writes of a

> muddled and inconsistent approach to those species which have travelled from where they were first found. People may rail against many such migrants. Pejorative language may be used, calling such species invasive and aggressive aliens. They can be depicted as threatening beautiful and virtuous native species. In a triumph of values over science, we exempt those we like from this generality, favouring introduced cornfield annuals in our wildflower mixes, advising people to plant Buddleia, and organising snowdrop (Galanthus nivalis) walks.

He concludes:

> If we lift our eyes above the ecological horizon we will see a world which, socially and culturally, is a borderless mix. Nature strives to be like this, but we constantly try to constrain it. Instead we need to harness nature's resilience, resourcefulness and chaos, and stop pretending that it is frozen and static. We need to create the conditions for natural processes to flourish and stop trying to impose our own 'designer solutions'.

If readers still require convincing, try reading 'Non-native plants provide habitats for a variety of British insects' (Williams, 2019) and Padovani et al. (2020)'s 'Introduced plants as novel Anthropocene habitats for insects'.

6.4 Place and a Rational Case for the Emotions

I well remember, as a Norfolk person myself, how the local naturalist, Ted Ellis, (www.wheatfen.org/tethtml/tet.html), an 'amateur' and author much respected by scientists, was voted the Eastern Region's most popular and valued television personality through, I submit, his passion for nature. This means to me that the common factors between the scientists, conservationists and the public are arguably to do with discourses about emotional engagements.

In Debord's (1956, 1977) psychogeography writings he discusses a methodology developed in Paris which involves the *dérive* (literally drifting) where you can wander at will in relation to what attracts you in the city. The experience of wandering and the routeway relates thus to how one feels. To me this can equally be effected in the landscape with the attractions of views, shade, flowers, old trees and so on and relates to how places make us feel.

I became so engaged with the idea of psychogeography applied to natural settings that I published a paper on psychobiogeography as a 'Guest editorial' in the *Journal of Biogeography* (Trudgill, 2001a). Here, I asked what motivated Rothschild in his endeavour to preserve nature (Rothschild and Marren, 1997); my answer was that it was a passion and a preference. Sheail (1998: 5) records Rothschild's Society for the Promotion of Nature Reserves in 1912 as posited on the aims "to preserve for posterity" and to "encourage the love of Nature".

A key point is that the case for conservation is constructed by scientists in scientific terms which others can't necessarily share. However, not everyone shares the positive affective emotions about nature either. Thus, this is not about just asking the public how they feel – as in Burgess's (1992) and Harrison and Burgess's (1994) Essex marshes you might soon come across the construct of 'dismal wasteland' with a preference for shops and amusement: negative emotions about nature also abound.

The writings of Burgess (1992) can only tell me that the public filter put on ecological knowledge means that ecological science arguments are not necessarily the most effective conservation motivators. Burgess rehearses both the ecological and the emotive arguments. The ecological aspects included phrases such as 'unique ecological exhibit', 'heritage to be protected' and 'a nature museum to educate people'. The emotional appeal focussed on wildlife, flowers and birdsong, the area as a remnant of a vanished world and 'a haven of peace and tranquillity' together with a sense of wonder and enjoyment and the strong idea that the area should not be destroyed as it would be lost for ever.

There are 'feels right' and 'feels good' elements in both sets so one hesitates to posit that the ecological rationale is more clinical and less appealing than the emotional. However, there was still a feeling in the research findings that the emotional arguments were marginalised by the ecological arguments and scientific rationale. Burgess concluded that conservationists, who were seen as an 'elite' by the public, failed in their attempts to encourage people to make connections between the immediate realities of their daily lives and the largely abstract arguments about ecological significance. To me this means the scientists should make their case more accessible and use the language of a wide appeal.

In following this thread, during a public meeting at Slapton Ley Field Centre about the eroding shoreline at Slapton National Nature Reserve (Box 6.5), I ran a questionnaire adapted from Burgess's themes. Participants were asked an open question on what they thought was

Box 6.5 *Slapton Ley Nature Reserve*

Slapton Ley is a freshwater lake on the south coast of Devon, England, separated from Start Bay by a shingle beach, known as Slapton Sands. The Ley is fed by streams and the river Gara flowing into the north end of the lake. The site is a National Nature Reserve, a Site of Special Scientific Interest and a Geological Conservation Review site. The nature reserve covers over 200 hectares. The lake is the largest natural freshwater lake in south-west England, 2.4 km long with two sections: the Lower Ley and the Higher Ley. The A379 road between the Ley and the sea runs along the shingle ridge and was rebuilt after damage by coastal erosion in the early 2000s (Trudgill, 2009: '"You can't resist the sea": Evolving attitudes and responses to coastal erosion at Slapton, S Devon').

The Slapton Ley Nature Reserve is owned by the Whitley Wildlife Conservation Trust and managed by the Field Studies Council. Habitats include woodland, marshland, reedbeds, open water and shingle ridge. There is a significant population of Cetti's warbler (*Cettia cetti*) at the site; the bittern (*Botaurus stellaris*) has also been recorded. The shores of the Ley are the only UK site for strapwort (*Corrigiola litoralis*), a plant identified by Natural England as being at high risk of going extinct by 2020. Badgers, otters, dormice and bats are recorded together with 250 species of lichen and 2,000 species of fungi, 29 of which have been described as new to science.

(www.field-studies-council.org/locations/slaptonleynnr/
www.slnnr.org.uk)

important about the nature reserve and the replies included 'looking after nature', 'guardianship', 'peace', 'beauty', 'open space', 'walking', 'stopping the loss', 'important in our populated suburbanised world' and 'a special place'. There were no specific ecological or species-based responses; more there were personalised notions of the value and worth of nature – nature which gives both restoration and meaning but is under threat. They were then asked specifically to score the themes from Burgess quoted above. As detailed in Trudgill (2001a) the highest scoring phrases from thirty respondents were 'a haven of peace and tranquillity', 'quiet enjoyment for years to come', 'endless opportunities for people to wonder at the beauties of the natural world' and 'a feeling of being with nature, naturalness' 'Flowers and bird song, views and vistas and a kind of living heritage to be protected and studied' also featured highly together with 'once you've destroyed all the wildlife, it's gone for good, a nature museum to educate people for a wider concern for nature'. Aspects such as 'importance of the global ecosystem, biodiversity and rare species' scored lower.

It seems that the local and the immediately tangible are key aspects. While these results came from a small group of respondents (thirty), it reinforces the idea that ecosystem scientists have some way to go in placing their arguments in terms of any priority, even with a self-selected group with a conservation interest, and also in terms of making more accessible arguments about the relationships of organisms with their habitats. It also reinforces the idea of a 'common currency' between ecologists and others in terms of generalised notions concerning peace, tranquillity, wonder, enjoyment and a feeling of being with nature.

Elton (1958: 145) wrote about the case for conserving the variety of nature, which he saw as "because it is the right relation between man and living things, because it gives opportunity for richer experience . . . and an attempt to harmonize divergent attitudes . . . – a wise principle of co-existence". Porteous (1996: 265) wrote that "the world will not be changed for the better in any fundamental way by coercion, legislation or even top-down education" but on a "spiritual enterprise" in the "texture" of "small, . . . life-decisions made by millions of people. You can try to think and sense for yourself . . . intuit and feel for yourself, embrace wild culture . . . with a sense of spirituality and feelings of attachment. In this way, landscapes may not only delight us but also become our fields of care (Evernden, 1985)."

This concurs with the findings of Kaplan and Kaplan (1989) who studied people's reactions to and preferences for photographic views.

They concluded that the preference judgements reflected a very rapid assessment of what one could do in the scene and how one might feel. Aspects of prospect, depth, focus and coherence were also important: a tangible sense of 'being there' ranks higher than the more abstract meanings of place such as biodiversity and uniqueness. Thus, one might propose that tangible, sensory and feeling aspects dominate the psychogeographic response, with more abstract constructs and ideas acting only to temper, modify or qualify the response.

Robert Lackey of the US Environmental Protection Agency is "concerned that we . . . are slipping into a morass that risks marginalizing the contribution of science to public policy" (Lackey, 2007: 12). Interesting: I am concerned that we are not consulting our values enough. Can't there be more science and more emotional engagement? There seems to be a lack of use of good science and lack of poetic emotion when what is needed is a good body of scientific conservation evidence and a recognition of the power of emotional engagement in conservation motivation. One problem is image – rabid eco-activists in woolly jumpers are so easy to caricature and dismiss. It would be lovely if people could stand up, look respectable and talk about the importance of emotional engagement in a quiet, confident, measured and unhurried way so that others might listen. But oh no, the media would hate that – activists have to be photographed looking angry and waving banners while the smartly dressed person justifies themself by quoting selective bits of science.

Consider what happens if a nature reserve is under threat in some way. The birdwatching lobby readily articulates a case for preservation, including arguments about access and recreation, even financial income from visitors, and can be heard. Wanting it as a place in which to dream is not so easily articulated. The two are not mutually exclusive but I continue to wonder why we commonly hear representations about species and rarity at public enquiries about land use planning rather than readings of poetry about feelings and senses of place.

This is all the more strange since there are now sufficient writings to show that it is through the emotions that people connect with the environment (Milton, 2002; Trudgill, 2001a, 2001b, 2008) – and it is through the expression of these feelings, for example through poetry, whereby we connect with each other about such deeper feelings. It thus becomes interesting why we appear to allow 'rational' connections with the environment. In a key set of writings, Kals and Müller (2012) discuss the relationships between emotions and the environment. They write that the special role of emotions has not always been sufficiently taken into account and record in the evolution of ideas in environmental psychology: "a phase of strong cognitive bias, mainly omitting emotions" which went

> hand in hand with the development of models aiming to explain environmentally relevant behavior without integrating emotions. In line with the explanation of human behavior in other action fields, the significant role of emotions was, consequently, for a long time overlooked. Instead behavioral decisions were often construed as rational processes, based for example, on judgement-expectation values. (Kals and Müller, 2012: 128–129)

They then go on to develop the discussion of a cognitive model of emotions. This stresses the understanding of emotions as consequences of cognitive processes:

> The core idea indicates that it is not an event itself or bodily reactions that directly elicit emotions but their individual interpretations, which means that the same stimulus can lead to different emotions. It is argued that cognitions do not need to be conscious, reflected and formulated thoughts but can also embrace automatic and pre-conscious processes. (Kals and Müller, 2012: 131)

A cognitive model of emotions has advantages for understanding environmentally relevant emotions:

> A cognitive model of emotions can explain that different people react differently to towards the same event ... and that there is intrapersonal variance in the emotional reaction toward the same event at different times, based on different appraisals of an event .... Cognitive models imply an idea of humans as acting individuals who can gain control over their emotions by reflecting and re-framing cognitive schemas and automatic appraisals. (Kals and Müller, 2012: 131)

They then discuss the taxonomy of emotions and move to a categorisation (points adapted from Kals and Müller, 2012: 131–133):

- Emotion derived from worries about environmental threats.
- Emotions associated with behaviour (e.g. disgust at littering, pleasure at buying organic food).
- Affective connection to nature. This may involve time spent in contact with nature; senses of restoration and fascination; a feeling of something greater than yourself, which can be especially associated with wilderness; a sense of recognition of the compatibility between human inclinations and nature; and a sense of identity.

- Moral emotions concerning behaviour affecting the environment and which go beyond self-interest but also a sense of social responsibility and moral convictions, especially about conservation.

In their paper the authors conclude (Kals and Müller, 2012: 145): "In many social contexts, emotions are still taboo or are devaluated as 'irrational'." However, they argue that cognitive emotion models, and associated empirical evidence, speak strongly against this position. Their discussion includes (p. 135) a critique of the rational choice model citing Abell's (1992) useful paper: 'Is rational choice theory a rational choice of theory?'. Here, the 'social trap' or 'tragedy of the commons' or 'socio-ecological dilemma' is explained in that individuals behave selfishly rather than altruistically because it is seen as 'rational'; that immediate short-term interests for the individual 'win' over long-term, not immediately tangible societal interests; so a common resource is depleted without thought for the future thus avoiding pro-ecological behaviour and showing ecological risky behaviour. A further rationalisation may be in that if individuals do behave altruistically and act to preserve a common resource then this is seen as masked self-interest. However, some individuals and groups act pro-environmentally despite high personal costs. The cognitive emotion model admits that people are happier when striving for self-transcending goals and act in a way which protects the global environment without receiving any direct or personal gain.

To me this seems as if self-interest is viewed as inherently rational while altruism is not – in the long term, of course, this can be seen as just as rational – it just refers to a different set of axioms involving common interest rather than self-interest. I do, however, see the process involved where the 'selfish' emotion rationalisation can be replaced through reflection/cognition by the altruistic rationalisation. This then confirms the idea of "humans as acting individuals who can gain control over their emotions by reflecting and re-framing cognitive schemas and automatic appraisals" as cited above.

Now let's imagine a lovely wooded area with a stream.

A) You can't put a road through it/build houses over it because there are forty-nine species here, three of them rare.
B) You can't put a road through it/build houses on it because the following poem encapsulates what this area means to me:

In the motion of the very leaves of spring,
in the blue air, there is found

a secret correspondence with the heart
there is eloquence in the tongueless wind, melody in the flowing brooks
and in the rustling of the reeds beside them
By their inconceivable relation to something in the soul, they awaken the
spirits to a dance of endless rapture, and bring tears of mysterious
tenderness to the eyes
(Shelley, 'On Love', 1801)

Which of these works for you? Either should because they both have an emotional appeal. However, the numerical one appears more rational and you don't mind 'coming out' and saying it. It is special to that area. But the second is just as rational – it is how you feel about the place which is special to you, just as special to that area. Indeed, if this was a public enquiry the adjudicator might say 'do these species exist elsewhere?' and the answer may be 'yes'. But 'do these special feelings and memories abide elsewhere?' and then the answer may well be 'no'. Ah, but then the argument might become 'can it be shared by others?' – then if it could be, the case is weightier. So, we can agree on the numerical importance of species; indeed biodiversity is a much-rehearsed mantra (but don't mention that species come and go and that they may be lost with no noticeable effects or you will lose the case). And many may not agree on your special memories – at least not the powerful with vested interests.

But what if many people have special memories, which may all be different but have the same root for their feelings for and memories of that place? Then that should carry weight too. OK, so we are carrying the species forward for the future – why is that weightier than carrying our memories forward so that children and grandchildren and their descendants can have similar memories in the future? Why is it that if there is [the emotional experience of] a rare protected snail then this might carry the day – and indeed it might be enshrined in statutes and stop the development, yet a personal emotional experience of place may not?

Both should be important.

6.5 Chapter Summary

- The decline of species numbers and area of wildlife habitats is well documented.
- This decline is seen in relation to the loss of wild areas.
- There is a significant place for nature in domesticated landscapes and cities.

- Whole landscapes and seascapes are significant in terms of conservation priorities such as the spatial mobility of species but also in terms of aesthetic and historical meanings.
- Gardens provide places where we interact with nature on our terms, much as we might in highly managed nature reserves. In the example of Wicken Fen, Cambridgeshire: "the early intention to preserve nature was soon followed by the realisation of the loss of desired habitats and the need for intervention" and in an East Anglian television programme: "This region is famous for its Nature Reserves … and it takes a lot of hard work to keep them looking like nature intended."
- There is a strong 'sense of what should be where' which, while understandable, can be a problem in the context of species distributions adapting to environmental changes.
- There is a need for a good body of scientific conservation evidence and a recognition of the power of emotional engagement in conservation motivation. Both should be important.

Part IV
Why Conserve Nature?

7 · *Possibilities*

7.1 Beyond Biodiversity

Perspectives on the Meanings of Biodiversity

We tend to think that diversity is good, and indeed we seem to find it psychologically attractive and intellectually interesting. But what does *bio*diversity mean? It can be applied to some form of enumeration – the number of species – or simply be used as a portmanteau word, referring to 'wildlife'. In thinking about what biodiversity means, tellingly, Perlman and Adelson (1997): 25) ask: "If biodiversity is good, is more biodiversity always better than less biodiversity?". Why does having more species matter? In Chapter 1 we asked whether functionality was really the key to why species matter – after all, different species can perform similar functions. And if the functionality of an ecosystem varies, then the system is different – but again we conflate such changes with worth and value judgements. Preference and prejudice seem to confound our thinking.

I once had a very specific insight into an instance of why biodiversity matters. For some twenty-five years or so I helped to run the nature reserve at Slapton Ley in South Devon (www.slnnr.org.uk) and see also Trudgill (2009). As a member of the Slapton Ley Nature Reserve Management Committee I well remember how there were earlier arguments about whether the place should be conserved for the species espoused by different sets of people ('my' birds, 'my' insects, 'my' plants or whatever) but when the mantra of 'biodiversity' arose in the 1980s then everybody seemed happier and nodded and smiled at each other, rapidly agreeing to manage different areas for different species and taking such measures as cutting grassy areas in different rotations from yearly to once every several years to encourage different habitats. It was thus clear that the place should be managed to make things as diverse as possible – and so everyone's agenda was allowed. Thus, without being unduly cynical, I felt that the endeavour was somewhat about the resolution of specialist interests with their competing narratives and personally held values with their associated emotions, rather than necessarily about any generalised notion of the desire to preserve nature. Such a widely held tenet as the latter was perhaps seen as something rather lesser in terms of a specialist argument. Be that as it may, the result was indeed an increase in the range and number of species which, if nothing else, made the area more attractive to a wide range of people who were variously excited and happy with their sightings and findings. I decline to hazard an evaluation as to whether the 'ecosystem functioned better' or was 'more stable' as I'm far from sure what criteria I would use to measure such things. When events such as storms and other extreme weather occurred changes certainly followed, as they ever have, but it made me think that while the emotive mantras of 'functioning' and' stability' were motivational, they were elusive whereas biodiversity could be much more readily grasped as a concept, encouraged as a policy and visibly sensed as a result. It is easy to see why biodiversity as an emotive mantra became rapidly adopted.

Since the 1980s, the concept of biodiversity has become firmly entrenched (e.g. https://en.wikipedia.org/wiki/Biodiversity) and, as such, has now become the subject of critical review. The evaluation by Morar, Toadvine and Bohannan (2017: 16–17) entitled 'Biodiversity at twenty-five years: Revolution or red herring?' is especially useful. They chart how biodiversity became a focus for scientific research and environmental policy, but is "rarely questioned" in terms of "either its descriptive basis or its prescriptive import[ance]". They question whether it has provided "any clearly established relationship with those aspects of nature about which we care the most". They note that "the evidence for a relation between biodiversity and ecosystem function is inconclusive at best" and that "the concept's abstractness . . . readily lends itself to a wide range of value interpretations".

They suggest that the apparent objectivity of the concept of biodiversity leads the public and policy makers to believe that decisions based on it are "value-neutral and free from any ideological commitments". They continue that "the veneer of objectivity masks the normative decisions" and "obscures the relationship between the concept and experienced values". They dislike the way in which "empirical facts can substitute for ethical judgments", taking the latter away from policy makers and the public, leaving decision-making in the hands of "scientific and technical experts", thereby compromising "the goals of conservation". They propose that this normative role should be avoided but instead "we pay renewed attention to our experiences of what we value in nature, and that we promote an inclusively democratic approach to the value judgments that underlie conservation policy."

Of the several reviews, notable is that by Casetta, Marques da Silva and Vecchi (2019): *From Assessing to Conserving Biodiversity*. This provides a very wide-ranging critique of the utility of the concept of biodiversity. In the volume, the abstract nature of the term biodiversity is critiqued by Meinard, Coq and Schmid (2019) in 'The vagueness of "biodiversity" and its implications in conservation practice'. The authors conclude (pp, 353–354) that "the vagueness of the term actually complicates [the] task of conservation practitioners" and feel that there should be "a dynamic definition of 'biodiversity practices'" and these can be understood "as a coherent collaborative effort from various disciplines to tackle environmental or conservation problems commonly identified on the basis of coherent value-laden aspirations". A key point is about the critical discussion (p. 371): "We should seize every opportunity to discuss and criticize the definitions put forward by the other biodiversity scientists." Interestingly, they end with the thought that: "Although they have never formally articulated it, art theoreticians and artists have historically followed a similar path, which proved to be very fruitful. Our hope is that biodiversity scientists can learn from this example."

Sarkar (2019: 375) asks 'What should "biodiversity" be?', noting that "there is no consensus on the question of what, precisely, biodiversity is supposed to be". He sees a tension between "biodiversity as a global heritage" and biodiversity as "embodying local values" and gives precedence to the latter while noting the issues of "all natural features ... being dubbed as biodiversity" as well as those of "restriction to biotic elements, attention to variability ... taxonomic spread ... and measurability". He feels that: "The biotic elements could be taxa, community types, or even non-standard land cover units such as sacred groves", that is, those features of local significance.

Continuing the questioning approach to the nature of the concept of biodiversity, Reydon (2019: 167) trenchantly asks: 'Are species good units for biodiversity studies and conservation efforts?' The author feels that species are "not good units of biodiversity" and should not be the basic unit involved. The logic of the approach is that there is considerable disagreement on how to define the notion of species for use in practice. Moreover, it seems that different organism groups are best classified using different definitions of 'species', such that species of organisms in very different domains of biodiversity are not generally comparable units. A "pragmatic notion of 'species' that can be used as an epistemic tool in the context of biodiversity studies" is discussed in an approach that involves emphasising (p. 189) "local populations and other groups of organisms as parts of landscapes and ecosystems".

Equally trenchantly, Dussault (2019: 297) questions the relationship between biodiversity and ecosystem function in 'Functional biodiversity and the concept of ecological function'. The author shows that some simplistic notion of numerical biodiversity and ecosystem functioning is inadequate. The paper critiques the ideas of ecological functions in relation to the presence of organisms in ecosystems and the conception of "ecological functions of organisms as use and service functions rather than design functions". There are ideas of "causal role" and "organizational accounts" of ecological functions. The conclusion is (pp. 298–299) that there are "functional effect groups" of organisms involved in some aspects of both "causal role" and "organizational account" of ecological functions. To my mind, this interesting paper is well beyond the notions of 'more means better' and of 'keystone species', with the idea of functional effect groups being well worth further attention. I was going to write: It certainly throws a new light on the question of 'what species should we save' – but in fact it possibly throws a new darkness onto the question. The idea of 'keystone species' made the answer easy, as did the 'all species matter', but functional groupings needs a more subtle answer – and looks ahead to the next section of connectivity and dependency.

Connectivity, Dependency and the Fundamental but Neglected Example of Soil Biota

Thus equipped with these examples of the critiques of biodiversity, we can well see the value of the title of this section: 'Beyond Biodiversity'. But where does this take us? If we are now well beyond ideas of biodiversity as numerical counting but have a realisation of organisation and groups of organisms with functional effects, to my mind we come to rest once again in this book on the idea that nature shows contingent conjunctions and dependency. This means that things happen to be juxtaposed the way they are in a place by the route through time that they got there – they thus depend on spatial interaction through prior states. The spatial interaction is not limited to proximal effects. Material which is transported by agencies such as wind, water or animals/humans can arrive at a site from both near and far. It also means that there is a dependency through connectivity – there are interactions which tend to have far more wide-reaching effects than the presence of any particular species alone. To me, this means that conservation could be focussing on connectivity in systems as much as on what has perhaps become a traditional 'list of species' approach; however, I am far from sure what 'focussing on connectivity' might entail.

To illustrate, let me examine the example of soils and soil biota. In so much conservation we tend to focus on the easily visible – the plants and animals above ground. Yet one way or another everything which is above ground depends to a greater or lesser extent to that which is below the surface. Soil conservation has tended to be undertaken in an agricultural context and is often focussed on attempting to minimise soil erosion. However, there seems to be not enough attention paid to the soils themselves and this seems especially true of soil organisms. In 'Soil biodiversity, nature conservation and sustainability', Usher (2005b: 363) writes: "Soils have hardly featured in conservation thinking" and proposes that "soils and their biota [are] far more important than the protection of individual soil types or individual species". While much of what he writes can be seen in the context of sustainable development, it certainly, to my mind, has universal application and importance. Tellingly, while not explicitly abandoning the concept of biodiversity in favour of the concept of connectivity, he writes (Usher, 2005b: 373): "In the conservation of soil biota, it seems inappropriate to focus on rare species, endemic species, or other 'significant' species because of their charismatic character or keystone role in ecosystems, but pertinent to consider the functioning of the soil ecosystem." In other words, instead of focussing on some equivalent of the "panda, corncrake or lady's slipper orchid" in soil we should cherish the whole system because of its functioning. This, I submit, also gives us pause for thought about our attitudes to the ways in which we conserve the above-ground ecosystems.

Usher (2005b: 373) admits that: "We still do not understand . . . just how species rich the soil needs to be to perform its function reliably" – a statement which raises several interesting questions, most obviously what does 'reliably' mean. It seems to be that there is a gradation here – if there are few decomposers – as when a soil is waterlogged and anaerobic – then organic matter accumulates – as in peat. So, I would argue that we are focussing on functional groups again, and in that case the relative abundance of organisms which act to decompose organic matter. It is well known that there are a number of types of organisms involved, from the insects and fungi which break down woody, lignified tissues, through earthworms and other creatures which ingest leaf matter to bacteria which tend to be involved in the more complete breakdown of organic matter (see, e.g., Kononova, 1966).

The case of soil fungi is particularly interesting. There is a group referred to as mycorrhiza – derived from the Greek for fungus and root – which have been known about for some time. They form associations of fungi with plant roots which was studied by Franciszek Kamieński (1882) and by Frank (1885) who coined the term mycorrhiza (and see also the English translation: Frank and Trappe, 2005). From Frank (1885: 129): "Der ganze Körper ist also weder Baumwurzel noch Pilz allein, sondern ähnlich wie der Thallus der Flechten, eine Vereinigung zweier verschiedener Wesen zu einem einheitlichen morphologischen Organ, welches vielleicht passend als Pilzwurzel, Mycorhiza bezeichnet werden kann" [The whole body is thus neither tree root nor fungus alone, but similar to the thallus of lichens, a union of two different organisms into a single morphological organ, which can be aptly designated as a 'fungus root', a mycorrhiza].

In 'Mycorrhizal ecology and evolution: The past, the present, and the future', van der Heijden et al. (2015: 1406) show how mycorrhiza are found in fossil records and that almost all land plants form symbiotic associations with mycorrhizal fungi. They cite estimates which "suggest that there are c. 50 000 fungal species that form mycorrhizal associations with c. 250 000 plant species". They show how the organisms play "a key role in terrestrial ecosystems as they regulate nutrient and carbon cycles, and influence soil structure and ecosystem multifunctionality. Up to 80% of plant N [nitrogen] and P [phosphorus] is provided by mycorrhizal fungi" – many plant species depend on them for growth and survival. The early work on the establishment of forest trees recognised that the survival of newly planted tree seedlings depended upon the presence of mycorrhiza (Ackers, 1938: 178) and their role is acknowledged in early works on soil science (Russell, 1959: 74–78; Russell, 1962: 232–239).

The mycorrhizal fungal communities form complex underground multi-species networks. It has now become clear that not just nutrients but also 'chemical messengers' or 'infochemicals' may pass through this network, including those which can trigger defence mechanisms against pathogens or herbivores (see, e.g., Gilbert and Johnson, 2017; Johnson and Gilbert, 2017; Liang et al., 2020). This has given rise not only to a broader awareness among scientific research workers but also to the somewhat romantic idea of 'trees talking to each other'. Such popular notions are espoused in the idea of a 'wood-wide web'. The roles of fungi have also come to wider public attention through books such as Merlin Sheldrake's (2020) *Entangled Life: How fungi make our worlds, change our minds and shape our future*. Notwithstanding the slight air of mysticism involved, the sense of ecosystem connectivity is firmly established. The considerable significance of the soil ecosystem is clear, not only for plant nutrition and ecology but also for carbon sequestration and climate interactions, as discussed by, for example, Steidinger et al. (2019) in 'Climatic controls of decomposition drive the global biogeography of forest-tree symbioses'.

Loss of forest and woodland can indeed be seen as a decrease in biodiversity – a loss in the numbers of species. However, it should now be clear that there is loss of so much more. Not only is there a loss of interconnectivity between different organisms, there is a loss of connectivity between organisms and their environment – a connectivity which acts to mitigate the effect of the environment on organisms but also to regulate aspects of the environment, especially through carbon sequestration. This latter point is critical when we consider deforestation for conversion to agriculture. Without the addition of organic matter to the soil, biological activity decreases, earthworm population declines and so soil structure is weaker, infiltration of rain decreases and runoff, flooding and erosion increase. I remember once a student project where they counted the earthworms in 3 cubic metre plots in the soils of an organic farm and replicate plots on the same soil and crop in the soils of an adjacent non-organic farm. In the former were several hundred earthworms per cubic metre; in the latter the counts for the three plots were 0, 1 and 2 respectively. In this sense, indeed biodiversity counts do matter – in the sense that they are a surrogate for – and indicator of – connectivity, activity and function in ecosystems. However, I am more minded by the concept of functional effect groups than necessarily any one species, in other words it is the worms as a group which are important – and within them there are several different species, often living at different depths and ingesting organic matter in varying stages of decomposition (Wallwork, 1970: 59–66).

This gives to me an answer to the points raised in Chapter 1 – it is actually the functional groups that matter rather than the species. In Chapter 1 the alternatives which were discussed were that if one species is removed it can be argued that (1) the system collapses, (2) another species steps in to take its place or (3) there can be no difference. In other words, if there was only one earthworm species, then (1) would be true, but as there are several then (2) and (3) can be true – but, more tellingly, if the overall numbers of that functional group decline then indeed (1) is true: the whole system declines. I think we can usefully add the concept of functional groups to our conservation needs alongside that of keystone species.

It is striking that we will go to extraordinary lengths to save charismatic animals from declining yet we cannot feed earthworms and other soil biota with the simple addition of organic matter to our soils – all the more strange when our food and our lives depend upon soil biological processes in so many ways, as Darwin himself realised in his book *The Formation of Vegetable Mould through the Action of Earthworms, with Observation of Their Habits* (Darwin, 1882). It is perhaps a shame that *The Origin of Species* and *The Voyage of the Beagle* have grabbed all the attention when it is the knowledge which is contained in *Vegetable Mould and Earthworms* on which the continuation of life on our planet and of our civilisation depends.

Here, I can only refer back to Section 4.3 on cultural attitudes to soil – seen as dirt in many ways and taken for granted. There is the idea that 'the earth shall endure and blossom forth in spring' (from *Das Lied von der Erde* by Mahler). Without nurturing soil biota there is a very good chance that it will not. The sense of something vulnerable is missing with soils, as was also evident with the seas. Perhaps usefully time to revisit nature in our imagination.

7.2 The Power of Nature in Our Imagination

Bernard Williams on the Sense of Something beyond Our Power

Nature as an enduring power beyond us is a strong and recurring concept. It is evident that Wordsworth knew about and alluded to the processes of weathering and decay of rocks in nature through his association with the geologist Adam Sedgewick, as discussed in Section 4.3. However, in the River Duddon sonnets he reassures us that the stream "shall for ever glide; the form remains, the function never dies" while "We men . . . must vanish":

I see what was, and is, and will abide;
Still glides the Stream, and shall for ever glide;
The Form remains, the Function never dies;
While we, the brave, the mighty, and the wise,

We Men, who in our morn of youth defied
The elements, must vanish;—be it so!
(from *Valedictory Sonnet to the River Duddon*, Wordsworth, 1820)

So, even though Wordsworth realised through observing rock decay that the constancy of nature is an illusion, he also realises that the river never ceases its work and will be there in some form long after we have gone. W. H. Auden refers to 'we the inconstant ones' when talking of the metaphor of a limestone landscape in *In Praise of Limestone*. The Reverend A. M. Toplady's 1763 'Rock of Ages' hymn and the Biblical Psalm 121 'I shall lift up mine eyes to the hills' both have the same sense reassurance from nature. The idea of a 'power beyond us' is a very deep one.

Caspar David Friedrich's picture, *The Dreamer* (1820–1840) (Figure 7.1) for me shows the crumbling ruins of the Oybin Monastery with nature not only viewed beyond man's efforts but also taking them over as they crumble. There are many other interpretations, especially of the lone figure with something of the dreamer contemplating nature as a spiritual experience, but to me there is a sense of nature enduring.

In the book *Making Sense of Humanity* by Bernard Williams (1995) he has a short chapter on the environment. It contains a succinct set of thoughts about our approaches to nature. To my mind the most compelling thing he says is: "We have to use our power to preserve a sense of what is not in our power" (Williams, 1995: 240). This is quite riveting. It is not about subjugating nature by our power, controlling it, bending it to our will; it is about using our power to let something which is beyond us happen. He adds: "What many conservation interests want to preserve is a nature that is not controlled, shaped or willed by us, a nature which, as against culture, can be thought of as just there." However, while we can destroy wilderness, we cannot create it, only allow it to happen as best we can. He writes that even when we preserve wilderness, what "is preserved is a definite, delimited, wilderness" and "anything we leave untouched, we have already touched".

In other words, while wilderness is an artifice, we should nonetheless try to preserve what we can. Additionally, note that he writes: "preserve a sense of what is not in our power". This is an important nuance as re-writing it without the word sense as 'we have to use our power to preserve what is not in our power' admits none of the points about wilderness already being 'touched' above. It also indicates that whether or not nature is touched, untouched, beyond us or not, it is the sense of beyondness which is really important.

Figure 7.1 The Dreamer by Caspar David Friedrich (Heritage Images / Contributor / Hulton Fine Art Collection / Getty Images). *A black and white version of this figure will appear in some formats. For the colour version, please refer to the plate section.*

So, the questions then revolve around whether it is an actual state which is being preserved or merely a sense of a state. While the latter seems irrefutable it is perhaps not 'merely' as I have written for it is that very sense which is so powerful – more or less irrespective of any actual state.

I argue elsewhere that preserving processes (e.g. processes of renewal) is liable to be more successful than trying to preserve particular states and their assemblages of species. Wordsworth wrote, above: "Still glides the Stream, and shall for ever glide;/ The Form remains, the Function never dies"; in truth the function is what is unchanging but the form through which it is expressed can be manifest and changeable. But it is nonetheless the form to which we are attracted and invest value. Trying to preserve function in terms of the processes such as renewal, decomposition, growth, dispersal and migration is probably going to work as we would then be working with nature. Trying to preserve form in terms of say vegetation type needs far greater effort and trying to preserve form in a particular location is even more difficult. Nature has changed in form and location radically throughout geological history and so this is a plea for not corralling nature into fossil vignettes in particular locations but to let it range over all the earth where it will, changing as it goes.

However, preserving a *sense* of a state is a different endeavour from preserving an actual state and not completely futile. Indeed, it is very motivating. Flawed though they may be 'wilderness' and 'balance of nature' are so motivational that they are worth pursuing even if one is intelligently aware of their limitations if applied unthinkingly. Given our pervading influence, wilderness as a state is therefore arguable but nevertheless the concept is usefully motivational – and there can be that sense of wilderness despite man's influence. We can bring a sense of wilderness to those areas which are still putatively wild and cherish them in terms of wild processes. The balance of nature is not a state of putative harmony but a process whereby mutual interaction occurs – and as such we can help by preserving nature's capacity to mutually interact. That is about conserving nature's functions, but none of this is about preserving actual 'pristine', 'balanced' or 'harmonious' states, rather it is about keeping a *sense* of these states in wilderness areas. That way we can help to keep and enhance the ecological functioning of an area which scientific investigation has sought to reveal as well as the significance and meaning of an area which studies of our culture reveal.

I feel that these points are useful because while I believe that nothing is indeed completely untouched any more, my answer to that is: 'so what'. If you say that everything is tainted it may lead you to do nothing as it means that nothing is worth bothering with as it is all ruined anyway. However, it is arguably much better that we try to keep whatever passes for wilderness as wild and as untouched as possible. Therefore, when we are dealing with concepts such as 'natural' and 'wilderness' I seem to be judging the validity of these concepts in terms of the consequences of holding these concepts and their associated value systems. So, it is, for me, not so much whether or not there is any untouched or real wilderness left, it is that trying to preserve a sense of wilderness increases the wilderness value of that area.

As Attenborough (2020) says, we have lost forever the completely untouched wilderness, we have lost untainted nature (McKibben, 1989) – but let's get on with cherishing that which we have left. And let's not lament that it is all tainted, what Proctor (1995) called a 'purificationist logic', let's get on with making it less tainted than it is now. And we must remember that the sense of nature 'touched' by us is a derivative of the sense of guilt derived from the Edenic myth as discussed elsewhere. If we rid ourselves of that thought, we then can rejoice in nature much more – and even want to preserve it more. Bernard Williams's anthropocentrism is very wise as both the wildness and the sense of wilderness now have to be man-made. But preserving that sense of wildness and wilderness – that sense of something which is beyond our power – is all important.

I can't help thinking that this is what the climate change lobby is all about. It is not so much about the actual evidence of our actions causing climate change, what is psychologically powerful is the *sense* that our actions are causing climate change. This offends the idea that nature *should* be beyond our power. In *The End of Nature* by Bill McKibben (1989) he writes: "Nature's independence is its meaning", concluding that if we deprive nature of its independence then that is fatal to the meaning of nature. He describes nature as a force previously independent of human beings, but which is now directly affected by the actions of people:

> If the waves crash up against the beach, eroding dunes and destroying homes, it is not the awesome power of Mother Nature. It is the awesome power of Mother Nature as altered by the awesome power of man, who has overpowered in a century the processes that have been slowly evolving and changing of their own accord since the earth was born. (McKibben, 1989: 51)

When students have asked me the question: 'Is mankind part of nature?' I have said that we are inextricably linked to and within nature and thus simultaneously our own entity and also part of something beyond us. The dual consequences of this involve dismay at the loss of something which is above and beyond us, beyond our power, and the simultaneous realisation that we also, therefore, have it in our power to redress. So, the human-induced climate change narrative simultaneously regrets that nature is influenced by us which can offend our cherished idea of a power beyond us but finds comfort that we can do something about it; the inverse is that climate change is natural which is then nature beyond us, just as it should be, but thus beyond our power which can offend our conceit. Culpability, responsibility and ability to rectify go hand in hand; McKibben offers defiant reflex action or a more humble way of living.

This is why the debates are so heated. The idea that nature is beyond our power is such a powerful one, however, that many cling to it, amassing all the evidence which they can find to prove that everything is natural, it is no warmer than at some time in the past, it is all part of nature and, in other words, it is still beyond our power. So, we have 'nature is screwed up by us, we must put it right' versus 'nature's fine, leave it alone'. But both come round to the same point – on the one hand once we have 'put it right' it can then be (best) left alone to get on with doing what it is doing, flourish in its own way while we stand back – on the other the stance of the second point of view gets there straight away without bothering with rectification. The sense of nature as a power beyond us is deeply fundamental and has a lot to answer for.

However, that power exists in the mind, books and poems – that is, in the imagination. So also dwells therein the necessity with which we imbue nature. The next time you find yourself wondering why something happens – for example, why does a particular creature behave as it does – ask yourself why you are asking that question. You have been condition and positioned – brainwashed – into thinking that there is a 'reason for everything', as Marek Kohn (2004) put it. Now maybe there is no particular purpose – maybe it is all in our imagination.

As an example – and I mean to do no more than try to describe a process, rather than be judgemental about it – individuals of the great tit (*Parus major*), a bird in the UK, have a wide variety of calls. The birds, in common with many, are thought to proclaim their territory using song. But somehow this 'wide variety' apparently needs to be explained, and it is said that 'this is because' other birds are then fooled by the wide variety into thinking that there are more birds around than there are and move on. Yes, OK, plausible. It never seems to occur to an investigator that it just has a wide variety of calls. No reason. Now of course an investigator can investigate and test the idea; does the bird with the widest variety of calls have the largest territory? We could even design investigations to try to disprove the idea – that would be more telling. Yes/No supports/detracts.

If it detracts it must be some other reason. If you can't find a reason, then it is a puzzle. Do you see what is going on? The thought that maybe it is a random genetic variation of no significance might possibly occur later in the thought process, but it is certainly not the first thought. We are creatures that are always asking 'why?'. We always have to have a narrative, yes – it can be 'territory', 'a puzzle' or 'random' – fine, but the imperative of the narrative is paramount. If we ask a question we must find an answer, and ask we do. But more, there is the seduction of reason. There has to be a reason – and if not the 'unreason' narrative still implies a search for reason. In this case, there is an assumption of reason in that there has to be some advantage to a behaviour otherwise it would not exist. We so rarely enjoy saying the answer is 'just because it does', or 'because there is no particular disadvantage'. It is unthinkable that there is no reason. Otherwise what would the investigator do? Sit back and enjoy the song? Note that I am indeed trying not to judge this process, partly because I know many open-minded investigators who indeed agree that you can push things too far – or 'over read' them – and that our interpretation can be way ahead of our evidence. I am writing for the sake of self-realisation about a process which takes place. We cannot resist asking 'why?' and we cannot resist finding an answer, even if the only answer we can find is 'puzzling'.

This is thus not to deny the significance of asking questions nor is it to denigrate the real importance of scientific investigation. It is to highlight what we do when we ask questions. In this context, we can show this further by making a contrast with what happens when we don't ask questions. I have seen a television programme where a presenter was discussing philosophy and sat there holding a stone, expounding Zen Buddhism. He expressed the importance of meditation which stripped away all the constructions – in Zen the self is between the object and you seeing the object as opposed to you seeing all the possible meanings. The self stands in the way and with no sense of self, you could see what was out there without logic or analysis. Perceptions stand in the way and seeing nature for what it is can be achieved by meditation. Thus, his stone was not igneous, metamorphic or whatever, it was simply a stone with shape, form and colour. So, we didn't ask any questions and we have a sense of the stone but we have little understanding of the significance and meaning of the stone. This is because significance and meaning are related to the answers we find as a result of asking questions. Nevertheless, we can still sense the stone – and a sense of something beyond us – and we can find a sense of a power in that something beyond us if we are so minded to. Does questioning get in the way of sensing something beyond us? It need not, but it can do. Also, the answers we find can increase a sense of something beyond us. There is no necessity in understanding, just different pathways which can be taken.

A sense of awe and power beyond our reasoning can be found in many writings, together with discussions of how this might relate to our questioning and how we see things. In *Notations of the Wild* Gyorgi Voros (1997: 7) wrote on the ecology in the poetry of the American poet Wallace Stevens (1879–1955, see, e.g., www.poetryfoundation.org/poems-and-poets/poets/detail/wallace-stevens). Voros felt that Stevens was mesmerized by "the flickering presence of something wild, primordial, pre-Oedipal, preverbal . . . he peered toward something yet more distant and elemental – pre-Adamic nature unadorned by human conception, scoured of impastoed [thickly layered] human meanings, unmediated, authentic, and whole". This was expressed by Stevens as "the poem of pure reality untouched by trope or deviation, straight to the word, straight to the transfixing object, to the object at the exactest point at which it is itself" and in "the cry of leaves that do not transcend themselves". A key point was seen as: "only in the imagination could the absence of imagination be imagined". Whether we can ever separate 'what is out there' from 'how we see it' is highly debateable, however, but I am fond of being rescued from this apparent dilemma by quoting Whatmore and Boucher (1993: 167) who feel that '*nature cannot be (re) produced outside social relations, neither is it reducible to them*' (my italics). This happily allows us to feel a sense of power beyond us and avoid the discussion of whether it is actually there or not.

I conclude that any interpretation – and in many ways the evidence for it – begins and ends in our imagination – and that we do so much love a story which makes sense. But does that 'making sense' serve us well when it necessarily involves finding a reason? Maybe we miss something while we are busy being seduced by our ideas? One can but argue, however, that a sense of a power beyond us can serve us well in many ways but also that it can delude us in others. Again, as with so many aspects of nature, we should have the self-realisation of how we think and try to harness this sense of a power beyond us in a way which both enhances nature itself and our enjoyment of it.

Meanings of Nature: Re-enchantment, Pluralism and Education

In 2002 Alister McGrath published a book called *The Reenchantment of Nature: The denial of religion and the ecological crisis* but in 2003 it was republished with the more positive forward-looking title of *The Reenchantment of nature: Science, religion and the human sense of wonder*. Part of the negativity is illustrated by the quotation he uses from Soulé (1995) on 'The social siege of nature': "Nature ... is under siege – of two kinds, one is overt, the other covert. The overt is physical ... bulldozers, chainsaws, plows, livestock ... the covert is ideological and therefore social; it serves to justify ... the physical assault" (McGrath, 2003: 73). I feel that part of the issues these writers are seeking to redress stems from a restricted view: nature as commodity or hindrance. A wider view of nature may lead to a more varied outcome and pluralism of meaning in the cause of a more progressive conservation ethic. Indeed, Lorimer (2012) argues that with what he calls a 'multinatural geography' we get away from a concept of 'Nature' and embrace a multiplicity of biodiversities.

In developing such a pluralistic idea we might usefully follow on from the ideas discussed by Perlman and Adelson (1997) on biodiversity, Kellert's (1993) 'Biological basis for human values of nature', Meinig's (1979) 'seeing eye' (as discussed in Chapter 1) and Macnaghten and Urry's (1998) sensing nature together with Porteous's (1996) *Environmental Aesthetics*. The range of ideas expressed in these writings means that a woodland, for example, can be seen as many things. A stand of timber for wood (furniture, building, fuel). It can be seen as an ecosystem. The diagram with boxes and arrows becomes mandatory (and I should know; see Trudgill, 1988, *Soil and Vegetation Systems*). Here, nature is constructed as a functioning system, with food chains, relationships, gaps, regrowth, feedbacks with notions of stability and other narratives. Maybe it can look after itself, maybe we have to intervene to facilitate it, maybe we want to intervene to give it a preferred state, maybe we want to preserve it because it is a rarity and one of few remaining examples of its type. It might just contain a cure for cancer. We can also see it as a wilderness with the duality of something dark and threatening needing conquering or of something of release and wandering (see also Table 4.1 on woods and forests in poetry).

None of these is mutually exclusive, as Perlman and Adelson (1997: 43–44) point out. These authors conclude with a need to "recognise the many forms of worth in biodiversity" in a pluralistic approach which, as they see it, legitimates utilitarian, ecological, aesthetic, emotive and moralistic senses of worth, in the fashion of Kekes's chapter (1994) on 'Pluralism and the value of life'. When considering, say, the classical 'by-pass road through a nature reserve' dilemma, involved are beauty, landscape, feeling and a sense of place and history, not just Sites of Special Scientific Interest and the rare snail, emotive as the latter might be for some.

However, a plurality of meanings in conservation is perhaps unusual and there is often a (contestable) dominant meaning (see, e.g., Mason, 1997, 'Democratising nature? The political morality of wilderness preservationists'). The proposition I have here is that speciesism alone is not enough to motivate for conservation: aesthetic, emotive and moralistic arguments are also involved and often present stronger arguments. Engendering a generalised conservation ethic thus involves a democratised plurality of allowed meanings which must refer to the wide range of held societal values if all sections of society are to be 'taken on board'. This may involve a spatial separation of activities where there are conflicts or multiple allowed meanings at one site. The emphasis on the importance of 'patch' dynamics (Pickett and White, 1985) even means that timber extraction (in patches) is not incompatible with conservation.

We have available an evidential website about the tangible benefits of conservation, largely seen in terms of increasing biodiversity: www.conservationevidence.com/. Equally worthwhile are the substantive volumes: Sutherland and Hill (1995) *Managing Habitats for Conservation* and Sutherland (1998) *Conservation Science and Action* and his more recent Sutherland (2006) 'Predicting the ecological consequences of environmental change: A review of methods'. Writings such as these, and many others, are fundamental and necessary for the conservation endeavour, but not sufficient for a wider pluralistic endeavour. They miss something important which is seen more in the article by Watson (2003) 'Performing place in nature reserves' in the edited volume of Szerszynski, Heim and Waterton (2003) *Nature Performed: Environment, culture and performance*. This book allows for a plurality of nature and for the multiple meanings which many people can engage with.

Relevant here is the paper by Matulis and Moyer (2016) who write on 'Beyond inclusive conservation: The value of pluralism, the need for agonism, and the case for social instrumentalism'. The authors recognise some of the issues inherent in attempts to allow for pluralism and ask for a greater recognition of conflict. They advocate an *agonistic* approach which recognises the validity of the other's point of view. To understand this concept the commonly cited example is where there is a sporting contest, but the opposing sides have a mutual admiration for each other – in other words a defeat for one side is at the hands of a worthy opponent. This is a deeply interesting idea as we all too readily fall into the clichés of greedy capitalists versus NIMBY conservationists where the opposing sides are mutually regarded as deeply unworthy. The art form lies in providing an arena where the differences may be confronted. They write (Matulis and Moyer 2016: 284): "Consensus as a goal should be abandoned, and instead conflict embraced. This entails voicing dissent, as well as actively engaging with dissent when it is voiced. Alternative framings and radical views should be articulated and differentiated, rather than relegated to separate arenas or appropriated into the mainstream." They write positively (Matulis and Moyer 2016: 285):

> The many and varied actions performed under the banner of conservation have the capacity to explore and strengthen human-nature relations, provide opportunities for knowledge exchange, and inspire emerging forms of stewardship. . . . a commitment to pluralism is needed to keep many of them [the ideas] afloat. In contrast, attempts to reign in such diverse activities so they might align with a more specific common vision would be oppressive and ultimately self-defeating. . . . agonism demands acknowledgement of the power dynamics at play among differently interested groups.

This seems like a deeply intelligent approach.

I look back to look forward. I remember being taken by my parents on outings with the Norfolk naturalists. This society of enthusiasts was full of specialists but everybody actually seemed interested in everything and took a wide view, asking people with specialist knowledge what things were. As a youngster I readily absorbed lots of this knowledge. It never occurred to me that there were any limits – we just saw and marvelled at everything; I also read literature and poetry – and enjoyed science. It all seemed one joyous fusion of existence and a celebration of the natural world. I wrote lists of birds seen, kept careful records and wrote poetry about nature.

Then somehow I learnt to keep poetry in one box and science in another. This isn't some kind of complaint about first learning from nature when young and then being corrupted by society, as could be spurred on by interpretations of Rousseau's writings, because I never lost the love of nature and I didn't lose my sense of wonder. I just didn't show them during lessons. Indeed, the process was one of addition rather than subtraction in that being possessed of a love for nature and *also* of scientific knowledge, then I could find myself marvelling at soaring bird flight and relishing the thought that science had helped me to understand how feathers worked. But I dutifully ticked the knowledge boxes and got the good marks, while keeping the other thing to myself. So, my separation of science from poetry started early: lessons in school were

Biology or English, Art or Chemistry, never that exciting mix where you can range from one to another so creatively. Then at University this continued as I think it was because the 'science' was part of the recognised expectations I laboured under, where an interest in poetry, art and gardens had no currency in the everyday structure I found myself in; instead I did these myself, separately from my studies. I studied Botany, Zoology and Geography; became a Geographer, did science at work, lectured on soils and agriculture and the environment and kept that quite separate from my interests in writing, art and gardens.

It wasn't till I came to Cambridge about two-thirds of the way through my academic career than I began to re-unite myself; partly through lecturing on not just biogeography and conservation but also by being able to lecture on nature in poetry, literature, art and gardens as well as in ecology and conservation. As I discuss in the acknowledgements to this book, most helpful was having a 'Third Space' by which I mean a room in a Cambridge College. The Geography Department was where I largely did science; home is where I kept natural history, poetry and art; however, having this Third Space in College where I felt I could do anything I liked and was free from expectations other than being involved in some kind of intellectual discourse, was so important for me. There, I could do, be and write anything I liked and managed to bring together my varied books and interests and write my book on *The Terrestrial Biosphere: Environmental change, ecosystem science, attitudes and values* (Trudgill, 2001b), fusing science and culture. This built from my earlier *Barriers to a Better Environment* book (Trudgill, 1990) and was encouraged by a review of that book by Simmons (1993b: 151) who wrote positively about my ability to progress from the natural sciences to the world of human affairs in a seamless manner and handling such "a wide variety of material with a facility that most of us will envy". In fact, to me, that interest in the social and cultural side had always been there, but more hidden. Thus, in writing the book I re-gained what I had found in my earlier years and lost through education and the channelled specialisation I had undergone. As Leopold (1949: 158) wrote: "Education, I fear, is learning to see one thing by going blind to another."

While that was true for me, I find another part of his rather bleak assessment that "The place for dismemberment is university" Leopold (1949: 153) need not be true. While I know very well what he means, being at Cambridge allowed me to be a naturalist again as well as fostering my interests in human society and culture. I indeed look up to the early naturalists, Gilbert White (1789, 1795) perhaps being one of the most famous ones, who looked at everything and knew no boundaries. I was bought up in the knowledge of Norfolk naturalists through reading Arthur Patterson (Patterson, 1930) and learning from Ted Ellis. Recently, Philip Stott (2016) wrote about a book by Andrea Wulf (2015) on Humboldt – surely a scientist who married a spirit of scientific enquiry with a sense of soul and wonder. Stott sees Humboldt as a founding giant and asks us to regain his "sense of wonder about our world, while recognising that we will only see it through our own distorting vision" (p. 6). Furthermore, Steinbeck is a hero of mine, being able to span the ecological and the literary, not just in the well-known *Grapes of Wrath* (Steinbeck, 1939) but in a lesser known book which I found really significant.

The Log from the Sea of Cortez

In Steinbeck's *The Log from the Sea of Cortez* ([1951]1960) there are writings on marine biology stemming from his association with scientist Ed Ricketts on the California Coast (see also Lannoo, 2010 and Tamm, 2004). The author writes: "A man looking at reality brings his own limitations to the world" (Steinbeck, [1951]1960: 146).

He takes up the theme of a man who "has strength and energy of mind" when looking at a tide pool, who can see both the microcosm and the macrocosm: "digs back to electrons and leaps space into the universe" in a timeless way: "Then ecology has a synonym which is ALL" (Steinbeck, [1951]1960: 146). He continues this theme later in the book (p. 267):

> What we know as life meets and enters what we think of as non-life: barnacle and rock, rock and earth, earth and tree, tree and rain and air. And the units nestle in the whole and are inseparable from it. . . . And it is a strange thing that most of the feeling we call religious, most of the mystical outcrying which is one of the most prized and used and desired reactions of our species, is really the understanding and the attempt to say that man is related to the whole thing, related inextricably to all reality, known and unknowable. This is a simple thing to say, but the profound feeling of it made a Jesus, a St Augustine, a St Francis, a Roger Bacon, a Charles Darwin, and an Einstein. Each of them in his own tempo and with his own voice discovered and reaffirmed with astonishment the knowledge that all things are one thing and that one thing is all things – plankton, a shimmering phosphorescence on the sea and the spinning planets and the expanding universe, all bound together by the elastic string of time. It is advisable to look from the tide pool to the stars and then back to the tide pool again.

There is much wisdom in Steinbeck's writings.

7.3 Reimagining Nature

Insights from Peter Kareiva, Ken Thompson and Fred Pearce

In this context, I would now like to turn to three books sitting on my desk as I write – the substantial 2003 volume edited by Peter Kareiva and Simon Levin on *The Importance of Species: Perspectives on expendability and triage*, the 2010 book by Ken Thompson: *Do We Need Pandas? The uncomfortable truth about biodiversity* and the 2015 book by Fred Pearce: *The New Wild: Why invasive species will be nature's salvation*. These three items present substantial challenges to many oft-rehearsed narratives.

In Kareiva and Levin's book they report on a great deal of experimental work and reflect on the theories which relate to the importance of species. Their use of the words 'importance', 'expendability' and 'triage' in the title admits that we are in a management, decision-making context where we wish to predict the consequences of our actions, be they inadvertent or deliberate, and whether they are conservation-orientated or not. In this book, Doak and Marvier (2003: 141) have a section on predicting the effects of species loss on community stability. As is usually the case with writings on stability, I can find no real discussion of why stability is important though it is defined in terms of stability "of aggregate community properties (e.g. total community abundance) or . . . community composition". They are careful to say that for their models "our results are driven by our assumptions". And they find that rank abundance prior to an extinction was a very useful predictor of outcome. They also, however, refer to the chapter by Simberloff (2003b) in the same volume on 'Community and ecosystem impacts of single-species extinctions' showing that several extremely abundant species have been lost with no dramatic effects recorded. This is notwithstanding the pioneering work of Paine (1966, 1969) on keystone species where the removal of a top 'keystone' predator leads to a complete change in a marine ecosystem – the removal of the sea star *Pisaster ochreous* converted a diverse rocky shore into a uniform mussel bed. Interestingly the editors (Kareiva and Levin, 2003: 347–351) in their 'Conclusion: Bob Paine's contributions to science of assessing species importance: Past, present, and future?' expressed 'uniform' in a negative manner: "a monotonous coverage of mussels" (p. 348). So that is: diversity good; single species/uniformity bad. And while Simberloff (2003b: 237) notes that for past extinctions, the effects have varied widely, his chapter ends with the guilt trip of "finally it should be noted that virtually all introductions and extinctions were caused by the activities of one keystone species, *Homo sapiens*". Doak and Marvier (2003: 158) also sensibly note that the effects of loss vary with the species loss, some being more important than others. They again cite Paine's work and write that "it is now widely appreciated that certain keystone species exert effects on communities or ecosystems that are disproportionately large relative to the species' abundance".

They continue: "Thus in some cases, real communities are strongly altered by the loss of a single species but in other cases not and the magnitude of the effects appears to depend upon the specific traits of the deleted species or on the nuances of how the deleted species interacted with others in the community, rather than on the changes in the numbers per se." That seems to me to be one of the most sensible things I have read about species in a lot of the relevant literature. It is a nice statement with no emotional narratives, confining the outcome to 'the magnitude of the effect' and not confusing the statement with value judgements about 'importance' and 'stability'. Nicely, the book contains discussions on whether species are expendable or not, and one chapter by Egbert Giles Leigh Jr concludes that "preconceived notions of what is important often prove to be deceptive. Whether we can learn enough natural history to predict the effects of most extinctions is open to question" (Leigh, 2003: 257–258).

In Ken Thompson's *Do We Need Pandas?* book he considers the question: "Are species necessary?" (Thompson, 2010: 98). He quotes from one of my favourite books, Steinbeck's *Log from the Sea of Cortez* ([1951]1960). Many people know Steinbeck's ([1939]1995) *Grapes of Wrath* book but fewer know his marine biological writings about his association with scientist Ed Ricketts on the California Coast. The specific writing quoted is as illuminating as many of the passages in *The Log*. It includes the phrases:

> The disappearance of plankton, although the components are microscopic, would probably in a short time eliminate every living thing in the sea and change the whole of man's life, if it did not through a seismic disturbance of balance eliminate all life on the globe. For these little animals, in their incalculable numbers, are probably the base food supply of the world. But the extinction of one of the rare animals, so avidly sought and caught and named, would probably go unnoticed in the cellular world. (Steinbeck, [1951]1960: 266)

There is such wisdom here one wonders whether the vast range of experiments undertaken since he wrote these words ever achieved any greater insight.

Figure 7.2 Georges-Louis Leclerc, Comte de Buffon (1707–1788), French naturalist (UniversalImagesGroup / Contributor / Universal Images Group / Getty Images)

I also like the other quotation mentioned earlier in the book that Thompson uses in a chapter heading from the great French naturalist Buffon (Figure 7.2; see also Trudgill, 2012c). "This is the most delicate and most important point in scientific studies, to know how to distinguish well what there is of the real in a subject and that which we add to it arbitrarily as we consider it; to recognise clearly which properties belong to the subject and which properties we only imagine it to have" (Buffon, 1749).

This topic is as relevant today as it was then. This is in many ways a trenchant, stimulating, cleansing and self-examining book but again like so many such writings it can be imbued with sententious narratives which are peppered around in the loaded words like 'restored' and 'recovered' which shows that he immediately fails to heed Buffon's advice: "Life on earth recovered from previous mass extinctions, but it took around 5 million years for diversity to be restored" (Thompson, 2010: 99) – so, there we are again, abundance is good and right, loss is bad and things have to recover and be restored. Why this should be so we are not told directly, but refreshingly he sees the necessity of the relationship between diversity and productivity as an outdated idea and sees high productivity as a questionable goal. He also refreshingly admits that productivity is a human value and he maintains that many of our scientific arguments do simply reflect human values in terms of the uncontested and unexamined axioms which underpin much of the work. He also nicely distinguishes between scientific arguments about function and stewardship arguments. So, we can think how nice it is to want to protect a range of species and also think about functionality and search for answers to questions like 'are species necessary?' in that context. The answers depend upon which ones they are and how you define necessary – to what ends and to what function.

Thompson continues, however: "we all agree that ecosystems work well only if they contain the right species" and falls down again – ecosystems of course don't actually exist, they are a concept, they don't 'work' – how can you define that? – and 'right' species really means a particular set of functions – but even then say, for example, if there are no decomposers, well then maybe you have a peat bog of accumulated organic matter. So, why do decomposers matter? Do pandas matter – well, yes, culturally and morally, and no in terms of functional criteria, if you like. He ends on positive upbeat notes, however, looking ahead to a more intelligent approach where we look at not only function but also beauty, cultural importance and the evolutionary significance of nature as well as the powerful economic arguments.

Fred Pearce's book is no less stimulating. He demolishes the myths of the pristine, wonders about species, points out that of course invasive species are the successful ones and the species which survived in the past could have been seen as invasive if we had been around to make that judgement. He nicely quotes Kareiva, as discussed above, as well as the work of Simberloff. Here we are getting somewhere:

> Conservationists need to take a hard look at themselves and their priorities. They must put aside their old certainties and ditch their obsessions with lost causes, discredited theories and mythical pristine ecosystems. . . . One of the few conservationists I have met who is willing to make the change is Peter Kareiva, Chief Scientist of the Nature Conservancy in the US . . . ironically his members . . . are the most wedded to the old ecology – the 'shed the old paradigms' – Kareiva [feels that] 'Conservation's continuing focus on preserving islands of [old] ecosystems in the age of Anthropocene is both anachronistic and counterproductive.' (Pearce, 2015: 230–232)

He writes further: "There are hard choices to be made. Conservationists suggest that protecting each last individual native species is somehow essential in maintaining the 'ecological' services' that nature provides for us . . .. But that argument is a romantic illusion." An essence of Pearce's whole argument in the book is that if you wish for ecosystem services (carbon storage, watershed protection, pollination, seed dispersal, protecting soils and preventing erosion), then we should look to the successful species which flourish and that this increasingly means looking to plants hitherto classified as aliens and invaders. He writes:

> Conservationists have 'grossly overstated the fragility of nature, arguing that once an ecosystem is altered, it is gone forever' Kareiva says. The argument is that a narrow pursuit of evidence of this 'harm' has biased ecological research, driven by invasion biologists . . . and has blinkered researchers. And so their pervasive belief that stability is the norm and change somehow abnormal. Neither is true. Nature is rarely in a steady state. It is the dynamics that matter, and for too long researchers have denied this. Saving threatened species and restoring the earth [to] how it used to be – both are doomed. The first misses the point and the second is impossible.

He feels that managed ecosystems are becoming like Disneyland (see also Whitley, 2008, 2012).

He looks to the rest of the world outside the parks or what are really 'theme parks'; the areas he calls The New Wild. He cites the writings of the ecologist Chris Thomas (pp. 233–240) and writes:

> Thomas accepts that we will sometime recoil at the kind of dynamic and unpredictable change he is talking about. Things are happening so fast that we see ecological transformations in our individual lifetimes, it is human nature to be worried about that. I sometimes pull up alien weeds that I see in the fields around where I live. But that is an emotional response. Intellectually, I see nothing wrong with most of them.
>
> We should, he said, 'not confuse change with damage, or think of alien species as bad and natives as good'. Nature is always changing and adapting. Species are going to have to move – [it is] simply the ongoing change that constantly marks out nature. The narrow preservationist agenda will reduce rather than increase the capacity of nature to respond to environmental changes that we are inflicting on the world. We need to think less about keeping things just the way they were – because it is impossible – and more about promoting the new. (Pearce, 2015: 239)

This is one of the most realistic assessments I have read.

Romantic Illusions and Wildlife Films

Jamie Lorimer's 2015 book *Wildlife in the Anthropocene* also takes this idea and develops it extensively as discussed further below. However, before we discuss Lorimer's important book, I would now like to return to Drury (1998) and consider some more of his words in these contexts as they seem very relevant here. In *Chance and Change* he discusses (p. 7) how "we should see what '*is*', not '*what ought to be*'" and writes: "When your views on the world . . . are being challenged and you begin to feel uncomfortable because of a contradiction you've detected that is threatening your current model of the world or some aspect of it, pay attention. You are about to learn something" (p. 201). He exemplifies this with: "The model of stable communities . . . where each species is a critical element . . . and could have irreparable damage if it is lost . . . has been largely discredited. [But it led to the] ecological imperative of preservation" (p. 184). A conclusion is that people then designed to prevent the loss of species as part of this. However, he questions the premise by asking: "What effects will be caused by the removal of a species? Will the extinction of a conspicuous species have any effect?" (p. 185). My deduction is that he is sceptical that it necessarily will. Indeed, he writes that "eliminating gulls from a number of outer islands where terns might nest will have no effect" (p. 188). If we follow Drury, there may well be functional changes in ecosystems (just as Tansley originally allowed for) and things will be different. The challenge is that we can't quite swallow this – our cultural attachments rest in nostalgia – have we not been positioned to think about 'what ought to be there'?

Drury asks (p. 7) that "we should see what 'is', not 'what ought to be'" and continues that nature is not in a "hallowed state" (p. 190) based on ideals which are constructs of the human imagination. What is needed is a probabilistic approach based on modification based on natural selection, "because natural systems encompass a large amount of variation, successful individuals use a variety of resources to spread over a geographic range. . . . Populations may go extinct in one place and move to (or survive if there already) another place" (p. 186). "If we can predict [this] we can make enlightened judgements instead of leaning on mysticism" (p. 197). This call is backed up by his assessment that: "Chance and change are ubiquitous, selection means that parents produce an excess of offspring, death and disturbance are necessary for life – for the fittest to continue – this, not 'order', is what allows species to ride out the tribulations of this imperfect world" (p. 199) and "death, disturbance and extinction have been the rule. We should get on with the job of protecting and encouraging the delightful array of living things" (p. xix) – but realise that "nature works on the basis of one-to-one species interaction, variability and chance" (p. 1). Scientifically, this does seem to offer an interesting way forward; however, culturally, at least in popular culture as displayed on television natural history programmes, we are way, way different from Drury's view. It will now be useful to consider Lorimer's writings having set the scene for new ways of thinking and the resistance to them.

TV wildlife programmes, in what Lorimer (2015) terms 'mediated ecology' never cease to amaze me in their selective empathy and intentionality. To me it is always striking how partisan every programme is – so often we might focus on the lives of one species and then all the other species are either enemies or food. We might then see another programme which homes in on another species and then the perspective of the whole thing changes in an equally verifiable way – what was the darling of one show becomes the enemy or the food. It is like a pantomime – we (seem to be meant to) feel shock and horror when the baby something is eaten by the something else and we boo and hiss at the evil predator – but then the roles can be swapped depending on how the programme is structured. Such sentiment, such powerful narratives. So, some birds raise some chicks – we follow them, we get involved, we empathise. They are surviving. Hurray! But then some nasty evil predator comes along and eats the chicks. How terribly sad; mournful music plays. But lo! Watch another programme and what was the evil predator now in turn becomes a beleaguered survivor, struggling for food – we watch it trying to catch something to eat, we empathise. And, then, how wonderful, it comes across some hapless bird chicks which it can catch and take back to its cubs to eat – and they will survive and we see them eating and play. What joy!

What rubbish! What an extraordinary morality play it is. But hang on a minute, what exactly is wrong with that: What truth! also. Anthropomorphism is both indefensible in its subjectivity and defensible in the absolutely realistic way we understand the lives of animals through our own feelings which, after all, are not that different or, unsurprisingly, have a lot in common with, the lives of animals and their assumed emotions. And if we didn't engage with animals like this, then much of the conservation cause would be lost. However, even the promotion of conservation thus is a flawed endeavour as it is very unequal – who wishes to conserve flies and earwigs?

In terms of children's books and therefore presumably visual narratives, I have found two immensely valuable sources which, to me, encapsulate the dimensions of the relevant discussions about anthropomorphism.

First, Ganea et al. (2014) have written 'Do cavies talk? The effect of anthropomorphic picture books on children's knowledge about animals'. They say:

> Many books for young children present animals in fantastical and unrealistic ways, such as wearing clothes, talking and engaging in human-like activities. This research examined whether anthropomorphism in children's books affects children's learning and conceptions of animals, by specifically assessing the impact of depictions (a bird wearing clothes and reading a book) and language (bird described as talking and as having human intentions).

Is this a useful engagement or a pernicious distraction?

> The results show that the language used to describe animals in books has an effect on children's tendency to attribute human-like traits to animals, and that anthropomorphic storybooks affect younger children's learning of novel facts about animals. These results indicate that anthropomorphized animals in books may not only lead to less learning but also influence children's conceptual knowledge of animals.

They have a key question: "In other words, does seeing animals talk and engage in human-like activities in children's picture books affect children's understanding of the biological and psychological properties of real non-human animals?" They find that

> adding fantastical elements in picture books could lead children to adopt an anthropocentric view of the natural world. Picture books are a significant source of information about the biological world for young children and yet the majority of books for young children present the natural world in highly distorted ways. Animal characters exhibit human characteristics and their natural environments are distorted, thus raising the question of how these representations of animals in picture books affect children's understanding of the biological world. Books that anthropomorphize animals may lead children to take a scientifically inaccurate view of the natural world by attributing human-like characteristics to non-human animals. This effect may be a result of seeing depictions of animals like humans (wearing clothes and engaging in human-like activities) and/or hearing descriptions of animals that include references to intentional human-like states and activities.

The riposte comes from a blog by Waldman (2014):

> Some of the best children's books out there have animal main characters: *Winnie the Pooh*, the *Very Hungry Caterpillar*, the *Jungle Book*, *Sylvester and the Magic*

Pebble, the *Story of Ferdinand*. Same with fiction for slightly older kids – books that build mouse fortresses and make spiders talk. But a study published this week in the journal *Frontiers in Psychology* warns that stories in which animals behave like humans can distort a child's view of the natural world.

The author's case is: "Scaffolding familiar traits onto alien subjects is a powerful way to promote learning, one that children do naturally from the age of 12 to 24 months." And imaginative play, she claims, has cognitive benefits. She cites Albert Einstein:

'If you want your children to be intelligent, read them fairy tales. If you want them to be more intelligent, read them more fairy tales.' Just as important, anthropomorphizing is a type of metaphor-making that allows kids to both identify with the characters they're reading about (so that they more readily apply the text's lessons to their own life, as in an Aesop's fable) and practice acknowledging outside perspectives. Reading literature fosters empathy . . . and it does so by awakening people to the echoes of themselves in others.

And there you have it – and actually I do feel that both writers have a case. Anthropomorphism and emotional attachments are contested issues. It is clear that there is a call for dispassionate endeavours but also that motivation and empathy are strongly related to identification with the subject. In his masterful chapter on wildlife on screen in relation to conservation Jamie Lorimer (2015) explores aspects of the phenomena involving sentimentality, sympathy, awe, curiosity and difference.

The way TV nature films play identifiable villains and heroes with animals is thus revealing. Lions are normally heroes, as are cheetahs and other some other big cat predators; definitions of strength, stealth, cunning and speed. The antelopes are the hapless food – they might get lucky but we are rarely asked to empathise with them. We are normally on the side of elephants too – such peaceable plant eaters. Pandas win hands down. Hyenas are more difficult. Then we turn to the vulnerable and we are on their side and the big predators become villains. Meerkats are of course people in disguise – why don't we feel sorry for the scorpions they are eating?

Where do we go from here? So, everything is trying to survive and that's about it. However, there is this overwhelming compulsion to identify and empathise. We support the vulnerable, admire the strong, regret the hapless and unlucky – it is as simple as that. Where does this get us? Do we plead for dispassionate nature films or do we engage? As I have said elsewhere (Trudgill, 2001a) it is the very identification which gives us the empathy, the engagement and the wish or even strong desire to conserve. Programme makers know this, that's why they do it. It is biologically illogical but motivationally compelling. And there you have it – the compelling illogicality of nature films. So be it. It was ever thus.

7.4 Inspiration from Nature and a Sense of Place

Nature, Place and Meaning

Josef Keulartz, developing from his *The Struggle for Nature: A critique of radical ecology* (Keulartz, 1998) and his 'Using metaphors in restoring nature' (Keulartz, 2007), has a relevant discussion in 'The emergence of enlightened anthropocentrism in ecological restoration' (Keulartz, 2012). He starts his paper by quoting the Bernard Williams thoughts which we started this chapter with: "A nature which is preserved by us is no longer a nature that is simply not controlled .... The paradox is that we have to use our power to preserve a sense of what is not in our power" (Williams, 1995: 240). Keulartz's thesis moves on from this, and is that:

> Over the past decade a shift can be noticed from ecological restoration to ecological design, where ecological design stands for a technocratic approach that courts hubris and mastery rather than humility and self-restraint. .... The new technocratic approach may be best characterized as enlightened (or prudential) anthropocentrism, where nature is only allowed that degree of agency which is required to deliver the services that are essential for human well-being. It is not only questionable if we have the scientific and technical abilities to purposeful design ecosystems that will serve our needs, but also if the new approach will be sufficient to protect biodiversity in the long run. (Keulartz, 2012: 48)

The paper is essentially a plea for the promotion of the intrinsic value of ecosystems rather than their instrumental value: "An anthropocentric approach may not protect biodiversity sufficiently because it emphasizes the instrumental value of biodiversity at the expense of its intrinsic value" (Keulartz, 2012: 65).

He cautions that the control elements of so-called enlightened anthropocentrism are really anything but enlightened. It is thus interesting to muse on what anthropocentrism means and about the putative dichotomy between intrinsic and anthropocentric values (see also Lackey's discussion in 'Societal values and the proper role of restoration ecologists'; Lackey, 2004). To me the whole situation is again summed up by Whatmore and Boucher (1993: 167–168) in a quotation I have used before in this book and I use it here in an extended and part paraphrased form:

> Nature cannot be (re)produced outside social relations, neither is it reducible to them. Rather the biological and physical dynamics of life forms and processes need to be recognized on their own terms, conceptually independent of human social agency [producing specific structures of nature/social articulation which] are spatially as well as historically specific. . . . As a living complex of life forms natural relations are always spatially embedded and thereby interact with, and condition, human social relations to varying extents and in different ways in specific times and places.

This rather rises usefully above the intrinsic nature–anthropocentric dichotomy by covering both aspects in an interactive and place specific and historically specific way. The value system is therefore recognisably reflexive within the contextualising social value. Just as with the recognition of ecosystems as a contingent state of conjunctions – things which happen to be together at a place showing dependency but not necessity – so the value system is a contingent state of conjunctions. Again, this does not make life easy as it involves place and historically specific evaluations rather than an easier generalisation.

This to me gives further insight into the planning process, or rather what the planning process should involve, in that associations are very place specific (and indeed Trudgill and Richards, 1997 called for more context-dependent policy). Thus, if the case is to be made for a road through a wildlife area and the rebuff of the conservation case is that 'nature can easily be elsewhere', the actual answer is 'yes, some form of nature could indeed be (recreated) elsewhere' but this is not – and never can be – that piece of nature at that place. That will have evolved on that site over centuries (and indeed with multiple human inputs) and is thus is an assemblage of unique historical associations (Ashmore and Knapp, 1999, on the *Archaeology of Landscape*). This is not an argument for never building anything anywhere but an argument for due consideration to be given to the whole assemblage which constitutes the landscape rather than just any one of its constituent parts.

However, climate change and environment change can both be causes of, and results of, landscape change (see, e.g., Sack, 1990; Thomas, 1956, 1970; Turner et al., 1990). Defining landscape change in its broadest sense of both direct deliberate choice made by people and also changes in vegetation and landscape processes brought about by climate change, we can see that this is a topic which is important to a sense of place (see, e.g., Braun, 2002: *The Intemperate Rain Forest*, especially ch. 4, 'Landscapes of loss and mourning'; Cosgrove and Daniels, 1988: *The Iconography of Landscape*; Craik, 1986, 'Psychological reflections on landscape'; and Penning-Rowsell and Lowenthal, 1986, *Landscape Meaning and Values*).

Earlier in this chapter we argued that preservation of process is perhaps easier to achieve than preservation of form; however, here we are now arguing for the preservation of place – but this is actually about preservation of meanings so the question becomes one of how far are meanings tied to forms? How far can meanings be preserved in the landscape if everything is changing? Where climate change and other environmental change affect a sense of place, this can indeed give rise to associated psychological stress because of a loss of meanings. The idea of landscape change and loss of a sense of place and associated meanings is under-emphasised relative to the commoner emphasis on species loss.

Environment editor at *The Guardian* for twenty-seven years, John Vidal wrote in his retirement year 2016 that he had spent "half a lifetime writing for the Guardian about the decline of the natural world". He reflected that he wanted to emphasise the media preoccupation with "charismatic species, so often the focus of television programmes" while there was a comparative neglect of what he calls "trashing of the planet": "We weep at the disappearance of endangered species but avert our eyes to the causes of Earth's destruction" (Vidal, 2016). His article is online under the heading 'The seven deadly things we're doing to trash the planet (and human life with it)'. It focusses on consumerism, corporate power, poverty and inequality as drivers of environmental degradation, changing landscapes – and the sense of our place in them.

My summary of his key drivers of environmental degradation is as follows.

- Hyper-consumerism
- Corporate powers
- Transport and the associated infrastructure
- Human population
- Losing soil
- Inequality
- Poverty

He concludes: "We do not have to live with these. Wildlife documentaries never point the finger at them and this makes us forget that we humans, too, are living in nature. Either we can wring our hands and carry on watching ever more gorgeous images of wildlife and see nature carry on declining, or we can intervene."

Solastalgia and Meanings of Place

The more immediate distress related to the loss of the specific benefits of nature have been referred to by the use of the term solastalgia. This idea was developed by an Australian, Glenn Albrecht, in 2003 in the context of "the pain or sickness caused by the loss or lack of solace and the sense of isolation connected to the present state of one's home and territory" (Albrecht, 2005: 45). Here, the environment people are accustomed to changes around them through such agencies as mining development or climate change, with attendant feelings of powerlessness to influence the changes (Albrecht, 2005; Albrecht et al., 2007).

Robert Macfarlane (2016) picked up on the theme of solastalgia when writing about literary responses to the Anthropocene: "Solastalgia is not a malady specific to the present – we might think of John Clare as a solastalgic poet, witnessing his native Northamptonshire countryside disrupted by enclosure in the 1810s – but it has flourished recently." Macfarlane then quotes Albrecht: "'A worldwide increase in ecosystem distress syndromes . . . is matched by a corresponding increase in human distress syndromes.'" Macfarlane continues: "Solastalgia speaks of a modern uncanny, in which a familiar place is rendered unrecognisable by climate change or corporate action: the home become[s] suddenly unhomely around its inhabitants." He writes of the Anthropocene and regrets a popular discourse which is "often just a virtue signal that merely mandates the user to proceed with the work of consumption" but concludes that the Anthropocene can jolt us into new ways of thinking: "In its unsettlement of the entrenched binaries of modernity (nature and culture; object and subject), and its provocative alienation of familiar anthropocentric scales and times, it opens up rather than foreclosing progressive thought."

So, we find the generalised "trashing of the planet" upsetting but do little but wring our hands and settle down to watch comforting sanitised nature programmes on TV with anthropocentric and anthropomorphic commentaries. Or we become motivated, activated and protest and then are seen as a 'green' and can be dismissed as extreme by vested, corporate interests. Is it such a bleak dichotomy? There is no necessity in this – the polarisation is the easy story and the manufactured opposing views and distress lead us to believe that there are opposing views and so debate is replaced by argument and confirmation bias, ignoring any evidence which does not fit some stance. As Macfarlane argues, it need not be thus. There can be quiet, careful consideration, balanced discussions, informed insights. Environmental actions nested alongside people's needs, wishes and hopes; environmental improvements which enhance people's lives.

There are indeed very positive writings in the opposite direction to Anthropocene solastalgia by offering a sense of roots in the land and a sense of place. This is not necessarily with any nostalgia and does not involve going back to the past but simultaneously admits that ideas can usefully stand the test of time and change. There are aspects of this human relationship with the land in eco-critical literature, bioregionalism and no small amount in some popular fiction and children's stories.

Aspects of this thread are encapsulated in a write-up in *The Guardian* newspaper which, while it has the often rehearsed narratives, does ask us to think more about the land itself under the title 'We imagine how it feels to be a character, why can't we imagine how the land feels?' (Kingsnorth, 2016). A basis of the article is that climate change and mass extinctions suggest that we have been telling the wrong stories and that writers need to reconnect with the natural world. The author writes:

> The supposedly secular west still clings to the Abrahamic notion that only humans possess consciousness – or souls – and that this gives us the right, or the duty, to run the world. The scientists investigating animal and plant consciousness, though, may be taking us back to older ways of seeing by very modern means. The living world around us may turn out to be much more sentient, aware and connected than we have allowed ourselves to believe.

He turns to Californian poet Robinson Jeffers, citing the end of his poem 'Carmel Point', and gives a prescription:

> We must uncentre our minds from ourselves;
> We must unhumanise our views a little, and become confident,
> As the rock and ocean that we were made from.

> It seems a good time for writers to begin writing about the rock and ocean as if they had a part to play. The novel looks pretty exhausted these days. Could this be its new frontier?

He gave the example of the Lani [the local people] in West Papua who sang a song of thanks, of belonging, lamenting that:

When European minds experience this kind of thing, they are never quite sure what to do with it. It's been so long since we had a sense that we dwelled in a living landscape that we don't have the words to frame what we see. Too often, we go in one of two directions, either sentimentalising the experience or dismissing it as superstition.

His is a call for the land to be represented and celebrated as these people do.

Elsewhere, older writers certainly knew about a sense of place, though it was not necessarily called that; for example, Massingham's 1936 book: *English Downland* and others in the Batsford *The Face of Britain* series (see also Abelson, 1988, *A Mirror of England*; Matless, 1998, *Landscape and Englishness*; Short, 2005, *Imagined Country*; and Barrell, 1972, *The Idea of Landscape and the Sense of Place 1730–1840: An approach to the poetry of John Clare*). The writings of W. H. Hudson are well known for creating a sense of place and of nature in it, particularly with reference to Wiltshire. The contributions of his books, notably Hudson (1903), *Hampshire Days*; (1909) *Afoot in England*; and (1910) *A Shepherd's Life* are discussed by many, for example Ronner (1986) on *W. H. Hudson: The man, the novelist, the naturalist* and Rosenbaum (1944), 'William Henry Hudson: Bibliografía'. They emphasise how he helped foster the back-to-nature movement of the 1920s and 1930s.

A sense of history and literary associations is also important, for example, the case of the view of Godrevy Lighthouse at St Ives. This inspired Virginia Woolf when she wrote her 1972 novel *To the Lighthouse*, even though she actually set the novel elsewhere. Development which blocked the view was lamented as Woolf used to gaze from the window of nearby Talland House in St Ives and it was said that visitors come specifically to the area for the literary association of that particular view – it was said that this amounted to a pilgrimage and that destroying the view was cultural vandalism (see, e.g., Barnett, 2015).

A sense of place was also understood and emphasised as *genius loci* (https://en.wikipedia.org/wiki/Genius_loci) by artist Paul Nash (1949) in *Outline: An autobiography and other writings*; see also www.tate.org.uk/whats-on/tate-britain/exhibition/paul-nash/room-guide/room-three/. "There are places, just as there are people and objects and works of art, whose relationship of parts creates a mystery, an enchantment, which cannot be analysed" (https://art-tales.org/paul-nash-tate-britain-spiritual-power-place/). This relationship is beautifully described in the book by Myers (2018), *Under the Rock: The poetry of place*. Furthermore, I now see the idea of *genius loci* revived in modern storytelling, especially for young people, for example both Garth Nix and Nicky Singer create special worlds: https://en.wikipedia.org/wiki/Old_Kingdom_(book_series); http://nickysinger.com/new/island/. Studies of place in children's literature include Jane Suzanne Carroll's (2012) *Landscape in children's literature*. She sees landscape as the integration of unchanging and irreducible physical elements or '*topoi*' (which, while derived from the Greek *topos* for place, can be variously defined as involving a literary motif or thread of argument). She identifies and analyses four kinds of space that are the component elements of the physical environments of British children's fantasy: sacred spaces, green spaces, roadways and lapsed spaces. She sees origins of these elements in medieval vernacular texts and follows them through to contemporary children's literature. Additionally, topoanalytical studies of literary landscapes sees geographical places within socio-historical contexts. It is possible to consider that the displacement of people from the land to an urban environment has not displaced the need for a sense of place and that this need is then being met by fantasy writings involving a strong sense of location giving an abstract but very real sense of place.

Contact with Nature

Environmental Education has always been an interest of mine (Trudgill, 1999) and I can see that the protagonists of the importance of a positive nature experience for the young are many, including the involvement of spiritual ideas (Palmer, 1998 in 'Spiritual ideas, environmental concerns and educational practice') and classically the book by Louv (2005) *Last Child in the Woods*. There are also fundamentally important books by David Sobel involving a sense of place: Sobel (1996), *Beyond Ecophobia: Reclaiming the heart in nature education*; (2004) *Place-Based Education: Connecting classrooms and communities*; (2008) *Childhood and Nature: Design principles for educators* (see also www.amazon.co.uk/David-Sobel/e/B001IQZIWU).

The key elements were encapsulated in an online article by David Sobel in 1998 where he asserts that: "If we want children to flourish we need to give them time to connect with nature and love the Earth before we ask them to save it." He writes of the alienation from nature and place through teaching of abstract problems which engenders fear and distance, termed *ecophobia*, rather than involvement:

> [E]cophobia – a fear of ecological problems and the natural world. Fear of oil spills, rainforest destruction, whale hunting, acid rain, the ozone hole, and Lyme disease. Fear of just being outside. If we prematurely ask children to deal with problems beyond their understanding and control, then I think we cut them off from the possible sources of their strength. ... children learn distancing techniques, ways to cut themselves off from [abuse] and pain. My fear is that our environmentally correct curriculum will end up distancing children from, rather than connecting them with, the natural world. The natural world is being abused, and they just don't want to have to deal with it.

His approach lies in the positive engagement with nature which progresses and changes as the child grows up but is always located locally and related to surrounding nature. "I propose that there are healthy ways to foster environmentally aware, empowered students. We can cure the malaise of ecophobia with ecophilia – supporting children's biological tendency to bond with the natural world."

He feels that empathy with the natural world can be enhanced in early childhood through allowing time for nature. As children grow up they can progress to exploring the nearby world, and knowing your local area and using maps gives them immersion, solitude and interaction in a close, knowable world rather than just with distant ecosystems and environmental problems.

Supporters of the general idea of the importance of contact with nature range from the analytical study by Tunnicliffe and Reiss (1999) on 'The place of living organisms in children's lives' to a recent column by the writer Ben Fogle (2015). Here, he writes of his personal experience and then moves to his prescription:

> The wilderness rescued me. I have been shaped by my experiences in the great outdoors. Feeling comfortable in the wild gave me the confidence to be who I am, not who others want me to be. There is a natural simplicity to nature; it is far more tactile and tangible than the classroom. It's a leveller; it strengthened my character and set me back on track. It's time to turn everything on its head and classrooms inside out ... we should focus on wellbeing and encouraging our children to connect with the natural world. I'm not suggesting the abolition of the exam system, but we could certainly cut back to allow more time for children to explore the world around them.

For many years I was a member of the Executive Committee of the Field Studies Council and I tried to raise money for the FSC (www.field-studies-council.org) Kids Fund, which stopped in 2020 during the pandemic.

The Kids Fund website said:

> We believe that the only way you can learn about and appreciate the environment is by getting outside, experiencing it . . . and having some fun. Sadly many young people do not get the chance to experience the outdoors or to take part in activities to increase appreciation and understanding of the environment. FSC Kids Fund provides financial support for groups of disadvantaged young people who would like to visit one of our centres for an FSC experience. FSC Kids Fund aims to:
>
> - bring environmental understanding to disadvantaged young people by providing financial support for them to attend a course at an FSC learning location.
> - help disadvantaged young people to attend an FSC course who may otherwise be excluded due to some form of disadvantage – health, mobility, deprivation or financial.

Worthy as this all is, the FSC course, while often transformative and having a long-lasting effect, is usually only of a short duration, so Ben Fogle is right when he says there should be more in the classroom, and we can readily build on David Sobel's ideas more in schools so that people can relate to nature better.

It seems that an implicit belief that you are part of nature does indeed increase a sense of care about nature. Schultz et al. (2004) take up the theme that attitudes about environmental issues are rooted in the degree to which people believe that they are part of the natural environment, a distinction between egoistic concerns, which focus on self, and biospheric concerns, which focus on all living things. The authors argue that the type of concerns a person develops about environmental issues is associated with the extent to which the individual believes that they are part of nature and that this connection is implicit and exists outside of conscious awareness. Results of their work showed that an implicit connectedness to nature was associated with a moderate positive relationship with biospheric concerns and a negative relationship with egoistic concerns.

Developmental psychology and children's affiliation with nature is explicitly discussed by Kahn (1997) in the context of the Biophilia Hypothesis. The work is exemplified by summaries of what he calls Homocentric and Biocentric views in terms of Environmental Justification Categories. These include the Homocentric appeal to how effects on the environment affect human beings, with personal, welfare, educative, justice and aesthetic aspects, and the Biocentric appeal to a larger ecological community of which humans may be a part. This includes aspects of the intrinsic value of life forms, the aspect of justice: "nature has rights/deserves respect" and what the author calls an "unelaborated harm to nature" (p. 41) with a generalised appeal without specific reference to whether appeals for nature derive from a homocentric or biocentric orientation. This includes harming unknown creatures, losing forests, making creatures extinct and harming ecosystems. Such appeals are seen as highly motivational.

We started this section with what was essentially a lament about disassociation from the land – an Anthropocene solastalgia. This is a relatively easy, hand-wringing exercise. However, I can but conclude that there are enough positive ideas around to give us more hope and inspiration. We need not have a situation where our only connection with nature is sitting around watching lovely nature programmes on TV while around us nature is being destroyed. Indeed, it will be very beneficial for us to get out and be involved more; not only will it be good for nature, it will be good for us, as many psychological studies show.

Well-Being, Nature and Place

We covered several aspects of environmental psychology earlier in the book but here we can focus on the specific idea that psychological studies have reinforced rather than detracted from the generalised notion of therapy and benefit through contact with nature. For example, Zhanga, Howell and Iyerc (2014) and Zhanga et al. (2014) showed that proximity to beautiful nature – even just beautiful plants in a room – lead to more positive emotions with greater prosociality exemplified by increased helping behaviour and generosity.

Zelenski and Nisbet (2014) found that subjective connection with nature, or nature relatedness, is similar to other environmental worldview measures in predicting sustainable attitudes and behaviours, yet is unique in predicting happiness. Nature relatedness remained a significant distinct predictor of many happiness indicators, even after controlling for other connections. Results support the notion that nature relatedness could be a path to human happiness and environmental sustainability.

Herzog et al. (1997) found that restorative environments were beneficial to reflection and attentional recovery, while Kidner (2007) writes of a critical ecology of psychological distress in the context of depression and the natural world. Ulrich (1979) demonstrated a link between visual landscape and psychological well-being and (1984) charted how a view through a window may influence recovery from surgery while Ulrich et al. (1991) researched into nature and stress recovery. Valtchanov and Ellard (2015) confirmed the way in which humans have a preference for images of nature over images of built environments which they felt could partially explain the restoration response to natural environments. Leong, Fischer and McClure (2014: 57) ask 'Are nature lovers more innovative?' and conclude that: "Students who were more connected with nature preferred innovative and holistic cognitive styles" and that the authors have established a link between connectedness with nature and cognitive styles.

Connectedness and direct experience are much discussed. Duerden and Witt (2010) found that indirect experience led to an increase of knowledge more than a change of attitude whereas direct experience led to similar changes in both. Van der Werff, Steg and Keizer (2013) discussed how environmental self-identity was related to preferences, intentions and behaviour. Hinds and Sparks (2008) study the role of affective connection and identity in engaging with the natural environment.

The role of place is specifically discussed by Beery and Wolf-Watz (2014) in 'Nature to place: Rethinking the environmental connectedness'. I think that this paper is of fundamental importance and provides a significant way forward as the authors present a substantial insight into the relationship between people and nature which involves place.

The authors discuss environmental connectedness as being based on nature experience and involving emotional attachment to nature with the presumption that it leads to pro-environmental behaviour. This assumes that we tend to wish to conserve that which we are emotionally attached to. However, they question whether a sense of connectedness necessarily leads to pro-environment actions, or whether it merely lays down a propensity to act – and even if it is a necessary prerequisite. They write of the "the need to 'place' environmental connectedness" and are impressed by the way in which place bonding and place attachment involves the emotional bond between an individual and particular settings. This bonding embraces both physical and social-cultural dimensions and they argue that there are significant results regarding possible relationships between place meaning, place attachment and pro-environmental behaviour (Beery and Wolf-Watz, 2014: 203). They conclude that "this research, along with the reasoning presented in this article, highlights the importance of rethinking the general assumptions of the environmental connectedness perspective, in favor of the concept of place".

Their prescription is that

> the nebulous category of nature should be replaced with the relational concept of place. In fact, it can be stated with certainty that 'nature encounter' always takes place somewhere, remembering that the previously noted environmental luminaries Henry David Thoreau [[1854] 1981], John Muir, and Aldo Leopold [1949] grounded their thoughts and writings in the experience of particular places: i.e. long term experiences in and attachment to Walden, Yosemite, and the farm in Wisconsin's Sand County.

They feel that while encounters with place do not necessarily foster care for a place "there are still reasons to believe that recreational settings, places, may facilitate and frame interpersonal relationships, social formation, and behavior" and that "deliberate investigation of lived experience, i.e. stories of place affiliation, may be able to provide better understanding into the conditions and context necessary for motivation of proenvironmental behavior" (Beery and Wolf-Watz, 2014: 203).

Place attachment is reviewed by Lewicka (2011), especially the developments since the publication of Altman and Low (1992) on *Place Attachment*. The importance of meaning-making is stressed: "a sense of place is a natural condition of human existence (dwelling = being)" (Lewicka, 2011: 209), though this is then mediated by a whole range of other factors such as a sense of social connectedness, length of residence, mobility and security. Indeed, Tam (2013) writes of concepts and measures related to connection to nature, concluding that some multidimensional ways of conceptualizing connection to nature are promising.

Additionally, *Places Journal* (https://placesjournal.org/about-places-journal) focusses on the future of architecture, landscape and urbanism, promoting equitable cities and resilient landscapes. The scope covers environmental health, social inequity, climate change, resource scarcity, human migration, rapid technological innovation and the erosion of the public sphere.

Nature, Self and Place Revisited

At the end of Chapter 5 we saw some poetic descriptions of place and meanings and then asked: "Are you still going to build a road though this place, concrete it over, dump rubbish in it?" An answer is: "Yes people will. But why?"

Maybe one aspect is because we don't listen to one another – nor do we recognise the validity of each other's viewpoints as Matulis and Moyer (2016) argue in their paper on a need for agonism – or worth of our opponents. Perhaps we need some more epistemic humility.

There is also the view that trying to change minds without an attendant attempt at understanding the other's point of view can be futile, for example Sodha (2017). The article claims that outrage not only doesn't change minds: "outrage, far from winning people over ... merely entrenches ... ways of thinking". There are people who just don't care and will never see another point of view.

One approach to 'winning people over' has, however, been, rather than stressing the moral stance of the imperative to preserve nature, instead to attempt to 'speak their own language' to people who deal with money and to attempt to commodify the worth of nature. Such attempts make a valuation of nature a reason for conserving it. A classic paper was Costanza et al. (1997) on 'The value of the world's ecosystem services and natural capital'. Ecologists even had a go at this endeavour, for example Odum (1978) on *The Value of Wetlands*. However, there are severe limits to this approach as was discussed, for example, by Norton (1988) on 'Commodity, amenity and morality: The limits of quantification in valuing biodiversity'.

Today, we are so much better at being more realistic about the need to make effective cases for conservation, for example the excellent paper by Rose et al. (2016) on 'Honest advocacy for nature: Presenting a persuasive narrative for conservation'. Here, the authors write of politically salient frames through which to communicate, using clear, accessible language and conducting rigorous science using an authoritative team of experts.

Additionally, however, I am still minded of Cindy Katz's (1998) question in 'Whose nature, whose culture? Private productions of space and the "reservation" of nature' and my own paper about the democratisation of a conservation ethic (Trudgill, 2001a). I was impressed by the human-centred approach of Willis (2015: 422–425) on 'A human needs approach to revealing nature's benefits for visitors to the coast'. The author writes of: "The positive influence on psychological well-being of interactions in nature – self-esteem, feelings of rejuvenation and renewal as well as stress reduction" and lists human need categories:

- Aesthetic appreciation
- Leisure and recreation
- Need to know and understand
- Freedom and escapism
- Self-actualisation
- Transcendence
- Belonging and connectivity.

This, to me, is what we should be considering, for surely they have universal relevance.

I think that the depth of meaning in the landscape is fundamental to a sense of place – and to the aspects of aesthetics, knowing, transcendence, belonging and connectivity cited above. Part of this is the long history of human use of the landscape, as Massingham (1936) describes. The depth of meaning in the landscape derived from centuries of human use is integral to the book by Ashmore and Knapp (1999) on the *Archaeology of Landscape*. They show the deep connection of the landscape to the prehistoric past which is both literal and metaphorical.

Another depth of meaning comes from the more recent history of uses, as described by Landry (2001) on *The Invention of the Countryside: Hunting, walking and ecology in English Literature, 1671–1831*. Here, there is a rather benign relationship between nature and pleasure. Another perspective is provided by Bell and Evans (1997) on 'Greening "the heart of England":– Redemptive science, citizenship and "symbol of hope for the nation"'. The literature aspect we have discussed elsewhere but the sense of place and the links with literature are emphasised by Alcorn (1977) in 'Spirit of place: The novel' (ch. 4 in his book *The Nature Novel from Hardy to Lawrence*) and especially in Canton (2013) in *Out of Essex: Re-imagining a literary landscape*, covering the literary associations with Shakespeare, Defoe, John Clare, Conrad and J. A. Baker among others. Landscape values are of course reflected in the authors' writings and in turn influence the reader in their sense of values, both reinforcing and awakening landscape values. These aspects are well discussed in the pioneering and fundamental books of Penning-Rowsell and Lowenthal (1986): *Landscape Meaning and Values* and Barnes and Duncan (1992): *Writing Worlds: Discourse, text and metaphor in the representation of landscape*. A regionally specific book is *Knowing Your Place: East Anglian landscapes and literature* (Tolhurst, 2009). Other key texts include the seminal *Topophilia* (Tuan, 1974) and his later book *Space and Place* (Tuan, 1977).

These ideas involving landscape and a sense of place have in many ways become focussed in writings on ecocriticism and bioregionalism. Tom Lynch writes on these topics in his own book (Lynch, 2008) *Xerophilia* and in his jointly edited book (Lynch, Glotfelty and Armbruster, 2012): *The Bioregional Imagination: Literature, ecology and place.* In the former (p. 17) Lynch writes: "Bioregionalism prepares us to begin to be at home in this landscape." In the latter book there are four aspects identified. "Reinhabiting", which looks at living-in-place and restoring damaged environments; "Rereading" looks at bioregional literary criticism; "Reimagining" seeks to make bioregionalism evolve using wider text sources and perspectives; and "Renewal" addresses bioregional pedagogy, including local habitat studies and the role of the Internet.

Additionally, Sale (1991) in *Dwellers in the Land* writes about traditional peoples: "The Bioregional Vision proposes how these dwellers teach us how to become dwellers in the land" (p. 420) as they "understand place, kinds of soil and rocks, source of the water we drink, different kinds of wind, insects, birds, mammals, plants and trees; cycle of the seasons, times to plant and harvest and forage." This has echoes of Jonathan Bate in *The Song of the Earth* (Bate, 2000) who, as seen earlier in this book, feels that: "The poet's way of articulating the relationship between human kind and the environment, person and place is . . .experiential . . . [over and above] *narratives* of dwelling, a poem may be a *revelation* of dwelling" (Bate, 2000: 267, original emphasis).

In *LifePlace: Bioregional thought and practice*, Thayer (2003: 1) urges us to discover "where are we?" as an antidote to our rootless, stressful modern lives. Focussing on the personal rewards and the social benefits of reinhabiting the natural world on a local scale, he shows how the spirit of bioregionalism springs from learning the history of a place, from participating in its local economy, from living in housing designed in the context of the region. He asks: how can we instil a love of place and knowledge of the local into our education system? The topics include grounding, living, reinhabiting, fulfilling, imagining, trading (with natural values), planning (a life-work place), building, learning, acting and taking personal responsibility.

Geographers have long emphasised and celebrated the importance of landscape in many ways from *The Land of Britain* (Stamp, 1962) to Daniels et al.'s (2011) *Envisioning Landscapes, Making Worlds: Geography and the humanities.* Matless's (2014) *In the Nature of Landscape*, as in his earlier book (Matless, 1998) *Landscape and Englishness*, sees landscape as a cultural production and thus a place of cultural resonance. Marsden's

(2014) *Rising Ground: A search for the spirit of place* charts how places can have a strong reaction within us, with layers of stories and meanings in relation to history and associations. Stilgoe (2015) asks *What Is Landscape?* This is about the ways the clues can be read and meaning discovered. Mitchell (2002) discusses the political significance of landscape in *Landscape and Power* and similarly Darby (2000) writes of geographies of nation and class in England in *Landscape and Identity*. Gallagher (1994) writes of *The Power of Place: How our surroundings shape our thoughts, emotions and actions*.

It is this emotional and spiritual significance which I would wish to emphasise. In *The Language of Landscape* Spirn (1998) writes that landscape is meaningful and expressive, indeed that landscape is language. People identify with aspects of the landscape as Sommer (2003) shows in his essay on 'Trees and human identity' and Rival (1998) compiles a dossier on the huge cultural significance of trees in the landscape. Macfarlane (2015) in *Landmarks* writes of the power of words to shape our sense of place and he cites the thoughts of Oliver Rackham (Macfarlane, 2015: 9) about not only the significance of wildlife and vegetation but the significance of beauty, freedom and above all meaning.

Meaning to me is indeed the key. Dimbleby (1994) in Polley and Woodman's (1994) *Spirit of Nature: Poetry of the earth* writes on 'The environment and the human spirit' and cites several examples of poems linking people to land and nature. He focusses on the writings of John Fowles especially in *The Tree* (Fowles, 2000; see also Aubrey, 1999). Fowles writes of the dangers of categorisation, taming and possession especially when applied to the landscape. This he sees as alienation from the unpredictable, the unaccountable and the intuitive where, to him, the tree symbolises the wild side of our psyche. He writes (Fowles, 2000: 56–57) of the legacy of scientists and, while not detracting from their achievements, as a luddite might do, he notes some consequences: "This addiction to finding a reason, a function, a quantifiable yield, has now infiltrated all aspects of our lives – and become effectively synonymous with pleasure. The modern version of hell is purposelessness." He feels that: "Nature suffers particularly in this, and our indifference and hostility to it is closely connected with the fact that its only purpose appears to be being and surviving." He moves on from the functional viewpoint to say that: "But most of this functional purpose is hidden to the non-scientist, indecipherable; and the immense variety of nature appears to hide nothing. Nothing but a green chaos at its core – which we brilliantly purposive apes can use and exploit as we please, with a free conscience…" He writes, in essence about the paucity of the numeral [biodiversity] approach. He proposes that woods "may not carry more species than some other environments, but they are far richer in sensory impressions" (Fowles, 2000: 63).

To me, when anyone writes of scientific understanding of purpose, that is just one narrative. Science is just one narrative. That is just one way of understanding. I cited Botkin's (1990: 89) stance earlier in the book when we were thinking about narratives of ecology: "we are acting on our beliefs rather than on our knowledge". This is not to denigrate either scientific understanding or acting on our beliefs; this was more an observation about process and not intended to denigrate one set of narratives at the expense of the other. Be our beliefs well founded or unfounded, they are powerful. What we know is always limited. What we know should illuminate and counter ignorance, but there are many things involved in understanding – science and knowledge and poetry, emotion, sentiment and senses of well-being. Just because these are different it does not say that they are opposable. They should be seen as complementary – and acknowledged as legitimate.

Let us not deny the importance of science and let us not deny the importance of an emotional attachment to sense of place. Let us not dismiss feelings and a sense of place in the cause of some putative rationality. Let us see that dismissal for what it is – someone trying to get their own way will argue anything and the assumed rationality can be seen as overcoming an emotion. However, acknowledging an emotional sense of place is perfectly rational because it is a normal characteristic of people. Additionally, an emotional appeal could be used to deny the science and the assumed rationality – the triumph of belief over what some people think we know. Let us see that also for what it is – the argument of someone who wants to get their own way and will argue anything, deny evidence and shout down, ignore or refuse to acknowledge what they wish to.

It is a big ask, but I think we have to think about being more open – to ideas, to arguments and to see the use of narratives – be they factual, emotional or scientific as secondary tools to our volition. So, let us not bandy with narratives without first examining our volition – what is in our heads, what is in our purpose, our consciousness, remembering how we have been positioned to experience the real and that we do not have to think the way that we do, we have choices. And let us remember that both knowledge and beliefs are important and engage with both.

Remember also that nature is not always something cuddly and sanitised nor always awesome and impressive. If it is these, then we run the risk of cherishing only what media makers have given us in the guise of what they believe we wish to see. Recently, Hale (2016) has published a book: *The Wild and the Wicked*. Here, the author writes of the value of nature even when it is seen as indifferent and hostile. Indeed, Taylor (1986) in his book *Respect for Nature: A theory of environmental ethics* has already said that our respect for nature should be independent of its attractiveness to us:

> The attitude of respect is not a private relationship between the person who has the attitude and that toward which the attitude is taken, as the love of nature is. . . . This contrast between respect and love has fundamental significance for our understanding of what is required for the attitude of respect to be rationally justified. Since the ground of respect does not lie in the emotional appeal that living things might have for us, the fact that an animal or plant is attractive to us is not relevant to our adopting the attitude of respect towards it or to our expressing such an attitude in a way we treat it. Some things in the natural world may be more beautiful, more interesting or more pleasing to us than others. Some may be unattractive, uninteresting, and even repulsive to us. But if we have respect for nature their attractiveness or unattractiveness in no way affects our impartial concern for their well-being. (Taylor, 1986: 91)

William Cronon (1995: 89) wrote a seminal paper: 'The trouble with wilderness; or, getting back to the wrong nature'. He nicely and seamlessly discuses both science and poetic writings and quotes the ecological poet Gary Snyder about what is in your mind:

> As Gary Snyder has wisely said, 'A person with a clear heart and open mind can experience the wilderness anywhere on earth. It is a quality of one's own consciousness. The planet is a wild place and always will be' (quoted in *New York Times*, Week in Review, 18 September 1994, p. 6). To think ourselves capable of causing 'the end of nature' is an act of great hubris, for it means forgetting the wildness that dwells everywhere within and around us.

Cronon continues:

> Learning to honor the wild – learning to remember and acknowledge the autonomy of the other – means striving for critical self-consciousness in all of our actions. It means that deep reflection and respect must accompany each act of use. It means too that we must always consider the possibility of non-use. It means looking at the part of nature we intend to turn toward our own ends and asking whether we can use it again and again and again – sustainably – without

its being diminished in the process. It means never imagining that we can flee into a mythical wilderness to escape history and the obligation to take responsibility for our own actions that history inescapably entails. Most of all, it means practicing remembrance and gratitude, for thanksgiving is the simplest and most basic of ways for us to recollect the nature, the culture, and the history that have come together to make the world as we know it.

There seems to be a call for more rationality, more realism in nature conservation. Fine, that is important. Also, a call for more realisation about the significance of landscape – good, that is important too. But also most important, to me, are the spiritual and psychological benefits of nature.

Being in nature as therapy, especially when walking, is well established in a variety of writings, for example 'Walking' by Henry David Thoreau (1862). 'Walking', sometimes referred to as 'The Wild', is a lecture by Henry David Thoreau first delivered at the Concord Lyceum on 23 April 1851. Written and added to between 1851 and 1860, Thoreau read the piece a total of ten times, more than any other of his lectures. 'Walking' was first published as an essay in the *Atlantic Monthly* after his death in 1862. Ronald Blythe (1999) quotes Andrew Young (1958): "Solvitur ambulando – you can sort it out by walking . . . a companionable path was more apt for a curative release than a road, since solitude, peace and close contact with nature, as well as the action of walking, are all important . . . problems unravel . . . but through the body's surroundings as well as the body's action" (Blythe, 1999): 23). It is interesting that this phrase has evolved into something about therapy through walking. It originates from the idea that a problem is solved by a practical experiment where in classical times Diogenes is said to have replied to Zeno's paradoxes on the unreality of motion by standing up and walking away. However, it works equally well in this context – 'you can solve it by walking' is perfectly good as a mantra for tackling stress. In my book on the *Terrestrial Biosphere* (Trudgill, 2001b: 146–147) I write in a poem on a weekend walk out of the city how walking dissolved stress for me:

stressed by stress . . .
. . . gridlock
of emotions with impossibilities
But then the steady rhythm footfall senses back
Focus and reality grow . . .
then light, relaxed and laughing free:
Going back to nature.

I do feel that there should also be more emphasis on the psychological benefits of nature – there seem to have been so many studies in environmental psychology to this effect that it should not be dismissed. The psychological benefit of nature is not a whim of eco woolly people or whimsical poets which can be dismissed in the name of economic progress, it is fundamental to us all; it is the recognition of the real and actual benefits which contact with nature brings. Whether it be the plant in the office, the garden, the park, nature reserve, woodland, countryside or the wilderness with mountain, desert, forest and coast, which bit of nature and in what place and in what state is always going to be a matter of individual preference and thereby contested. But we are better off with nature – it is good for us.

As Laurens van der Post (1986) wrote, "conservation is a deep need in the soul of man . . . man needed it almost more than the animals did" (p. 139). "Nature will always take care of itself even without man. But man without nature is unthinkable and, known or unknown, his spirit needs it: needs it for its survival, sanity and increase, as his body does" (p. 141). Loss of nature is thus a loss of culture and a loss of self. Indeed, Proctor's (1996) paper on conservation is imbued with the idea of an inextricable nature–culture intertwining.

Richard Jefferies wrote of his favourite haunt, Liddington Hill near Coate where he was born:

> There is a hill to which I used to resort at such periods. The labour of walking three miles to it, all the while gradually ascending, seemed to clear my blood of the heaviness accumulated at home. On a warm summer day the slow continued rise required continual effort, which carried away the sense of oppression. The familiar everyday scene was soon out of sight; I came to other trees, meadows, and fields; I began to breathe a new air and to have a fresher aspiration. I restrained my soul till I reached the sward of the hill; psyche, the soul that longed to be loose. I would write psyche always instead of soul to avoid meanings which have become attached to the word soul, but it is awkward to do so. Clumsy indeed are all words the moment the wooden stage of commonplace life is left. I restrained psyche, my soul, till I reached and put my foot on the grass at the beginning of the green hill itself. Moving up the sweet short turf, at every step my heart seemed to obtain a wider horizon of feeling; with every inhalation of rich pure air, a deeper desire. The very light of the sun was whiter and more brilliant here. By the time I had reached the summit I had entirely forgotten the petty circumstances and the annoyances of existence. I felt myself, myself. (*The Story of My Heart*, by Richard Jefferies ([1883]1938: 18–19; see also: www.richardjefferiessociety.org)

This quiet, gentle, thoughtful voice is uplifting. But still people will cite other imperatives which deny this experience. To help us understand this, I recommend Toner Raimi and Leary's (2014) writing on *Belief Superiority in the Environmental Domain*. They found that those with more extreme views showed a higher degree of belief superiority – the belief that one's beliefs are superior to other viewpoints – and a greater tendency to argue with others and a greater resistance to competing viewpoints. Such a lack of openness they found to be a great barrier to learning.

The gentle, quiet thoughtful voice is so readily drowned out by the easy cliché. Don't let it be.

Nature, Romanticism and Dark Ecology

Morton (2007) argues in *Ecology without Nature* that we might do better if we ditched our concepts about nature, especially the more romantic ones. This can only be welcomed if it frees us up from the stranglehold of romanticism which is the – often unacknowledged – foundation of so many writings. Such is analysed in so many places but two useful volumes are, to my mind Merrill's (1989) *The Romance of Victorian Natural History* and Harris's (2015) *Romantic Moderns: English writers, artists and the imagination from Virginia Woolf to John Piper*. Morton also writes on dark ecology (2008, 2010, 2016) which turns its back on some unattainable utopian ideal. His main aim seems to be to free thinking from the constriction of previous conceptions of nature, particularly those which see nature as something hallowed and placed on a pedestal: what he calls a "utopian image of nature which does not really exist" (2007: 24) but which has been celebrated "as a way of healing what modern society has damaged" (2007: 22). He calls for a more exploratory approach and one which encompasses freedom of artistic expression.

This one could see as a natural extension of Heidegger's *The Origin of the Work of Art* (1950) where art is a means of creating truth in a culture by being not merely representational, but actually producing a community's shared understanding, with the attendant observation that each work of art changes the meaning of existence for the observer. However, art as a means of breaking free of the past and also as a means of reinforcing values (e.g. of some idyllic landscape) are both evident and neither of these ideas contradict the concept that they are not transformative of the individual or a culture.

In terms of 'ecology without nature' Evernden (1992) expresses this well:

We must remember that nature itself was *our* creation [his italics]. That we now regard nature as an independent object is because we regard virtually everything as material objects. We seem predisposed to regard whatever we encounter, in direct experience or in thought, as an externally existing entity independent of our own willing and creation. Indeed, objects gain credibility for us as the traces of our authorship are progressively eliminated. But in fact the absorption of ourselves into Nature is simply the absorption of ourselves into ourselves, or rather, our own conception of how it 'ought' to be. The paradox we encounter, of this perpetual oscillation between the domains of nature and culture, arises from a fundamental error. The dualism cannot actually be resolved, *because it never existed* [his italics]. The dualism we fret over only exists because of our own decision, not only to constrict the nature-tube into two domains, but to create the container in the first place. One might even say that there is no 'nature', and there never has been. (Evernden, 1992: 99)

This, together with: "When Richard Jeffries concluded, at the end of a life of trying to understand the creatures he greatly admired, that he could not 'know' nature, he liberated himself from a lifelong deceit" (Evernden, 1992: 129). This discussion has to me resonances in two places. The first is a quotation from Donald Worster (1992) who was writing in the context of the Hoover Dam being built over the Colorado River: "What an utter foolishness it is to believe that any mastery over nature has really been won" (Worster, 1992: 77) and: "Human domination over nature is quite simply an illusion, a passing dream by a naive species. It is an illusion that has cost us much, ensnared us in our own designs, given us a few boasts to make about our courage and genius, but all the same it is an illusion" (Worster, 1992; 78).

The second is a set of thoughts from Richard Jefferies ([1883]1938: 131 and see also www.richardjefferiessociety.org):

In human affairs everything happens by chance – that is, in defiance of human ideas, and without any direction of an intelligence. A man bathes in a pool, a crocodile seizes and lacerates his flesh. If any one maintains that an intelligence directed that cruelty, I can only reply that his mind is under an illusion. A man is caught by a revolving shaft and torn to pieces, limb from limb. There is no directing intelligence in human affairs, no protection, and no assistance. Those who act uprightly are not rewarded, but they and their children often wander in the utmost indigence. Those who do evil are not always punished, but frequently flourish and have happy children. Rewards and punishments are purely human institutions, and if government be relaxed they entirely disappear. No intelligence whatever interferes in human affairs. There is a most senseless belief now prevalent that effort, and work, and cleverness, perseverance and industry, are invariably successful. Were this the case, every man would enjoy a competence, at least, and be free from the cares of money. This is an illusion almost equal to the superstition of a directing intelligence, which every fact and every consideration disproves. (www.victorianweb.org/authors/jefferies/1.html)

He also rejects design in nature (p. 127):

In this lies my objection to the logic of science. The arguments proceed from premises to conclusions, and end with the assumption 'it therefore follows'. But I say that, however carefully the argument be built up, even though apparently flawless, there is no such thing at present as 'it must follow'. Human ideas at present naturally form a plan, and a balanced design; they might be indicated by a geometrical figure, an upright straight line in the centre, and branching from that straight line curves on either hand exactly equal to each other. In drawing that is how we are taught, to balance the outline or curves on one side with the curves on the other. In nature and in fact there is no such thing. The stem of a tree represents the upright line, but the branches do not balance; those on one side are larger or longer than those on the other. Nothing is straight, but all things curved, crooked, and unequal.

Then there are the bleak thoughts about standing by and doing nothing (p. 134):

From every human being whose body has been racked by pain; from every human being who has suffered from accident or disease; from every human being drowned, burned or slain by negligence, there goes up continually increasing cry louder than thunder. An awe-inspiring cry dread to listen to, which no one dares to listen to, against which ears are stopped by the wax of superstition and the wax of criminal selfishness: – These miseries are your doing, because you have mind and thought and could have prevented them. You can prevent them in the future. You do not even try.

So, we have a romantic nature on the one hand, a dark ecology on the other; we have all our illusions – and we have the power to change the things which are under our influence which can usefully involve art. And we have nature as therapy.

Ways Forward – and Some 'Good Myths to Have'?

I am encouraged. There are plenty of indications of positive ways forward.

For starters there is Ian McCallum's (2005) uplifting book on *Ecological Intelligence: Rediscovering ourselves in nature*. While the older romantic poems are well rehearsed, who could not be uplifted and moved by the more recent meaningful poetry of Kathleen Raine (e.g. Keeble, 2000), Mary Oliver and Owen Sheers to name but a few? As I write I find that there is a site about nature reducing depression and obesity on Facebook: www.theguardian.com/society/2017/mar/21/access-nature-reduces-depression-obesity-european-report?CMP=Share_AndroidApp_Facebook and that nature is not a vague abstraction, it has personal meaning: www.theguardian.com/environment/2016/nov/01/nature-conservation-development-protest-logh-beg-lodge-hill-country-diary?CMP=share_btn_link and another about incorporating nature into measures of well-being: https://theconversation.com/measures-of-poverty-and-well-being-still-ignore-the-environment-this-must-change-74248 with useful links to: Millennium Ecosystem Assessment (2005), *Ecosystems and Human Well-Being* – synthesis and studies showing the significance of nature to our well-being:

- Berman, Jonides and Kaplan (2008) on 'The cognitive benefits of interacting with nature' in *Psychological Science*.
- Berman et al. (2012) on 'Interacting with nature improves cognition and affect for individuals with depression' in the *Journal of Affective Disorders*.
- Hedlund-de Witt, de Boer and Boersema (2014) on 'Exploring inner and outer worlds: A quantitative study of worldviews, environmental attitudes, and sustainable lifestyles' in the *Journal of Environmental Psychology*.

I take great heart from these and the books published about nature and place and the associated love, beauty and joy and the contribution of these to our well-being. These aspects are encapsulated in Rachel Carson's (1956) admirable *The Sense of Wonder*. In these contexts, a signal book is Richard Mabey's (2005) *Nature Cure* where, depressed, he goes to live in Norfolk and gradually finds himself again through contact with nature and the land. More recently, there is the sterling book by Fiona Reynolds (2016) on *The Fight for Beauty: Our path to a better future* with a vision for our environment, our society and our future and Michael McCarthy's (2016) *The Moth Snowstorm: Nature and joy*. In this genre, Harrison (2020) in *The Stubborn Light of Things: A nature diary* celebrates a move from the city to the country and the *Diary of a Young Naturalist* by Dara McAnulty (2020) is much celebrated as representing the best of the current youthful engagement with nature, winning the 2020 Wainwright Prize for nature writing. Engagingly, Helen Macdonald (2020: 136) writes in *Vesper Flights* that: "Swifts are magical in the manner of all things that exist just a little beyond our understanding", reaffirming a sense of wonder.

In many of these writings, there are modern-day resonances of that ecological milestone: Aldo Leopold's (1949) *A Sand County Almanac.* In this he defines his land ethic: "A thing is right when it tends to preserve the integrity, stability, and beauty of the biotic community. It is wrong when it tends otherwise" (pp. 224–225). A more modern approach is that, if taken literally, this would require interventions to prevent naturally occurring changes and that 'stability' and 'integrity' are myths with motivating power rather than being capable of precise definition. There are changes all the time from external causes and from progressive changes within a system. The endeavour is more to stand back and 'let nature flourish' in its own way rather than necessarily wield our preferences and our predilection for the status quo.

There is however an interesting aspect of change which involves people's memories and how one generation regards the situation they grew up in as normal despite those of an older generation being able to say how things have changed from when they were younger. This has been referred to as shifting baseline syndrome (SBS), defined as "a persistent downgrading of perceived 'normal' environmental conditions with every sequential generation, leading to under-estimation of the true magnitude of long-term environmental change on a global scale" (Jones et al., 2020: 1131). This is usually regarded negatively in the sense of older people lamenting that younger people don't know about what they feel they have lost but it could be regarded positively in the sense of younger people adapting to changed situations and making the best of what they have got. The relevance of this for conservation was discussion by Papworth et al. (2009) and updated with more examples by Jones et al. (2020) in 'Evidence for shifting baseline syndrome in conservation'. The authors felt that SBS is a real problem for those using human perceptions of change to inform conservation policy-making or management because of its influence on participatory monitoring, local ecological knowledge, community-based conservation and conservation education. They studied situations where biological change had happened and identified both generational amnesia, where knowledge extinction had occurred because younger generations were not aware of past biological conditions, and personal amnesia, where knowledge extinction occurred as individuals forgot their own experience. If age- or experience-related differences in perception are then found, generational amnesia may be occurring and if individuals believe current conditions also occurred in the past, then personal amnesia may be occurring. This highlights the importance of inter-generational dialogue and of keeping records which are widely available. However, it appears that even among well-informed people, SBS may also occur, as shown by Muldrow, Parsons and Jonas (2020) in 'Shifting baseline syndrome among coral reef scientists'.

This is interesting because it highlights the need for awareness of loss which cannot be personally felt, but also gives the possibility that once there is such an awareness then this will hopefully increase the resolve that there should be no further losses. However, it tempers the loss by the fact that younger people who are unaware of the loss can be perfectly content, which highlights the importance of education about loss and the importance of the generalised ethos of conservation involving a sense of still being able to do something to keep something of value rather than being powerless to do anything about it.

If we go back to Laurens van der Post's (1986: 139) "conservation is a deep need in the soul of man: man without nature is unthinkable and, known or unknown, his spirit needs it: needs it for its survival, sanity and increase, as his body does" we can then think of J. Baird Callicott's (1995) suggestion that nature's value is intrinsic and subjective, that is to say that it has intrinsic value because we value it intrinsically as opposed to just instrumentally. We can also dwell on Simon James's (2016: 213) paper where he argues that "nature should be protected, not because it is a means to anthropocentric ends, but because it is part of something about human life that is of value: because, that is, its value is anthropocentric and constitutive rather than anthropocentric and instrumental" – it should be protected for its own sake because we value it thus. As I said around the start of this book: "Nature is there for its own sake and not for mine, though I make it what it is for me" (Trudgill, 2003a). We can also cite Deborah Cracknell's (2019) "taking care of the oceans so they take care of us" which can easily become "taking care of nature so it takes care of us". Now, having been through all the stuff in the book and especially reaching back to Evernden's thoughts we started with about the "conceptual prison" and "letting nature be", I can now rewrite what I think we should all be saying: "nature is there; I value it; I'd like to let it be."

I don't think nature is some kind of indulgence which can only be enjoyed by those who can afford to. Sure, there are Western obsessions about nature while so many in the world struggle in conflict and deprivation. But nature is deep and universal in humanity and fundamental to us all and so the narratives of nature matter to us all. Take care over them.

There is no meaning in nature other than that which we bring to it. Many meanings are woven round myths which do not stand up to scrutiny. So, if myths like the 'balance of nature being upset' are strong motivators, so be it. Even if we cannot precisely tell what it means in specific situations, there are, however, some good myths to have.

If we are motivated by the meanings of powerful myths, I would vote for the myth that we depend on and are responsible for nature.

Think deeply, think well. Think how you have been positioned to experience the real.

Remember you don't have to think the way that you do. Think about judging the validity of concepts in terms of the consequences of holding them and their associated value systems.

There is a wide range of narratives that show dependency on your axioms and context but they have no necessity to exist. You can choose what to think and what to agree with – and remember there will be consequences of what you think.

You can simultaneously realise that how people react to you tells you as much about them as about you and that you can tell what you believe is revealed by what you do and the effect you have on others – and by the effect you have on your surroundings and by how people react to you – and how your surroundings are changed by you and how you are changed by your surroundings.

Think well, think wisely, you choose what you think, you choose what you do and you choose how you affect people and the places around you.

Evernden (1992), as indicated above, writes:

> When Richard Jefferies concluded, at the end of a life of trying to understand the creatures he greatly admired, that he could not 'know' nature, he liberated himself from a lifelong deceit. . . . He gave up the pretence to knowledge that delimits what a creature may be, and which protects us thereafter from the uncertainties of strangeness: we hide from the wild by making it 'natural'.

Evernden then reflects on the nature of what we think we know and on Jefferies's approach to that: "Inevitably, what we know is largely our own symbolic representations, which will behave as they were designed to. But of that which they purport to represent, they tell but a partial story at best. To accept, at last, his own failure to comprehend the world was no doubt a great disappointment to Jefferies." Evernden sees, however, that this was not a cause for dismay to Jefferies, who wrote: "I look at the sunshine and feel that there is no contracted order: there is divine chaos, and, in it, limitless hope and possibilities" (Evernden, 1992: 130).

Jordan Peterson writes of the "deadly force of chaos" and the "tyranny of order", with the forces of chaos being kept at bay by social order and culture – but that order itself can become deadly if allowed unregulated or permanent expression (Peterson, 1999: 91). Peterson feels we need a balance between tolerable novelty and flexible security so that neither chaos nor tyranny prevail. Jefferies's revelation is that while order is what we give to nature, divine chaos is not to be feared, therefore giving us the possibility that our imposed order should have a light touch: let nature happen.

Which, of course, is just another set of contested narratives, but at least you should know that by now.

Revelation

If you read all that has been written
You know everything*.
But what do you see?
(*but you can't, so you don't
and there is much to know which is not written)

If your eyes are open*
You see everything.
But what do you know?
(*but they are not, so you can't)

If your mind is open*
You can see anything
And you can know anything
(*but it is isn't so you can't)

But if the light of ancient stars
shines age-old though the silvered edges
of new-born leaves
and meets your eyes
you can see something you cannot know
yet you know something you cannot see.

(S. Trudgill, 2006)

7.5 Why Conserve Nature? Threads and Signposts

Threads and Exhortations

When we look at the threads of arguments running through any discussion, we can see that people pick out the threads which appeal to them – and also that different people can pick up the same threads as each other but then weave different stories with them. So it is with nature conservation, which people inevitably discuss within the limitations of their varied perceptions, wishes and abilities. This variety means that there is never going to be one easily identifiable path showing the way ahead. However, I think we might offer some signposts to the directions we could usefully take; signposts which may well mean different things to different people but nonetheless can lead in the direction of effective actions. There will always be disagreements and indifference but, rather than seeing meanings as competing with each other and vying for dominance, we can most usefully work with the situation where multiple meanings and motivations can coexist and lead to a range of worthwhile action. Human nature is such that I think some kind of utopia where nature is universally cherished is unlikely but equally human nature is such that the positive will to conserve nature means that a complete dystopia is also unlikely.

However, the concepts of utopia and dystopia are threaded through many arguments and play significant parts in the public dialogue. There is the nostalgic concept of 'how good things once were', the dystopian concept of 'how bad things could get' and the utopian exhortation of 'how good things could be if only we could act' (often with a recipe for action attached). How far these three states are actually illusory is debatable but not so relevant as the real power they may wield over us. The threads are often run together and certainly the dystopian one gives the utopian more impetus. There is a good example of 'unspoilt earth' wrecked by 'human havoc' and the prospect of 'a better future' in a social media post by *earth glory official*. Here, if the earth's history of forty-six billion years is imagined as forty-six years then humans have been around for only the last four hours, with the industrial revolution beginning only one minute ago but we have destroyed more than 50 per cent of the world's forests in this short time (www.facebook.com/earthgloryofficial). The exhortation is then to redress this by planting a tree. There follows a train of people posting that they have planted a tree. It is certain that such exhortations have an effect and make people feel good if they meet the exhortation.

The exhortations may be rather generalised and unfocussed, or very specific and it is possible that the latter might be more effective. A generalised one is that it is being argued that the Covid-19 virus pandemic is symptomatic of our fractured and disrespectful relationship with nature. This is being widely rehearsed but one wonders at the impact unless there are attendant specific manifestations of the exhortation. Somewhat more specific is the common example of the concept of tipping points. This is a finely balanced state which is claimed to be present – and 'unless we act now' then an irreversible change will happen. These tipping points are often heralded as 'just around the corner', but while these are much rehearsed there seems not to be widespread agreement that they necessarily exist unless we actually can be seen to have passed one with evidence that is clear for all to see. Even then, as is the case with recent coverage of the Greenland ice cap, the response can be rather diffuse as it is seen as supporting the general case that 'we must reduce CO_2 emissions'. Similar exhortations about climate change and exhortations about zero carbon come from the writing of and on Greta Thunberg (Box 7.1) and Extinction Rebellion (Box 7.2) and how we and everything on earth are all going to suffer if we do not act now.

However, there are also sceptical writings about the causal factors and, equally, there are writings on why there is nothing to worry about at all because we can adapt to changed conditions OK. So, there are

Box 7.1 *Greta Thunberg*

Swedish environmental activist, born 3 January 2003.

- Her action began as she felt that governments were not responding enough to the United Nations Paris Agreement on climate change.
- In August 2018, age 15, she started *Skolstrejk för klimatet* (school strike for climate).
- In 2018 she addressed the United Nations Climate Change Conference.
- In 2019 she sailed to North America to attend the 2019 UN Climate Action Summit and her speech there, in which she included the phrase "how dare you", received wide publicity.

(www.bbc.co.uk/news/world-europe-49918719; Thunberg, 2019; Thunberg, Sanchez Vegara and Weckmann, 2020)

Box 7.2 *Extinction Rebellion*

https://extinctionrebellion.uk/

Extinction Rebellion (abbreviated as XR) has the aim of avoiding tipping points in the climate system and biodiversity loss, together with the attendant risk of social and ecological collapse. It uses non-violent civil disobedience to compel government action on these matters.

Established in the United Kingdom in May 2018, XR uses a circled hourglass, known as the extinction symbol, to serve as a warning that time is rapidly running out for many species. Its original aims were stated as:

- Government must tell the truth by declaring a climate and ecological emergency, working with other institutions to communicate the urgency for change.
- Government must act now to halt biodiversity loss and reduce greenhouse gas emissions to net zero by 2025.
- Government must create, and be led by the decisions of, a citizens' assembly on climate and ecological justice.

(www.bbc.co.uk/news/uk-48607989; Extinction Rebellion, 2019; see also www.facebook.com/XRebellionUK)

arguments that we should act now to get things back to how they were otherwise a bleak future awaits us or that our adaptability will see us through. It seems that somehow, either way we might get to utopia. However, Gray (2008) in *Black Mass: Apocalyptic religion and the death of utopia* argues that utopian ideals are the actual problem. He feels that it is this very chasing of a non-existent and unrealistic utopia, together with our misplaced faith in our ability to change the world, which has actually made it worse. It does seem true that each politician promises to make everything better – and we fall for what Gray calls this 'pernicious myth' every time. He sees apocalypse as an anthropocentric myth and part of the narrative of catastrophe and redemption. There are certainly many narratives of impeding catastrophe and ways of redemption around, justifying what Gray refers to as cults, each with their own narratives of self-justification. Some of the endeavours seek to drown out or silence other voices and make them non-legitimate. It seems that the idea from Voltaire (from his biographer, Evelyn Beatrice Hall writing as

S. G. Tallentyre, 1906) that even though you disapprove and disagree with something someone is saying, you should defend their right to say it, is itself being drowned out.

As part of the narratives of catastrophe, more specific exhortations involve pollution by plastics. Here, life-cycle analysis of products to cut down on waste of packaging and containers after use has been argued as a way forward for many years. However, policies still seem to lag behind this awareness. Nevertheless, there will still be many who are indifferent – or more often will agree but not necessarily act, either at an individual or at a policy level. The gap between popular narratives and action is often referred to as the value-action gap, as was discussed by Blake (1999) in 'Overcoming the "value-action gap" in environmental policy' and Owens (2000) in 'Engaging the public: Information and deliberation in environmental policy'. However, in many ways concern about plastic has been moving steadily to centre stage, aided by media coverage.

This shift to centre stage seems to be part of a general process which indicates how future policy shifts may happen. Public opinion can change and something which starts as a fringe argument can become widely acceptable and occupy centre stage. Politicians tend to be reluctant to act on fringe arguments held by only a few but act more readily if something is seen as being 'in the window' of what is acceptable, sensible and popular. This is seen in the idea of an Overton Window as conceived by Joseph Overton (1960–2003) from the Mackinac Center for Public Policy, Michigan. Here, the idea is that the range of views can be classified according to the following schema, becoming more mainstream as the list progresses:

Unthinkable
Radical
Acceptable
Sensible
Popular
Policy

This is discussed by Lehman (2010) in *An Introduction to the Overton Window of Political Possibility* and by the political commentator Joshua Treviño (www.dailykos.com/stories/2006/5/9/208784/-). An attendant idea is that the extremes of radical views and changing circumstances pull the spectrum one way or another so that what was unacceptable and radical at one time becomes located in the mainstream 'window' of policy at a later date. So, here is one signpost – the lobbies from the fringe activities of today need careful consideration as they may be tomorrow's mainstream.

This is an attractive proposition and evidence for it can certainly be found. However, the complexities of all the different threads of arguments and counter-arguments means that such a progression from fringe to mainstream is unlikely to be simple. If we think of Extinction Rebellion, for example, many find its basic concerns acceptable and sensible but some of its ideas about implementation currently rather radical and some unthinkable. However, this is likely to change in the future. So, while climate change is a widely accepted concept, the precise causes, dimensions and manifestations can be disputed and there is still a way to go in finding widely acceptable remedies, relevant policies and effective actions. To illustrate this, I see what is being argued in the name of climate change and I dread some of the options, especially covering good farmland soil in solar panels and the seas and wild moors in wind farms, let alone the disasters of tidal barrages if they impair the habitats for the millions of wildfowl and wading birds which depend upon our estuaries. This, to me, speaks of trying to find ways of producing just as much energy without the CO_2 rather than following a pathway of decreasing the use of energy which would have less environmental impact than such technologies. The solutions should not only be effective but also they should not cause harm in different ways. Progress lies in making the solutions as widely acceptable and popular as the basic concerns are.

So, it can be seen that while the threads of the arguments are varied, some ways may be more effective than others – and while exhortations may fall on both deaf and receptive ears, the deaf ears of today may well become the receptive ears of tomorrow.

2020 Visions

At the Intergovernmental Science-Policy Platform on Biodiversity and Ecosystem Services (IPBES), meeting 29 April–4 May 2019 in Paris, the IPBES Chair, Sir Robert Watson, said: "The overwhelming evidence of the IPBES Global Assessment, from a wide range of different fields of knowledge, presents an ominous picture" (UN, 2019). In the meeting it was observed that: "Nature is declining globally at rates unprecedented in human history – and the rate of species extinctions is accelerating, with grave impacts on people around the world now likely."

The meeting stressed that this profoundly impacts human well-being: "The health of ecosystems on which we and all other species depend is deteriorating more rapidly than ever. We are eroding the very foundations of our economies, livelihoods, food security, health and quality of life worldwide." However, the report also stresses that it is not too late to make a difference. While expecting opposition from those who have "interests vested in the status quo" it feels that "such opposition can be overcome for the broader public good" (UN, 2019).

The Convention on Biological Diversity was signed by 150 government leaders at the 1992 Rio Earth Summit. The Convention recognized that biological diversity is about more than plants, animals and micro-organisms and their ecosystems – it is about people and our need for food security, medicines, fresh air and water, shelter and a clean and healthy environment in which to live. In 2010 visions for 2020 were presented. At a conference held on 29 October 2010, in Nagoya, Aichi Prefecture, Japan, a revised and updated Strategic Plan for Biodiversity was adopted, including the Aichi Biodiversity Targets, for the 2011–2020 period (Convention on Biological Diversity, 2020; Box 7.3).

When 2020 arrived it appeared that none of these had been met. The assessments of the failure are exemplified in the following – from Earth.org (2020): 'World fails to meet single Aichi biodiversity target to stop destruction of nature – UN' and a similar assessment in the *New Scientist* by Vaughan (2020): '"Massive failure": The world has missed all its biodiversity targets'.

By that time two other threads had also arrived. First, the valuing of nature during lockdowns, exemplified by McCarthy, Mynott and Marren (2020) in *The Consolation of Nature: Spring in the time of coronavirus*. Second was the publication of several more radically thinking articles involving the simultaneous enhancement of biodiversity and of the human condition. About 300 experts were consulted for the publication of the paper 'An agenda for research and action towards diverse and just futures for life on Earth' (Wyborn et al., 2020a). Their essential stance is that: "Decades of research and policy interventions on biodiversity have insufficiently addressed the dual issues of biodiversity degradation and social justice." The 'failure' of the Aichi targets above seems to be notable in this respect.

The authors call for "a collective task of 'revisiting biodiversity' towards the goal of sustaining diverse and just futures for life on Earth". Their insight is that "biodiversity research and action is underpinned by choices about how problems are conceptualized". They recognize "knowledge, action, and ethics as inseparable" and they propose four thematic areas for future research (Box 7.4).

Box 7.3 *Targets to be reached by 2020*

Derived from Convention on Biological Diversity (2020):

Strategic Goal A: Address the underlying causes of biodiversity loss – address government and society.

1. People should be aware of the values of biodiversity and the steps they can take to conserve and use it sustainably.
2. Biodiversity values should be integrated into development and poverty reduction strategies.
3. Incentives harmful to biodiversity should be eliminated/ reformed, while those for conservation and sustainability should be developed.
4. Governments, business and stakeholders should ensure that the impacts of use of natural resources are within ecological limits.

Strategic Goal B: Reduce the direct pressures on biodiversity and promote sustainable use.

5. Halve the rate of loss of all natural habitats. Degradation and fragmentation should be significantly reduced.
6. Fish and other aquatic stocks to be managed and harvested sustainably.
7. Areas under agriculture, aquaculture and forestry to be managed sustainably, with conservation of biodiversity.
8. Pollution, including from excess nutrients should not be detrimental to ecosystem function and biodiversity.
9. Invasive alien species should be controlled or eradicated; and pathways managed to prevent their spread.
10. Anthropogenic pressures on coral reefs should be minimized so as to maintain their integrity and functioning.

Strategic Goal C: To safeguard ecosystems, species and genetic diversity.

11. Significant proportions of aquatic areas should be effectively and equitably managed and integrated.
12. Prevent the extinction of known threatened species and improve their status.
13. Maintain the genetic diversity of cultivated plants, domesticated animals and other valuable species.

Strategic Goal D: Enhance the benefits to all from biodiversity and ecosystem services.

14. Restore/safeguard ecosystems services for women, indigenous communities, the poor and the vulnerable.
15. Enhance ecosystem resilience to increase climate change mitigation and combat desertification.
16. Operationalise protocols on the access to genetic resources and the fair and equitable sharing of benefits.

Strategic Goal E: Enhance participatory planning, knowledge management and capacity building.

17. Develop and implement participatory biodiversity strategy and action plan.
18. Respect traditional knowledge with the full and effective participation of indigenous and local communities.
19. Improve the sharing and application of biodiversity knowledge and the consequences of its loss.
20. Increase the mobilization of finance for effectively implementing this Plan for Biodiversity 2011–2020.

Box 7.4 *Points derived from Wyborn et al. (2020a)*

1. Revisit biodiversity narratives. Challenge the notion of "the separation of humans, cultures, economies, and societies from nature".
2. See "humanity and biodiversity as tied together".
3. Derive better accounting for the "interacting structures of economic and financial systems as core drivers of biodiversity loss".
4. Re-configure relationships "between human and non-human communities". "Focus on dialogue among biodiversity communities" and foster "just and diverse futures for human and non-human life on Earth".

In a further paper, Wyborn et al. (2020b: 670): 'Imagining transformative biodiversity futures', again these authors cite successive failures, noting that 2020 was: "Posited to be a 'super year' for biodiversity with various international meetings and the conclusion of the Convention on Biological Diversity's ten-year Aichi Targets." However, they point out that 2020 will be "remembered for very different reasons: catastrophic fires, the COVID-19 pandemic, floods, locust outbreaks, a drastic drop in oil prices and widespread food insecurity". They point out that it is the poor who have suffered most together with "other marginalized groups – women, Indigenous communities and people of colour". They also fear that while "carbon emissions may be down … there are growing concerns that nature will be forgotten in the rush to rebuild devastated economies".

They consider possible futures including "zero conflict, obliterated nature and societal collapse" but there are many other possibilities. They see the key aspects involve "contrasting world views that shape who has power, what values are prioritized and which bits of biodiversity 'matter'" and ask for greater imagination in finding better futures for nature and humanity together.

A further radical revisiting of the conservation narratives is seen in the book by Büscher and Fletcher (2020): *The Conservation Revolution: Radical ideas for saving nature beyond the Anthropocene*. The authors feel that while: "Many believe conservation requires full integration into capitalist production processes" and call for conservation to "go beyond protected areas and faith in markets" instead they coin the phrase "convivial conservation" which will "incorporate the needs of humans and nonhumans within integrated and just landscapes" (p. 15).

I remain intrigued by the writings about how indigenous peoples have been involved in the tropical rainforest since prehistoric times. This has been headlined in various sources, including Meyer (2017): 'The Amazon rainforest was profoundly changed by ancient humans' which reports that "the region's ecology is a product of 8,000 years of indigenous agriculture". The work is also described in the paper by Levis et al. (2017) on 'Persistent effects of pre-Columbian plant domestication on Amazonian forest composition'. Not only does this knock on the head the persistent and in many ways pernicious idea of a 'pristine' rainforest (see also Stott, 1997) which has led to a 'purificationist logic' (Proctor, 1995, 1996) which encourages the exclusion of people; it shows how people have been a part of nature and can continue to be. The authors found that: "Plants domesticated by pre-Columbian peoples are much more likely to be dominant in Amazonian forests than other species" (Levis et al., 2017: 925). Even more interestingly, in pure biodiversity terms, forests close to archaeological sites often have a higher abundance and richness of domesticated species". The authors can but conclude that "modern-day Amazonian tree communities across the basin remain largely structured by historical human use".

While this is an example which relates to the specific area of the earth, it nevertheless provides a salutary thought about meeting both human needs and enhancing biodiversity.

Visions of the Future: Signposts on the Path to Enhancing Nature and Human Welfare Together

The varying degrees of optimism and pessimism about the future are very evident. I have before me several books and papers which point to the range. On the one hand, there is a very strong sense of our limitations. These can come from the general tone of books such as Gray's (2002) *Straw Dogs: Thoughts on humans and other animals* and (2008) *Black Mass: Apocalyptic religion and the death of utopia*. On the other hand, there is Rutger Bregman's (2020) positive *Humankind: A hopeful history* and Lily Cole's (2020) *Who Cares Wins: Reasons for optimism in our changing world* with the upbeat chapter on 'Playing God or re-wilding', including a section on favouring natural regeneration. Both sets of ideas are illustrated with supportive examples. The former set is often called 'realistic', the latter 'naïve'; however, I think somewhere in between there can be a better future and that both sets are important. Just because things are different, it does not mean that they are necessarily opposable. I have always believed that a good way ahead is to have the simultaneous continual upwelling of belief that you will succeed coupled with the thought that you might not. Without the former you don't aim high and without the latter you are unwary of the pitfalls. Such a balance gives a sense of 'realistic naivety', if you like, or you might call it 'world-weary hope' or 'pragmatic optimism'.

The other kind of balance which appeals to me is one which works with a varied and diverse human nature but never loses sight of making things better for both people and nature – seeing them as part of a whole rather than opposable. This needs a positive belief in human capabilities, such as that which Bregman's *Humankind* espouses. To me a good future is where we look after nature and the welfare of people together. In this context, Moss and Kinne (2012) provide a real signpost by discussing the importance of reconciling human progress with the protection of nature in *Liberation Ecology: The reconciliation of natural and human cultures*.

Balancing threads of arguments becomes an important endeavour. We can pick up the thread of the paper by Costanza et al. (1997) where the idea is promoted that nature will flourish if we can value it economically. I am sure that despite the ethical arguments ranged against that, there is a place for this argument, though monetising everything can, indeed, be seen as rather bleak. However, the idea of making a profit at the same time as conserving nature must, surely, be a good one. It is a matter of balance, like everything else. New Zealand Prime Minister Jacinda Ardern provided a good signpost when she said: "Economic growth accompanied by worsening social outcomes is not success – it is failure" (twitter.com/jacindaardern; McCarthy, 2019). That doesn't argue against economic growth but also argues for simultaneous better human well-being. We can also pick up the thread from Jonathan Bate (2000) in *The Song of the Earth* where he feels that poetry is the place where we can save the earth – a conclusion I coincidentally also came to (Trudgill, 2001b: 263) in *The Terrestrial Biosphere: Environmental change, ecosystem science, attitudes and values*. Indeed, poetry too has its place. Acting on both a flourishing economy which promotes human well-being and promoting poetry as inspiration together is surely a good way forward. I restate that things which are different are not opposable. Enhancing both economic survival and cultural values is surely effective if used in a complementary rather than competitive fashion.

So, we need the benefits of civilisation – as Wendell Berry (2017: 160) wrote, "people cannot live apart from nature . . . and yet, people cannot live in nature without changing it. [We] depend upon nature, and [we] change it", as well as: "Pure nature is not good for humans to live in [; we need] basic human amenities – [such as] clothing, shelter, cooked food. . ." He also adds that: "It is equally true that a condition that is purely human is not good for people to live in, and people do not want to live for very long in it." So, we also need the drive and inspiration of David Attenborough (2020) who in *A Life on Our Planet: My witness statement and vision for the future* wrote:

> As a young man, I felt I was out there in the wild, experiencing the untouched natural world – but it was an illusion. The tragedy of our time has been happening all around us, barely noticeable from day to day – the loss of our planet's wild places, its biodiversity . . . if we act now, we can yet put it right. We have one final chance to create the perfect home for ourselves and restore the wonderful world we inherited. All we need is the will do so. (from book advertisement on Amazon: www.amazon.co.uk/Life-Our-Planet-Witness-Statement/dp/1529108276)

This really sums up the key points, as, from his lifetime of experience, only Attenborough can "create the perfect home for ourselves and restore the wonderful world we inherited". An excellent signpost: the world as home and wonder are both important.

In terms of engendering enthusiasm for nature and enhancing cultural values, I am very minded of Mark Cocker's (2007: 170 *et seq.*) *Crow Country* where he devotes some pages to how conservationists developed their passion. He focusses especially on Derek Ratcliffe (1929–2005) and Desmond Nethersole-Thompson (1908–1989), describing the immersion and engagement in a sense of curiosity leading to a deep and positive feeling for the things we investigate. Here, again, we focus on the importance of involvement to enhance people's sense of the value of nature. Additionally, Peter Marren (2002: 316) in *Nature Conservation* concludes his book by referring to "the nature conservation industry" in almost pejorative tones. He seems to take a side-swipe at the 'Management Plan' by saying that: "It is good for us to be reminded that nature is [an] infinitely more complex and tested scheme than anything we try to impose on it." This seems to presage the growth of the idea of 'letting nature be' and he suggests that we should dump "the burden of care" and "just enjoy nature for its own sake". Indeed, rewilding has become more centre stage at the moment though the degree of management involved – or needed – can be debated. In *Feral: Rewilding the land, the sea and human life* George Monbiot (2013) writes how ecosystem restoration can revitalise and enrich our lives. He discusses restoration of forests and bringing back missing species such as wolves, lynx, wolverines and wild boar, offering an alternative to a 'silent spring': the chance of a 'raucous summer' in which ecological processes resume and humans draw closer to the natural world. The endeavours range from changing farmland (e.g. Tree, 2018, and Somerleyton Estate in Suffolk: www.edp24.co.uk/business/farming/bbc-countryfile-visits-somerleyton-estate-1-6802532) to the re-introduction of beavers (Gow, 2020) and other wild animals in the UK, including case studies and examples covered in *Rebirding: Rewilding Britain and its birds* by Benedict Macdonald (2019); *Rewilding: Real life stories of returning British and Irish wildlife to balance* by David Woodfall (2019) and *The Missing Lynx: The past and future of Britain's lost mammals* by Ross Barnett (2019). The book by Jepson and Cain (2020): *Rewilding: The radical new science of ecological recovery* sets something of a bench mark by combining scientific insights with practical innovations – and the material included covers ideas on reviving ecological processes which benefit people as well as nature from urban areas to the remoter parts of the planet.

However, the variety of 'benefits to people' will be contested, so there is always a need for education. Here, I am thinking of the benefits of high speed rail travel, like the UK HS2 and the consequent loss of some ancient woodlands. I think we haven't got the idea of bioheritage across enough – when I said to someone "you wouldn't knock down St Paul's Cathedral to put a railway through, would you?" the reply was "of course not, it is irreplaceable, but woods are different, trees can be replanted elsewhere and re-grow". So, if trees are seen as replaceable and heritage buildings aren't, it seems like the idea of irreplaceable woods which are inherited from the past and have developed as ecosystems full of wildlife over time is something which people need more education about.

There are other writings showing these kinds of signposts to ways ahead. W. G. Sebald (2002: 81) in *After Nature* explores the lives of three men connected by their questioning of humankind's place in the natural world. From the efforts of each, "an order arises, in places beautiful and comforting, though more cruel, too, than the previous state of ignorance". Berry (2015) in *The Dream of the Earth* promotes a new intellectual-ethical framework by positing planetary well-being as the measure of all human activity. Kellert (2012) in *Birthright: People and nature in the modern world*, chapter 7 on 'Spirituality', describes how human health and well-being are inextricably linked to nature. He promotes the idea that "physical health, and capacities for affection, aversion, intellect, control, aesthetics, exploitation, spirituality, and communication are deeply contingent on the quality of our connections to the natural world" (www.amazon.co.uk/Birthright-People-Nature-Modern-World/dp/0300205791). Taylor (2010) in *Dark Green Religion: Nature, spirituality and the planetary future* examines those involved in 'ecopsychology' and "emphasizes the depth of believers' passion and also suggests a potential shadow side: besides uplifting and inspiring, such religion might mislead, deceive, or in some cases precipitate violence". He draws on "Western philosophy, Asian thought, and Native American traditions, as well as physics and biology ... to foster mutually enhancing human-Earth relationships" (www.goodreads.com/book/show/7414775-dark-green-religion).

Finally, Shirley (2019) in 'Nature's place – what should live where?' concludes that:

> If we lift our eyes above the 'ecological horizon' we will see a world which, socially and culturally, is a borderless mix. Nature strives to be like this, but we constantly try to constrain it. Instead we need to harness nature's resilience, resourcefulness and chaos, and stop pretending that it is frozen and static. We need to create the conditions for natural processes to flourish and stop trying to impose our own 'designer solutions'.

These all seem to be questioning our place in nature and to promote the idea of enhancing the processes of nature to occur – for nature's sake, and for our own sake. We know from the geological past that nature, in terms of life forms, will survive in some way and in some form in the face of whatever changes occur, albeit involving many losses of specific life forms on the way. That is why there is a functional argument that we should conserve the processes of nature rather than any specific form, culturally attached to specific forms as we might be. The argument for preserving species is therefore as much culture as it is a clinical one that species are needed for nature to survive. However many species are lost, unless the earth is made to be totally uninhabitable, nature (here meaning life forms) will survive in some form – it has done ever since life arose on the planet. Our question of 'why conserve nature?' thus brings different answers in terms of 'why conserve the processes of nature?' and 'why conserve the forms of nature?' Quite where we stand on this spectrum of survivability ourselves is difficult to foresee – though we can see that while we are culturally attached to our species, nature can survive without us, indeed it did so for millions of years. So, the arguments become more ones of the survivability of nature and the survivability of our species. The former might seem more likely than the latter. We thus find further support for the answer to 'why conserve nature?' as one of the fact that we need it – it is our support system; add to that the joy and wonder which can be felt at experiencing the diversity of nature and helping it to flourish and you have both existential and cultural reasons for conserving nature.

I am encouraged by the existence of the charity People Need Nature (peopleneednature.org.uk) which promotes the value of nature for people in their everyday lives: nature as a source of inspiration, as a source of solace; and nature enriching people's spiritual lives. It also works to influence public thinking and policy to place a greater value on nature for these things. The charity has also been working with the Young Poets Network on encouraging poetry about people's place in nature, including poems appreciating the trees by the motorway, the river by the factory, the flowers growing in brick (https://ypn.poetrysociety.org.uk/workshop/people-need-nature-gboyega-odubanjo/). The PNN website promotes the idea that: "Nature doesn't need human beings – it will survive without us. We need nature to thrive and survive." This sentiment is echoed by Maslin (2021) in *How to Save Our Planet* in that we need to save the planet both from us and for us. Additionally, the economic value of biodiversity has been emphasised in an encouraging review: *The Economics of Biodiversity: The Dasgupta review* (Dasgupta, 2021). This all sounds like Salk's (1973) *Survival of the Wisest* to me.

In *Arctic Dreams* Lopez (2014: 245) discusses the work of Novak (2007): *Nature and Culture: American landscape and painting, 1825–1875.* In thinking about the relationship between landscape and art Lopez cites: "Atmospheres of painting suggesting a private rather than a public encounter with the land. An actual spiritual presence in the landscape" and celebrates what Novak terms "a loss of ego" with the words: "The artist disappears. The authority of the work lies, instead, with the land." Something we might bear in mind more.

So, why conserve nature?

Do we wish to be the species that protects and cherishes other species or the species which removes other species?

Do we wish to be the species which cherishes the wilder areas of the planet or do we wish to be the one which makes our artefacts even more pervasive than they already are?

Do we wish to be the species which cherishes the life-support system this planet offers or do we wish to diminish this system?

Are future peoples going to look back at us and see us as 'good ancestors' (Krznaric, 2020)?

The manifestations of the answers are many, but the questions are simple enough.

7.6 Chapter Summary

- The concept of biodiversity has an abstractness which leads to a wide range of interpretations which is not necessarily helpful. Species vary in their significance. 'Keystone species' means that an ecosystem would tend to change radically if it were removed.

- Biodiversity counts can be a useful surrogate for – and indicator of – connectivity, activity, process and function in ecosystems.
- Dussault (2019: 297) proposes that there are "functional effect groups" of organisms playing a causal role in ecological functions. There is a dependency through connectivity: with interactions having wide-reaching effects.
- There is connectivity in soil through mycorrhizal fungal networks around plant roots – the 'wood-wide web'. This is important for plant nutrition, defences and carbon sequestration.
- The concept of functional effect groups means that if one species of such a group is removed it could be argued that another could step in to take its place or there could just be no evident difference in function. But if the population size/species numbers of a functional group, such as earthworms, decrease then whole systems would be liable to change in terms of function.
- Preserving processes (e.g. processes of renewal) is liable to be more worthwhile than trying to preserve states: create conditions for natural processes rather than imposing 'designer solutions'.
- "We have to use our power to preserve a sense of what is not in our power" (Williams, 1995: 240). Use our power to let something which is beyond us happen.
- A commitment to pluralism of ideas provides opportunities for knowledge exchange and stewardship – while recognising the power dynamics between differently interested groups.
- Nature is always changing in response to environmental change. A preservationist agenda of trying to keep things the way they are reduces this ability to respond.
- With wildlife films, a tension can arise between a more dispassionate view of biological observation and the idea that we do indeed share many characteristics in common with animals. Anthropomorphisation can engage the viewer and provide a conservation motivation.
- A sense of place is an important aspect of conservation. Solastalgia refers to the loss of a person's place in the world through change: a familiar place is rendered unrecognisable by climate change or corporate action – the home becomes unhomely around its inhabitants.
- The sense of place relates to the history of a place and to the stories of that place, often expressed through writings. The depth of meaning in the landscape involves aesthetics, knowing, transcendence, belonging and connectivity.

- David Attenborough: "We have one final chance to create the perfect home for ourselves and restore the wonderful world we inherited. All we need is the will do so" – and for those who have power and influence to make it happen.
- 'Why conserve nature?' We need it – it is our support system. Add to that the joy and wonder which can be felt at experiencing the diversity of nature and helping it to flourish and you have both existential and cultural reasons for conserving nature. We should have in mind the dual goals of human progress and the protection of nature.

Bibliography

Abell, P. (1992). Is rational choice theory a rational choice of theory? In Coleman, J. S. and Farar, T., eds., *Rational Choice Theory: Advocacy and criticism*. Thousand Oaks, CA: Sage. 183–207.

Abelson, E. (1988). *A Mirror of England: An anthology of the writings of H. J. Massingham*. Rapidan, VA: Hartland Publications.

Abulafia, D. (2019). *The Boundless Sea: A human history of the oceans*. London: Allen Lane.

Ackers, C. P. (1938). *Practical British Forestry*. London: Oxford University Press.

Adams, W. M. (1986). *Nature's Place*. London: Allen & Unwin.

Adams, W. M. (1997). Rationalization and conservation: Ecology and the management of nature in the United Kingdom. *Transactions of the Institute of British Geographers*, 22, 277–291.

Adams, W. M. (2003). When nature won't stay still: Conservation, equilibrium and control. In Adams, W. M. and Mulligan, M., eds., *Decolonizing Nature: Strategies for conservation in a post-colonial era*. London: Earthscan. 220–246.

Adams, W. M. (2014). Conservation poetry: A field guide. *Thinking Like a Human: Conservation for the 21st century* [blog], 17 October. https://thinkinglikeahuman.com/

Agyeman, J. (1995). *People, Places and Plants*. Crediton: Southgate Publishers.

Agyeman, J. (1998). Native good, alien bad? The city as an equal opportunity habitat. *Green Teacher*, 34, 28–33.

Albrecht, G. (2005). Solastalgia, a new concept in human health and identity. *Philosophy Activism Nature*, 3, 41–44.

Albrecht, G., Sartore, G.-M., Connor, L. et al. (2007). Solastalgia: The distress caused by environmental change. *Australasian Psychiatry*, 15(Suppl. 1), S95–S98.

Alcorn, J. (1977). *The Nature Novel from Hardy to Lawrence*. London: Macmillan Press.

Allen, D. E. (2010). *Books and Naturalists*. London: Collins New Naturalist 112.

Allwood, J. M. and Cullen, J. (2019). *Sustainable Materials without the Hot Air: Making building products efficiently and with less material*. Cambridge: UIT Cambridge Ltd.

Altman, I. and Low, S. M. (1992). *Place Attachment*. Human Behavior and Environment, 12. New York: Plenum Press.

Altman, I. and Wohlwill, J. F., eds. (1977). *Human Behavior and Environment*. Advances in Theory and Research, 2. New York: Plenum Press.

Altman, I. and Wohlwill, J. F., eds. (1983). *Human Behavior and the Natural Environment*. Human Behavior and Environment, 6. New York: Plenum Press.

American Psychiatric Association, ed. (2000). Anxiety disorders. In *Diagnostic and Statistical Manual of Mental Disorders* (4th ed., text rev.). Washington, DC: American Psychiatric Association. 450–456.

American Psychiatric Association, ed. (2013). Avoidant personality disorder, 30182 (F606). *Diagnostic and Statistical Manual of Mental Disorders* (5th ed.). Washington, DC: American Psychiatric Association. 672–675.

Anderson, K. and Smith, S. (2001). Editorial: Emotional geographies. *Transactions of the Institute of British Geographers*, 26, 7–10.

Andrews, M., ed. (1994). *The Picturesque Literary Sources and Documents, Vol. I: The idea of the picturesque and the vogue for scenic tourism*. London: Helm Information.

Andrews, M. (1999). *Landscape and Western Art*. Oxford: Oxford University Press.

Anker, P. (2001). *Imperial Ecology: Environmental order in the British Empire 1895–1945*. Cambridge, MA: Harvard University Press.

Anonymous. (2016). Professor Sir David MacKay, physicist – obituary. *The Telegraph*, 15 April. www.telegraph.co.uk/obituaries/2016/04/15/professor-sir-david-mackay-physicist–obituary/

Appleton, G. (n.d.). Little egret. *British Trust for Ornithology*. www.bto.org/about-birds/species-focus/little-egret

Appleton, J. (1975). *The Experience of Landscape*. London: Wiley.

Appleton, J. (1996). *The Experience of Landscape* (2nd rev. ed.). London: Wiley.

Arias, A. H. and Botté, S. E. (2020). *Coastal and Deep Ocean Pollution*. Boca Raton, FL: CRC Press (Taylor & Francis).

Armitage, S. and Dee, T. (2009). *The Poetry of Birds*. London: Viking Penguin.

Armour, T. and Tempany, A. (2020). *Nature of the City: Green infrastructure from the ground up*. London: RIBA Publishing.

Arnold, A. (2015). *Narratives of Climate Change: Outline of a systematic approach to narrative analysis in cultural sociology* [Dissertation]. University of Stuttgart. elib.uni-stuttgart.de/bitstream/11682/8757/1/Arnold_2015_Narratives_of_Climate_Change_Dissertation.pdf

Arntzen, S. and Brady, E., eds. (2008). *Humans in the Land: The ethics and aesthetics of the cultural landscape*. Oslo: Unipub.

Ashmore, W. and Knapp, A. B. (1999). *Archaeology of Landscape: Contemporary perspectives*. London: Blackwell.

Athanasiou, T. (1996). *Slow Reckoning: The ecology of a divided planet*. New York; London: Vintage.

Attenborough, D. (2020). *A Life on Our Planet: My witness statement and a vision for the future*. London: Witness Books/Penguin Random House.

Aubrey, J. R. (1999). *John Fowles and Nature: Fourteen perspectives on landscape*. Madison, NJ: Fairleigh Dickinson University Press.

Averill, J. R. (1990). Inner feelings, works of the flesh, the beast within, diseases of the mind, driving force, and putting on a show: Six metaphors of emotion and their theoretical extensions. In Leary, D., ed., *Metaphors in the History of Psychology*. Cambridge: Cambridge University Press. 104–132.

Bailey, R. (2017). Georgia Tech climatologist Judith Curry resigns over 'the CRAZINESS in the field of climate science': She is a prominent critic of the 'consensus' that man-made climate change is an impending catastrophe. *Reason*, 4 January. http://reason.com/blog/2017/01/04/georgia-tech-climatologist-judith-curry

Baker, J. A. (1967). *The Peregrine*. London: Collins.

Baker, J. A. (2005). *The Peregrine, with Introduction by Robert Macfarlane*. New York: New York Review Books.

Baker, K., ed. (2000). *The Faber Book of Landscape Poetry*. London: Faber & Faber.

Baker, M. (1971). *Discovering the Folklore of Plants*. Tring: Shire Publications.

Baker, S. (2019). 'The biggest problem is greed' says conservationist Jane Goodall. *DW*, 12 July. www.dw.com/en/environmental-protection-the-biggest-problem-is-greed-says-conservationist-jane-goodall/a-49556942

Balmer, D., Gillings, S., Caffrey, B., Swann, B., Downie, I. and Fuller, R. (2013). *Bird Atlas 2007–11*. Thetford: BTO Books.

Barnes, S. (2018). *The Meaning of Birds*. New York: Pegasus Books.

Barnes, T. and Duncan, J., eds. (1992). *Writing Worlds: Discourse, text and metaphor in the representation of landscape*. London: Routledge.

Barnett, D. (2015). Virginia Woolf fans fight to save view that inspired 'To the Lighthouse'. *The Independent*, 7 November. www.independent.co.uk/arts-entertainment/books/news/virginia-woolf-fans-fight-to-save-view-that-inspired-to-the-lighthouse-a6725621.html

Barnett, R. (2019). *The Missing Lynx: The past and future of Britain's lost mammals*. London: Bloomsbury.

Barrell, J. (1972). *The Idea of Landscape and the Sense of Place 1730–1840: An approach to the poetry of John Clare*. Cambridge: Cambridge University Press.

Barringer, T. (2015). Poetry. In Van Hout, N. and Merle du Bourg, A., eds., *Rubens and His Legacy*. London: Royal Academy of Arts. 262–264.

Bate, J. (1991). *Romantic Ecology: Wordsworth and the environmental tradition*. London: Routledge.

Bate, J. (2000). *The Song of the Earth*. London: Picador.

Bate, J. (2003). *John Clare: A biography*. London: Picador.

Bate, J. (2020). *Radical Wordsworth: The poet who changed the world*. London: William Collins.

Batten, H. M. (1924). *Dramas of the Wild Folk*. London: S. S. Partridge & Co., Ltd.

Battistini, M. (2005). *Symbols and Allegories in Art*. Los Angeles: Getty Publications.

BBC. (2018). *Blue Planet II*, episode 4: Plastic Pollution Awareness, 24 January. www.youtube.com/watch?v=xLx4fVsYdTI

Beamish, T. (1970). *Aldabra Alone*. London: George Allen & Unwin.

Beardsworth, A. and Bryman, A. (2001). The wild animal in late modernity: The case of the Disneyization of zoos. *Tourist Studies*, 1, 83–104.

Beavan, A. H. (1905). *Animals I Have Known*. London: T. Fisher Unwin.

Beery, T. B. and Wolf-Watz, D. (2014). Nature to place: Rethinking the environmental connectedness. *Journal of Environmental Psychology*, 40, 198–205.

Beinart, W., Middleton, K. and Pooley, S., eds. (2013). *Wild Things: Nature and the social imagination*. Cambridge: White Horse Press.

Bell, M. and Evans, D. M. (1997). Greening 'the heart of England': Redemptive science, citizenship and 'symbol of hope for the nation'. *Environment and Planning D: Society and Space*, 15, 257–279.

Bell, P. A., Greene, T. C., Fisher, J. D. and Baum, A. (1996). *Environmental Psychology*. New York: Harcourt Brace.

Berger, A. A. (1997). *Narratives in Popular Culture, Media and Everyday Life*. Thousand Oaks, CA: Sage.

Berman, M. G., Jonides, J. and Kaplan, S. (2008). The cognitive benefits of interacting with nature. *Psychological Science*, 19, 1207–1212.

Berman, M. G., Kross, E., Krpan, K. M. et al. (2012). Interacting with nature improves cognition and affect for individuals with depression. *Journal of Affective Disorders*, 140, 300–305.

Bernauer, J. W. (1987). Michel Foucault's ecstatic thinking. In Bernauer, J. and Rasmussen, D., eds., *The Final Foucault*. Cambridge, MA: The MIT Press. 45–82.

Bernauer, J. W. (1992). Beyond life and death: On Foucault's post-Auschwitz ethic. In Armstrong, T. J., ed. (trans.), *Michel Foucault, Philosopher*. Hemel Hempstead: Harvester Wheatsheaf. 260–279.

Berto, R. (2005). Exposure to restorative environments helps restore attentional capacity. *Journal of Environmental Psychology*, 25, 249–259.

Berry, T. (2015). *The Dream of the Earth*. San Francisco: Sierra Club.

Berry, W. (2017). *The World-Ending Fire*. London: Penguin.

Berry, W. (2018). *The Peace of Wild Things*. London: Penguin.

Beute, F. and de Kort, Y. A. W. (2014). Natural resistance: Exposure to nature and self-regulation, mood, and physiology after ego-depletion. *Journal of Environmental Psychology*, 40, 167–178.

Biddulph, S. (1994). *Manhood: An action plan for changing men's lives*. Stroud: Hawthorn Press.

Bircham, P. (2007). *A History of Ornithology*. London: Collins New Naturalist 104.

Bishop, P. (1992). Rhetoric, memory and power: Depth psychology and postmodern geography. *Environment and Planning D: Society and Space*, 10, 5–22.

Blackbourn, D. (2007). *The Conquest of Nature: Water, landscape, and the making of modern Germany*. New York: W. W. Norton & Company.

Blackburn, S. (1998). *Ruling Passions*. Oxford: Oxford University Press.

Blake, J. (1999). Overcoming the 'value-action gap' in environmental policy: Tensions between national policy and local experience. *Local Environment*, 4(3), 257–278.

Blewett, A. (2018). Medicine for contemporary ills: A 'dose of nature'?. *ECOS*, 39(6). www.ecos.org.uk/ecos-396-medicine-for-contemporary-ills-a-dose-of-nature/

Bly, R. (1990). *Iron John: Men and masculinity*. Reading, MA: Addison-Wesley.

Blythe, R. (1999). *Going to Meet George and Other Outings*. Ebrington: Long Barn Books.

Bocking, S. (2015). Ecological concepts: Seeing, placing, imposing. *Geoforum*, 65, 489–492.

Boer, R. (2012). *The Earthy Nature of the Bible: Fleshly readings of sex, masculinity, and carnality*. London: Palgrave Macmillan.

Böhme [Boehme], J. (1621). *De Signatura Rerum, or, The Signature of All Things: Shewing the sign and signification of The several forms and shapes in the creation And what the Beginning, ruin, and cure of everything is. It proceeds out of Eternity into time, and again out of time into eternity, And comprizes all mysteries*. Subsequent republications, e.g. (2008) *The Signature of All Things*. Santa Cruz, CA: Evinity Publishing Inc.

Bonnett, A. (1996). The new primitives: Identity, landscape and cultural appropriation in the mythopoetic men's movement. *Antipode*, 28, 273–291.

Bonnett, A. (2003). *Psychogeography*. London: Continuum International Publishing Group – Academic.

Booker, C. (2015). The real 'deniers' in the climate change debate are the warmists. *Daily Telegraph*, 1 August. www.telegraph.co.uk/comment/11778376/The-real-deniers-in-the-climate-change-debate-are-the-warmists.html/

Bormann, F. H. and Likens, G. E. (1979). *Pattern and Process in a Forested Ecosystem*. Berlin: Springer-Verlag.

Botkin, D. B. (1990). *Discordant Harmonies: A new ecology for the twenty-first century*. Oxford: Oxford University Press.

Boyd, W. (1990). *Brazzaville Beach*. London: Sinclair-Stevenson.

Bramwell, A. (1989a). *The Literary Ecologist*. New Haven, CT: Yale University Press.

Bramwell. A. (1989b). *Ecology in the 20th Century: A history*. New Haven, CT: Yale University Press.

Bratman. G. N., Daily, G. C., Levy, B. J. and Gross, J. J. (2015). The benefits of nature experience: Improved affect and cognition. *Landscape and Urban Planning*, 138, 41–50.

Braubach, M., Egorov, A., Mudu, P., Wolf, T., Ward Thompson, C. and Martuzzi, M. (2017). Effects of urban green space on environmental health, equity and resilience. In Kabisch, N., Korn, H., Stadler, J. and Bonn, A., eds., *Nature-Based Solutions to Climate Change Adaptation in Urban Areas: Linkages between science, policy and practice*. Theory and Practice of Urban Sustainability Transitions. Cham: Springer Open. 187–205.

Braun, B. (2002). *The Intemperate Rain Forest: Nature, culture and power on Canada's west coast*. Minneapolis: University of Minnesota Press.

Braun-Blanquet, J., Fuller, G. D. and Conard, H. S. (1932). *Plant Sociology: The study of plant communities*. New York: McGraw-Hill.

Bregman, R. (2020). *Humankind: A hopeful history*. London: Bloomsbury.

Briggs, J., Badri, M. and Mekki, A.-B. (1999). Indigenous knowledge and vegetation use among the Bedouin in the Eastern Desert of Egypt. *Applied Geography*, 19, 87–103.

British Trust for Ornithology. (2013). *Bird Atlas 2007–2011*. Thetford: BTO Books.

Brockmeir, J. and Carbaugh, D., eds. (2001). *Narratives and Identity*. Amsterdam: John Benjamins Publishing Company.

Brøgger, F. C. (2009). The cultural contamination of the language of nature: Dos Passos' *Manhattan Transfer* and Jeffers' nature poems. *Nordlit*, 24, 135–149.

Bronowski, J. (1973). *The Ascent of Man*. London: British Broadcasting Corporation.

Brooke, R. (1912 et al.). *Collected Poems*, quoted from Marsh (1942) – see below.

Bryson, B. (1997). *A Walk in the Woods*. London: Doubleday.

Buckley-Archer, L. (2014). *The River Singers* by Tom Moorhouse – review. *The Guardian*, 11 January. www.theguardiancom/books/2014/jan/11/river-singers-tom-moorhouse-review/

Buffon, Georges-Louis Leclerc. (1749). *Premier discours. De la manière d'étudier et de traiter l'Histoire Naturelle*. Paris: De L'Imprimerie Royale.

Burger, J. M. (1998). Solitude. In Friedman, H. S., ed., *Encyclopedia of Mental Health*, Vol. 3, 563–569. San Diego: Academic Press.

Burgess, J. (1992). The cultural politics of nature conservation and economic development. In Anderson, K. and Gale, F., eds., *Inventing Places: Studies in cultural geography*. London: Wiley. 235–251.

Burke, K. (1941). *Philosophy of Literary Form*. Baton Rouge: Louisiana State University Press.

Büscher, B. and Fletcher, R. (2020). *The Conservation Revolution: Radical ideas for saving nature beyond the Anthropocene*. New York; London: Verso.

Callicott, J. B. (1995). Intrinsic value in nature: A metaethical analysis. *The Electronic Journal of Analytic Philosophy*, 3. http://ejap.louisiana.edu/EJAP/1995.spring/callicott.1995.spring.html

Cameron, L. (1999). Histories of disturbance. *Radical History Review*, 74, 4–24.

Cameron, L. and Earley, S. (2015). The ecosystem: Movements, connections, tensions and translations. *Geoforum*, 65, 473–481.

Cameron, L. and Forrester, J. (2000a). 'A nice type of English scientist': Tansley, Freud and a psychoanalytic dream. *History Workshop Journal*, 48, 64–100.

Cameron, L. and Forrester, J. (2000b). Tansley's psychoanalytical network: An episode out of the early history of psychoanalysis in England. *Psychoanalysis and History*, 2, 189–256.

Campbell, L. and Wiesen, A., eds. (2011). *Restorative Commons: Creating health and well-being through urban landscapes*. Washington, DC: United States Department of Agriculture.

Canton, J. (2013). *Out of Essex: Re-imagining a literary landscape*. Oxford: Signal Books.

Carabine, K. (1998). Introduction. In Conrad, J., *Three Sea Stories: 'Typhoon', 'Falk' and 'The Shadow Line'*. Hertfordshire: Wordsworth Editions Ltd. vii–xxxviii.

Carroll, J. S. (2012). *Landscape in Children's Literature*. New York; London: Routledge.

Carson, R. (1956). *The Sense of Wonder*. New York: Harper & Row.

Carson, R. (1962). *Silent Spring*. London: Penguin.

Carson, R. (1964). *The Sea*. London: MacGibbon & Kee Ltd.

Casetta, E., Marques da Silva, J. and Vecchi, D., eds. (2019). *From Assessing to Conserving Biodiversity*. History, Philosophy and Theory of the Life Sciences, 24. Cham: Springer Nature.

Cayton, K. (2012). *The Misleading Mind: How we create our own problems and how Buddhist psychology can help us solve them*. Novato, CA: New World Library.

Charles, A. D. (2020). *Outraged: Why everyone is shouting and no one is talking*. London: Bloomsbury Circus.

Chawla, L. (1999). Life paths into effective environmental action. *The Journal of Environmental Education*, 31, 15–26.

Clark, K. (1976). *Landscapes into Art*. London: John Murray.

Clark, T. (2011). *Hokusai's Great Wave*. London: The British Museum Press.

Clayton, S., ed. (2012). *Oxford Handbook of Environmental Psychology*. Oxford: Oxford University Press.

Clayton, S. and Myers, G., eds. (2015). *Conservation Psychology: Understanding and promoting human care for nature*. New York; London: Wiley-Blackwell.

Clayton, S. and Opotow, S., eds. (2003). *Identity and the Natural Environment: The psychological significance of nature*. Cambridge, MA: The MIT Press.

Clayton, S. D. and Saunders, C. D. (2012). Introduction: Environmental and conservation psychology. In Clayton, S., ed., *Oxford Handbook of Environmental Psychology*. Oxford: Oxford University Press. 1–10.

Clements, F. E. (1904). *The Development and Structure of Vegetation. Botanical Seminar: VII Studies in the Vegetation of the State, III Botanical Survey of Nebraska*. Lincoln, NE: University Publishing.

Clements, F. E. (1909). Darwin's influence upon plant geography and ecology. *The American Naturalist*, 43, 143–151.

Clements, F. E. (1916). *Plant Succession: An analysis of the development of vegetation*. Washington, DC: Carnegie Institute.

Clements, F. E. (1928). *Plant Succession and Indicators*. New York: H. W. Wilson.

Clements, F. E. (1935). Experimental ecology in the public service. *Ecology*, 16, 342–363.

Clements, F. E. (1936). Nature and structure of the climax. *Journal of Ecology*, 24, 252–284.

Clements, F. E. and Shelford, V. E. (1939). *Bioecology*. New York: Wiley.

Cocker, M. (2007). *Crow Country*. London: Jonathan Cape.

Cocker, M. and Mabey, R. (2005). *Birds Britannica*. London: Chatto & Windus.

Colautti, R. I. and MacIsaac, H. J. (2004). A neutral terminology to define 'invasive' species. *Diversity and Distributions*, 10, 135–141.

Cole, H. A. (1971). Objectives of biological pollution studies. *Philosophical Transactions of the Royal Society of London B*, 177, 277–278.

Cole, H. A. (1979). Pollution of the sea and its effects. *Proceedings of the Royal Society of London B*, 205, 167–230.

Cole, L. (2020). *Who Cares Wins: Reasons for optimism in our changing world*. London: Penguin.

Collingham, Y. and Huntley, B. (2000). Impacts of habitat fragmentation and patch size upon migration rates. *Ecological Applications*, 10, 131–144.

Colwell, M. (2018). *Curlew Moon*. London: William Collins.

Convention on Biological Diversity. (2020). *Aichi Biodiversity Targets*. www.cbd.int/sp/targets/

Cooper, A. (1988). *Doubt and Identity in Romantic Poetry*. New Haven, CT: Yale University Press.

Cooper, D. E. (2006). *A Philosophy of Gardens*. Oxford: Oxford University Press.

Cooper, D. E. and Palmer, J. A., eds. (1998). *Spirit of the Environment: Religion, value and environmental concern*. London: Routledge.

Cooper, G. (2001). Must there be a balance of nature? *Biology and Philosophy*, 16, 481–506.

Cosgrove, D. (1990). Environmental thought and action: Pre-modern and post-modern. *Transactions of the Institute of British Geography*, 15, 344–358.

Cosgrove, D. (2008). Images and imagination in 20th-century environmentalism: From the Sierras to the Poles. *Environment and Planning A*, 40, 1862–1880.

Cosgrove, D. and Daniels, S., eds. (1988). *The Iconography of Landscape*. Cambridge: Cambridge University Press.

Costanza, R., d'Arge, R., de Groot, R. et al. (1997). The value of the world's ecosystem services and natural capital. *Nature*, 387, 253–260.

Court, W. E. (1985). The doctrine of signatures or similitudes. *Trends in Pharmacological Sciences*, 6, 225–227.

Cracknell, D. (2019). *By the Sea: The therapeutic benefits of being in, on and by the water.* London: Aster.

Craik, K. H. (1986). Psychological reflections on landscape. In Penning-Rowsell, E. C. and Lowenthal, D., eds. *Landscape Meaning and Values*. London: Allen & Unwin. 48–63.

Craik, K. H. (1970). Environmental psychology. In Craik, K., Kleinmutz, R., Rosnow, R., Rosenthal, J., Cheyne, J. and Walters, R., eds., *New Directions in Psychology*, Vol. 4. New York: Holt, Rinehart and Winston. 1–222.

Crawford, R. (2002). *Poetry, Enclosure and the Vernacular Landscape 1700–1830.* Cambridge: Cambridge University Press.

Cronon, W. (1992). A place for stories: Nature, history and narrative. *Journal of American History*, 78, 1347–1376.

Cronon, W. (1995). The trouble with wilderness; or, getting back to the wrong nature. In Cronon, W., ed., *Uncommon Ground: Rethinking the human place in nature.* New York: W. W. Norton & Company. 69–90.

Cuddington, K. (2001). The 'balance of nature' metaphor and equilibrium in population ecology. *Biology and Philosophy*, 16, 463–479.

Culpeper, N. (1653). *Complete Herbal.* Available editions include: Culpeper, N. (1995), *Culpeper's Complete Herbal: A book of natural remedies of ancient ills.* London: The Wordsworth Collection Reference Library NTC/Contemporary Publishing Company.

Curtis, A. (2011). The use and abuse of vegetational concepts. Part II of *All Watched Over by Machines of Loving Grace*, BBC Television, 13 May. BBC documentary series written and produced by Adam Curtis.

Daitch, V., Kweon, B.-S., Larsen, L., Tyler, E. and Vining, J. (1996). Personal environmental histories: Expressions of self and place. *Human Ecology Review*, 3, SHE-VIII Proceedings – 1: Human Ecology: 'Livelihood and Liveability'. 19–31.

Daniels, S. (1993). *Fields of Vision: Landscape imagery and national identity in England and the United States.* Cambridge: Polity Press.

Daniels, S. and Endfield, G. H. (2009). Narratives of climate change: Introduction. *Journal of Historical Geography*, 35, 215–222.

Daniels, S., DeLyser, D., Entrikin, J. N. and Richardson, D., eds. (2011). *Envisioning Landscapes, Making Worlds: Geography and the humanities.* London: Routledge.

Darby, W. J. (2000). *Landscape and Identity: Geographies of nation and class in England.* Oxford: Berg.

Darier, É. (1999). Foucault against environmental ethics. In Darier, É., ed., *Discourses of the Environment.* London: Blackwell. 217–240.

Darwin, C. (1882). *The Formation of Vegetable Mould through the Action of Worms, with Observation of Their Habits.* London: John Murray.

Dasgupta, P. (2021). *The Economics of Biodiversity: The Dasgupta review.* London: HM Treasury.

Davies, D. (1988). The evocative symbolism of trees. In Cosgrove, D. and Daniels, S., eds., *The Iconography of Landscape*. Cambridge: Cambridge University Press. 32–42.

Davies, G. (2000). Science, observation and entertainment: Competing visions of postwar British natural history television, 1946–1967. *Ecumene*, 7, 432–459.

Davies, P. C. W. (1980). *Other Worlds: A portrait of nature in rebellion – space, superspace and the quantum universe*. New York: Simon & Schuster; 1990 London: Penguin Science Paperback).

Davis-Berman, J. and Berman, D. S. (1993). Therapeutic wilderness programs: Issues of professionalization in an emerging field. *Journal of Contemporary Psychotherapy*, 23, 127–134.

Dawkins, R. (1989). *The Extended Phenotype*. Oxford: Oxford University Press.

Dawkins, R. (1996). *The Blind Watchmaker*. New York: W. W. Norton & Company.

Deakin, R. (1999). *Waterlog: A swimmer's journey through Britain*. London: Chatto & Windus.

Deakin, R. (2007). *Wildwood: A journey through trees*. London: Hamish Hamilton.

Deakin, R. (2008). *Notes from Walnut Tree Farm*. London: Hamish Hamilton.

Debord, G. (1956). *Theory of Dérive*. Reprinted in Knabb, K. (1981), *Situationist International Anthology*. Berkeley, CA: Bureau of Public Secrets (see listings: www.notboredorg/bibliographyhtml).

Debord, G. (1977). *Society of the Spectacle*. Paris; London: Rebel Press AIM Publications.

De Bruyn, B. (2012). *Wolfgang Iser: A companion*. Berlin; Boston: De Gruyter.

de la Vega, E., Chalk, T. B., Wilson, P. A., Bysani, R. B. and Foster, G. L. (2020). Atmospheric CO_2 during the Mid-Piacenzian Warm Period and the M2 glaciation. *Science Report*, 10, 11002. doi.org/10.1038/s41598–020-67154-8

De Luc, J. A. (1806). Letter quoted in Rennie (1807) *Essays on the Natural History and Origin of Peat Moss* (cited from Clements, 1916, above).

Dennison, M. (2018). *Eternal Boy: The life of Kenneth Grahame*. London: Apollo Books, Head of Zeus.

de Witt, A. H. [Cited differently in different sources] see herein under Hedlund-de Witt.

Diamond, A. W. and Filion, F. L. (1987). *The Value of Birds*. Proceedings of a Symposium and Workshop XIX World Conference of the International Council for Bird Preservation, 1986, Queens University, Kingston, Ontario, Canada: ICBP Technical Publication No. 6.

Dimbleby, J. (1994). The environment and the human spirit. In Polley, R. and Woodman, J., eds., *Spirit of Nature: Poetry of the earth*. Tiverton: Devon Books. 64–68.

Doak, D. and Marvier, M. (2003). Predicting the effects of species loss on community stability. In Kareiva, P. and Levin, S. A., eds., *The Importance of Species: Perspectives on expendability and triage*. Princeton, NJ: Princeton University Press. 140–160.

Dolan, P. (2019). *Happy Ever After: Escaping the myth of the perfect life*. London: Allen Lane.

Doyle, J. (2011). *Mediating Climate Change*. Farnham: Ashgate.

Drury, W. H. (1998). *Chance and Change: Ecology for conservationists*. Berkeley: University of California Press.

Duerden, M. D. and Witt, P. A. (2010). The impact of direct and indirect experiences on the development of environmental knowledge, attitudes and behaviour. *Journal of Environmental Psychology*, 30, 379–392.

Dunn, S. T. (1905). *The Alien Flora of Britain*. London: West, Newman.

Dussault, A. C. (2019). Functional biodiversity and the concept of ecological function. In Casetta, E., Marques da Silva, J. and Vecchi, D., eds., *From Assessing to Conserving Biodiversity*. History, Philosophy and Theory of the Life Sciences, 24. Cham: Springer Nature. 297–316.

Dymond, D. (1990). *The Norfolk Landscape*. Bury St Edmunds: The Alastair Press.

Eagleton, T. (2000). *The Idea of Culture*. London: Blackwell Publishers.

Earth.org. (2020). World fails to meet single Aichi biodiversity target to stop destruction of nature – UN. 16 September. https://earth.org/un-report-aichi-targets/

Ebbesmeyer, C. C. (2006). Beachcombing science from bath toys. *Beachcombers' Alert*. Seattle, WA: 2005, archived 3 August 2006. http://beachcombersalert.org/RubberDuckies.html

Ebbesmeyer, C. C. and Ingraham, W. J. Jr. (1994). Pacific toy spill fuels ocean current pathways research. *Earth in Space*, 7(2), 7–9, 14. Archived 2006. https://web.archive.org/web/20061005100806/ www.agu.org/sci_soc/ducks.html; https://web.archive.org/web/20061110180943/ www.beachcombers.org/RubberDuckies.html

Eisenstein, C. (2018). *Climate: A new story*. Berkeley, CA: North Atlantic Books.

Eisenstein, C. (2013). *The More Beautiful World Our Hearts Know Is Possible*. Berkeley, CA: North Atlantic Books.

Elton, C. S. (1958). *The Ecology of Invasions by Animals and Plants*. London: Chapman & Hall.

Emerson, R. W. (1836). *Nature*. New York: James Munroe and Company.

Estés, C. P. (1992). *Women Who Run with the Wolves*. London: Random Books.

Evans, P. (2014). *Herbaceous: Illustrations by Kurt Jackson*. Toller Fratrum: Little Toller Books.

Evernden, N. (1985). *The Natural Alien*. Toronto: University of Toronto Press.

Evernden, N. (1992). *The Social Creation of Nature*. Baltimore: Johns Hopkins.

Extinction Rebellion. (2019). *This Is Not a Drill*. London: Penguin Books, Penguin Random House.

Fara, P. (2003a). *Sex, Botany and Empire*. Cambridge: Icon.

Fara, P. (2003b). Carl Linnaeus: Pictures and propaganda. *Endeavour*, 27, 14–15.

Fara, P. (2003c). Errata. *Endeavour*, 27, 109.

Ferber, M. (1999). *A Dictionary of Literary Symbols*. Cambridge: Cambridge University Press.

Feyerabend, P. (1999). *Conquest of Abundance: A tale of abstraction versus the richness of being*. Chicago: University of Chicago Press.

Fiedler, P. I., White, P. S. and Leidy, R. A. (1997). The paradigm shift in ecology and its implications for conservation. In Pickett, S. T. A., Ostfield, R. S., Shachak, M. and Likens, G. E., eds., *The Ecological Basis of Conservation:*

Heterogeneity, ecosystems and biodiversity. New York; London: Chapman & Hall. 83–92.

Finn, F. and Robinson, E. K. (n.d. but commonly cited as *c*.1920). *Birds of Our Country: Their eggs, nests, life, haunts and identification*. London: Hutchinson & Co.

Fischedicks, K. S. (1995). *Practices and Pluralism: A socio-historical analysis of early vegetation science, 1900–1950*. Amsterdam: KSF.

Fisher, P. (1998). *Wonder, the Rainbow, and the Aesthetics of Rare Experiences*. Cambridge, MA: Harvard University Press.

Fitter, C. (1995). *Poetry, Space, Landscape: Toward a new theory*. Cambridge: Cambridge University Press.

Fitter, R. S. R. (1945). *London's Natural History*. London: Collins New Naturalist 3.

Fitter, R. S. R. (1971). Black redstarts breeding in Britain 1964–68. *British Birds*, 64, 117–124.

Fogle, B. (2015). We need fewer exams and more wilderness in education. *The Guardian*, 17 December. www.theguardian.com/teacher-network/2015/dec/17/we-need-fewer-exams-and-more-wilderness-in-education?CMP=share_btn_fb

Foster, C. (2016). *Being a Beast*. London: Profile Books.

Foucault, M. (1971). *L'ordre du discours*. Paris: Gallimard. 1971 trans. "The Discourse on Language", appendix 215–237 in *Archaeology of Knowledge*, New York: Pantheon, 1972; see also Routledge, 1972, 2002.

Fowles, J. (2000). *The Tree*. London: Random House.

Frank, A. B. (1885). Über die auf Wurzelsymbiose beruhende Ernährung gewisser Bäume durch unterirdische Pilze [On the nourishing, via root symbiosis, of certain trees by underground fungi]. *Berichte der Deutschen Botanischen Gesellschaft* (in German), 3, 128–145.

Frank, A. B. and Trappe, J. M. (2005). On the nutritional dependence of certain trees on root symbiosis with below ground fungi (an English translation of A.B. Frank's classic paper of 1885). *Mycorrhiza*, 15, 267–275.

Friday, L., ed. (1997). *Wicken Fen: The making of a wetland nature reserve*. Colchester: Harley Books.

Friday, L. and Harvey, H. J. (1997). Sedge, litter and droves. In Friday, L., ed., *Wicken Fen: The making of a wetland nature reserve*. Colchester: Harley Books. 60–81.

Gaard, G. (2014). What's the story? Competing narratives of climate change and climate justice. *Forum for World Literature Studies*, 6, 272–291.

Gallagher, W. (1994). *The Power of Place: How our surroundings shape our thoughts, emotions, and actions*. New York: Harper Perennial.

Gandy, M. (2002). *Concrete and Clay: Reworking nature in New York City*. Cambridge, MA: The MIT Press.

Gandy, M. (2013). Marginalia: Aesthetics, ecology and urban wastelands. *Annals of the Association of American Geographers*, 103, 1301–1316.

Gandy, M. and Jasper, S., eds. (2020). *The Botanical City*. Berlin: Jovis Verlag.

Ganea, P. A., Canfield, C. F., Simons-Ghafari, K. and Chou, T. (2014). Do cavies talk? The effect of anthropomorphic picture books on children's knowledge about animals. *Frontiers in Psychology*, 10 April. doi.org/10.3389/fpsyg.2014.00283; http://journalfrontiersinorg/article/103389/fpsyg201400283/full

Gilbert, L. and Johnson, D. (2017). Plant–plant communication through common mycorrhizal networks. In Becard, G., ed., *How Plants Communicate with Their Biotic Environment*. Advances in Botanical Research, 82. Cambridge, MA: Academic Press. 83–97.

Glacken, C. J. (1967). *Traces on the Rhodian Shore: Nature and culture in western thought from ancient times to the end of the eighteenth century*. Los Angeles: University of California Press.

Godwin, H. (1975). *A History of the British Flora*. Cambridge: Cambridge University Press.

Gomez, M. (2000). *Essential Constable*. Bath: Paragon.

Good, P., Caesar, J., Bernie, D. et al. (2011). A review of recent developments in climate change science, Part I: Understanding of future change in the large-scale climate system. *Progress in Physical Geography*, 35, 281–296.

Goode, D. (2014). *Nature in Towns and Cities*. London: Collins New Naturalist 127.

Gould, H. F. (1841). The Bird Uncaged. In *Poems*. Boston, MA: Hilliard, Gray and Co. 93. http://name.umdl.umich.edu/BAD5889.0003.001

Gould, S. J. (1989). *Wonderful Life: The Burgess shale and the nature of history*. New York: W. W. Norton & Company.

Gould, S. J. (2004). The evolution of life on earth. *Scientific American*, 290, 93–100.

Gould, S. J. and Vrba, E. (1982). Exaptation – a missing term in the science of form. *Paleobiology*, 8, 4–15.

Gow, D. (2020). *Bringing Back the Beaver: The story of one man's quest to rewild Britain's waterways*. London: Chelsea Green Publishing.

Grahame, K. (1908). *The Wind in the Willows* (originally *Willows Whistle*). London: Methuen. Quotations from 1968 reprint of 1961 ed.

Gray, J. (2002). *Straw Dogs: Thoughts on humans and other animals*. London: Granta Books.

Gray, J. (2008). *Black Mass: Apocalyptic religion and the death of utopia*. London: Penguin.

Greitemeyer, T. (2013). Beware of climate change skeptic films. *Journal of Environmental Psychology*, 35, 105–109.

Grigson, G. (1958). *The Englishman's Flora*. London: Hart-Davis, MacGibbon. 1975 ed.

Gullone, E. (2000). The Biophilia Hypothesis and life in the 21st century: Increasing mental health or increasing pathology? *Journal of Happiness Studies*, 1, 293–322.

Hajer, M. (1995). *The Politics of Environmental Discourse*. Oxford: Oxford University Press.

Hale, B. (2016). *The Wild and the Wicked*. Cambridge, MA: The MIT Press.

Hall, D. W. (2014). *Romantic Naturalists, Early Environmentalists: An ecocritical Study, 1789–1912*. London: Routledge.

Hall, J. (1996). *Dictionary of Subjects and Symbols in Art*. London: John Murray.

Hammitt, W. E. and Madden, M. A. (1989). Cognitive dimensions of wilderness privacy: A field test and further explanation. *Leisure Sciences*, 11, 293–301.

Hample, M. (2016). Have climate sceptics taken the bait? What deconstruction of instrumental climate records can tell us about the politics of climate change. *Area*, 48, 244–248.

Hamsun, K. (1935). *The Growth of Soil*. London: Pan. 1980 ed.

Harding, S. (1986). *The Science Question in Feminism*. Ithaca, NY: Cornell University Press.

Hardy, A. C. (1958). *The Open Sea: Part I – The world of plankton*. London: Collins New Naturalist 34.

Hardy, A. C. (1959). *The Open Sea: Part II – Fish and fisheries*. London: Collins New Naturalist 37.

Hardy, T. (1898). In a wood. In *Wessex Poems and Other Verses*. New York: Harper. 39. www.bartlebycom/121/39html

Harman, P. M. (2009). *The Culture of Nature in Britain 1680–1860*. New Haven, CT: Yale University Press.

Harré, R. J., Brockmeier and Mühlhäusler, P. (1999). *Greenspeak: A study of environmental discourse*. Thousand Oaks, CA: Sage.

Harris, A. (2015). *Romantic Moderns: English writers, artists and the imagination from Virginia Woolf to John Piper*. London: Thames & Hudson.

Harrison, C. M. and Burgess, J. (1994). Social constructions of nature: A case study of conflicts over the development of Rainham Marshes. *Transactions of the Institute of British Geographers*, 19, 291–310.

Harrison, G. B. (1938). Introduction. In *Richard Jefferies: The story of my heart* (first published 1883). London: Penguin Illustrated Classics. 9–13.

Harrison, M. (2020). *The Stubborn Light of Things: A nature diary*. London: Faber & Faber.

Hartig, T. (2007). Three steps to understanding restorative environments as health resources. In Thompson, C. W. and Travlou, P., eds., *Open Space: People space*. London: Taylor & Francis. 163–179.

Hartig, T., Böök, A., Garvill, J., Olsson, T. and Gärling, T. (1996). Environmental influences on psychological restoration. *Scandinavian Journal of Psychology*, 37, 378–393.

Hartig, T., Evans, G., Jamner, L., Davis, D. and Gärling, T. (2003). Tracking restoration in natural and urban field settings. *Journal of Environmental Psychology*, 23, 109–123.

Hartig, T., Korpela, K., Evans, G. W. and Gärling, T. (1997). A measure of restorative quality in environments. *Scandinavian Housing and Planning Research*, 14, 175–194.

Hartig, T., Mang, M. and Evans, G. W. (1991). Restorative effects of natural environment experiences. *Environment and Behavior*, 23, 3–26.

Hartig, T., Mitchell, R., de Vries, S. and Frumkin, H. (2014). Nature and health. *Annual Review of Public Health*, 35, 207–228.

Hartman, R. P. (2010). *Ernst Haeckel: Art forms in nature*. Berlin: Prestel Verlag.

Hassall, C. (1964). *Rupert Brooke: A biography*. London: Faber & Faber.

Hedlund-de Witt,* A., de Boer, J. and Boersema, J. J. (2014). Exploring inner and outer worlds: A quantitative study of worldviews, environmental attitudes, and sustainable lifestyles. *Journal of Environmental Psychology*, 37, 40–54. [* In some sources cited as de Witt, A. H.]

Heidegger, M. (1950). *Der Ursprung des Kunstwerkes*, Reclam, Philipp, jun. GmbH, Verlag. 15–87. Trans. Hofstader, A. (1971), The origin of the work of art. In *Poetry, Language, Thought*. New York: Harper and Row. 143–212. Reprinted as Farrell, D. and Krell, D. F., eds. (2008), New York: Harper Collins 1st Harper Perennial Modern Thought ed.

Helsinger, E. (1997). *Rural Scenes and National Representation: Britain*. Princeton, NJ: Princeton University Press.

Henrey, B. (1975). *British Botanical and Horticultural Literature before 1800.* 3 vols. Oxford: Oxford University Press.

Herman, D., Jahn, M. and Ryan, M.-L., eds. (2010). *Routledge Encyclopedia of Narrative Theory*. New York; London: Routledge.

Herrick, R. (1648). To the virgins, to make much of time (Gather ye rosebuds). First published in 1648 as number 208 in a volume of verse entitled *Hesperides*. www.poets.org/poetsorg/poem/virgins-make-much-time

Herzog, T. R., Black, A. M., Kimberlee, A. F. and Knotts, D. J. (1997). Reflection and attentional recovery as distinctive benefits of restorative environments. *Journal of Environmental Psychology*, 17, 165–170.

Hinds, J. and Sparks, P. (2008). Engaging with the natural environment: The role of affective connection and identity. *Journal of Environmental Psychology*, 28, 109–120.

Hirsh, S. (2015). Jane Goodall on the power of "reaching people's hearts" as climate activism. *Green Matters*, 22 October. www.greenmatters.com/p/jane-goodall-climate-activism

Hitchmough, J. (2004). Naturalistic herbaceous vegetation for urban landscapes. In Dunnett, N. and Hitchmough, J., eds., *The Dynamic Landscape: Design, ecology and management of naturalistic urban planting*. London: Taylor & Francis. 172–245.

Hitchmough, J. (2005). What value exotic plant species? *ECOS*, 26, 28–32.

Hitchmough, J. (2008). New approaches to ecologically based, designed urban plant communities in Britain: Do these have any relevance in the USA? *Cities and the Environment*, 1, Article 10.

Hitchmough, J. and Dunnett, N. (2004). Introduction to naturalistic planting in urban landscapes. In Dunnett, N. and Hitchmough, J., eds., *The Dynamic Landscape: Design, ecology and management of naturalistic urban planting*. London: Taylor & Francis. 1–32.

Hoffman, A. J. (2011). Talking past each other? Cultural framing of sceptical and convinced logics in the climate change debate. *Organization and Environment*, 24, 3–33.

Hohn, D. (2012). *Moby-Duck: The true story of 28,800 bath toys lost at sea and of the beachcombers, oceanographers, environmentalists, and fools, including the author, who went in search of them*. New York: Viking.

Holdgate, M. W. and Woodman, M. J. (1978). *The Breakdown and Restoration of Ecosystems*. Berlin; Heidelberg: Plenum Springer Nature.

Hollings, C. S. (1986). The resilience of terrestrial ecosystems: Local surprise and global change. In Clark, W. C. and Mann, R. E., eds., *Sustainable Development and the Biosphere*. Cambridge: Cambridge University Press. 217–232.

Holloway, S. J. and Glue, D. E. (1999). *Site Action Plan for Black Redstarts Phoenicurus ochruros in the Deptford Creek Area, Greenwich, London*. BTO Research Report No. 212. Thetford: British Trust for Ornithology.

Horrell, D. G., Hunt, C. and Southgate, C. (2008). Appeals to the Bible in ecotheology and environmental ethics: A typology of hermeneutical stances. *Studies in Christian Ethics*, 21, 219–238.

Hoskins, W. G. (1955). *The Making of the English Landscape*. London: Hodder & Stoughton.

Hudson, W. H. (1903). *Hampshire Days*. London: Longmans, Green & Co.

Hudson, W. H. (1909). *Afoot in England*. London: Hutchinson & Co.

Hudson, W. H. (1910). *A Shepherd's Life*. London: Methuen & Co.

Hugo, V. (1866). *Toilers of the Sea* (*Les travailleurs de la mer*). London: Routledge & Sons; quotations from 1911 Everyman ed. London: J. M. Dent.

Hulme, M. (2009). *Why We Disagree about Climate Change*. Cambridge: Cambridge University Press.

Hulme, M. (2014). Attributing weather extremes to climate change: A review. *Progress in Physical Geography*, 38, 499–511.

Hulme, M. (2019). *Contemporary Climate Change Debates*. London: Routledge/Taylor & Francis.

Hulme, M. (2020). Why Extinction Rebellion's tactics are deeply misguided. mikehulme.org, 20 February. https://mikehulme.org/why-extinction-rebellions-tactics-are-deeply-misguided/

Huntley, B. (1998). The dynamic response of plants to environmental change and the resulting risks of extinction. In Mace, G. M., Balmford, A. and Ginsburg, J., eds., *Conservation in a Changing World*. Cambridge: Cambridge University Press. 69–85.

Impelluso, L. (2004). *Nature and Its Symbols*. Los Angeles: Getty Publications.

Impelluso, L. (2007). *Gardens in Art*. Los Angeles: Getty Publications.

Intergovernmental Panel on Climate Change. *Reports*. 1990 onwards: www.ipcc.ch/reports/

Iser, W. (1972). The reading process: A phenomenological approach. *New Literary History*, 3, 279–299.

Jackson, K. (2016). When asked to show evidence of man-made warming, scientists can't do it. *Investors Business Daily Politics*, 25 October. www.investors.com/politics/commentary/when-asked-to-show-evidence-of-man-made-warming-scientists-cant-do-it/

James, P. D. (1986). Interview with P. D. James. *The Face* Magazine, 80, December.

James, S. P. (2016). Protecting nature for the sake of human beings. *Ratio*, 29, 213–227. www.ingentaconnect.com/content/bpl/rati/2016/00000029/00000002/art00007

Jax, K. (2010). *Ecosystem Functioning*. Cambridge: Cambridge University Press.

Jefferies, R. (1938). *The Story of My Heart*. London: Penguin Illustrated Classics ed. (first published 1883).

Jeffers, R. (1989). Sinverguenza. In *The Collected Poetry of Robinson Jeffers, Vol. 2: 1928–1938*. Redwood City, CA: Stanford University Press. 458.

Jepson, P. and Cain, B. (2020). *Rewilding: The radical new science of ecological recovery*. London: Icon Books.

Jex, C. (2016). Scientist: No evidence of extreme drought and floods in the twentieth century. Climate records show no evidence of increasing extremes in wet-dry climate in the twentieth century that is projected by current climate models, shows new study. *Science Nordic*, 6 April. https://sciencenordic.com/climate-change-climate-history-rainfall/scientist-no-evidence-of-extreme-drought-and-floods-in-the-twentieth-century/1431910

Job, D. (1999). Multicultural biogeography. In Job, D., Day, C. and Smyth, T., eds., *Beyond the Bikesheds: Fresh approaches to field work in the school locality*. Sheffield: Geographical Association. 75–78.

Johnson, D. and Gilbert, L. (2017). Mycorrhizal fungal networks as plant communication systems. In Dighton, J. and White, J. F., eds., *The Fungal Community: Its organization and role in the ecosystem* (4th ed.). Boca Raton, FL: CRC Press. 539–548.

Johnson, N. C. (2011). *Nature Displaced, Nature Displayed: Order and beauty in botanical gardens*. London: I. B. Taurus.

Jones, L. P., Turvey, S. T., Massimino, D. and Papworth, S. K. (2020). Investigating the implications of shifting baseline syndrome on conservation. *People and Nature*, 2, 1131–1144. doi.org/10.1002/pan3.10140

Jongman, R. and Pungetti, G. (2004). *Ecological Networks and Greenways: Concept, design, implementation*. Cambridge: Cambridge University Press.

Jorgensen, A., Hitchmough, J. and Dunnett, N. (2007). Woodland as a setting for housing-appreciation and fear and the contribution to residential satisfaction and place identity in Warrington New Town, UK. *Landscape and Urban Planning*, 79, 273–287.

Kahn, P. H. (1997). Developmental psychology and the Biophilia Hypothesis: Children's affiliation with nature. *Developmental Review*, 17, 1–61.

Kahn, P. H. (2001). *The Human Relationship with Nature: Development and culture*. Cambridge, MA: The MIT Press.

Kals, E. and Müller, M. M. (2012). Emotion and environment. In Clayton, S., ed., *The Oxford Handbook of Environmental and Conservation Psychology*. Oxford: Oxford University Press. 128–149.

Kamieński, F. (1882). Les organes végétatifs de *Monotropa hypopitys L. Mémoires de la Société nat. des Sciences naturelles et mathém. de Cherbourg*, ser. 3, tom. 24. (Republished and translated in Berch, S. M., Massicotte, H. B. and Tackaberry, L. E. (2005), Re-publication of a translation of 'The vegetative organs of Monotropa hypopitys L.' published by F. Kamienski in 1882, with an update on Monotropa mycorrhizas. Archived 20 December 2016 at the Wayback Machine Mycorrhiza 15:323–332.)

Kantor, M. (2003). *Distancing: A guide to avoidance and avoidant personality disorder*. Westport, CT: Praeger Publishers. (Revised from 1993 ed.).

Kaplan, S. (1995). The restorative benefits of nature: Towards an integrative framework. *Journal of Environmental Psychology*, 15, 169–182.

Kaplan, S. and Berman, M. G. (2010). Directed attention as a common resource for executive functioning and self-regulation. *Perspectives on Psychological Science*, 5, 43–57.

Kaplan, S. and Kaplan, R. (1989). *Cognition and Environment: Functioning in an uncertain world*. Ann Arbor, MI: Ulrich's.

Kareiva, P. and Levin, S. A., eds. (2003). *The Importance of Species: Perspectives on expendability and triage*. Princeton, NJ: Princeton University Press.

Katcher, A. and Wilkins, G. (1993). Dialogue with animals: Its nature and culture. In Kellert, S. R. and Wilson, E. O., eds., *The Biophilia Hypothesis*. Washington, DC: Island Press. 173–200.

Katz, C. (1998). Whose nature, whose culture? Private productions of space and the 'reservation' of nature. In Braun, B. and Castree, N., eds., *Remaking Reality: Nature at the millennium*. London: Routledge. 46–63.

Kavanagh, P. (1947). Stony grey soil. In *A Soul for Sale*. London: Macmillan. 26.

Kearns, G. (1998). The virtuous circle of facts and values in the New Western History. *Annals of the Association of American Geographers*, 88, 377–409.

Keeble, E., ed. (2000). *The Collected Poems of Kathleen Raine*. Ipswich: Golgonooza Press.

Kekes, J. (1994). Pluralism and the value of life. In Paul, E. F. and Miller, F. F., eds., *Cultural Pluralism and Moral Knowledge*. Cambridge: Cambridge University Press. 44–60.

Kellert, S. R. (1993). The biological basis for human values of nature. In Kellert, S. R. and Wilson, E. O., eds., *The Biophilia Hypothesis*. Washington, DC: Island Press. 42–69.

Kellert, S. R. (2012). *Birthright: People and nature in the modern world*. New Haven, CT: Yale University Press.

Kellert, S. R. and Wilson, E. O. (1993). *The Biophilia Hypothesis*. Washington, DC: Island Press.

Kerr, R. (2013). In the hot seat. *Science*, 342, 688–689.

Keulartz, J. (1998). *The Struggle for Nature: A critique of radical ecology*. London: Routledge.

Keulartz, J. (2007). Using metaphors in restoring nature. *Nature and Culture*, 2, 27–48.

Keulartz, J. (2012). The emergence of enlightened anthropocentrism in ecological restoration. *Nature and Culture*, 7, 48–71.

Kidner, D. (2007). Depression and the natural world: Towards a critical ecology of psychological distress. *Critical Psychology*, 19, 123–146.

King, A. M. (2003). *Bloom: The botanical vernacular in the English novel*. Oxford: Oxford University Press.

Kingsnorth, P. (2016). Paul Kingsnorth: 'We imagine how it feels to be a character, why can't we imagine how the land feels?' *The Guardian*, Books, 23 July 2016, modified 20 September 2016. www.theguardian.com/books/2016/jul/23/paul-kingsnorth-imagine-how-land-feels

Kingsolver, B. (2012). *Flight Behaviour*. London: Faber & Faber.

Klonk, C. (1996). *Science and the Perception of Nature: British landscape art in the late eighteenth and early nineteenth centuries*. New Haven, CT: Yale University Press.

Knight, M. (1955). *A Cuckoo in the House*. London: Methuen.

Koch, P. (1994). *Solitude: A philosophical encounter*. Chicago: Open Court.

Kohn, M. (2004). *A Reason for Everything: Natural selection and the English imagination*. London: Faber & Faber.

Kononova, M. M. (1966). *Soil Organic Matter*. Oxford: Pergamon.

Kornberg, H. (1982). Oil pollution of the sea: An assessment. *Philosophical Transactions of the Royal Society of London B*, 297, 429–432.

Krakauer, J. (1996). *Into the Wild*. London: Villard (Random House). Quotations in text from 1998 ed. London: Pan Books.

Kricher, J. (2009). *The Balance of Nature: Ecology's enduring myth*. Princeton, NJ: Princeton University Press.

Kriz, K. D. (1997). *The Idea of the English Landscape Painter: Genius as alibi in the early nineteenth century*. New Haven, CT: Yale University Press.

Krznaric, R. (2020). *The Good Ancestor: How to think long term in a short-term world*. London: Ebury Press (Penguin).

Lackey, R. T. (2001). Values, policy and ecosystem health. *Bio-Science*, 51, 437–443.

Lackey, R. T. (2004). Societal values and the proper role of restoration ecologists. *Frontiers in Ecology and the Environment*, 2, 45–46.

Lackey, R. T. (2007). Science, scientists, and policy advocacy. US Environmental Protection Agency Papers, No. 142. https://digitalcommons.unl.edu/usepapapers/142

Lakoff, G. and Johnson, M. (1980). *Metaphors We Live By*. Chicago: University of Chicago Press.

Landor, W. S. (1849). *Dying Speech of an Old Philosopher*. www.poetryfoundation.org/poems-and-poets/poems/detail/44562

Landry, D. (2001). *The Invention of the Countryside: Hunting, walking and ecology in English literature, 1671–1831*. Basingstoke: Palgrave.

Lannoo, M. J. (2010). *Leopold's Shack and Rickett's Lab: The emergence of environmentalism*. Berkeley: University of California Press.

Larson, R. W. (1990). The solitary side of life: An examination of the time people spend alone from childhood to old age. *Developmental Review*, 10, 155–183.

Latour, B. (1994a). Pragmatogonies – a mythical account of how humans and nonhumans swap properties. *American Behavioural Scientist*, 37, 791–808.

Latour, B. (1994b). On technical mediation – philosophy, sociology, genealogy. *Common Knowledge*, 3, 29–64.

Latour, B. (2004). *Politics of Nature: How to bring the sciences into politics*. Cambridge, MA: Harvard University Press.

Lawton, J. (2010). *Making Space for Nature*. London: DEFRA (Department of Environment, Food and Rural Affairs).

Leary, D., ed. (1990). *Metaphors in the History of Psychology*. Cambridge: Cambridge University Press.

Lefebvre, H. (1991). *Production of Space* [trans. D. Nicholson-Smith from the original *La production de l'espace*, 1905]. Oxford: Basil Blackwell.

Lehman, J. G. (2010). *An Introduction to the Overton Window of Political Possibility*. Midland, MI: Mackinac Center for Public Policy. www.mackinac.org/12481

Leigh, E. G. Jr. (2003). Social conflict, biological ignorance, and trying to agree which species are expendable. In Kareiva, P. and Levin, S. A., eds., *The Importance of Species: Perspectives on expendability and triage*. Princeton, NJ: Princeton University Press. 239–259.

Lejano, R., Ingram, M. and Ingram, I. (2013). *The Power of Narrative in Environmental Networks*. Cambridge, MA: The MIT Press.

Lekan, T. M. (2004). *Imagining the Nation in Nature: Landscape preservation and German identity, 1885–1945*. Cambridge, MA: Harvard University Press.

Lenoir, T. (1997). *Instituting Science: The cultural production of scientific disciplines*. Redwood City, CA: Stanford University Press.

Leong, L. Y. C., Fischer, R. and McClure, J. (2014). Are nature lovers more innovative? The relationship between connectedness with nature and cognitive styles. *Journal of Environmental Psychology*, 40, 57–63.

Leopold, A. (1949). *A Sand County Almanac*. Oxford: Oxford University Press.

Levis, C., Costa, F. R. C., Bongers, F. et al. (2017). Persistent effects of pre-Columbian plant domestication on Amazonian forest composition. *Science*, 355, 925–931.

Lew, J. (2017). Women who changed the way we see nature. *MNN*, 19 January. www.mnn.com/earth-matters/wilderness-resources/stories/women-who-changed-way-we-see-nature [Updated source: Lew, J. (2020), *Treehugger*, 6 March, www.treehugger.com/women-who-changed-way-we-see-nature-4863368]

Lewicka, M. (2011). Place attachment: How far have we come in the last 40 years? *Journal of Environmental Psychology*, 31, 207–230.

Liang, M., Johnson, M., Burslem, F. R. P. D. et al. (2020). Soil fungal networks maintain local dominance of ectomycorrhizal trees. *Nature Communication*, 11, 2636. doi.org/10.1038/s41467-020-16507-y

Lindenmuth, B. (2012). Narrative traps. *Do Some Damage*, 3 September. www.dosomedamage.com/2012/09/narrative-traps.html

Ljungqvist, F. C., Krusic, P. J., Sundqvist, H. S., Zorita, E., Brattström, G. and Frank, D. (2016). Northern Hemisphere hydroclimate variability over the past twelve centuries. *Nature*, 532, 94–98. www.nature.com/nature/journal/v532/n7597/full/nature17418.html

Lock, J. M., Friday, L. E. and Bennett, T. J. (1997). The management of the Fen. In Friday, L., ed., *Wicken Fen: The making of a wetland nature reserve*. Colchester: Harley Books. 213–254.

Lock, L. and Cook, K. (1998). The little egret in Britain: A successful colonist. *British Birds*, 91(7), 273–280.

Lomborg, B. (2020). *False Alarm: How climate change panic costs us trillions, hurts the poor, and fails to fix the planet*. New York: Basic Books-Hachette.

London, J. (1903). *The Call of the Wild*. New York: MacMillan.

London, J. (1939). *White Fang*. London: Methuen.

Long, C. R., Seburn, M., Averill, J. R. and More, T. A. (2003). Solitude experiences: Varieties, settings, and individual differences. *Personality and Social Psychology Bulletin*, 29, 578–583.

Lopez, B. (2014). *Arctic Dreams*. London: Vintage.

Lorimer, J. (2006). Nonhuman charisma: Which species trigger our emotions and why? *ECOS*, 27, 20–27.

Lorimer, J. (2007). Nonhuman charisma. *Environment and Planning D: Society and Space*, 25, 911–932.

Lorimer, J. (2012). Multinatural geography for the Anthropocene. *Progress in Human Geography*, 36, 593–612.

Lorimer, J. (2015). *Wildlife in the Anthropocene: Conservation after nature*. Minneapolis: University of Minnesota Press.

Louafi, K. (2013). *Green Islands in the City: 25 ideas for urban gardens*. Berlin: Jovis Verlag.

Louv, R. (2005). *Last Child in the Woods: Saving our children from nature-deficit disorder*. New York: Workman Publishing Company.

Ludwin, R. (1999). *Cascadia Megathrust Earthquakes in Pacific Northwest Indian Myths and Legends*. University of Washington Dept of Earth and Space Sciences. 29 December Draft. www.mrbrewerorg/Documents/Theses/IslandWood/Web/PDFs/EARTHQUAKEMYTHS%20AND%20LEGENDSpdf

Lynch, T. (2008). *Xerophilia*. Lubbock: Texas Tech University Press.

Lynch, T., Glotfelty, C. and Armbruster, K., eds. (2012). *The Bioregional Imagination: Literature ecology and place*. Athens, GA: University of Georgia Press.

Lyon, J. and Buffon, Georges-Louis Leclerc. (2012). The 'Initial Discourse' to Buffon's "Histoire Naturelle": The first complete English translation. *Journal of the History of Biology*, 9, 133–181.

Mabey, R. (1980). *The Common Ground: A place for nature in Britain's future?* London: Hutchinson.

Mabey, R. (1998). *Flora Britannica: The concise edition*. London: Random House.

Mabey, R. (2005). *Nature Cure*. London: Vintage Books.

Mabey, R. (2010). *Weeds: How vagabond plants gatecrashed civilisation and changed the way we think about nature*. London: Profile Books.

Mabey, R. (2013). In defence of nature writing. *The Guardian*, 18 July. www .theguardiancom/books/2013/jul/18/richard-mabey-defence-nature-writing

Mabey, R. (2015). *The Cabaret of Plants: Botany and the imagination*. London: Profile Books.

Macdonald, B. (2019). *Rebirding: Rewilding Britain and its birds*. London: Pelagic Publishing.

Macdonald, H. (2006). *Falcon*. London: Reaktion Books Ltd.

Macdonald, H. (2014). *H Is for Hawk*. London: Jonathan Cape.

Macdonald, H. (2020). *Vesper Flights*. London: Jonathan Cape.

Macfarlane, R. (2003). *Mountains of the Mind*. London: Granta.

Macfarlane, R. (2005). Introduction to Baker, A. H., *The Peregrine*. New York: New York Review Books. vii–xv.

Macfarlane, R. (2007). *The Wild Places*. London: Granta.

Macfarlane, R. (2012). *The Old Ways: A journey on foot*. London: Hamish Hamilton.

Macfarlane, R. (2014). Introduction to Watkins, A., *The Old Straight Track* (first published 1925). London: Head of Zeus. xxi–xxv.

Macfarlane, R. (2015). *Landmarks*. London: Hamish Hamilton.

Macfarlane, R. (2016). Generation Anthropocene: How humans have altered the planet for ever. *The Guardian*, 1 April, amended on 6 April. www. theguardian com/books/2016/apr/01/generation-anthropocene-altered-planet-for-ever

Macfarlane, R. (2019). Should this tree have the same rights as you? *The Guardian*, 2 November. www.theguardian.com/books/2019/nov/02/trees-have-rights-too-robert-macfarlane-on-the-new-laws-of-nature.

Mack, J. (2011). *The Sea: A cultural history*. London: Reaktion Books.

MacKay, D. (2009). *Sustainable Energy – without the hot air*. Cambridge: UIT Cambridge Ltd. See also under Anonymous (2016) above.

MacLean, G., Landry, D. and Ward, J. P., eds. (1999). *The Country and the City Revisited: England and the politics of culture*. Cambridge: Cambridge University Press.

Macnaghten, P. and Urry, J. (1998). *Contested Natures*. London: Sage.

Maguire, S. (2003). *Flora Poetica: The Chatto book of botanical verse*. London: Chatto & Windus.

Mahood, M. (2008). *The Poet as Botanist*. Cambridge: Cambridge University Press.

Maitland, S. (2012). *Gossip from the Forest: The tangled roots of our forest and fairytales*. London: Granta Books.

Mancha, R. M. and Yoder, C. Y. (2015). Cultural antecedents of green behavioural intent: An environmental theory of planned behaviour. *Journal of Environmental Psychology*, 43, 145–154.

Marin, L. (2006). The narrative trap: The conquest of power. *Economy and Society*, 229–251. Published online 28 July. doi.org/10.1080/03085148700000005

Marcus, G. (1989). *Lipstick Traces: A secret history of the twentieth century*. London: Secker & Warburg.

Marren, P. (2002). *Nature Conservation: A review of the conservation of wildlife in Britain 1950–2001*. London: Collins New Naturalist 91.

Marsden, P. (2014). *Rising Ground: A search for the spirit of place*. London: Granta Publications.

Marsh, E. (1942). *Rupert Brooke: The collected poems* (with a memoir by Edward Marsh). London; Beccles: William Clowes and Sons Ltd.

Marsh, G. P. (1864). *Man and Nature, or, physical geography as modified by human activity* (1965 ed.). Lowenthal, D., ed., Cambridge, MA: Harvard University Press.

Maslin, M. (2021). *How to Save Our Planet: The facts*. London: Penguin.

Mason, M. (1997). Democratising nature? The political morality of wilderness preservationists. *Environmental Values*, 6, 281–306.

Massingham, H. J. (1924). *Sanctuaries for Birds and How to Make Them*. London: G. Bell.

Massingham, H. J. (1936). *English Downland*. London: B. T. Batsford – The Face of Britain Series.

Mather, G. (2014). *The Psychology of Visual Art: Eye, brain and art*. Cambridge: Cambridge University Press.

Matless, D. (1998). *Landscape and Englishness*. London: Reaktion Books.

Matless, D. (2014). *In the Nature of Landscape: Cultural geography of the Norfolk Broads*. London: Wiley Blackwell.

Matulis, B. S. and Moyer, J. R. (2016). Beyond inclusive conservation: The value of pluralism, the need for agonism, and the case for social instrumentalism. *Conservation Letters: A Journal for the Society of Conservation Biology*, 10, 279–287. doi.org/10.1111/conl.12281

Maxwell, G. (1960). *Ring of Bright Water*. London: Longman Green and Co.

May, A. (2016). CO_2, good or bad? *Watts Up With That?*, 5 December. https://wattsupwiththat.com/2016/12/05/co2-good-or-bad/

May, J. (1996). In search of authenticity off and on the beaten track. *Environment and Planning, D: Society and Space*, 14, 709–736.

Maycock, P. F. (1967). Jozef Paczoski: Founder of the science of phytosociology. *Ecology*, 48, 1031–1034.

McAnulty, D. (2020). *Diary of a Young Naturalist*. Dorset: Little Toller Books.

McCallum, I. (2005). *Ecological Intelligence: Rediscovering ourselves in nature*. Golden, CO: Fulcrum.

McCarthy, J. (2019). Jacinda Ardern says economic growth is pointless if people aren't thriving. *Global Citizen*, 25 September. www.globalcitizen.org/en/content/jacinda-ardern-goalkeepers-unga-2019/

McCarthy, M. (2016). *The Moth Snowstorm: Nature and joy*. London: John Murray.

McCarthy, M., Mynott, J. and Marren, P. (2020). *The Consolation of Nature: Spring in the time of coronavirus*. London: Hodder & Stoughton.

McClatchy, J. D. (2001). *Poems of the Sea*. London: Everyman's Library (Alfred A. Knopf; Penguin Random House).

McComas, K. and Shanahan, J. (1999). Telling stories about global climate change: Measuring the impact of narratives on issue cycles. *Communication Research*, 26, 30–57.

McDonald, R. I., Chai, H. Y. and Newell, B. (2015). Personal experience and the 'psychological distance' of climate change: An integrative review. *Journal of Environmental Psychology*, 44, 109–118.

McGrath, A. (2002). *The Reenchantment of Nature: The denial of religion and the ecological crisis*. New York: Doubleday.

McGrath, A. (2003). *The Reenchantment of Nature: Science, religion and the human sense of wonder*. London: Hodder & Stoughton.

McKibben, W. (1989). *The End of Nature*. London. 1989 Anchor; 1990 Random House.

McMahan, E. A. and Estes, D. (2015). The effect of contact with natural environments on positive and negative affect: A meta-analysis. *Journal of Positive Psychology*, 10, 507–519.

Meinard, Y., Coq, S. and Schmid, B. (2019). The vagueness of 'biodiversity' and its implications in conservation practice. In Casetta, E., Marques da Silva, J. and Vecchi, D., eds., *From Assessing to Conserving Biodiversity*. History, Philosophy and Theory of the Life Sciences, 24. Cham: Springer Nature. 353–374.

Meinig, D. W. (1979). *The Interpretation of Ordinary Landscapes*. Oxford: Oxford University Press.

Mellanby, K. (1981). *Farming and Wildlife*. London: Collins New Naturalist 67.

Mellor, L. (2014). The lure of wilderness. In Westling, L., ed., *The Cambridge Companion to Literature and Environment*. Cambridge: Cambridge University Press. 104–117.

Mentz, S. (2009). Toward a blue cultural studies: The sea, maritime culture, and early modern English literature. *Literature Compass*, 6, 997–1013.

Merrill, L. L. (1989). *The Romance of Victorian Natural History*. Oxford: Oxford University Press.

Meyer, R. (2017). The Amazon Rainforest was profoundly changed by ancient humans. *The Atlantic*, 2 March. www.theatlantic.com/science/archive/2017/03/its-now-clear-that-ancient-humans-helped-enrich-the-amazon/518439/.

Miles, J. (1965). *Pathetic Fallacy in the Nineteenth Century: A study of the changing relationship between object and emotion*. New York: Octagon Books Inc.

Millennium Ecosystem Assessment. (2005). *Ecosystems and Human Well-Being*. Synthesis. Washington, DC: Island Press World Resources Institute.

Milton, J. (1667). *Paradise Lost*. See also: Milton, J. (1674), *Paradise Lost* (2nd ed.), London; Milton, J. (2000), *Paradise Lost*. New York: Penguin.

Milton, K. (2002). *Loving Nature: Towards an ecology of emotion*. London: Routledge.

Mitchell, W. J. T. (2002). *Landscape and Power*. Chicago: University of Chicago Press.

Modell, A. (1993). *The Private Self*. Cambridge, MA: Harvard University Press.

Monbiot, G. (2013). *Feral: Rewilding the land, the sea and human life*. London: Allen Lane.

Monsarrat, N. (1951). *The Cruel Sea*. London: Cassell.

Moon, K., Blackman, D., Adams, V., et al. (2019). Expanding the role of social science in conservation through an engagement with philosophy, methodology, and methods. *Methods in Ecology and Evolution*, 10, 294–302.

Mooney, H. A. and Hobbs, J. (2000). *Invasive Species in a Changing World*. Washington, DC: Island Press.

Moorhouse, T. (2014). *The River Singers*. Oxford: Oxford University Press.

Morar, N., Toadvine, T. and Bohannan, B. J. M. (2017). Biodiversity at twenty-five years: Revolution or red herring? *Ethics, Policy and Environment*, 18, 16–29.

Morton, T. (2007). *Ecology without Nature: Rethinking environmental aesthetics*. Cambridge, MA: Harvard University Press.

Morton, T. (2008). John Clare's dark ecology. *Studies in Romanticism*, 47, 179–193.

Morton, T. (2010). *The Ecological Thought*. Cambridge, MA: Harvard University Press.

Morton, T. (2016). *Dark Ecology: For a logic of future coexistence*. New York: Columbia University Press.

Moss, B. R. and Kinne, O., eds. (2012). *Liberation Ecology: The reconciliation of natural and human cultures*: Oldendorf: International Ecology Institute, Excellence in Ecology 24.

Mühlhäusler, P. (1995). The interdependence of linguistics and biological diversity. In Myers, D., ed., *The Politics of Multiculturalism in the Asia Pacific Northern Territory*. Darwin: Charles Darwin University Press. 154–161.

Mühlhäusler, P. (2000). Humboldt, Whorf and the roots of ecolinguistics. In Putz, M. and Verspoor, M. J., eds., *Explorations in Linguistic Relativity*. Current Issues in Linguistic Theory, 199. Amsterdam: John Benjamins. 89–99.

Muldrow, M. Jr., Parsons, E. C. M. and Jonas, R. (2020). Shifting baseline syndrome among coral reef scientists. *Humanities and Social Sciences Communications*, 7, Article 42. doi.org/10.1057/s41599–020-0526-0

Murphy, P. D., ed. (1998). *Literature of Nature: An international sourcebook*. Chicago: Fitzroy Dearborn Publishers.

Myers, B. (2018). *Under the Rock: The poetry of place*. London: Elliott and Thompson Ltd.

Nagel, T. (1986). *The View from Nowhere*. Oxford: Oxford University Press.

Nagy, K. and Johnson, P. D. II, eds. (2013). *Trash Animals: How we live with nature's filthy, feral, invasive, and unwanted species*. Minneapolis: University of Minnesota Press.

Nash, P. (1949). *Outline: An autobiography and other writings*. London: Faber & Faber.

Nash, R. (1967). *Wilderness and the American Mind*. New Haven, CT: Yale University Press (5th ed. 2014).

National Biodiversity Network. (2019). *State of Nature*. Nottingham: National Biodiversity Network. https://nbn.org.uk/stateofnature2019/; https://nbn.org.uk/wp-content/uploads/2019/09/State-of-Nature-2019-UK-full-report.pdf; https://nbn.org.uk/wp-content/uploads/2019/09/State-of-Nature-2019-UK-summary.pdf

Necker, L. A. (1832). Observations on some remarkable optical phaenomena seen in Switzerland; and on an optical phaenomenon which occurs on viewing a figure of a crystal or geometrical solid. *London and Edinburgh Philosophical Magazine and Journal of Science*, 1, 329–337.

Ngwenya, N., Helfand, R., Mcnamara, A. et al. (2020). A call for collective crisis leadership. *Oryx*, 54, 431–432. doi.org/10.1017/S0030605320000496

Nightingale, A. J. (2016). Adaptive scholarship and situated knowledges: Hybrid methodologies and plural epistemologies in climate change and adaptation research. *Area*, 48, 41–47.

Nin, A. (1961). *Seduction of the Minotaur.* Athens, OH: Swallow Press; Ohio University Press.

Noakes, V. (1985). *Edward Lear: The life of a wanderer.* London: BBC Crown Publications.

Norton, B. (1988). Commodity, amenity and morality: The limits of quantification in valuing biodiversity. In Wilson, E. O., ed., *Biodiversity*. Washington, DC: National Academy Press. 200–205.

Novak, B. (2007). *Nature and Culture: American landscape and painting, 1825–1875.* New York; London: Oxford University Press.

Odum, H. T. (1971). *Environment, Power and Society*. Chichester: Wiley.

Odum, E. P. (1978). *The Value of Wetlands: A hierarchical approach.* Proceedings of the National Symposium on Wetlands. New York: American Water Resources Association.

Oliver, P. J. (1997). The breeding birds of inner London, 1966–94. *British Birds*, 90, 211–225.

Olney, J. (1972). *Metaphors of Self: The meaning of autobiography*. Princeton, NJ: Princeton University Press.

Orians, G. H. (1986). An ecological and evolutionary approach to landscape aesthetics. In Penning-Rowsell, E. and Lowenthal, D., eds., *Landscape Meaning and Values*. London: Allen & Unwin. 3–25.

Orians, G. H. (2014). *Snakes, Sunrises and Shakespeare: How evolution shapes our loves and fears*. Chicago: University of Chicago Press.

Orsman, C. (1999). *South: An Antarctic journey*. London: Faber & Faber.

Ortony, A., ed. (1993). *Metaphor and Thought.* Cambridge: Cambridge University Press.

Osler, M. (1990). An essayist in the garden. (Quoted from Wheeler, 1998, below, 21–22, cited as 'A word about boxes'.) *Hortus*, 16.

Oswald, F. I. (1884). Changes in the climate of North America. *The North American Review*, 138, 362–373.

Owens, S. (2000). Engaging the public: Information and deliberation in environmental policy. *Environment and Planning A*, 32, 1141–1148.

Owens, S. (2015). *Knowledge, Policy, and Expertise: The UK Royal Commission on Environmental Pollution 1970–2011.* Oxford: Oxford University Press.

Owens, S. (2020). *Spirit of Place: Artists, writers & the British landscape.* London: Thames & Hudson.

Padovani, R. J., Salisbury, A., Bostock, H., Roy, D. B. and Thomas, C. D. (2020). Introduced plants as novel Anthropocene habitats for insects. *Global Change Biology*, 26, 971–988. doi.org/10.1111/gcb.14915

Pahl-Wostl, C. (1995). *The Dynamic Nature of Ecosystems: Chaos and order entwined.* London: Wiley.

Paine, R. T. (1966). Food web complexity and species diversity. *The American Naturalist*, 100, 65–75.

Paine, R. T. (1969). A note on trophic complexity and community stability. *The American Naturalist*, 103, 91–93.

Palmer, C. (2011). Place-historical narratives: Road – or roadblock – to sustainability? *Ethics, Policy and Environment*, 14, 345–359.

Palmer, J. (1998). Spiritual ideas, environmental concerns and educational practice. In Cooper, D. E. and Palmer, J., eds., *Spirit of the Environment: Religion, value and environmental concern*. London: Routledge. 146–167.

Pang, A. S.-K. (1996). Gender, culture and astrophysical fieldwork: Elizabeth Campbell and the Lick Observatory-Crocker Eclipse Expeditions. In Kuklick, H. and Kohler, R. E., eds., *Science in the Field*. Chicago: University of Chicago Press. 15–43.

Papworth, S. K., Rist, J., Coad, L. and Milner-Gulland, E. J. (2009). Evidence for shifting baseline syndrome in conservation. *Conservation Letters*, 2, 93–100.

Park, C. (2017). *Wedded to the Rocks: The life and work of Adam Sedgwick (1785–1873)*. Lancaster; Chris Park/Scotts Valley, CA: CreateSpace/Amazon.com.

Patterson, A. H. (1930). *A Norfolk Naturalist: Observations on birds, mammals and fishes*. London: Methuen.

Peake, M. (1946). *Titus Groan*. London: Penguin Books. 1968 ed.

Pearce, F. (2015). *The New Wild: Why invasive species will be nature's salvation*. London: Icon.

Penning-Rowsell, E. and Lowenthal, D. (1986). *Landscape Meaning and Values*. London: Allen & Unwin.

Perlman, D. L. and Adelson, G. (1997). *Biodiversity: Exploring values and priorities in conservation*. Oxford: Blackwell Scientific Ltd.

Peterson, J. B. (1999). *Maps of Meaning: The architecture of belief*. New York; London: Routledge.

Peterson, J. B. (2018). *12 Rules for Life: An antidote to chaos*. London: Allen Lane.

Philippon, D. J. (2004). *Conserving Words: How American nature writers shaped the environmental movement*. Athens, GA: University of Georgia Press.

Pickett, S. T. A. and White, P. S. (1985). *The Ecology of Natural Disturbance and Patch Dynamics*. New York: Academic Press.

Pickett, S. T. A., Ostfield, R. S., Shachak, M. and Likens, G. E. (1997). Themes. In Pickett, S. T. A., Ostfield, R. S., Shachak, M. and Likens, G. E., eds., *The Ecological Basis of Conservation: Heterogeneity, ecosystems and biodiversity*. New York: Chapman & Hall. 81–82.

Pickston, M. (1968). *The Language of Flowers*. London: Michael Joseph.

Pielke, R. Jr, Prins, G., Rayner, S. and Sarewitz, D. (2007). Climate Change 2007: Lifting the taboo on adaptation. Renewed attention to policies for adapting to climate change cannot come too soon. Commentary. *Nature*, 445, 597–598. www.naturecom/nature/journal/v445/n7128/full/445597ahtml

Pimm, S. L. (1991). *The Balance of Nature? Ecological issues in the conservation of species and communities*. Chicago: University of Chicago Press.

Pinder, D. (2001). Ghostly footsteps: Voices, memories and walks in the city. *Ecumene*, 8, 1–19.

Pollan, M. (2001). *The Botany of Desire: A plant's-eye view of the world*. New York: Random House; 2002 London: Bloomsbury.

Pollan, M. (2002). *Second Nature: A gardener's education*. London: Bloomsbury (first published 1991 New York: Grove/Atlantic Press).

Polley, R. and Woodman, J. (1994). *Spirit of Nature: Poetry of the earth*. Tiverton: Devon Books.

Poole, S. (2007). *Unspeak: How words become weapons, how weapons become a message, and how that message becomes reality*. New York: Grove Press.

Poole, S. (2013). Is our love of nature writing bourgeois escapism? *The Guardian*, 6 July. www.theguardiancom/books/2013/jul/06/nature-writing-revival

Pope, A. (*c*.1700). *Ode on Solitude*. [Numerous collections and analyses: See, for example, Higgins, J. (1993). Turning readers into spectators: Pope's 'Ode on Solitude' and the frame of representation. *English Academy Review*, 10, 56–65.]

Porteous, J. D. (1990). *Landscapes of the Mind: Worlds of sense and metaphor*. Toronto: University of Toronto Press.

Porteous, J. D. (1996). *Environmental Aesthetics: Ideas, politics and planning*. London: Routledge.

Postma, D. W. (2006). *Why Care for Nature? In search of an ethical framework for environmental responsibility and education*. New York: Springer.

Potter, B. (1902). *The Tale of Peter Rabbit*. London: Frederick Warne & Co.

Potter, S. and Sargent, L. (1973). *Pedigree: Essays on the etymology of words from nature*. London: Collins New Naturalist 56.

Potts, T. and Meyers, A. (2009). Directors' foreword. In Donald, D. and Munro, J., eds., *Endless Forms: Charles Darwin, natural science and the visual arts*. New Haven, CT; London: Yale University Press. vii–ix.

Pratt, M. L. (1992). *Imperial Eyes: Travel writing and transculturation*. London: Routledge.

Proctor, J. D. (1995). Whose nature? The contested moral terrain of ancient forests. In Cronon, W., ed., *Uncommon Ground: Toward reinventing nature*. New York: W. W. Norton & Company. 269–297.

Proctor, J. D. (1996). Nature and the reproduction of endangered space: The spotted owl in the Pacific Northwest and southern California. *Environment and Planning D: Society and Space*, 14, 683–708.

Proshansky, H. M., Ittelson, W. H. and Rivlin, L. G., eds. (1970). *Environmental Psychology: Man and his physical setting*. New York: Holt, Rinehart and Winston.

Pulkkinen, L. (1990). Adult life-styles and their precursors in the social behaviour of children and adolescents. *European Journal of Personality*, 4, 237–251.

Raban, J. (1992). *The Oxford Book of the Sea*. Oxford: Oxford University Press.

Rackham, O. (1986). *The History of the Countryside*. London: Dent.

Rackham, O. (1990). *Trees and Woodlands in the British Landscape*. London: Dent.

Rackham, O. (1991). Landscape and the conservation of meaning. *Journal of the Royal Society of Arts*, 139, 903–915.

Rackham, O. (2003). *Ancient Woodland*. Dalbeattie: Castlepoint Press.

Rackham, O. (2006). *Woodlands*. London: Collins New Naturalist 100.

Readman, P. (2018). *Storied Ground: Landscape and the shaping of English national identity*. Cambridge: Cambridge University Press.

Rebanks, J. (2020). *English Pastoral: An inheritance*. London: Penguin.

Reed-Danahay, D. E. (1997). *Auto/Ethnography: Rewriting the self and the social*. Oxford; New York: Berg.

Rees, M. (2018). *On The Future: Prospects for humanity*. Princeton, NJ: Princeton University Press.

Reydon, T. A. C. (2019). Are species good units for biodiversity studies and conservation efforts? In Casetta, E., Marques da Silva, J. and Vecchi, D., eds., *From Assessing to Conserving Biodiversity*. History, Philosophy and Theory of the Life Sciences, 24. Cham: Springer Nature. 164–194.

Reynolds, F. (2016). *The Fight for Beauty: Our path to a better future*. London: Oneworld.

Riding, C. (2013). Introduction. In Riding, C. and Johns, R., eds., *Turner and the Sea*. London: Thames & Hudson. 11–23.

Ridley, M. (2013). Global lukewarming need not be catastrophic. *The Times*, 28 September. www.thetimes.co.uk/tto/opinion/columnists/article3881481ece

Ridley, M. (2015a). I am branded disgraceful, shameful, even scandalous, all for being a lukewarmer. *The Times*, 19 January. www.lancaster.ac.uk/staff/ecagrs/Hounded.pdf

Ridley, M. (2015b). Why we love a bit of Africa in our parkland. *The Times*, 28 December. www.thetimes.co.uk/tto/opinion/columnists/article4650587ece

Ridley, M. (2017). Politics and science are a toxic combination. *The Times*, 6 February. www.thetimes.co.uk/article/politics-and-science-are-a-toxic-combination-706jm3hqv

Ritchie, J. M. (1983). *German Literature under National Socialism*. London: Croom Helm/Barnes and Noble.

Ritson, K. (2019). *The Shifting Sands of the North Sea Lowlands: Literary and historical imaginaries*. London: Routledge.

Rival, L., ed. (1998). *The Social Life of Trees: Anthropological perspectives on tree symbolism*. Oxford: Berg.

Robbins, J. (2020). Ecopsychology: How immersion in nature benefits your health. *Yale Environment 360*, 9 January. https://e360.yale.edu/features/ecopsychology-how-immersion-in-nature-benefits-your-health

Roberts, R. C. (2003). *Emotions: An essay in aid of moral psychology*. Cambridge: Cambridge University Press.

Roe, N. (2002). *The Politics of Nature: William Wordsworth and some of his contemporaries*. London: Palgrave.

Rolston III, H. (1979). Can and ought we to follow nature? *Environmental Ethics*, 1, 7–30.

Rolston III, H. (1997). Nature, the genesis of value and human understanding. *Environmental Values*, 6, 361–364.

Ronner, A. D. (1986). *W. H. Hudson: The man, the novelist, the naturalist*. New York: AMS Press.

Rorty, R. (1979). *Philosophy and the Mirror of Nature*. Princeton, NJ: University Press.

Rose, D. C. (2014). Five ways to enhance the impact of climate science. *Nature Climate Change*, 4, 522–524.

Rose, D. C., Brotherton, P. N. M., Owens, S. and Pryke, T. (2016). Honest advocacy for nature: Presenting a persuasive narrative for conservation. *Biodiversity and Conservation*, 27, 1703–1723.

Rosenbaum, S. C. (1944). William Henry Hudson: Bibliografía. *Revista Hispánica Moderna Año*, 10, 222–230. University of Pennsylvania Press. www-jstor-org.ezp.lib.cam.ac.uk/stable/i30205471

Roszak, T. (1972). *Where the Wasteland Ends: Politics and transcendence in post-industrial society*. New York: Doubleday.

Roszak, T., Gomes, M. E. and Kanner, A. D., eds. (1995). *Ecopsychology: Restoring the earth/healing the mind*. San Francisco: Sierra Club.

Rothman, D. J. (1995). 'I have fallen in love outward': Robinson Jeffers and the pathetic fallacy. *Hellas*, 61, 51.

Rothschild, M. and Marren, P. (1997). *Rothschild's Reserves: Time and fragile nature*. Colchester: Balaban Harley.

Royal Commission on Environmental Pollution. (1981). *Eighth Report: Oil pollution of the sea* (Cmnd. 8358). London: HMSO.

Royal Society. (2014). *Climate Change Evidence and Causes*. https://royalsociety.org/~/media/Royal_Society_Content/policy/projects/climate-evidence-causes/climate-change-evidence-causes.pdf

Rudiak-Gould, P. (2014). Climate change and accusation: Global warming and local blame in a small island state. *Current Anthropology*, 55, 365–386.

Russell, E. J. (1959). *The World of the Soil*. London: Collins New Naturalist 35.

Russell, E. W. (1962). *Soil Conditions and Plant Growth*. London: Longmans.

Ruskin, J. (1897). Of the pathetic fallacy in modern painting. In *Modern Painters, Vol. III: Of many things*. London: Smith Elder. 161–177.

Sack, R. D. (1990). The realm of meaning: The inadequacy of human-nature theory and the view of mass consumption. In Turner, B. L. II, Clark, W. C., Kates, R. W., Richards, J. F., Mathews, J. T. and Meyer, W. B., eds., *The Earth as Transformed by Human Action: Global and regional changes in the biosphere over the past 300 years*. Cambridge: Cambridge University Press. 659–671.

Sale, K. (1991). *Dwellers in the Land: The bioregional vision*. Philadelphia: The New Society.

Salisbury, E. (1961). *Weeds and Aliens*. London: Collins New Naturalist 43.

Salk, J. (1973). *The Survival of the Wisest*. New York: Harper & Row.

Sandbrook, C., Fisher, J. A., Holmes, G., Luque-Lora, R. and Keane, A. (2019). The global conservation movement is diverse but not divided. *Nature Sustainability*, 2, 316–323.

Sarewitz, D. and Pielke, R. (2000). Breaking the global-warming gridlock. *The Atlantic Monthly*, 286, 55–64. www.theatlantic.com/past/issues/2000/07/sarewitzhtm

Sarewitz, D. and Pielke, R. (2006). The neglected heart of science policy: Reconciling supply of and demand for science. *Environmental Science and Policy*, 10, 5–16.

Sarkar, S. (2019). What should 'biodiversity' be? In Casetta, E., Marques da Silva, J. and Vecchi, D., eds., *From Assessing to Conserving Biodiversity*. History, Philosophy and Theory of the Life Sciences, 24. Cham: Springer Nature. 375–399.

Satterfield, T., Slovic, P. and Gregory, R. (2000). Narrative valuation in a policy judgement context. *Ecological Economics*, 34, 315–331.

Saunders, C. (2003). The emerging field of conservation psychology. *Human Ecology Review*, 10, 137–149.

Sayer, G. (2005). Landscape, seascape, mindscape. In Scott, I., ed., *The Turn of the Tide: North Norfolk's saltmarsh coast*. Fakenham: JJG Publishing. 101–117.

Schama, S. (1995). *Landscape and Memory*. London: Fontana.

Schleicher, J., Zaehringer, J. G., Fastré, C., Vira, B., Visconti, P. and Sandbrook, C. (2019). Protecting half of the planet could directly affect over one billion people. *Nature Sustainability*, 2, 1094–1096.

Schultz, P. W., Shrive, C., Tabanico, J. J. and Khazian, A. M. (2004). Implicit connections with nature. *Journal of Environmental Psychology*, 24, 31–42.

Sebald, W. G. (2002). *After Nature*. London: Hamish Hamilton.

Seton, E. T. (1906). *Wild Animals I Have Known*. London: David Nutt.

Shafer, C. S. and Hammitt, W. E. (1995). Congruency among experience dimensions, condition indicators, and coping behaviors in wilderness. *Leisure Sciences*, 17, 263–279.

Shanahan, J., Pelstring, L. and McComas, K. (2010). Using narratives to think about environmental attitude and behaviour: An exploratory study. *Society & Natural Resources*, 12, 405–419.

Shanahan, M. (2007). *Talking about a Revolution: Climate change and the media*. COP13 Briefing and Opinion Papers. London: IIED.

Shapin, S. (1998). Placing the view from nowhere: Historical and sociological problems in the location of science. *Transactions of the Institute of British Geographers*, 23, 5–12.

Sharma, S. (2002). *George Eliot's Novels: Language and meaning*. London: Sarup & Sons.

Shawe-Taylor, D. (2010). *Dutch Landscapes*. London: Royal Collection Publications/ Scala Publishers.

Shea, C. (2015). Jane Goodall on how to get people to hear your message. *Canadian Business*, 22 October. www.canadianbusiness.com/leadership/jane-goodall-on-branding/

Sheail, J. (1976). *Nature in Trust*. London: Blackie.

Sheail, J. (1995). Guest editorial: The ecologist and environmental history – a British perspective. *Journal of Biogeography*, 22, 953–966.

Sheail, J. (1998). *Nature Conservation in Britain: The formative years*. London: The Stationery Office.

Sheldrake, M. (2020). *Entangled Life: How fungi make our worlds, change our minds and shape our future*. London: Random House.

Shelley, P. B. (1801). On Love. P. B. Shelley fragments in Shelley, M. W., ed., *The Keepsake*, 1829(1828). www.rc.umd.edu/editions/mws/lastman/pbsfragshtm

Shepard, P. (1967). *Man and the Landscape: An historic view of the esthetics of nature*. Athens, GA: University of Georgia Press.

Shirky, C. (2008). *Here Comes Everybody: The power of organizing without organizations*. London: Penguin.

Shirley, P. (2019). Nature's place – what should live where? *ECOS*, 40(3). www.ecos.org.uk/ecos-403-natures-place-what-should-live-where/

Short, J. R. (2005). *Imagined Country: Environment, culture and society*. Syracuse, NY: Syracuse University Press.

Shrader-Frechette, K. (2001). Non-indigenous species and ecological explanation. *Biology and Philosophy*, 16, 507–519.

Sidney, Philip, Sir. (1593). O sweet woods the delight of solitarines! In *The Complete Works* (1912). Poems first printed in a folio of 1593: *The Second Ecloges*.

Silvertown, J. (2009). *An Orchard Invisible: A natural history of seeds*. Chicago: University of Chicago Press.

Simberloff, D. (2003a). Confronting introduced species: A form of xenophobia? *Biological Invasions*, 5, 179–192.

Simberloff, D. (2003b). Community and ecosystem impacts of single-species extinctions. In Kareiva, P. and Levin, S. A., eds., *The Importance of Species: Perspectives on expendability and triage*. Princeton, NJ: Princeton University Press. 221–237.

Simmons, I. G. (1993a). *Interpreting Nature: Cultural constructions of the environment*. London: Routledge.

Simmons, I. G. (1993b). Review: 'Barriers to a better environment. What stops us solving environmental problems? S. Trudgill 1990'. *Transactions of the Institute of British Geographers*, 18, 151.

Simmons, I. G. (1993c). *Environmental History: A concise introduction*. Oxford: Blackwell.

Slaymaker, O. (2001). Why so much concern about climate change and so little attention to land use change? *The Canadian Geographer*, 45, 71–78.

Smith, J. E. (1968). *'Torrey Canyon' Pollution and Marine Life*. A report by the Plymouth Laboratory of the Marine Biological Association of the United Kingdom. Cambridge: Cambridge University Press.

Smith, P. and Howe, N. (2015). *Climate Change as Social Drama*. Cambridge: Cambridge University Press.

Smyth, R. (2015). Plashy Fens: The limitations of nature writing. *Times Literary Supplement*, 8 May. www.the-tls.co.uk/articles/nature-writing-richard-smyth/

Sobel, D. (1996). *Beyond Ecophobia: Reclaiming the heart in nature education*. Massachusetts: The Orion Society Nature Literacy Series 4.

Sobel, D. (1998). Beyond ecophobia. *Yes! Magazine*, 2 November. www.yesmagazineorg/issues/education-for-life/803

Sobel, D. (2004). *Place-Based Education: Connecting classrooms and communities*. Great Barrington, MA: The Orion Society Nature Literacy Series 4.

Sobel, D. (2008). *Childhood and Nature: Design principles for educators*. Portland, MA: Stenhouse.

Sodha, S. (2017). Outrage makes you feel good, but doesn't change minds. *The Guardian*, 2 April. www.theguardian.com/commentisfree/2017/apr/01/outrage-makes-you-feel-good-but-doesnt-change-minds?CMP=fb_gu

Sommer, R. (2003). Trees and human identity. In Clayton, S. and Opotow, S., eds., *Identity and the Natural Environment: The psychological significance of nature*. Cambridge, MA: The MIT Press. 179–204.

Soulé, M. (1995). The social siege of nature. In Soulé, M. E. and Lease, G., eds., *Reinventing Nature? Response to postmodern deconstructionism*. Washington, DC: Island Press. 137–169.

Spencer, T. and Lane, S. (2016). Reflections on the IPCC and global change science: Time for more (physical) geographical tradition. *The Canadian Geographer*, 61, 124–135.

Spender, S. (1997). *World within World: The autobiography of Stephen Spender*. London: Faber & Faber.

Spirn, A. W. (1998). *The Language of Landscape*. New Haven, CT: Yale University Press.

Staats, H. and Hartig, T. (2004). Alone or with a friend: A social context for psychological restoration and environmental preferences. *Journal of Environmental Psychology*, 24, 199–211.

Stamp, L. D. (1962). *The Land of Britain: Its use and misuse*. London: Longman.

Steer, J. (2015). *The Reconciliation of Introduced Species in New Zealand: Understandings from three 'exceptional' case studies*. Unpublished PhD thesis, The University of Auckland, New Zealand. https://researchspaceaucklandacnz/handle/2292/27449

Steers, J. A. (1962). *The Sea Coast*. London: Collins New Naturalist 25.

Steidinger, B. S., Crowther, T. W., Liang, J. et al. (2019). Climatic controls of decomposition drive the global biogeography of forest-tree symbioses. *Nature*, 569, 404–408.

Stein, H. F. (1987). *Developmental Time, Cultural Space: Studies in psychogeography*. Norman: University of Oklahoma Press.

Steinbeck, J. (1939). *The Grapes of Wrath*. New York: The Viking Press-James Lloyd. 1995 Mandarin Paperbacks ed.

Steinbeck, J. (1951). *The Log from the Sea of Cortez*. London: Pan Books. 1960 ed.

Stewart, I. and Nield, T. (2013). Earth stories: Context and narrative in the communication of popular geoscience. *Proceedings of the Geologists' Association*, 124, 699–712.

Stilgoe, J. R. (2015). *What Is Landscape?* Cambridge, MA: The MIT Press.

Stocking, M., Perkin, S. and Brown, K. (2014). Co-existing with nature in a developing world. In Morse, S. and Stocking, M., eds., *People and Nature: Development for the future*. London: Routledge. 155–185.

Stoddard, R. H. (1880). *The Poems*. New York: Charles Scribner.

Storm, T. (1888). *Der Schimmelreiter*. Paetel. Wright, J. (1964) *The Rider on the White Horse*. New York: New York Review of Books.

Storr, A. (1989). *Solitude: A return to the self*. London: Ballantine Books. 1997 Harper Collins paperback ed.; first published 1988 as *The School of Genius*. London: André Deutsch Ltd.

Stott, P. (1997). Dynamic tropical forestry in an unstable world. *Commonwealth Forestry Review*, 76, 207–209.

Stott, P. (2016). Physical geographies. Past, present, and future. *Progress in Physical Geography*, 40, 3–6.

Stow, D. (2004). *Encyclopedia of the Oceans*. Oxford: Oxford University Press.

Stuart-Smith, S. (2020). *The Well Gardened Mind: Rediscovering nature in the modern world*. London: William Collins.

Sutherland, W. J., ed. (1998). *Conservation Science and Action*. Oxford: Blackwell Science Ltd.

Sutherland, W. J. (2006). Predicting the ecological consequences of environmental change: A review of methods. *Journal of Applied Ecology*, 43, 599–616.

Sutherland, W. J. and Hill, D. A. (1995). *Managing Habitats for Conservation*. Cambridge: Cambridge University Press.

Sutherland, W. J., Dicks, L. V., Everard, M. and Geneletti, D. (2018). Qualitative methods for ecologists and conservation scientists. *Methods in Ecology and Evolution*, 9, 7–9.

Swim, J. K., Markowitz, E. M. and Bloodhart, B. (2012). Psychology and climate change: Beliefs, impacts, and human contributions. In Clayton, S., ed., *Oxford Handbook of Environmental Psychology*. Oxford: Oxford University Press. 645–669.

Szerszynski, B., Heim, W. and Waterton, C., eds. (2003). *Nature Performed: Environment, culture and performance*. Oxford: Blackwell.

Tallentyre, S. G. [pseudonym for Hall, E. B.] (1906). *The Friends of Voltaire*. London: Smith, Elder & Co.

Tam, K.-P. (2013). Concepts and measures related to connection to nature: Similarities and differences. *Journal of Environmental Psychology*, 34, 64–78.

Tamm, E. E. (2004). *Beyond the Outer Shores: The untold odyssey of Ed Ricketts, the pioneering ecologist who inspired John Steinbeck and Joseph Campbell*. New York: Thunder's Mouth Press.

Tansey, C. J., Hadfield, J. D. and Phillimore, A. B. (2017). Estimating the ability of plants to plastically track temperature-mediated shifts in the spring phenological optimum. *Global Change Biology*, 23, 1–14. doi.org/10.1111/gcb.13624; http://onlinelibrary.wiley.com/doi/10.1111/gcb.13624/abstract

Tansley, A. G. (1920). The classification of vegetation and concept of development. *Journal of Ecology*, 8, 118–149.

Tansley, A. G. (1923). *Practical Plant Ecology*. London: George Allen & Unwin (republished in 1946 as *Introduction to Plant Ecology*).

Tansley, A. G. (1929). Succession, the concept and its value. *Proceedings of the International Congress of Plant Sciences 1926*, 677–686.

Tansley, A. G. (1935). The use and abuse of vegetational concepts and terms. *Ecology*, 16, 284–307.

Tansley, A. G. (1939). British ecology during the past quarter century: The plant community and the ecosystem. *Journal of Ecology*, 27, 513–530.

Tappolet, C. (2006). Critical review of Roberts, R. C. 2003 *Emotions: An essay in aid of moral psychology*. *Ethics*, 117, 143–147.

Tate, P. (2007). *Flights of Fancy: Birds in myth, legend and superstition*. New York: Random House.

Taylor, B. (2010). *Dark Green Religion: Nature, spirituality and the planetary future*. Berkeley: University of California Press.

Taylor, P. W. (1986). *Respect for Nature: A theory of environmental ethics*. Princeton, NJ: Princeton University Press.

Tennessen, C. M. and Cimprich, B. (1995). Views to nature: Effects on attention. *Journal of Environmental Psychology*, 15, 77–85.

Thayer, R. L. (1976). Visual ecology: Revitalizing the aesthetics of landscape architecture. *Landscape*, 20, 37–43.

Thayer, R. L. (2003). *LifePlace: Bioregional thought and practice*. Berkeley: University of California Press.

Thomas, R. S. (1995). Bird watching. In *No Truce with the Furies*. Hexham: Bloodaxe Books.

Thomas, W. L., ed. with the collaboration of Sauer, C. O., Bates, M. and Mumford, L. (1956). *Man's Role in Changing the Face of the Earth*. Chicago: Published for the Wenner-Gren Foundation for Anthropological Research and the National Science Foundation by the University of Chicago Press.

Thomas, W. L. Jr, ed. with the collaboration of Sauer, C. O., Bates, M. and Mumford, L. (1970). *Man's Role in Changing the Face of the Earth.* Chicago; London: Published for the Wenner-Gren Foundation for Anthropological Research and the National Science Foundation by the University of Chicago Press. Vol. 1, Vol. 2.

Thomashow, M. (1995). *Ecological Identity: Becoming a reflective environmentalist.* Cambridge, MA: The MIT Press.

Thompson, H. S. (1997). *The Proud Highway: Saga of a desperate Southern gentleman, 1955–1967.* New York: Bloomsbury.

Thompson, K. (2010). *Do We Need Pandas? The uncomfortable truth about biodiversity.* Cambridge: Green Books.

Thoreau, H. D. (1862). Walking. *Atlantic Monthly.*

Thoreau, H. D. (1981). Walden. In Krutch, J. W., ed., *Walden and other writings by Henry David Thoreau.* (Original work published 1854). New York: Bantam. 105–341.

Thunberg, G. (2019). *No One Is Too Small to Make a Difference.* London: Francis Lincoln Children's Books.

Thunberg, G., Sanchez Vegara, M. I. and Weckmann, A. (2020). *Little People, BIG DREAMS.* London: Penguin.

Tolhurst, P., ed. (2009). *Knowing Your Place: East Anglian landscapes and literature.* Norwich: Black Dog Books.

Toner Raimi, K. and Leary, M. (2014). Belief superiority in the environmental domain: Attitude extremity and reactions to fracking. *Journal of Environmental Psychology*, 40, 76–85.

Tree, I. (2018). *Wilding: The return of nature to a British farm.* London: Picador.

Trudgill, S. T. (1988). *Soil and Vegetation Systems.* Oxford: Oxford University Press.

Trudgill, S. T. (1990). *Barriers to a Better Environment: What stops us solving environmental problems?* London: Belhaven Press.

Trudgill, S. T. (1999). Environmental Education, Ethics and Citizenship Conference held at the Royal Geographical Society with the Institute of British Geographers 20 May 1998. Introduction and Postscript. *Ethics, Place and Environment*, 2, 81–82, 87–89.

Trudgill, S. T. (2001a). Psychobiogeography: Meanings of nature and motivations for a democratised conservation ethic. *Journal of Biogeography*, 28, 677–698.

Trudgill, S. T. (2001b). *The Terrestrial Biosphere: Environmental change, ecosystem science, attitudes and values.* London: Pearson.

Trudgill, S. T. (2003a). Meaning, knowledge, constructs and fieldwork in physical geography. In Trudgill, S. T. and Roy, A., eds., *Contemporary Meanings in Physical Geography: From what to why?* London: Arnold. 25–46.

Trudgill, S. T. (2003b). Conclusion. In Trudgill, S. T. and Roy, A., eds., *Contemporary Meanings in Physical Geography: From what to why?* London: Arnold. 269–277.

Trudgill, S. T. (2006). Dirt cheap: Cultural constructs of soil. *Journal of Geography in Higher Education*, 301, 7–14.

Trudgill, S. T. (2007). Classics Revisited. 'Tansley, A. G. 1935: The use and abuse of vegetational concepts and terms. *Ecology* 16, 284–307'. *Progress in Physical Geography*, 31, 501–507.

Trudgill, S. T. (2008). A requiem for the British flora? Emotional biogeographies and environmental change. *Area*, 401, 99–107.

Trudgill, S. T. (2009). 'You can't resist the sea': Evolving attitudes and responses to coastal erosion at Slapton, S Devon. *Geography*, 94, 48–57.

Trudgill, S. T. (2012a). Do theories tell us what to see? The 19th-century observations of Darwin, Ramsay and Bonney on glacial features. *Progress in Physical Geography*, 364, 558–566.

Trudgill, S. T. (2012b). Nature's clothing and spontaneous generation? The observations of Thoreau and Dureau de la Malle on plant succession. *Progress in Physical Geography*, 365, 707–714.

Trudgill, S. T. (2012c). 'The interactions between all neighbouring organisms': The roles of Charles Darwin, Ernst Haeckel and Eugenius Warming in the evolution of ideas on plant dynamics. *Progress in Physical Geography*, 86, 853–861.

Trudgill, S. T. (2020). Pioneering fieldwork heroes in the life sciences. In Burt, T. P. and Thompson, D., eds., *Curious about Nature: A passion for fieldwork*. Cambridge: Cambridge University Press. 87–115.

Trudgill, S. T. and Richards, K. S. (1997). Environmental science and policy: Generalisation and context sensitivity. *Transactions of the Institute of British Geographers*, 22, 5–12.

Trudgill, S. T. and Roy, A., eds. (2003). *Contemporary Meanings in Physical Geography: From what to why?* London: Arnold.

Trudgill, S. T., Jeffery, A. and Parker, J. (2010). Climate change and the resilience of the domestic lawn. *Journal of Applied Geography*, 30, 177–190.

Tuan, Y.-F. (1974). *Topophilia: A study of environmental perception, attitudes and values*. New York: Columbia University Press.

Tuan, Y.-F. (1977). *Space and Place: The experience of perspective*. Minneapolis: University of Minnesota Press.

Tunnicliffe, S. D. and Reiss, M. J. (1999). The place of living organisms in children's lives. *Ethics, Place and Environment*, 2, 108–114.

Turner, B. L. II., Clark, W. C., Kates, R. W., Richards, J. F., Mathews, J. T. and Meyer, W. B., eds. (1990). *The Earth as Transformed by Human Action: Global and regional changes in the biosphere over the past 300 years*. Cambridge: Cambridge University Press.

Turner, J. F. (1992). *Rupert Brooke: The splendour and the pain*. London: Breese Books.

Turner, L. (2019). *Out of the Woods*. London: Weidenfield & Nicholson.

Ulrich, R. S. (1979). Visual landscapes and psychological well-being. *Landscape Research*, 4, 17–23.

Ulrich, R. S. (1981). Natural versus urban scenes: Some psychophysiological effects. *Environment and Behavior*, 13, 523–556.

Ulrich, R. S. (1984). View through a window may influence recovery from surgery. *Science*, 224, 420–421.

Ulrich, R. S., Simons, R., Losito, B., Fiorito, E., Miles, M. and Zelson, M. (1991). Stress recovery during exposure to natural and urban environments. *Journal of Environmental Psychology*, 11, 201–230.

UN. (2019). *The Global Assessment Report on Biodiversity and Ecosystem Services*. www.un.org/sustainabledevelopment/blog/2019/05/nature-decline-unprecedented-report/ https://news.un.org/en/story/2019/05/1037941

Usher, M. B., ed. (1986). *Wildlife Conservation Evaluation*. London: Chapman & Hall.

Usher, M. B. (1996). The soil ecosystem and sustainability. In Taylor, A. G., Gordon, J. E. and Usher, M B., eds., *Soils, Sustainability and the Natural Heritage*. Edinburgh: Her Majesty's Stationery Office. 22–43.

Usher, M. B. (2001). Earth science and the natural heritage: A synthesis. In Gordon, J. E and Leys, K. F., eds., *Earth Science and the Natural Heritage: Interactions and integrated management*. Edinburgh: The Stationery Office. 314–324.

Usher, M. B. (2005a). Conserving European biodiversity in the context of climate change. *T-PVS 21*. Strasbourg: Council of Europe Publishing, Strasbourg.

Usher, M. B. (2005b). Soil biodiversity, nature conservation and sustainability. In Bardgett, R. D., Usher, M. B. and Hopkins, D. W., eds., *Biological Diversity and Function in Soils*. Cambridge: Cambridge University Press (for the British Ecological Society). 363–378.

Valdés, M. J., ed. (1991). *A Ricoeur Reader: Reflection and imagination*. Toronto: University of Toronto Press.

Valtchanov, D. and Ellard, C. G. (2015). Cognitive and affective responses to natural scenes: Effects of low level visual properties on preference, cognitive load and eye movements. *Journal of Environmental Psychology*, 43, 184–195.

van der Heijden, M. G. A., Martin, F. M., Selosse, M.-A. and Sanders, I. R. (2015). Mycorrhizal ecology and evolution: The past, the present, and the future. *New Phytologist*, 205, 1406–1423.

van der Post, L. (1986). *A Walk with a White Bushman*. London: Penguin.

van der Werff, E., Steg, L. and Keizer, K. (2013). The value of environmental self-identity: The relationship between biospheric values, environmental self-identity and environmental preferences, intentions and behaviour. *Journal of Environmental Psychology*, 34, 55–63.

Van Matre, S. (1974). *Acclimatizing: A personal and reflective approach to a natural relationship*. Martinsville, IN: American Camping Association.

Van Matre, S. (1979). *Sunship Earth: An acclimatization program for outdoor learning*. Martinsville, IN: American Camping Association.

Van Matre, S. (1983). *The Earth Speaks*. Warrenville, IL: Acclimatization Experiences Institute.

Vaughan, A. (2020). 'Massive failure': The world has missed all its biodiversity targets. *New Scientist*, 15 September. www.newscientist.com/article/2254460-massive-failure-the-world-has-missed-all-its-biodiversity-targets/

Vickery, R. (2019). *Vickery's Folk Flora: An A–Z of the folklore and uses of British and Irish plants*. London: Weidenfeld & Nicolson.

Vidal, J. (2016). The seven deadly things we're doing to trash the planet (and human life with it). *The Guardian*, 19 December. www.theguardian.com/commentisfree/2016/dec/19/seven-deadly-things-trash-planet-human-life?CMP=Share_iOSApp_Other

Vining, J. (2003). The connection to other animals and caring for nature. *Human Ecology Review*, 10, 87–99.

Vitebsky, P. (2005). *Reindeer People*. London: Harper Perennial.

Voros, G. (1997). *Notations of the Wild*. Iowa City: University of Iowa Press.

Wainwright, A. (1992). *A Pennine Journey: The story of a long walk in 1938*. London: Penguin Books.

Waldman, K. (2014). Researchers want children's books to stop anthropomorphizing animals. That's a terrible idea. *Slate*, 28 March. https://slate.com/culture/2014/03/animals-in-kids-books-should-have-human-characteristics-a-defense-of-anthropomorphization.html

Wallace, R. (1983). Bird study. In *Tunes for Bears to Dance To*. Pittsburgh, PA: University of Pittsburgh Press.

Wallach, A. D., Batavia, C., Bekoff, M. et al. (2020). Recognizing personhood in compassionate conservation. *Conservation Biology*, 34, 1097–1106. https://conbio.onlinelibrary.wiley.com/doi/abs/10.1111/cobi.13494

Wallwork, J. A. (1970). *The Ecology of Soil Organisms*. London: McGraw-Hill.

Ward Thompson, C. (2002). Urban open space in the 21st century. *Landscape and Urban Planning*, 60, 59–72.

Ward Thompson, C. (2016). Editorial: Landscape and Health Special Issue. *Landscape Research*, 41, 591–597.

Ward Thompson, C., Elizalde, A., Cummins, S. et al. (2019). Enhancing health through access to nature: How effective are interventions in woodlands in deprived urban communities? A quasi-experimental study in Scotland, UK. *Sustainability*, 11, 12.

Watson, M. (2003). Performing place in nature reserves. In Szerszynski, B., Heim, W. and Waterton, C., eds., *Nature Performed: Environment, culture and performance*. Oxford: Blackwell. 145–160.

Watts, G., Hannah, D. M. and Watkinson, A. (2015a). Introduction to the special issue on the impact of climate change on water in the UK. *Progress in Physical Geography*, 39, 3–5.

Watts, G., Battarbee, R. W., Bloomfield, J. P. et al. (2015b). Climate change and water in the UK – past changes and future prospects. *Progress in Physical Geography*, 39, 6–28.

Westling, L. (2014). *The Cambridge Companion to Literature and Environment*. Cambridge: Cambridge University Press.

Whatmore, S. J. and Boucher, S. (1993). Bargaining with nature: The discourse and practice of environmental planning gain. *Transactions of the Institute of British Geographers*, 18, 166–188.

Wheeler, D., ed. (1998). *The Penguin Book of Garden Writing*. London: Penguin.

Whipple, T. (2020). Join the dots for a glimpse of the Almighty. *The Times*, 10 September. www.thetimes.co.uk/article/join-the-dots-for-a-glimpse-of-the-almighty-lzl2lkqh8

White, G. (1789). *The Natural History and Antiquities of Selborne*. London: Cassell & Company.

White, G. (1795). *A Naturalist's Calendar, with observations in various branches of natural history, extracted from the papers of the late Rev Gilbert White of Selborne, Hampshire, Senior Fellow of Oriel College, Oxford*. London: B. and J. White.

White, L. (1967). The historical roots of our ecological crisis. *Science*, 155, 1203–1207.

White, T. H. (1951). *The Goshawk*. London: Jonathan Cape.

White, T. H. (1958). *The Once and Future King*. London: Collins.

Whitley, D. (2008). *The Idea of Nature in Disney Animation*. Aldershot; Burlington, VA: Ashgate.

Whitley, D. (2012). *The Idea of Nature in Disney Animation: From Snow White to WALL•E*. Aldershot; Burlington, VA: Ashgate.

Whitmarsh, L. (2009). Behavioural responses to climate change: Asymmetry of intentions and impacts. *Journal of Environmental Psychology*, 29, 13–23.

Whitney, G. G. (1994). *From Coastal Wilderness to Fruited Plain: A history of environmental change in temperate North America from 1500 to the present*. Cambridge: Cambridge University Press.

Wilber, K. (2000). *Sex, Ecology and Spirituality: The spirit of evolution*. Boston; London: Shambala.

Williams, B. (1995). *Making Sense of Humanity*. Cambridge: Cambridge University Press.

Williams, R. (1973). *The Country and the City*. London: Chatto & Windus.

Williams, S. (2019). Non-native plants provide habitats for a variety of British insects. *Centre for Ecology and Hydrology*. www.ceh.ac.uk/news-and-media/news/non-native-plants-habitats-british-insects

Williamson, A. (1995). *Henry Williamson: Tarka and the last romantic*. Stroud: Alan Sutton Publishing Ltd.

Williamson, H. (Hugh) (1771). An attempt to Account for the Change of Climate, Which Has Been Observed in the Middle Colonies in North-America. *Transactions of the American Philosophical Society*, 1, 272–280. www.jstororg/stable/1005036

Williamson, H. (Henry) see www.henrywilliamson.co.uk/bibliography/booksbyhw

Williamson, H. (1921). *The Beautiful Years*. Collins, 1921; revised ed. Faber, 1929; Dutton, USA, 1929.

Williamson, H. (1922a). *Dandelion Days*. Collins, 1922; revised ed. Faber, 1930; Dutton, USA, 1930.

Williamson, H. (1922b). *The Lone Swallows*. Collins, 1922; revised ed. illustrated by C. F. Tunnicliffe, Putnam, 1933.

Williamson, H. (1923). *The Peregrine's Saga, and Other Stories of the Country*. Green Collins, 1923; published as *The Sun Brothers*, Dutton, USA, 1925; revised ed. illustrated by C. F. Tunnicliffe, Putnam, 1934.

Williamson, H. (1924a). *The Dream of Fair Women*. Collins, 1924; Dutton, USA, 1924; revised ed. Faber, 1931; Dutton, USA, 1931.

Williamson, H. (1924b). *The Pathway*. Cape, 1928; Dutton, USA, 1929.

Williamson, H. (1927). *Tarka the Otter: His joyful water-life and death in the country of the two rivers*. Putnam, 1927; Dutton, USA, 1928; revised ed. illustrated by C. F. Tunnicliffe, Putnam, 1932; Penguin, 1937; Puffin, 1949 to present day; ed. illustrated by film stills, introduction by Richard Williamson, Bodley Head, 1978; ed. illustrated by photographs by Simon McBride, introduction by Richard Williamson, Webb and Bower, 1985; The Folio Society, 1995.

Williamson, H. (1928). *The Pathway*. Cape, 1928; Dutton, USA, 1929; Pears Collins, 1921; revised ed. Faber, 1929; Dutton, USA, 1929.

Williamson, H. (1935). *Salar the Salmon*. Faber, 1935 ed. illustrated by C. F. Tunnicliffe; Penguin, 1936, 1949; ed. illustrated by Michael Loates, with introduction by Richard Williamson, Webb and Bower, 1987.

Williamson, H. (1945). *The Lone Swallows and Other Essays of Boyhood and Youth*. London: Putnam and Co illustrated ed. (first published 1922b – see above).

Willis, C. (2015). A human needs approach to revealing nature's benefits for visitors to the coast. *Area*, 47, 422–428.

Wilson, J. K. (2012). *The German Forest: Nature, identity, and the contestation of a national symbol, 1871–1914*. Toronto: University of Toronto Press.

Winnicott, D. (1958). The capacity to be alone. *International Journal of Psychoanalysis*, 39, 416–420.

Wohlwill, J. (1970). The emerging discipline of environmental psychology. *American Psychologist*, 25, 303–312.

Wood, L. A. (1986). Loneliness. In Harré, R., ed., *The Social Construction of Emotions*. Oxford: Blackwell. 184–208.

Woodfall, D. (2019). *Rewilding: Real life stories of returning British and Irish wildlife to balance*. London: William Collins.

Woodward, I., Aebischer, N., Burnell, D. et al. (2020). APEP 4: Population estimates of birds in Great Britain and the United Kingdom. *British Birds*, 113, 69–104.

Wordsworth, W. (1820). *The River Duddon: A series of sonnets*. London: Longman, Hurst, Rees, Orme and Brown.

Worster, D. (1992). *Under Western Skies: Nature and history in the American West*. New York; Oxford: Oxford University Press.

Worster, D. (1994). *Nature's Economy: A history of ecological ideas*. Cambridge: Cambridge University Press.

Wulf, A. (2015). *The Invention of Nature: The adventures of Alexander von Humboldt – The lost hero of science*. London: John Murray.

Wyatt, J. (1995). *Wordsworth and the Geologists*. Cambridge: Cambridge University Press.

Wyborn, C., Montana, J., Kalas, N. et al. (2020a). An agenda for research and action towards diverse and just futures for life on Earth. *Conservation Biology*, 26 November. doi.org/10.1111/cobi.13671

Wyborn, C., Davila, F., Pereira, L. et al. (2020b). Imagining transformative biodiversity futures. *Nature Sustainability*, 3, 670–672.

Wynne, B. (1996). May the sheep safely graze? A reflexive view of the expert-lay knowledge divide. In Lash, S., Szeszynski, B. and Wynne, B., eds., *Risk, Environment and Modernity: Towards a new ecology*. London: Sage. 44–87.

Wypijewski, J., ed. (1997). *Painting by Numbers: Komar and Melamid's scientific guide to art*. Berkeley: University of California Press.

Yaalon, D. H. (2000). Down to earth: Why soil – and soil science – matters. *Nature*, 407, 301.

Yonge, C. M. (1949). *The Sea Shore*. London: Collins New Naturalist 12.

Young, A. (1958). *Out of the World and Back: Into Hades and A Traveller in Time*. (Revised version of *Into Hades*). London: Rupert Hart-Davis.

Zechner, J. (2013). From poetry to politics: The Romantic roots of the 'German Forest'. In Beinart, W., Middleton, K. and Pooley, S., eds., *Wild Things: Nature and the social imagination*. Cambridge: White Horse Press. 185–210.

Zelenski, J. M. and Nisbet, E. K. (2014). Happiness and feeling connected: The distinct role of nature relatedness. *Environment and Behavior*, 46, 3–23.

Zhanga, J. W., Howell, R. T. and Iyerc, R. (2014). Engagement with natural beauty moderates the positive relation between connectedness with nature and psychological well-being. *Journal of Environmental Psychology*, 38, 55–63.

Zhanga, J. W., Piff, P. K., Iyerb, R., Kolevab, S. and Keltnera, D. (2014). An occasion for unselfing: Beautiful nature leads to prosociality. *Journal of Environmental Psychology*, 37, 61–72.

Zola, E. (1880). *La Terre*. Translation: Parmee, D. (1980), *The Earth*. London: Penguin.

Index